THE SACRED EXCHANGE

· THE ·
SACRED
EXCHANGE

Creating a Jewish
Money Ethic

Edited by
RABBI MARY L. ZAMORE
Foreword by Rabbi B. Elka Abrahamson

CCAR Challenge and Change Series

Library of Congress Cataloging-in-Publication Data

Names: Zamore, Mary L., 1969- editor. | Abrahamson, Elka, writer of added
   introduction.
Title: The sacred exchange : creating a Jewish money ethic / edited by Rabbi
   Mary L. Zamore ; foreword by Rabbi Elka Abrahamson.
Description: New York, NY : CCAR Press, [2019] | Series: CCAR challenge and
   change series | Includes bibliographical references and index.
Identifiers: LCCN 2019006519 (print) | LCCN 2019008001 (ebook) | ISBN
   9780881233346 | ISBN 9780881233339 (pbk. : alk. paper)
Subjects: LCSH: Money--Religious aspects--Judaism. | Economics--Religious
   aspects--Judaism. | Jewish ethics.
Classification: LCC BJ1279 (ebook) | LCC BJ1279 .S23 2019 (print) | DDC
   296.3/68--dc23
LC record available at https://lccn.loc.gov/2019006519

CCAR Press, 355 Lexington Avenue, New York, NY 10017
(212) 972-3636
www.ccarpress.org

Printed in the U.S.A.

10 9 8 7 6 5 4 3 2 1

Sacred Exchange Task Force

David Altshuler

Rabbi Nicole Auerbach

Rabbi Nikki DeBlosi

Rabbi Danny Burkeman

Rabbi Neal Gold

Rabbi Samuel N. Gordon

Rabbi Lisa Greene

Rabbi Ilene Haigh

Rabbi Sari Laufer

Rabbi Richard Levy

Rabbi John Linder

Rabbi David Lyon

Rabbi Douglas B. Sagal

Rabbi Hara E. Person
Publisher, CCAR Press

Rabbi Steven A. Fox
Chief Executive
Central Conference of American Rabbis

Contents

Contents · xi

Acknowledgments

My first anthology, *The Sacred Table: Creating a Jewish Food Ethic* (CCAR Press, 2011), has been the center of my teaching for many years. After its publication Rabbi Hara Person would periodically, yet persistently, ask when I would be ready to tackle another book. I thought about many other topics, knowing that I had to be ready to live with a new subject for a long time in an intense relationship. Despite researching and reflecting, nothing clicked for me. Then, I was invited by Rabbi Rebecca Sirbu and Shifra Bronznick to be part of cohort of female Jewish leaders to attend the Op-Ed Training, funded by Clal's Rabbis Without Borders and Advancing Women Professionals and the Jewish Community. It was through their training exercises that I realized that I had been thinking and teaching about money already. As I taught about Judaism and food, my focus had expanded to include the economic issues that intersect with food and Jewish ethics. My new topic for my next book appeared instantly. Thank you for the training, which led to this book.

I gratefully thank Rabbi Hara Person and the CCAR Press for believing in me so many years ago and continuing to do so. *The Sacred Exchange* represents my bat mitzvah work with the CCAR Press, as I have edited, written in, or otherwise contributed to thirteen publications. It is a pleasure to produce another anthology with Rabbi Person, Rabbi Beth Lieberman, Rabbi Sonja Pilz, Deborah Smilow, Sasha Smith, Ortal Bensky, Carly Linden, and Rabbi Dan Medwin, as well as publishing interns Vanessa Harper and Jessica Kerman. I also thank the book's task force members for their feedback and support from the review of my outline until the final reading of the manuscript: especially David Altshuler, Rabbi Nicole Auerbach, Rabbi Danny Burkeman, Rabbi Nikki DeBlosi, Rabbi Neal Gold, Rabbi Sam Gordon, Rabbi Lisa Greene, Rabbi Ilene Haigh, Rabbi Sari Laufer, Rabbi Richard Levy, Rabbi John Linder, Rabbi David Lyon, and Rabbi Doug Sagal.

Thank you to my friends Rabbi Batsheva Appel and Rabbi Neal Gold for forcing me to stay fast to this project even when my other work needed me equally. To keep me focused, Rabbi Gold, especially, spent hours reviewing my ideas with me, helping perfect them. My deepest thanks to the all authors; I am so blessed to have such talented, passionate people share their time and talent.

There are many at the CCAR who helped move this book forward. These include Rabbi David Stern, CCAR President; Rabbi Steven A. Fox, CCAR Chief Executive; Rabbi Don Goor, Chair of the Press Committee, as well as copy editor Debra Hirsch Corman and cover designer Barbara Leff.

Thank you to all of my teachers and mentors, especially Rabbi Charles Kroloff, whose guidance has been invaluable since the beginning of my rabbinate. Thank you to the Women's Rabbinic Network. I am blessed to work with such amazing leaders, our board members, and especially the presidents who served during the production of this book, Rabbis Ellen Nemhauser, Amy Memis-Foler, and Kelly Levy. Your encouragement means the world to me.

Thank you to my mother, Ellen Zamore, my most passionate proofreader and proudest parent out there. Thank you to my brother, Phillip Zamore, and his family, Catherine Colinvaux, Hannah, and Eli for their love and support. I remember my father, Leonard, knowing that his legacy continues daily.

Finally, the center of my heart: thank you to my love and partner in everything, Terje who always encourages my dreams, and to Aryeh for being proud of me and my work. Terje, an economist, has provided invaluable feedback, and Aryeh's editing advice on my writing is always insightful and welcomed. I could not do everything I do without both of your support and love.

Terje, I will add how blessed we are to celebrate twenty-five years of marriage, growing as a couple while growing as individuals, treasuring life together.

אשרינו   How greatly we are blessed!

מה טוב חלקנו   How good is our portion!

ומה נעים גורלנו   How pleasant is our lot!

ומה יפה ירשתנו   How beautiful is our heritage!

Foreword

Rabbi B. Elka Abrahamson

I recall with a measure of delight the day when, together with my rabbinical school classmates, we studied *Pirkei Avot* 3:21, *Im ein kemach, ein Torah*, "Where there is no bread [literally, no flour], there can be no Torah." Undergirding this mishnah is the principle that laboring to be a student of Torah is a noble pursuit, but not if one does so at the expense of material needs. A more colloquial version of the verse might be "But a rabbi's gotta eat." And the verse continues, as stunning Jewish texts are known to do, with the very opposite expression of the relationship between Torah learning and making a suitable living: *Im ein Torah, ein kemach*. Without Torah, the verse posits, of what good is financial success? In short, Jewish tradition teaches that a healthy Torah study–work balance leads to healthy living. For young rabbinical students, it was a relief to read that our ancestors affirmed our need to be paid for the passions we were pursuing. And it was uplifting to know that earning money, no matter one's profession, should never come at the cost of acquiring more knowledge.

Earning bread, *money*, is a topic we are instructed as children shouldn't enter polite conversation, along with, ironically, religion and politics. Perhaps we all should have ignored that elementary school list. Why? Because we must talk about all three of these topics as thoughtful and empathetic adults, particularly those of us exercising leadership or making decisions about spending in the Jewish community. Understanding our relationship with earning, spending, and giving away money is a complex journey that should start with, yes, polite dinner table conversation. My career path has taken to me to a unique position. As the president of the Wexner Foundation, I have the opportunity to work in a pluralist Jewish environment at an organization founded and guided by a visionary philanthropist. We talk about money often, not because we must raise funds, but because within our organization we think about how best to leverage our philanthropy. As a foundation, we know that funding is a privilege, one we do not take lightly. We understand the importance of partnerships, because through collaborative funding, we dramatically increase our impact. Leslie Wexner, the founder and co-chairman of the Wexner Foundation, is known to hold out his open palm where he holds an invisible but very real moral compass. It is checked against our funding priorities, which include these questions, worthy of all individuals gifting money: Are we spending our money to reflect the values we espouse? Is our spending aligned with *our* sacred mission? Are we having the results we intended? Are we doing good? Are we doing the right thing? These are the core questions that animate the timely and timeless collection in this volume, *The Sacred Exchange: Creating a Jewish Money Ethic.*

Indeed, these are essential questions we need to ask as Jews in an era when economic inequality in our communities is dramatic. We often use our sacred texts to exhort our people to fulfill the obligation to care for the vulnerable, and we routinely encourage those with privilege to support and lift up those in need. We talk about the importance of giving the gift of time, yet these additional questions come to mind: Are time and money of equal value? How do we find a balance? We possess varying degrees of capacity to give dollars. By what criteria do we make this determination? Is it the business of anyone else how we spend our money? In an age of virtual sharing so much of who we are, should we be more open about our philanthropy at all levels of giving? Can we speak with greater transparency when asking for dollars from others? Is it chutzpah to discuss the financial choices we observe others making, or is it an opportunity to frame a deep conversation about the power of the dollar? Do we embarrass others by pushing them to redirect their money, or might we open sacred conversations? This timely book offers guidance and sources, as it wisely challenges the reader to grapple with complex questions that are sure to generate appropriate, even if at times uncomfortable conversations about money, wealth, and equality. The essays in this volume are sure to create productive discomfort! The Torah itself envisioned a society in which the gap between the haves and the have-nots would be minimal. We are a long way from that vision. It is time to start the talk about fixing our world through a rigorous conversation about how to distribute wealth. Let us talk openly about our unique obligations and seize upon strategies to lessen—dare we dream—even close that gap.

Central to my own professional work is developing emerging leaders, both in the professional and the volunteer realm. The money conversations are never easy, especially for emerging adults who have not (yet) fully developed their relationship with money and few of whom are at ease asking for dollars from donors. Many new leaders are not sure how to broach this topic. Others are frustrated with the reluctance of their peers to donate to Jewish causes and to adequately fund institutions. Some are simply stymied by the high cost of Jewish engagement. It is widely acknowledged that establishing a lifelong Jewish identity comes with a high price tag, after adding tuitions, fees, memberships, and *s'machot*, joyous occasions. This too raises important questions for our community: Are we limiting the finest Jewish experiences to the rare few who can afford it? Are we too quick to chase the next big idea, leaving basic needs in the funding dustbin? And with all of the issues facing well-meaning donors, when will the Jewish community take seriously the challenge of Jewish poverty in our own communities?

Some of my favorite teachings reveal our sages' search for balance between honoring wealth and minimizing the importance of it. In the fifteenth-century *Sefer Halkarim* by Rabbi Joseph Albo, we are taught that the love of money and glory is one of three qualities that inhibits true repentance. Indeed, our tradition prescribes specific acts, some great and others small, to balance a desire to earn more with a commitment to giving away what we have. In the eighteenth century, Rabbi Yisrael Meir Kagan, the Chofetz Chaim, asserted that it is fitting to give to the poor the best that is on your table, while elsewhere we are taught to honor the wealthy with our finest seat at the table. So which is it? Our thoughtful and perpetually challenging tradition calls on us to find a balance. How do we leave the most honored space at our table for the wealthiest, the one who makes the most "dough," and adhere to the halachah, Jewish law, to leave the best food/bread on the table for the poorest one present? If taken together, one could suggest that two texts come to tell us that we are obligated to gather together, at the same table, honored guests, rich and poor, and that all be satisfied. Can we say the same of our communities? Have we figured out how to talk about money? Let's pull up a chair, open the book, and get started.

Opportunities for engaging in these important discussions abound in the chapters of *The Sacred Exchange: Creating a Jewish Money Ethic*. The authors provide us with a wealth of information and Jewish texts to enrich and guide our exploration of many weighty topics related to money and finding the proper balance for spending, earning, wasting, saving, donating, acknowledging those who give it, and satisfying those who do not. Forget whatever we learned as kids. We need to articulate our values around money from a Jewish perspective. It will do us good and, ultimately, will enable us to do more good in the world.

Introduction: We Can and Should Talk about Money

American culture seems to be all about money. We live in a society driven by consumerism; we are defined by our ability to earn money and spend it on status symbols; America is the land of economic opportunity, where we glorify the rags-to-riches stories of every generation. With a culture tethered to wealth, it would be easy to assume that we are acclimated to talking about money with great ease, but we are not. Anyone who has lived outside of America can easily recall that awkward moment when unflinchingly asked how much money you make or how much your house is worth. Here in America such questions are *verboten* for normative social interaction. In fact, the very inquiry can be taboo within families. Just ask your friends how many of them have shared their salary, debt, or home budgets with their parents or children. Furthermore, many of us do not even talk about money with our partners, rather depending on assumptions instead of clear financial planning.

Some attribute the American discomfort with money to the Puritan roots of our nation, but whatever the cause, it is clear that American Jews are not immune to this reticence. Most of us have absorbed the message from our greater culture that meaningful talk about wealth is not decorous. Although the Jewish canon of sacred texts has much to teach concerning our view of and use of money, modern American Jews have not adopted their forthright approach to money talk. Yet, we need to talk about money, not to build a modern golden calf, worshiping wealth, but to think deeply about the definition of wealth, the theology of plenty and poverty, employment ethics, personal finances, economic injustice, and *tzedakah*, among other important topics.

The Sacred Exchange: Creating a Jewish Money Ethic creates a rich, multifaceted conversation about wealth, surveying biblical, Rabbinic, and modern sources to focus on a broad spectrum of subjects. Together the chapters in this book challenge us to consider the Jewish values and ethics guiding our interactions with each other and the world through money. While the transcendent is explored, ultimately this book is rooted in the practical.

Divided into six parts, *The Sacred Exchange* starts with "Wealth: Wisdom from Our Texts," a deep exploration of our sacred texts' view of wealth. The five chapters composing the heart of this section work together to present a comprehensive set of texts with their spiritual and theological questions about wealth, poverty, gluttony, coveting, and contentment. The result is as much a conversation about wealth and money as an exploration of the human condition and meaning of life. Shifting toward the practical application of the material from part 1, "The Power of Money: *Tzedakah* and *Tzedek*" (part 2) is dedicated to the good we can do with our money through philanthropy and investments. These chapters examine not only the ethics of giving money, but also the vehicles through which we may want to donate. Reflecting Judaism's injunction to give *tzedakah* specifically to support Israel, part 3, "Israel," is committed to our relationship to Israel through money. Although its content is related to many chapters found throughout this book, Rabbi Edward Elkin's "Full Faith and Credit: Jewish Views on Debt and Bankruptcy" was placed in the Israel part of this book in recognition that the laws of credit are rooted in biblical Israel. Part 4,

"We Are All Employers," calls upon us to apply Jewish ethical teachings to our employment relationships, as well as the marketplace. The name of this section, "We Are All Employers," draws attention to the impact we each have on others through direct and indirect employment and business relationships. Also, in this part, Judith Rosenbaum, PhD, provides "Bread and Roses: Jewish Women Transform the American Labor Movement," illustrating the Jewish labor leaders who demanded better treatment of workers in the American workplace. In "Dreaming a New American Economy," Rabbi Andy Kahn reflects on the state of the modern economy and its impact on our fellow Americans; he then surveys some of the innovative remedies promising a better way for all.

While some may insist that religion and money should be kept far from one another, part 5, "Religious Life and Money," shows how intertwined these are—and that this is not a bad thing. Using the language of value proposition, Rabbi Leah Lewis offers a compelling argument in "The Value of Affiliation" for synagogue membership, while Rabbi Jennifer Gubitz's "Dividends of Meaning: Jewish Rituals for the Financial Life Cycle" challenges the Jewish community to create a new set of rituals as a method of engaging modern Jews. Finally, part 6, "Uncomfortable Conversations," takes our discomfort with money talk and embraces it completely, encouraging important conversations and teachings. The chapters in this section range from the examination by Joshua Holo, PhD, of the history of Jewish moneylending to Rabbi Amy B. Cohen and Rabbi Alan Freedman's "Embracing Dave Ramsey: A Financial Literacy Model for the Jewish Community" to "Ethical Estate Planning" by Rabbi Richard F. Address, DMin.

Each part of this book ends with two specially themed chapters. The first, entitled "Ethics in Focus," offers a targeted discussion on a specific issue related to the ethics of money, and the second, "Talking about Money," is a narrative thought piece illustrating the motif of the part of the book in which it is found.

The Sacred Exchange brings together scholars and thought leaders to provide a broad survey of the multifaceted discussion of Judaism and money. The resulting chapters are thought-provoking and enriching, sometimes surprising, always encouraging the reader to think deeply about one's relationship to the world through the vehicle of money. Enjoy reading these extraordinary writings, and then allow them to echo in your daily activities, conversations, and use of money.

Small Change

I learned about the Jewish obligation to tithe in religious school, right before my bat mitzvah, fifty years ago. Tithing was a mitzvah that captured my heart. We had very little growing up. I worked through high school, always tithing one-tenth of everything I earned or received as gifts. When I got married, I told my husband that I planned to tithe for both of us, and he agreed. I have shared the importance of tithing with my children and my students. Content with 90 percent, I give God 10 percent, not just because it is commanded, but because it feels right.

Rabbi Amy R. Perlin, Fairfax Station, VA

*　　*　　*

There are many ways to support Israel; however, as Reform/Progressive Jews, there is none better than supporting one of the fifty Progressive congregations around the country. My husband and I support several, because we as Israelis, together with American Jews, can ensure that Israel develops as the democratic and Jewish state of which we dream.

Planting trees or donating ambulances are worthwhile endeavors; they help ensure the material health of the State of Israel. However, by supporting congregations, we safeguard a pluralistic future for Israel; we ensure an equal place in Israeli society for women, open the doors for the LGBTQ population, and help repair the tears in Israeli society.

Our *tzedakah* directed toward Progressive congregations supports the spiritual health of the State of Israel.

Rabbi Donald Goor, Jerusalem, Israel

*   *   *

As a Jewish professional, I raised my children in a heavily Jewish environment. They attended JCC nursery school, day school, Jewish camp, BBYO trips, JCC Maccabi Games, and more. Often these were out of our financial league. Throughout their growing up, they watched as I filled out scholarship applications so they could participate fully in Jewish life.

It's not easy and also quite humbling to ask for financial aid, but the experience of receiving funds taught our family about the importance and value of *tzedakah*. I hope that my children, as they enter the workforce, will "pay it forward" and enable other children to have the experiences they were given.

Aliza Orent, New York, NY

*   *   *

As a labor organizer in the 1980s, I worked with hospital workers who fought hard for a living wage, affordable quality health care, and safer working conditions. Yet, at the core, from doctors and nurses to hospital aides and maintenance staff, what employees cared most deeply about was to be treated with respect and dignity and to care for their patients and families. Years later, at Torah study on Shabbat mornings, I connect these issues of fairness, justice, and human dignity as cornerstones of Judaism. This is what inspired me to become a rabbi—bringing words of Torah into the real world.

Rabbi John A. Linder, Paradise Valley, AZ

My spouse and I had a wonderful house. I worked five to seven part-time jobs as a rabbi, while she had a full-time job. Her employer, a synagogue, needed to make some financial adjustments and came to each staff member to negotiate. She asked that her cut be taken from non-salary benefits. Sadly, they refused. Her salary was cut, and we were unable to keep making our mortgage payments. We tried selling our house, but the bank refused to accept a short sale. When I got a job out of town, we simply walked away. The house was foreclosed on. As the bank kept coming after us, we had no choice but to file for bankruptcy. Thank God, it was only money!

Rabbi Robin Nafshi, Concord, NH

*   *   *

My *zayde*, Abraham Woroshilsky, gave my father a wooden box and instructed him to bury it in his grave when he died. My parents had no idea what was in it, but after Zayde died, my father opened the box and found a large stack of paper. They were IOUs from people who owed him money he never collected. My father closed the box and buried it as instructed.

JoAnn Hornsten, as told to her daughter
Rabbi Marla Hornsten, Detroit, MI

*   *   *

I was middle class, then I was poor. I learned the value of a dollar by working at sub-minimum wage before I was legally old enough to work (meaning, if you complained, you would lose your job). Money meant power, and I wanted the power money could bring. I wanted to have enough money to walk away.

I'd always considered my student loan debt a "mortgage on my brain." When I finished paying off my law school loans, I realized I didn't have to be a lawyer anymore unless I wanted to, which was an incredibly scary thought. Deciding to attend rabbinical school meant another $100,000 in student loans. No one better to invest in than me.

Rabbi Cookie Lea Olshein, West Palm Beach, FL

During the early years of my rabbinate, I felt significant discomfort asking for money during fundraising. That is, until I sat down one day, together with my temple president, took a deep breath, and asked a synagogue member for a quarter of a million dollars. Within sixty seconds of my ask, he said, "Rabbi, you have the hard job: counseling, teaching, mediating, and taking care of this large congregation. My job is easy—I just write the check."

What I learned is that we all have different relationships to money and that in this instance I was not bringing pressure, but rather offering this member an opportunity, a chance to make a palpable difference for good in the world.

Rabbi Charles A. Kroloff, Westfield, NJ

* * *

It's easy to lose sight of the responsibility that comes with abundance. There are people who have more than I do but still reject all calls—taxes, regulation, charity—society makes on their wealth. Nobody is self-made; we each build our fortune within a system that has been created by our common investment. But this system does not return equal rewards to each of us; for those who have built wealth, it has provided far more. We should recognize our roles as stewards of this abundance and give back with gratitude and humility.

"[God did all this, so you would never say to yourself,] 'My own power and the might of my own hand have won this wealth for me.' Remember that it is the Eternal your God who gives you power to get wealth, in fulfillment of the covenant made on oath with your ancestors, as is still the case" (Deuteronomy 8:17–18).

Eric Muhlheim, Los Angeles, CA

* * *

When I was thirty-eight, my husband and I and our two children went to Israel for my first year of rabbinical school. Having no excess savings, we took money out of a retirement account to live on. We were *very* happy and *very* poor. The year was the most amazing year of our lives. Without a car, we walked everywhere together and had such wonderful conversations. The most valuable lesson I learned that year was that money is just money. It has no relation to how happy you can be. I learned what really matters in life—family, community, and finding meaning in what you do.

Rabbi Michele Medwin, DMin, Monticello, NY

*   *   *

I daydream about my family's next house, often skimming real estate listings without much regard for price or location.

Recently, however, I reviewed listings around my synagogue. Instead of excitement, there was angst: someday, housing costs will force me from the city to the suburbs.

Could I stay a member then? For me, proximity is integral. It lets me visit a friend, go to shul, then to a restaurant and back, waving at faces as I pass. It instills an intangible sense of connectedness.

No, I couldn't. I'd find something else (reluctantly). Aren't most young families caught in the same bind?

Aaron H. Midler, Hyde Park, Chicago, IL

*   *   *

I am still amazed by my own naivete taking out student loans for rabbinical school. Thinking the interest rate is less than for a credit card. Thinking "I'll pay the interest while I am still in school." Thinking that the loans would be easy to repay since I had repaid loans for college.

Not understanding how quickly debt grows. Not understanding how consistently underpaid I would be. Not understanding that student loans are a debt that never goes away or that default could mean the garnishment of my salary.

Remembering the freedom of finally paying the last of the loans off: "... *matir asurim* ... who frees the captive."

Anonymous

From my parents I learned that everyone can be a philanthropist. We were a family of five living on $30,000 per year. The paycheck never stretched to the end of month. One year, my parents considered declaring bankruptcy. After my dad died, I remember going through his checkbook. Along with the mortgage and utility payments, it was littered with years of $36 donation checks to many Jewish and non-Jewish organizations. I was shocked. And proud. Judaism teaches that regardless of your income, every person can give *tzedakah*. Today, I, too, am a philanthropist.

Rabbi Beth Singer, San Francisco, CA

* * *

I was a salesman for ten years, and in that time I came to see that money is far more than currency. It's a symbol. It's a tool that allows us to do what we want. Some pursue money because it provides security. For others, money offers freedom. Others use money as *tzedakah*, to bring justice into the world. Power, choice, motivation, love, success—money represents all of these for different people, at different times in our lives. When I think about money in a basic way, I think about what I can buy with it. When I consider it more deeply, however, I think about what it allows me to do and who it allows me to be.

Rabbi Dean Shapiro, Tempe, AZ

* * *

After eighteen years, I left full-time synagogue life to pursue either my "passion" or a "*meshugenah* idea," depending on when you ask me. I converted a trolley bus into a mobile bookstore for kids. Once I became a small-business owner, I realized how detached from money I had been. With electronic deposits, my salary had magically appeared in my account. With credit cards, I never carried much cash. Now, selling a $17.99 hardback means $6.30 profit. An hour without a customer means I've earned nothing. And, when I bring a cash deposit to the bank teller, I feel proud.

Rabbi Deborah Bodin Cohen, Bethesda, MD

My autistic child is expensive. The cost of his care, therapies, medications, best programs, and services involves outrageous amounts. I love Judaism, traditions, Israel, etc., but the best place for our funds is investing in his best, most independent future. Religious schools do not come close. My heart is too involved in the care of my children to apply for aid and force upon all three children religious education. Some days my heart aches; I stole religion from them. Mostly I pray these siblings are capable of autonomy, finding traditions together involving love of religion and finding their blessings in *tikkun olam*.

Faith Michelle Dantowitz, Brookline, MA

* * *

One of my most painful life experiences was uncovering a massive embezzlement at my synagogue. The huge amount of money stolen was bad enough, but what was most troubling was dealing with the fallout. How to hold the "secret" among just a few until the prosecutor could make an arrest. How to inform the rabbi, the board, the congregation. How to explain how it happened. How to keep it from ever happening again. Using our Jewish lens to help guide our actions, we sought truthfulness, justice, and resolution. For me, even many years later, forgiveness is still a work in progress.

Laurie Spiegel, Florham Park, NJ

* * *

After my wife and I married, we invited guests to our new apartment. But we had little money and nothing fancy on which to serve. While we were browsing at a local shop, we came across a beautiful glass piece on which were engraved stars—on sale for five dollars, a sum we didn't take lightly. We agonized an entire day whether we should make the purchase. Over forty years later, we still have that plate. Whenever we are faced with a difficult financial challenge, we take out that plate: a reminder not to take for granted our material blessings.

Rabbi Kerry M. Olitzky, North Brunswick, NJ

xxxii • THE SACRED EXCHANGE

In one high school lesson on *tzedakah* I shared a teaching from the *Shulchan Aruch* that outlines priorities in giving: first to family, then to poor in one's community, and afterward to poor outside of your city. At the end of the class I gave each student an envelope with five dollars. Their assignment: donate the money to a worthy cause and report back where you gave. Some were Jewish, some were local, others not. While priority in giving was an important lesson, more so was learning how meaningful the cause was to the giver of the *tzedakah*.

Rabbi Amy L. Memis-Foler, Skokie, IL

*   *   *

In *The Opposite of Spoiled*, Ron Lieber suggests labeling three jars "spend," "save," "give." Dividing their allowance by three, children gain agency for how to spend their money. Recently, when preaching on *Parashat Vayak'heil*, I connected this lesson to the freewill gifts given for the *Mishkan*. A nine-year-old in the congregation appeared taken by Lieber's teaching. Walking off the bimah, I handed the jars to the boy. Quickly realizing he would now be on the hook for giving his son allowance according to Lieberman's formula, child's age = amount of allowance per week, his father said to me, "You just cost me $468." "You'll thank me later," I replied. How wonderful then when my phone buzzed with a picture of the three labeled jars and the words, "He's using them. It's a nice idea."

Rabbi Daniel B. Gropper, Harrison, NY

*   *   *

During an onsite interview to be an assistant rabbi, I was with a real estate agent and congregant on a tour of the affluent community. But as they showed me one house after another, it was clear that the median home price was in the millions and even a small fixer-upper would be well beyond the salary for the position, even without the burden of student loans. I pointed out something that looked more like apartments, possibly affordable. They replied, "Those? Those are the projects." When the offer came, I couldn't see myself in that community, in part because of finances.

Anonymous

*　　*　　*

Every year, when I review my expenses in preparing my taxes, I'm happiest when I've met my *tzedakah* goals. But there is something else that I always look for: Did I spend my money on time or space? On experiences or things? On building memories or acquiring stuff?

My goal is to spend my resources in ways that enhance relationships with those closest to me. Adventures, learning experiences, travel, encounters with those in need, always trump junk. Buber would say, "More I-Thou moments." Heschel would say, "Building a sanctuary in time." My mother always said, "Do I need another *shmateh?*"

Rabbi Karen Bender, Reseda, CA

*　　*　　*

As a business manager, I work with people who have unique skills (artists) that allow them to earn tremendous sums of money. What their unique skills don't teach them is financial literacy. Earning money and understanding how it will affect your life and the lives of everyone you care about are two very different things. Jewish ethical teaching is a wonderful tool for guiding people who have experienced a financial windfall. The average person doesn't relate, but having sudden great wealth creates opportunities fraught with ethical dilemmas. The Torah has many insights into how to navigate them.

Steve Landau, West Hills, CA

*　　*　　*

At first it was amazing, ordering any book and having it delivered to my door. And where I live, in Los Angeles, ride-sharing apps make life so much easier, especially for those who cannot drive. Who among us doesn't love big-box stores that deliver up-to-the-minute service and savings? But I wonder—are we stopping to consider what happens to individuals and businesses with deep knowledge and long-standing investment who lose their livelihoods when we choose these new providers? Our sages understood predatory pricing in their time, and their teachings might be worth revisiting today.

Rabbi Beth Lieberman, Los Angeles, CA

*   *   *

Not long ago I was in the local mall and noticed a twenty-dollar bill on the floor. With the injunction in *D'varim* to return lost items to their owners in mind, I turned it in to security. They were somewhat surprised, to say the least, but I told them that it was my religious obligation to do so. I went back a few days later, and it turned out it had been dropped by a young teen, who was incredibly grateful to have been able to retrieve it.

Rabbi Benjamin Lefkowitz, Warwick, RI

*   *   *

Hurricane Katrina resulted in displacement and destruction of homes for the majority of my congregants, as well as for me. Who could imagine that comfortable middle-class Jewish families could overnight need to be the recipients of food stamps, donated clothing, Red Cross and FEMA dollars, military ration packets, unemployment insurance, and the individual generosity of millions? My role as a rabbi became teaching our people not only to give *tzedakah*, but also accept it. Judaism reminds us that "the wheel of fortune is ever revolving" (*Kitzur Shulchan Aruch, Hilchot Tzedakah* 34:1).

Rabbi Bob Loewy, Metairie, LA

*   *   *

A friend says that her congregation thinks *tzedakah* is *tikkun olam*. Can money replace action, and is this substitution appropriate? If donating pays for expertise you don't have or supports a physically distant cause, then yes. More often, donors use money to distance themselves from "others." Repairing the world requires being involved in the world, getting dirty in its messiness. One cannot repair the world from a balcony, a place of privilege, throwing crumbs to those in need, or fight injustice through a pane of glass without breaking it. Yet, what Reform congregation doesn't serve a meal to the indigent, with a counter separating the two?

Muriel Lederman, Little Rock, AR

*   *   *

When I was a child, if the bus conductor didn't reach us before we arrived at our stop, my father *z"l* would always put the fare money in our *tzedakah* box. "It doesn't belong to us anymore." Nowadays, when receiving such an unexpected bonus from a supermarket or restaurant bill, my first thought is often, "Hurrah! What luck!!" The original miscalculation may not be my fault, but when I consider keeping that surplus, I hear my father's voice as if he were in the room beside me. "It does not belong to you."

Rabbi Ariel J. Friedlander, Modena, Italy

*   *   *

I was torn. Should I uproot my life and my partner's in order to follow my passion and become a rabbi? The decision was agonizing. I wished someone would say, "Don't you see? You *have* to do this!" On top of the emotional costs (abandoning my career, my beloved shul, my friends, my house), there was the cost of rabbinical school tuition.

That year, my grandfather's estate was divided among his six grandkids. Astoundingly, my share was *the precise amount* of rabbinical school tuition. I don't believe in *bashert*, ordained fate, but I did feel my grandfather saying, "Don't you see. . . ."

Rabbi Nicole K. Roberts, New South Wales, Australia

*   *   *

Four gift sets of Cross pens when I became bar mitzvah convinced my then thirteen-year-old self that cash would have been a much better option.

But that perception shifted with age. Cash is great, but I don't remember who gave me cash for my wedding. I *do* remember who bought me the toaster oven I really wanted and those really colorful handmade coffee mugs.

Life-cycle events are momentous. Putting thought into a gift that the recipient will remember should be commensurate with the effort it took to get to that day. Save the cash to tip your dog-walker.

Matthew Grob, New York, NY

* * *

In our family, the women worked in the world and at home.

My mother grew up in Dortmund, Germany, which was home to our upper-middle-class, liberal Jewish family for over four hundred years. One great-aunt, Charlotte, became a psychologist; another, Frida, a social worker; Trude, a businesswoman; and my grandmother Berta had wanted to be a doctor.

Hitler changed all that.

My mother, Senta Salomons Fox, finished only the eighth grade in Germany. When she came to America, Mom became a nanny, a seamstress, and then a masseuse. My parents married in 1943, but Mom always worked outside the home.

I too desired and needed to work. Wanting to change the world, I never considered what I would earn. Money made me anxious to think, talk, or learn about.

When I married, my husband was astounded at my ignorance. I've grown professionally, managed large budgets, and negotiated for higher salaries, proud that I can earn and spend. However, I'm still anxious and unsophisticated about money. It's not an aspect of feminism I have owned. May the next generation of women have the power, ownership, and pride in earning, spending, and managing money.

Rabbi Karen L. Fox, LCSW, Los Angeles, CA

* * *

Congregation B'nai Israel in Little Rock went from a "dues" model, which felt like taxation on "gifts of the heart," to an annual financial commitment pledged by each member entirely at the member's discretion. Annual membership income went up by well over 10 percent. Making the change was a huge leap for longtime leadership in a historic congregation and was spurred by the faith that our president placed in the congregation. Success indicated love for and engagement in the community.

Rabbi Barry H. Block, Little Rock, AR

*   *   *

During our holiest season of the High Holy Days, we employ *cheshbon hanefesh*, literally "the soul's arithmetic," taking account of our deeds in light of our values. It conveys Judaism's affirmation of the spiritual-ethical dimension over monetary materialism embodied in *cheshbon haguf*, "the body's arithmetic." In our society, with the greatest consumer-oriented materialism in history, we affirm the human hunger for the higher consumption of purpose and meaning.

The Hebrew word *shekel*, referring to the monetary unit, is kin to the word *shikul*, "consideration and evaluation." Life's reality of the necessity of the *shekel* is ultimately to be guided by satisfying our spiritual needs and ethical demands. Indeed, our lives' secular dimension is to be augmented by sacred consideration. "Small change" is contrasted with our heritage's call for "major change."

Rabbi Dr. Israel Zoberman, Virginia Beach, VA

*   *   *

I learned at least as much at Berkeley Hillel as I did in any college course. During my third year, I held a student seat on the board of directors, which had a minimum donation requirement for the "adults." Students also needed to make a gift—any amount, as long as it was significant and meaningful. I felt burdened and awed by this responsibility. I tried to quantify the meaning of Hillel. I could never donate enough to cover the pizzas I'd eaten, the mentoring I'd received, or the community where I'd learned to lead. It was a small donation on the ledgers, but a transformative one for me. It was the first donation check I had ever written.

Rabbi Jill Cozen-Harel, San Francisco, CA

When my grandfather died, I was fortunate to receive an inheritance. I used the majority of it for a house down payment. My sister-in-law Dana Kasen Gilbert suggested I purchase something special that would serve as a wonderful reminder of him. My grandfather loved ice cream, so buying lots of that would be delicious but not long-lasting. He played the organ for fun, and my children were learning piano. I bought a piano. All of my sons have played piano over the years. My youngest son, named for my sister and my grandfather, is now playing the piano often, and I am so grateful I purchased it.

Rabbi Faith Joy Dantowitz, Millburn, NJ

*   *   *

Years ago, waiting to pick up my son from Jewish day school, I overheard a conversation between two other mothers. The first was complaining about her household help, yet again. A young mother with three little children at home, she had two women helping her. However, on this day, this mom felt she was paying too much money for too little work. A bit older, the second mother listened patiently and then simply pronounced, "You don't need help; you need slaves." Needless to say, that response made quite an impression on me and, I hope, the first mother.

Rabbi Mary Zamore, Westfield, NJ

*   *   *

Tractate *Gittin* of the Talmud tells the story of two sheep trying to cross a river. One sheep is shorn and the other is not. The shorn sheep crossed to the other side without any noticeable effort whatsoever. The unshorn sheep, however, could not and did not cross. The Rabbis liken the shorn sheep to one who gives *tzedakah*, as he has lightened himself of possessiveness. The one who has not given is thus akin to the unshorn sheep, made heavy by excess, even greed. So it is for us. To give, whether money or time, is to lighten ourselves in a world that can often feel like a fast-flowing river. Our world frequently encourages the self above all else, while the Talmud urges us elsewhere, across the river to a place of selflessness.

Rabbi Benjamin David, Mount Laurel, NJ

*   *   *

It was an unusual thing to do. An inconvenient thing to do, especially for an impatient child. My mother checked her change and found it to be too much. Too many coins lay in her hand. So she marched back into the store to return the extra money. It didn't belong to her, she said. It wasn't right, she argued. Even though the owner of the large chain never would've known. Even though the cashier didn't care. My mother lived by the law of Leviticus: "Do not oppress your neighbor, nor rob him." She was a role model of righteousness.

Rabbi Adena Blum, Princeton Junction, NJ

*   *   *

RAYBAM'S Ladder of Teaching *Tzedakah* to Your Children (with apologies to RAMBAM)
1. Give *tzedakah* but keep it a secret.
2. Give and let your children know that you give.
3. Give and tell your children to whom you give.
4. Give and tell your children to whom you give and why.
5. Give and tell your children to whom and how you decide where to give.
6. Give and tell your children to whom, how you decide to whom, and how much you give.
7. Give and tell your children to whom and how you decide, both where, and how much of what you have to give.
8. Partner with your children, and decide together to whom and how much to give of your money and theirs.

Rabbi Joel N. Abraham, Fanwood, NJ

Part One

Wealth: Wisdom from Our Texts

While much of the discussion of money and Judaism easily jumps to the practical—*How much* tzedakah *should I give? Can we make Jewish living more affordable? How should we invest our money?*—these questions must be steeped in the foundational knowledge of what our sacred texts have to say about the Jewish view of wealth. Subjects examined include whether money is innately evil, how much our wealth is due to our own merit as opposed to being gifts from God, whether our possessions are truly our own or God's, what is the meaning of income disparity, what constitutes need or poverty, what is the Jewish view of greed, and what is contentment.

Opening this part of the book, the first four chapters present a comprehensive view of this topic, revealing various approaches and understandings in the sacred canon. While each author provides a unique view of the topic with interesting texts and questions, together the four chapters provide a deep look at Jewish values from ancient to modern times. These scholars emphasize that the Jewish sacred texts span multiple time periods, places, histories, and authors. Therefore, there is not one sole Jewish approach to wealth and its acquisition. As Rabbi Dvora Weisberg, PhD, writes, "These attitudes are not necessarily in opposition to each other; rather they can be seen as an acknowledgment of the complexity of the subject." These four chapters navigate the reader through this complexity, spurring much thought as the reader enjoys the interaction among the chapters and the values they present, as well as the questions they explore.

In "Wealth: Essential Teachings of Our Tradition," Rabbi Dvora Weisberg, PhD, provides the reader with a primer, reviewing the most important texts and themes related to wealth found in biblical and Rabbinic sources. No conversation about Judaism and wealth can begin without these teachings. Alyssa M. Gray, JD, PhD, builds on the foundation offered by Rabbi Weisberg. Her "Blessing and Challenge: A Further Look at the Sources" explores biblical, medieval, and modern Jewish sources to illustrate eight themes related to wealth, its blessing and challenge. Rabbi Amy Scheinerman, in her essay "How Much Is Enough?", juxtaposes ancient, medieval, and modern Jewish texts with non-Jewish sources to provide a thorough discussion of envy, satisfaction, and purpose. Rabbi Neal Gold's "Does Wealth Automatically Coarsen the Soul?" explores biblical through modern texts, integrating an examination of broader Jewish values to explore the spiritual challenge of wealth. Along the way, Rabbi Gold offers a fiery critique of the approach to wealth in the contemporary Jewish community, which should be kept in mind when reading Rabbi Douglas B. Sagal's chapter later in this book.

This part of the book continues with Rabbi Max Chaiken's "The Economic Theology of the Ten Commandments." This chapter mines the Ten Commandments to reflect the breadth of economic theology, revealing lesser-known lessons from this foundational text. Like every part of the book, part 1 ends with two themed chapters. The "Ethics in Focus" is Rabbi A. Brian Stoller's "When Donors Behave Badly: Guiding Principles for Jewish Institutions," which addresses the ethics of accepting money and vetting its source both before and after a donation has been given. In "Talking about Money: Financial Lessons from My Parents," Dr. Elana Altzman recalls the hard work and frugal ways of her parents as they emigrated from the former Soviet Union, seeking religious freedom. She wonders what lessons for better or worse have become part of her family's DNA.

1

WEALTH

Essential Teachings of Our Tradition

Rabbi Dvora Weisberg, PhD

Contemporary Judaism draws much of its information and inspiration from earlier texts and traditions. The Hebrew Bible and Rabbinic literature are our main source for the first thousand years of Jewish life and are regarded as the foundational texts of Judaism. Although these texts reflect an understanding of economics that is very different from that of the modern period, they help us ground our conversations about wealth in Jewish values.

Wealth is mentioned early and often in the *Tanach*, the Hebrew Bible. The first coins appeared in Greece around the sixth or fifth century BCE, but the absence of currency before then, in ancient Israel, did not prevent an understanding that acquiring possessions was something to be desired. The *Tanach* measures wealth in precious metals, land, flocks, and slaves and often mentions a person's possessions as an indication of power and status.

The books that compose the *Tanach* are not the work of a single author, nor do they derive from a single period of history. It is not surprising then that the *Tanach* offers multiple ways to think about wealth or the acquisition of wealth. These attitudes are not necessarily in opposition to each other; rather they can be seen as an acknowledgment of the complexity of the subject.

One approach suggests that wealth is a gift from God or a sign of divine favor. Although wealth is not one of the things God promises Abraham, and despite the fact that much of Abraham's wealth is the result of Sarah being taken into Pharaoh's house, we later learn that it was God who "blessed Abraham in every way" (Gen. 24:1). That explanation for Abraham's wealth is reiterated by his servant, who says, "The Eternal has blessed my master exceedingly and made him rich, giving him sheep and cattle, silver and gold" (Gen. 24:35). Similarly, God is the source of the riches that the Israelites take with them when they leave Egypt. The gold and silver they carry with them belonged to the Egyptians, but it is God who disposes the Egyptians to bestow gifts on the departing slaves (Exod. 12:36). In the wilderness, Moses promises the Israelites that they will be prosperous in the land of Canaan, providing they follow God's law; in this construct, wealth is an indication of God's blessing (Deut. 6:10–11, 7:13–14, 8:7–13).

This idea is accompanied by two warnings. The first is that an individual should not see wealth as the outcome of his labor alone. The Israelites are warned against becoming too comfortable.

> When you have eaten your fill, and have built fine houses to live in, and your herds and flocks have multiplied, and your silver and gold have increased, and everything you own has prospered, beware lest your heart grow haughty and you forget the Eternal your God— who freed you from the land of Egypt . . . and you say to your- selves, "My own power and the might of my own hand have won this wealth for me." Remember that it is the Eternal your God who gives you the power to get wealth. (Deut. 8:12–14, 8:17–18)

God is the source of wealth and blessing. Wealth is positive when it is understood as a blessing rather than a sign of one's own capacity for acquisition.

The second corollary is that good fortune brings with it responsi- bilities. The Torah acknowledges that even in an Israelite community blessed by God there will be individuals who will be in need. Those who have wealth are not entitled to regard those who do not as unde- serving of assistance. The Israelites are instructed to set aside portions of their harvest for "the Levite . . . the stranger, the fatherless, and the widow" (Deut. 14:29). Through loans, the remission of debts every seventh year, and generosity to the poor, the Israelites will merit God's continuing blessing.

The society portrayed in the Torah is an agrarian one, as indicated by both the division of the land of Canaan among the twelve tribes and the emphasis on the agricultural cycle and produce. The Torah does not imagine a classless society or one in which all are equally provided for. In urging the Israelites to provide for those mentioned above, the Torah acknowledges that those who do not own land are vulnerable. In addition, those with land may be forced to sell it or even to sell themselves into indentured servitude. Acknowledging the inevitability of poverty in society, the Torah promulgates laws that offer regular "resets" to prevent extreme economic disparity (Deut. 15:7–11). The cancellation of debts in the Sabbatical year, the return of land to its original owners, and the freeing of Israelites who were sold into indentured servitude in the Jubilee year ensure that wealth is less likely to be wholly concentrated in the hands of the few. At the very least, some people would be spared utter destitution.

For the Torah, wealth seems entirely good, assuming the one who possesses it understands its ultimate source and acts generously toward the less fortunate. The Book of Ecclesiastes offers a different view. The speaker in Ecclesiastes describes his drive to accumulate wealth:

> I multiplied my possessions. I built myself houses and I planted vineyards. I laid out gardens and groves. . . . I constructed pools of water. . . . I bought male and female slaves. . . . I also acquired more cattle. . . . I further amassed gold and silver and treasures of kings. . . . I gained more wealth than anyone before me in Jerusalem. . . . I withheld from my eyes nothing they asked for, and denied myself no enjoyment; rather, I got enjoyment out of all my wealth. (Eccles. 2:4–10)

After acquiring everything he could possibly want and more, the speaker enjoyed the possessions he had amassed. However, his pleasure in his wealth quickly dissipated. He came to realize that enjoyment "was all I got out of my wealth" (Eccles. 2:10). He soon realized that the pleasure he got from wealth was transitory; his wealth would eventually pass to someone else (Eccles. 6:2). Worse still, he discovered that wealth alone does not make a person happy (Eccles. 4:7–8).

Ecclesiastes serves as a warning that wealth and the pursuit of wealth do not ensure happiness. The classical prophets go a step further, warning that the desire for wealth can lead a person to disregard ethical standards. Isaiah castigates the leaders of Jerusalem, "every one avid for presents and greedy for gifts" who accept bribes to pervert justice (Isa. 1:23). Amos speaks of greed that causes the powerful to oppress the poor: "They have sold for silver those whose cause was just, and the needy for a pair of sandals" (Amos 2:6). It is not that wealth is inherently evil; rather, a preoccupation or obsession with acquiring wealth can blind individuals to the need to behave ethically. While the *Tanach* accepts income inequality, it recognizes the danger that the wealthy and powerful will oppress the poor or forget their obligation to care for those in need.

Like the *Tanach*, the major works of Rabbinic literature came together over hundreds of years and represent the views of many individuals. Rabbinic traditions about money, wealth, and poverty are multivocal. Additionally, they deal with these topics both from a legal point of view, formulating rules for civil law, business practices, and *tzedakah*, and from a theological/philosophical point of view.

Rabbinic literature, like the *Tanach*, assumes a much less complex economy than ours. Wealth is seen primarily in terms of real property: land, crops, and flocks. The urban workforce is made up of craftspeople and merchants. Coins have value assigned by the monetary system of the ruling powers and based on the metals from which they are made. Given the shift toward a more urban society, it is likely that the gap between rich and poor was wider in the Rabbinic period than it had been in ancient Israel. Rabbinic sources do not seek to eliminate that gap; rather they emphasize the responsibilities of the more fortunate toward those with less.

Rabbinic literature attests to the Rabbis' willingness, or perhaps preference, for a somewhat regulated or stabilized economy. The Babylonian Talmud speaks of a community's right to fix prices for basic commodities and to set standard wages and conditions for employees (BT *Bava Batra* 8b; *Mishnah Bava M'tzia* 7:1). The institution of *onaah*, literally "overreaching," referring to the laws regulating unfair pricing, prohibited charging more than one-sixth over the market value of an item or paying more than one-sixth under that market value; failure to follow this law invalidated the sale (*Mishnah Bava M'tzia* 4:3–4).

Rabbinic literature also suggests the Rabbis' discomfort with assets obtained without a visible contribution to society. The Mishnah disqualifies gamblers from serving as judges or witnesses; in explaining the disqualification, one sage indicates that money obtained without a clear transaction or buy-in by both parties is stolen property, while another sage explains that the gambler is not furthering public welfare (BT *Sanhedrin* 24b). The prohibition against lending to one's fellow Jews on interest limited ways that a person with discretionary assets could expand those assets without going into business or taking the risk of investing in someone else's business venture. In one story, Yochanan ben Zakkai meets an impoverished young woman. She identifies herself as the daughter and daughter-in-law of formerly wealthy men. Asked what happened to her family's wealth, she replies, "Rabbi, do they not say in Jerusalem, 'One who wishes to preserve his money should expend it [on *tzedakah*]'?" (BT *K'tubot* 66b). The young woman's cryptic reply suggests that giving *tzedakah* secures God's blessing, helping the wealthy person to remain wealthy; failure to give *tzedakah* might result in the rich person losing his or her wealth.

One question explored in Rabbinic literature is: How do we define or describe wealth and poverty? The most famous response is attributed to Shimon ben Zoma, who is reported to have said, "Who is rich? One who is happy with his portion" (*Pirkei Avot* 4:1). A more expansive discussion is found in the Babylonian Talmud:

> Our Rabbis taught: Who is rich? One who is content with his
> wealth—the words of Rabbi Meir. Rabbi Tarfon said: One who
> has one hundred vineyards, one hundred fields, and one hundred
> slaves working in them. Rabbi Akiva says: One who has a wife
> whose deeds are beautiful. Rabbi Yosei said: One who has a privy
> close to his table. (BT *Shabbat* 25b)

This passage teaches us several things about wealth. First, although
it may be possible to enumerate a person's possessions, seeing oneself
as rich is subjective. A person may have very little and still consider
herself a wealthy woman. Indoor plumbing—or an outhouse in the
backyard—might make a person feel like he has won the lottery. And
although the Rabbis cited in the Talmud do not say so explicitly, we
can imagine that the opposite is true as well: a person could have one
hundred fields and vineyards and still not think of himself as rich.

Just as wealth means different things to different people, so too does
need. Commenting on the words "lacking everything" in Deuteronomy
28:48, a number of rabbis attempt to define poverty:

> Rabbi Ammi said Rav said: Without a lamp and without a table.
> Rav Chisda said: Without a wife. Rav Sheshet said: Without a
> servant. Rav Nachman said: Without knowledge. A *Tanna* taught:
> Without salt and without fat. (BT *N'darim* 41a)

Just as in the previous passage, we see acknowledgment that some
people feel poor only when they lack the most basic furniture or ingre-
dients that make food more palatable, while others think the absence
of a servant renders them impoverished. And, not surprisingly, for at
least one rabbi, poverty is measured not by one's lack of material goods
but by lack of knowledge!

Is wealth always a sign of divine favor, and is poverty always an
indication of God's disfavor? This idea is dismissed in another Talmudic passage:

> Said Rava: Lifespan, children, and sustenance are not a matter of
> merit, but of luck. For Rabbah and Rav Chisda were both righ-
> teous sages—when either prayed, it rained—but Rav Chisda lived

ninety-two years, while Rabbah lived forty years. In the house of Rav Chisda, there were sixty wedding feasts, while in the house of Rabbah, there were sixty bereavements. In the house of Rav Chisda, there was bread made of fine flour even for the dogs and there were leftovers, while in the house of Rabbah there was coarse barley bread for humans and there was not enough. (BT *Mo-eid Katan* 28a)

The Rabbis' approach to the acquisition of resources is ambivalent, perhaps in part because the study of Torah, privileged by the Rabbis above all other endeavors, was not an occupation that led to wealth. Stories told about early sages often present their protagonists as extremely poor men who made great sacrifices to study Torah. In one story, the great sage Hillel is described as so poor that he could not afford the entry fee to the house of study. One cold day he resorted to lying on the skylight to listen to the great teachers of his day; he was found on the roof the next morning covered with snow (BT *Yoma* 35b). Rabbi Akiva is said to have been an illiterate shepherd who lived with his wife in dire poverty before he began to study (BT *K'tubot* 62b–63a; BT *N'darim* 50a). Another early rabbi, Eliezer ben Hyrcanus, was disinherited by his wealthy father because he chose to study Torah; when his father, impressed by his son's accomplishments as a scholar, relented, Eliezer reportedly expressed no interest in his father's property, claiming that all he wanted was Torah (*Avot D'Rabbi Natan* 6; *Pirkei D'Rabbi Eliezer* 1). Some rabbis are described as men who earned a living through manual labor while devoting as much time as possible to their studies.

At the same time, Rabbinic literature recognizes the value of wealth and the potential that wealth may enable Torah study, either by freeing its owner from the need to earn a living or through donations by the wealthy to those who study. The Babylonian Talmud encourages fathers to marry their daughters to Torah scholars (BT *P'sachim* 49b); a marriage between a rabbi and the daughter of a well-to-do family would provide the former with the means to study without concern for his livelihood. We read of Rabban Yochanan ben Zakkai entertaining the wealthy men of Jerusalem at his table; whether or not the story reflects the social reality of the earliest rabbis, it indicates that the narrator knew the value of associating with rich men.

Rabbinic literature recognizes the responsibility of those who are able to help maintain communal institutions and to provide for the needy. *Mishnah Pei-ah* includes basic parameters about eligibility for communal charity. It teaches, "One who has food (or funds to buy food) for two meals should not take from the soup kitchen. [One who has food] for fourteen meals should not take from the community fund" (*Mishnah Pei-ah* 8:7). The Mishnah continues:

> One who has 200 *zuz* should not take agricultural portions designated for the poor. If one has 200 *zuz* less one, even if a thousand people give to him at once, he may take. If [his property] is mortgaged to a creditor or his wife's marriage settlement, he may take. We do not force a person to sell his house and his household goods [in order to receive communal assistance]. One who has 50 *zuz* and is engaging in commerce with them should not take. (*Mishnah Pei-ah* 8:7–9)

The Mishnah offers us a glimpse into the Rabbis' thinking about what constitutes need or poverty. It sets 200 *zuz*, which commentators explain would allow a person to pay for basic needs for a year, as the threshold for receiving public assistance; a person with less than this amount is considered poor. The Mishnah also safeguards the dignity of the poor by excluding an individual's home and household goods from valuation in determining need. It also recognizes that money used to do business has a greater value to an individual than money not invested. These rules indicate the Rabbis of the Mishnah recognized that poverty existed in their communities, that the community had an obligation to assist its needy members, and that concern for human dignity and the realities of the economy had to be taken into consideration when formulating policies about public assistance.

Rabbinic discussions about *tzedakah* also teach us what the Sages assumed about the obligations of the wealthy toward those less fortunate. The Babylonian Talmud discusses the nature of the authority conferred on those who collect *tzedakah*. Although *tzedakah* collectors are described as oppressive when they attempt to secure donations from those unable to give to charity, they may apply pressure to those who are rich. The Talmud reports that one rabbi "forced" another to give 400 *zuz* to *tzedakah*; the latter's ability to make this substantial donation justified the pressure put on him to do so by his colleague (BT *Bava Batra* 8b).

Although never stated explicitly in Rabbinic sources, the relationship between money and power or autonomy is acknowledged. A father controls any assets earned or found by his minor daughter. Although women can own property and earn money, a married woman's earnings belong to her husband, who also has the right to enjoy income she receives from property she brings into the marriage (*Mishnah K'tubot* 4:4). Only when a woman is wholly autonomous—emancipated from her father, divorced, or widowed—does she control and benefit from her property. The institution of the *ketubah*, the sum a husband pledges to pay his wife should they get divorced or should he die, served to protect a woman both against frivolous divorce at a time when a husband could divorce his wife for any reason and without the latter's consent; it also protected a widow against complete dependence on her husband's heirs.

The foundational texts of Judaism, although reflecting economic systems much less complex than our own, are aware that a person's assets may reflect or bestow social status. There is no blanket condemnation of wealth, nor is there any sense that it indicates a person's moral superiority. Instead, Rabbinic texts focus on the obligations that come with having means; if a person fulfills those responsibilities, he or she is not required to give up his or her wealth. The adage "Who is rich? The one who is happy with his/her portion" can be read both as permission to take pleasure in what we have and as a reminder that the pursuit of money is not a substitute for or a guarantee of happiness.

2

BLESSING AND CHALLENGE

A Further Look at the Sources

ALYSSA M. GRAY, JD, PHD

The teachings of our tradition in large part agree that wealth is a blessing. However, a nuanced view of the sources provides us with clear-eyed cautions about the spiritual, psychological, and social costs that come with the pursuit of wealth and with our possession of it. This chapter's purpose is to concisely explore a selection of the ancient, medieval, and modern Jewish legal and other sources that illustrate this dual approach. The selected sources illustrate eight themes: (1) Jewish tradition's overall positive attitude toward the possession of wealth; (2) how (not) to accumulate wealth, ethically speaking; (3) the Rabbis' ambivalence about wealth, as seen through the lens of their traditions about how Moses became wealthy; (4) right and wrong attitudes people might have about wealth; (5) the destructive spiritual, psychological, and social effects of greed; (6) praiseworthy uses of wealth; (7) misuses of wealth; and (8) acknowledging and mitigating the outsized social impact that wealth can allow its possessors to have.

Being Wealthy Is a Good Thing

There is no shortage of biblical verses supporting this proposition. Let us look at the role that God's bestowal of the blessing of wealth plays in the crafting of the character of Abraham, the father of Israel. Wealth and divine favor go hand in hand. Abram leaves Haran with wealth (Gen. 12:5) and is described as rich in "livestock, silver, and gold" (Gen. 13:2). He is concerned that the king of Sodom not be able to take credit for his wealth (Gen. 14:23) but does accept silver and flocks from Abimelech (Gen. 20:14–16). His servant Eliezer opens his speech to Abraham's relatives about his mission to find a wife for Isaac by stressing that "the Eternal has blessed my master exceedingly and made him rich" (Gen. 24:35).

The Book of Proverbs later says that "in her [= Wisdom's] right hand is length of days; in her left, riches and honor" (Prov. 3:16). Wisdom "herself" later says, "Riches and honor belong to me, enduring wealth and success" (Prov. 8:18). The Babylonian Talmud (*Bava Batra* 25b) builds on Proverbs' linkage of wisdom, riches, and honor: while Rabbi Yitzchak teaches that one should face south while praying to obtain wisdom and north to obtain wealth, Rabbi Y'hoshua ben Levi teaches that one should always face south, as wisdom leads to wealth (citing Prov. 3:16). At the very least, this Talmudic passage demonstrates that seeking and acquiring wealth is viewed positively. Apropos, the Rabbis have a jaundiced view of self-impoverishment. A person should not spend more than 20 percent of one's possessions on charity, lest one become impoverished from it (BT *K'tubot* 50a). Rabbi Yochanan is described as having impoverished himself for Torah study, much to the unconcealed dismay of Rabbi Chiyya (*Vayikra Rabbah* 30:1).

How (Not) to Become Wealthy

Possessing wealth may be a positive thing, but the end does not justify any and all means of acquiring it. Obtaining wealth through the oppression of others, for example, is unjustified, even (or especially) if one wishes to use that wealth to give *tzedakah*. *P'sikta D'Rav Kahana* 10:10 critically describes an administrator of landed estates who would go out to the villages, collect money by force from his tenants, and then return to the city and proclaim, "Gather the poor, that I might do a mitzvah with them [i.e., give them charity]." Another example is overcharging the public for necessities. Making a profit as a middleman by high prices for dietary staples like wines, oils, and different kinds of flour was prohibited in the Land of Israel, as was profiting "twice" in eggs anywhere. One definition of "twice" was one egg dealer selling to another (BT *Bava Batra* 91a). "Necessities" can also be items required for religious purposes. *Mishnah K'ritot* 1:7 describes the sacrificial offerings that women had to bring to the Jerusalem Temple in the event of certain cases involving childbirth or other related events. Given the state of the law, which required women to bring a number of offerings, the price of a pair of doves (one of the required offerings) rose to the very expensive price of a golden *dinar*. Rabban Shimon ben Gamliel was outraged by this, and he determined to bring the cost down to a silver *dinar*, which he did by teaching the law in a way that reduced the number of offerings women had to bring. The price of a pair of doves then fell to a (much less expensive) quarter of a silver *dinar*.

Two passages in the Babylonian Talmud about ethical ways to obtain wealth notably include God as part of the equation. Rabbi Meir teaches in *Mishnah Kiddushin* 4:14 that a person should teach his child a "clean and easy" trade and "pray to the One to whom wealth and possessions belong." Rabbi Meir stresses that every trade carries the potential for wealth or poverty. These do not inhere in any trade; rather, "everything is according to one's merit." BT *Nidah* 70b squarely answers the question of what one must do in order to become wealthy, with the advice to do a lot of business and do so honestly. Following the Talmud's forthright acknowledgment that this path has not always been successful for everyone, the additional advice is given that one should also pray to God, who owns all silver and gold (citing Haggai 2:8). The contrast between these two passages is clear: the proper path to riches must include a pious awareness of God and God's role in the bestowal of wealth. Those who amass wealth improperly clearly lack that awareness of God; their improperly acquired wealth is not a blessing, certainly not to the people from whom they likely extorted it.

The "How Moses Became Wealthy" Traditions and Rabbinic Ambivalence about Wealth

On the one hand, the Rabbis were aware that acquiring wealth in the real world might involve engaging in compromising activities, possibly including the oppression and exploitation of other human beings. On the other hand, they lived in a culture in which leaders were expected to be wealthy, and they even retroject such a value onto the paradigmatic Jewish leader, Moses. But how could Moses—and by extension, other Jewish leaders—acquire the wealth expected of a communal leader, both practically and ethically? In answering this question, the Rabbis also tacitly signal their own ambivalence about wealth. *Sifrei B'midbar* 101, JT *Sh'kalim* 5:2, 49a, *Vayikra Rabbah* 32:2, and BT *N'darim* 38a all concern themselves with Moses's attainment of wealth. *Sifrei B'midbar* and BT *N'darim* attribute his wealth to God's allowing him to keep the leftover pieces of the hewn stone tablets for himself. According to JT *Sh'kalim* and *Vayikra Rabbah*, God created either a sapphire quarry (*Vayikra Rabbah*) or a quarry of precious stones and pearls (JT *Sh'kalim*) in Moses's tent, and "Moses became wealthy from it" (JT *Sh'kalim*). The key point is that either way, Moses's wealth is pristine in origin: it was either planted in the ground by God just for him, or it was generated through his keeping for himself the stony crumbled remains of his revelatory encounter with the Divine. The Rabbis' ambivalence about wealth here is tacit, yet clear: while being wealthy is good (and even necessary for a leader), acquiring that wealth directly from God's own hand rather than through practical means in the real world is ideal (albeit fantastical).

Right and Wrong Attitudes about One's Wealth

Naturally, Moses is also an exemplar of the right attitude to hold about wealth: *Vayikra Rabbah* 32:2 tells us that his divinely bestowed good fortune led him to declare, "It is the blessing of the Eternal that enriches, and no toil can increase it" (Prov. 10:22).

But Ecclesiastes 5:9–13 points us in the direction of a *wrong* attitude about wealth, notably, "a lover of money never has his fill of money" (v. 9). This wrong attitude is *cupidity*, the never-ending drive to accumulate merely for the sake of accumulation. Tempering cupidity is a notable preoccupation of Jewish jurists and sages. Writing in *Hilchot Dei-ot* 3:2 in his *Mishneh Torah*, Moses Maimonides (Spain/Egypt, 1138–1204) rules that when doing business or engaging in salaried labor, a person should not be motivated solely by the drive to accumulate money, but by the physical and social needs this money can help him satisfy, all of which will ultimately aid in his service of God. Relatedly, in *Hilchot T'shuvah* 7:3, Maimonides rules that we are obligated to do penance not only for sinful acts, but also for sinful character traits (*dei-ot*), among which is "the pursuit of money." With keen psychological insight, he notes that repenting of such character traits is more difficult than repenting for deeds, for "when a person is immersed in these [character traits] it is difficult to separate from them." The later Provençal Talmudic commentator and jurist Me'iri (ca. 1249–1315) writes in his *Beit HaB'chirah* (to BT *Bava Batra* 9a) that a person should not be pained by the prospect of parting with his money as charity; a person should not "exclusively exert effort in increasing one's money [only for the sake of such increase]." The early modern Bible commentator Rabbi Shlomo Ephraim Luntschitz (Prague, 1550–1619) comments on Genesis 4:17 ("He became the founder [*boneh*, 'builds' in the present tense] of a city, and he named the city after his son, Enoch") that

> for all who love the possessions of the earth like Cain and his companions: he goes on building and can't ever complete his edifice in his lifetime, because he never has enough . . . if he has one measure [of gold or silver] he craves [more] up to two hundred, as is known of the nature of those who love money. And, this being so, he goes on building forever, and has no rest all his days, he just wanders throughout the earth like Cain . . . most of his days he is chasing after wealth.[1]

Luntschitz comments in a similar vein on Genesis 33:9, "The evil ones, even though they have all the silver and gold in the world, it nevertheless appears to them as if they are still lacking." Luntschitz contrasts these "evil ones" with the "righteous," who "even if they have [only] a little, they suffice with it and are happy with their lot, and it appears to them as if they have everything." Luntschitz's characterization of the "righteous" echoes the earlier comments of Nachmanides (Catalonia, 1194–1270) on Genesis 25:8 ("And Abraham breathed his last . . . old and contented"): "This is a recounting of God's kindnesses toward the righteous. . . . [God ensures] that they should not passionately desire excess [possessions], as is said about them, 'You have given him his heart's desire' (Ps. 21:3)." Feverish desire and perpetual accumulation characterize the greedy; calm contentment and a focus on ultimate concerns characterize those who live righteously.

The Devastating Spiritual, Psychological, and Social Consequences of Greed

What of those who remain trapped by the feverish desire for possessions and a cycle of perpetual accumulation for its own sake? *Mishnah Avot* 2:7 states that the one who increases his possessions increases his worries. This increase in worry, if taken to an extreme, can become spiritually damaging. Commenting on Exodus 16:4 ("I will rain down bread for you from the sky . . . that I may thus test them"), Luntschitz points out that those who have more possessions than they actually need are too busy maintaining their lifestyle "to engage in Torah." We may discern another consequence of the endless drive for accumulation in a responsum of Rabbi Solomon ben Adret, the Rashba (Barcelona, 1235–1310)—the emergence of an "us and them" mentality, separating the very wealthy and the needy. Adret harshly criticizes people he labels the "magnificently wealthy" for their plan to dismantle the local social welfare apparatus and compel the local poor to beg, all because (as he sees it) they wished to save themselves the money needed to maintain it.[2]

Taken to an extreme, greed can fray social bonds so much that social breakdown results. JT *Yoma* 1:1, 38c claims that the Second Temple was destroyed in 70 CE despite widespread engagement in Torah study because the people "loved money" and hated each other without cause. Although the Jerusalem Talmud does not connect these two social ills, they can reasonably be seen as mutually reinforcing.

Unchecked greed can dehumanize the greedy. BT *Sanhedrin* 109a recounts that the people of Sodom would deposit bundles of fragrant spices with wealthy people, who would put the bundles in their treasure chests. At night the greedy people of Sodom would sniff out the bundles like dogs and tunnel to steal the treasures. They allowed their greed to distort their humanity and began behaving like animals. The end point of such untrammeled accumulation is rebellion against God; according to BT *Yoma* 86b, Moses held God responsible for Israel's worshiping the Golden Calf, because God gave them so much silver and gold when they left Egypt that they yelled, "Enough!" Their sense of spiritual self was entirely overwhelmed by the excess of gold and silver—and God was to blame! In the twentieth century, Rabbi Israel Meir Kagan warned that the unchecked pursuit of luxuries could lead people down a path of "robbery, violence, and also disgrace and shame."[3]

Appropriate and Praiseworthy Uses of Wealth

Wealth can—and should—be used for positive purposes. One example is spending generously on the beautiful performance of ritual commandments (BT *Shabbat* 133b; compare BT *Sukkah* 41b), referred to as *hidur mitzvah* (beautification of a mitzvah). Another example is giving *tzedakah*. The thirteenth-century compilation *Sefer Chasidim* quotes God as telling the wealthy that God gave them wealth to give it to the poor.[4] Writing about the Purim holiday, Maimonides stresses that a person should spend more on *matanot l'evyonim* (gifts to the poor) than on a lavish Purim meal and *mishloach manot* (sending of [food] portions) for one's friends.[5] Related but not identical to *tzedakah*, redeeming captives is labeled a *mitzvah rabbah*, a great mitzvah.[6] Further, using wealth to provide employment for the needy is also praiseworthy.[7] Finally, wealth can and should be used to support Torah scholars and study. Commenting on Deuteronomy 33:18 ("Rejoice, O Zebulun, on your journeys, and Issachar, in your tents"), Rashi (France, 1040–1105) describes Zebulun as a traveling businessman who supports Issachar's Torah study and shares in the latter's reward.[8]

Misuses of Wealth

To misuse wealth is, essentially, to squander it on that which is not needed, short lasting, and ultimately unimportant. Solomon Alami (Spain, ca. 1415) complained that the wealthy Jews of Spain spent money on "government officials, dance masters, court contractors, comedians, circus proprietors, doubtful characters of all colors and creeds," but not Torah scholars.[9] *Sefer Chasidim* states that giving money to the poor is better than spending it on beautiful exotic birds or even on the purchase of a second home (provided one's first home is fireproof).[10]

The Wealthy and Everyone Else

The wealthy can use their wealth in ways that have a great, even outsized impact on Jewish society (naturally, the classical Jewish sources are focused internally; a modern reader can apply this to all of society). Jewish legal sources over the centuries show a measure of discomfort with public, long-standing recognition of the wealthy for good works—recognition in the form of placing their names on edifices or the modern award of "plaques." Despite a history of lingering ambivalence extending into the twentieth century, Jewish legal scholars have tended to follow the *Shulchan Aruch*'s lead in permitting such recognition.[11] Recognition acknowledges and thanks generous donors and also encourages others to give.

The Babylonian Talmud tends to portray Babylonian rabbis as independently wealthy, or at least as independent of wealthy non-rabbis (BT *N'darim* 38a; BT *B'rachot* 10b). In BT *N'darim* 38a, this portrayal of independence is linked to Moses's portrayal as a serendipitously wealthy man; Moses, the paradigm of a rabbinic leader, is thus also the prime exemplar of rabbinic independence. Although the Talmud's motivation for this portrayal of Babylonian rabbis is not made explicit, related narrative portrayals of tensions between Babylonian rabbis and wealthy non-rabbis indicate that the Rabbis saw economic independence as integrally related to religious, spiritual, and intellectual independence.

This carries into medieval texts, as Maimonides rules that among the required characteristics of a rabbinic judge is "hatred of money" and that they "not even [be] anxious about their own money" and do not "pursue the accumulation of money."[12] A Jewish judge's angle of vision on justice should not be distorted by an obsession with wealth. Similarly, Rabbi Jacob ben Asher (Spain, ca. 1269–1343) later rules that communal arrangements for the payment of judges must be such that "the judges don't need to . . . ask anything of anyone . . . nor need anyone, *nor flatter anyone, nor be beholden to anyone.*"[13] To Jacob ben Asher, a judge must not be required to raise the funds needed to pay his salary himself, with all the inevitable compromises with and/or submission to powerful people in the community this might entail.

From this chapter's brief summary, we see that Jewish tradition views wealth as a blessing. The first half of Proverbs 10:22 can serve as a fit summary of that view: "It is the blessing of the Eternal that enriches." But centuries of immersion in the messy world of human actions, motivations, virtues, and weaknesses have led Jewish scholars, sages, and jurists to the realization that wealth is not an *unqualified* blessing. Wealth poses challenges to human beings, and grappling with and overcoming these challenges is key to living a truly God-minded, Torah-following, Jewish life.

NOTES

1. This and all references to Shlomo Ephraim Luntschitz are to his Torah commentary *K'li Yakar* (the "precious vessel"). This commentary is printed in editions of the standard rabbinic Bible (*Mikraot G'dolot*).
2. Solomon ben Adret, *Responsa* 3:380.
3. Israel Meir Kagan, *Biur Halachah* 529.
4. *Sefer Chasadim*, ed. Wistinetzki, paragraph 1345.
5. Maimonides, *Mishneh Torah, Hilchot M'gilah V'Chanukah* 2:17.
6. Rabbi David ibn Zimra, *Responsa* 1:40, based on BT *Bava Batra* 8a–b.
7. E.g., Maimonides, *Mishneh Torah, Hilchot Mat'not Aniyim* 10:7.
8. See also Moses Isserles's comments on *Shulchan Aruch, Yoreh Dei-ah* 246:1.
9. For this text, see Jacob Rader Marcus and Marc Saperstein, *The Jews in Christian Europe: A Source Book, 315–1791* (Pittsburgh: Hebrew Union College Press and University of Pittsburgh Press, 2015), 556–61.
10. *Sefer Chasadim*, ed. Wistinetzki, paragraphs 461–62.
11. Moses Isserles to *Shulchan Aruch, Yoreh Dei-ah* 249:13.
12. Maimonides, *Mishneh Torah, Hilchot Sanhedrin* 2:7.
13. Jacob ben Asher, *Arbaah Turim, Choshen Mishpat* 9; emphasis added.

3

HOW MUCH IS ENOUGH?

RABBI AMY SCHEINERMAN

The incomparable George Carlin is fondly remembered for his iconic "A Place for My Stuff" routine:

> That's the whole meaning of life, isn't it? Trying to find a place for your stuff. That's all your house is—your house is just a place for your stuff. . . . That's all your house is; it's a pile of stuff with a cover on it . . . a place to keep your stuff while you go out and get *more* stuff. Sometimes you've gotta move, you've gotta get a bigger house. Why? *Too much stuff?*[1]

Carlin was addressing a concern limited to affluent people prior to the advent of industrialism, but since then to a far broader swath of society. An early warning flare of the corrosive nature of materialism was raised by the early twentieth-century British economic historian and social critic R. H. Tawney, who coined the term "the acquisitive society" to title a book in which he claimed that capitalism and the modern industrial society promote selfish individualism and fuel insatiable materialism.[2] He further argued that highly skewed income distribution in a society "diverts energy from the creation of wealth to the multiplication of luxuries, so that, for example, while one-tenth of the people of England are overcrowded, a considerable part of them are engaged . . . in making rich men's hotels, luxurious yachts, and motorcars."[3] While capitalism and industrialization may have teamed up to promote a higher level of materialism than previously possible in human history, that level pales in comparison to what we find today. What is more, given human nature and our complicated relationship with coveting, satisfaction, and gratitude, Tawney's observation was hardly novel.

When the Torah inveighed against coveting, elevating the prohibition to the tenth of the Ten Commandments (Exod. 20:14; Deut. 5:18), the lives we live today and the extent of our preoccupation with possessions were hardly imaginable.[4] Now, in the twenty-first century, scientists are unsure whether craving "stuff" is baked into our biology or triggered by socially generated emotions. Chief among those emotions are the fear and shame we feel when we compare our status and possessions unfavorably to those of others. What is clear is that advertising has developed far beyond its original mission of fulfilling needs to become an industrial mammoth that creates and nurtures needs we never knew we had. Advertising cultivates in us a deep dissatisfaction that gives rise to "affluenza,"[5] the socially transmitted epidemic disease of consumerism, whose symptoms include anxiety, debt, and waste.[6]

The Christian socialist Tawney had opined, "A society is rich when material goods, including capital, are cheap, and human beings dear: indeed the word 'riches' has no other meaning."[7] His observations and warnings echo those articulated by Jewish thinkers long before capitalism and industrialism democratized excess.

The desire for wealth and material possessions and the attribute of cupidity are universally human qualities; they are by no means the exclusive province of any one society or epoch. However, the moral valence assigned to wealth, generosity, pleasure, satisfaction, and gratitude represents cultural values. Jewish tradition has long engaged in an ongoing conversation concerning the nature and effect of coveting, the meaning and purpose of wealth, and appropriate sources of pleasure and satisfaction. The fruits of that conversation help each of us, in every generation, wade through the swamp of human experiences and emotions that provoked Tawney, Carlin, and many others to weigh in on the challenge of wealth and materialism for both individuals and societies.

Coveting: What It Is and What Might It Cause Us to Do?

Genesis explains that humanity's foray from the protected Garden of Eden out into the world was spurred by desire: the people longed for the fruit of the Tree of Knowledge. Desire motivates action, but envy is a particularly powerful and dangerous form of desire. People have long pondered the meaning of the last of the *Aseret HaDib'rot* (Ten Commandments), which prohibits coveting, but rarely does anyone question the pernicious and dangerous nature of coveting. Each of the two versions of the prohibition on coveting in the Torah employs a common verb, but the second version also employs an additional verb:

> You shall not covet [*tachmod*] your neighbor's house: you shall not covet [*tachmod*] your neighbor's wife, nor male nor female slave, nor ox nor ass, nor anything that is your neighbor's. (Exod. 20:14)

> You shall not covet [*tachmod*] your neighbor's wife. You shall not crave [*titaveh*] your neighbor's house, or field, or male or female slave, or ox, or ass, or anything that is your neighbor's. (Deut. 5:18)

What do *tachmod* and *titaveh* mean, and how are they distinguished from one another? It is rare for Torah to legislate or prohibit an emotion, this being virtually impossible to judge and enforce.[8] Does Torah forbid an emotion or a behavior here? And in forbidding coveting, what emotional and behavioral fallout is Torah seeking to prevent?

In a fascinating and moving discussion of funerary practices in the second century, the Babylonian Talmud, *Mo-eid Katan* 27, grapples with the confluence of class distinction and the envy such distinctions arouse within the Jewish community and the emotional pain of shame and embarrassment that ensues:

Our Rabbis taught: Formerly, they would bring food to the house
of mourners in following manner: to the rich, in baskets of gold
and silver, and to the poor, in wicker baskets made of peeled willows. And the poor people were ashamed. The Sages, therefore,
instituted that all should be provided with food in wicker baskets
made of peeled willows, out of deference to the poor.

Our Rabbis taught: Formerly, they would provide drinks to the
house of mourners in the following manner: to the rich, in white
glass [which was very expensive], and to the poor, in colored glass.
And the poor people were ashamed. The Sages therefore instituted
that all should be provided with drinks in colored glass, out of deference to the poor. . . .

Formerly, the expense of carrying out the dead was harder on the
family than the death itself; the family therefore abandoned the
corpse and fled, until Rabban Gamliel [president of the Sanhe-
drin] disregarded his own dignity and had his body carried out in
flaxen shrouds. Afterward, all the people followed his lead and had
themselves carried out in flaxen shrouds. Rav Papa stated: And
nowadays, all follow the practice of being carried out even in a
paltry shroud that costs but a *zuz*.[9]

Rabban Gamliel, the leader of the community, who came from a
wealthy family, renounced the luxuries available to him and his family
in connection with burial and mourning practices in order to prevent
poor Jews from feeling ashamed that they could not provide the same
for their beloved deceased. He thereby established a premium on
simplicity and modesty in burial that remains to this day.

The Mishnah evinces concern for envy Jews might arouse among
their non-Jewish neighbors as well, because jealousy could spell danger
for Jews. *Mishnah Sotah* 9:14 reports that the Rabbis prohibited "the
bridegroom's crown" during the war of Vespasian and "bride's diadem"
(likely a tiara) during the war of Titus, banning a display of decorative
opulence the bride wore on the occasion of a wedding celebration
during particularly precarious times.

It appears that this passage in the Mishnah began a trend that cul-
minated in sumptuary laws limiting private expenditures on religious

grounds throughout the Middle Ages.[10] These laws were designed to alleviate both envy within the Jewish community and antisemitic accusations and attacks from without stemming from jealousy over perceived Jewish ostentation. The Rhine Synod of 1202–23, the Forli (Italy) conference of 1418, the Castilian synod at Valladolid in 1432, the Cracow ordinances of 1595, the Polish Council of the Four Lands ruling of 1607, the Lithuanian Council regulations of 1637, the sumptuary laws issued in Metz 1690–97, and regulations issued in Salonika, Mantua, and Rome in the sixteenth and seventeenth centuries were among the many laws passed by rabbis and community leaders limiting the size and opulence of banquet celebrations, as well as the lavishness of apparel and jewelry worn in public.

The eleventh-century philosopher Rabbi Bachya ibn Pakuda recognized that far too many Jews concerned themselves with outward ritual observances ("duties performed by limbs of the body") while ignoring the underlying ethical and spiritual ideas ("duties of the heart"). In *Chovot HaL'vavot* (*Duties of the Heart*), his work of religious philosophy, Ibn Pakuda pointedly asserted that living one's life focused on materialistic self-indulgence and luxuries distances one from God. He adjured his readers to employ their intellects to rule over their desires lest they be spiritually diminished.[11]

A century later, Moses Maimonides (Spain/Egypt, 1135–1204) pursued a different line of argument to resolve the question of what constitutes coveting. In his law code *Mishneh Torah* (*Hilchot G'zeilah Va-aveidah* 1:9–11), he explains that coveting can damage our relationships with other people:

> One who covets a servant, a maidservant, a house, or utensils belonging to another person, or any other item that he can purchase from him and pressures him with friends and requests until he agrees to sell it to him violates a negative commandment, although he pays much for it, Torah states, "You shall not covet. . . ."

What is more, coveting is an emotional state so intense it leads to proscribed behavior; therein lies Torah's prohibition. Maimonides continues by noting that the craving to obtain an object possessed by another might lead one to think, "How is it possible to acquire this from him?" and this thought may well lead to a forbidden act: "Craving leads to coveting, and coveting leads to robbery." Even worse, in extreme cases the person motivated by craving "will resort to murder."

Hence, Jewish thinkers have addressed a wide variety of outcomes of envy and coveting: on the inner emotional life of the one who experiences envy, on the spiritual life of one distracted by material acquisition, and on the behavior of one obsessed with the desire to acquire an object. Does this mean that material wealth is a curse? Can it be a blessing?

Wealth: A Blessing or a Curse?

Judaism does not reject materialism, glorify poverty, or sanctify asceticism. Rather, tradition teaches that God gave us life to enjoy and revel in. *Kohelet*, Ecclesiastes, teaches that the ordinary pleasures of life are God's blessings and the craving to amass wealth is a vain pursuit:

> There is nothing as worthwhile for a person than to eat and drink and enjoy the good that is afforded by one's labor. And even that, I noted, comes from God. For who eats and who enjoys but myself? To the one who pleases God, God has given the wisdom and shrewdness to enjoy life and to the one who displeases God, God has given the urge to gather and amass. . . . That too is futile and the pursuit of wind. (Eccles. 2:24–26)

Jewish tradition has always viewed wealth as a blessing. Hebrew Scripture holds that, together with long life and peace, wealth is deemed God's reward to those who obey the covenant.[12] Those blessed with wealth are expected to share their good fortune with those who are needy; for this, too, they will be rewarded:

> If . . . there is a needy person among you, one of your kin in any of your settlements in the land that the Eternal your God is giving you, do not harden your heart and shut your hand against your needy kin. Rather, you must open your hand and lend whatever

is sufficient to meet the need. Beware lest you harbor the base thought, "The seventh year, the year of remission, is approaching," so that you are mean and give nothing to your needy kin, who will cry out to the Eternal against you, and you will incur guilt. Give readily and have no regrets when you do so, for in return the Eternal your God will bless you in all your efforts and in all your undertakings. For there will never cease to be needy ones in your land, which is why I command you: open your hand to the poor and needy kin in your land. (Deut. 15:7–11)

Torah preserves, in Deuteronomy 16, an early calendar of the three Pilgrimage Festivals, Passover, Shavuot, and Sukkot. The practices of Passover are designed to invoke memories of slavery in Egypt, but on Shavuot and Sukkot the Israelites are specifically commanded to rejoice. On Shavuot: "You shall rejoice before the Eternal your God together with your son and daughter, your male servant and your female slave, the [family of the] Levite in your communities, and the stranger, the fatherless, and the widow in your midst, at the place where the Eternal your God will choose to establish the divine name" (Deut. 16:11). The commandment to rejoice implies holding a celebration, which requires money. *Midrash Tanchuma* (R'eih 18) uses this verse to emphasize the importance of generosity toward people who are not within one's immediate circle:[13]

> The Holy Blessed One says: You have four in your household—*your son and your daughter and your male servant and your female servant*—and I have four in My household—*the Levite and the stranger and the orphan and the widow.* All [eight] of them are [mentioned] in one verse [to teach that] if you make Mine happy, then I will take care of the members of your household.

In the minds of the Rabbis, our generosity is reciprocated—indeed rewarded—by God. Even more, God supplies people with wealth in order that they should share God's bounty with people in need. On the one hand, wealth makes more *tzedakah* possible. On the other hand, the theological assurance that God will not permit generosity toward poor people to impoverish one encourages increased giving.

The Rabbis confirmed this message in connection with tithes, as well. In biblical times, one-tenth of a farmer's produce was separated and donated to poor people in the third and sixth years of the seven-year *Sh'mitah* (Sabbatical) cycle. The Babylonian Talmud, *Taanit* 9a (and *Midrash Tanchuma Re-eh* 18) makes a clever wordplay based on the similarly sounding Hebrew words for "tithe" and "rich": "'You shall surely *aseir* [tithe]' (Deut. 14:22) in order that you become *ashir* [rich] and never come to lack anything."[14] In a similar vein, Rashi, Abraham ibn Ezra, and other commentators read Proverbs 11:24—"There is one who scatters and yet is given more; another stints from doing right and incurs loss"—as promoting the same view that those who share their wealth with poor people will be financially recompensed by heaven.[15] As these examples demonstrate, wealth is seen as a blessing in and of itself, but even more because it facilitates generosity toward those in need. The greater one's wealth, the more *tzedakah* one can do. Money can alleviate hunger, homelessness, and suffering. For the Rabbis, and the sages who followed them, the blessing of money is meant to be shared.

The Rabbis articulated and reinforced this theological formulation many times in many ways, perhaps because they were so keenly aware that the desire for wealth is often a powerful motivator. So too, envy, greed, and coveting play a significant role in shaping our desires and thus our behavior. Hence a parallel conversation about cupidity has been conducted since the Bible first promulgated the tenth commandment.

What Makes Us Happy?

We live in a culture awash in consumer products and inundated with marketing ploys to inspire our desire for them. We also live in an age of unprecedented income inequality coupled with a window providing a continual view into the lives of the "haves." This is a recipe for increased coveting and corresponding dissatisfaction and unhappiness. Tawney warned nearly a century ago, citing numbers that are laughable today, the effect of income inequality on people of modest means and society as a whole:

> As long as a minority has so large an income that part of it, if spent at all, must be spent on trivialities, so long will part of the human energy and mechanical equipment of the nation be diverted from serious work, which enriches it, to making trivialities, which impoverishes it since they can only be made at the cost of not making other things. And if the peers and millionaires who are now preaching the duty of production to miners and dock laborers desire that more wealth, not more waste, should be produced, the simplest way in which they can achieve their aim is to transfer to the public their whole incomes over (say) $5,000 a year, in order that it may be spent in setting to work, not gardeners, chauffeurs, domestic servants and shopkeepers in the West End of London, but builders, mechanics and teachers.[16]

The situation he described has only grown more acute with time. In the 1980s, professor of clinical psychology Paul L. Wachtel penned *The Poverty of Affluence: A Psychological Portrait of the American Way of Life*,[17] a pointed condemnation of American consumerism as a nefarious contributor to psychological, social, political, and environmental decimation. Wachtel argued that Americans were schooled to believe in unlimited economic growth, each generation destined to become wealthier than the one before. Yet unbridled affluence would come at a high price: lives filled with more and more consumer goods would require ever more time and labor to pay for them—at the cost of a life endowed with spiritual richness, wealth of family and community relationships, and time to renew ourselves in the natural world.

The response to these concerns was articulated long ago by Shimon ben Zoma, a second-century sage, who encapsulated profound wisdom in this teaching:

> Who is rich? The one who is happy with his lot, as it says, "When you enjoy the fruit of your labors, you will be happy and you shall prosper" (Ps. 128:2). "You will be happy" in this world and "you shall prosper" in the world-to-come.

The secret of happiness, which eludes far too many people, Ben Zoma teaches, is experiencing satisfaction with what you have and avoiding craving and envy, which give rise to cupidity and worse.[18]

Ben Zoma's teaching is not merely countercultural; it seems at first glance to violate human nature. Yet many people successfully find contentment amid a modest lifestyle and are not driven by envy. They know that craving and acquiring material possessions do not enrich their lives spiritually. For a moment such acquisitions may make them happy, but in the next moment they are likely to fixate on something else they do not yet have. What makes them stronger and more resilient? What brings them genuine contentment? Their "secret sauce" is often a sense of purpose that fills their lives with happiness and fulfillment. We humans need our lives to have meaning and purpose. The pursuit of meaningful goals and endeavors—for example, contributing to the welfare of others, artistic endeavors, learning and teaching, personal relationships, professional achievements—are deeply fulfilling and provide the happiness and satisfaction. If desire for "stuff" creates a "great emptiness," then a sense of purpose fills the void.

NOTES

1. George Carlin, "Stuff," YouTube, https://www.youtube.com/watch?v=4x_QkGPCL18. "A Place for My Stuff" was launched in 1981. The John F. Kennedy Center for Performing Arts named Carlin its 2008 honoree for the Mark Twain American Prize for American Humor four days before his death on June 22, 2008.
2. R. H. Tawney, *The Acquisitive Society* (London: Fabian Society, 1920). Tawney lived from 1880 to 1962.
3. Tawney, *The Acquisitive Society*, 37. Tawney wrote, "The purpose of industry is obvious. It is to supply man with things that are necessary, useful or beautiful, and thus bring life to body or spirit" (8).
4. George Carlin, in a routine on the Ten Commandments cynically opined, "*Thou shalt not covet thy neighbor's goods.* This one is just plain stupid. Coveting your neighbor's goods is what keeps the economy going. . . . Coveting creates jobs; leave it alone."

5. The term "affluenza" predates the well-publicized case of Texas teen-ager Ethan Couch, whose attorney defended him against the charge of DUI, killing four pedestrians, and injuring eleven by arguing that he "suffered" from "affluenza," which rendered him unable to comprehend the consequences of his actions.

6. Arguably, the classic tome on this topic is Vance Packard's *The Hidden Persuaders*, which documented the manipulative methods of the advertising industry.

7. Tawney, *Acquisitive Society*, 98.

8. When Torah commands "love," it means to act loyally. When Torah commands "rejoicing," it means to engage in a celebration. Certainly, emotions are involved, but the essence of each is behavioral.

9. A *zuz* is a nominal amount.

10. David Biale has argued that while Jewish sumptuary laws were motivated by the pressures from non-Jewish authorities. In addition, since clothing serves as an identity marker, regulations limiting Jews' sartorial choices ensured that they could be visually distinguished from their gentile neighbors. See Biale, "Homeland, Exile and the Boundaries of Jewish Identity," in *Boundaries, Identity and Belonging in Modern Judaism*, ed. Maria Diemling and Larry Ray (New York: Routledge, 2014), 22.

11. Julius Guttmann explains, "Radical asceticism would put an end to the continued existence of human society, and thus contradict the divine will which demands the preservation of life. . . . On the other hand, Bahya teaches a mitigated form of asceticism in accordance with both the will of the Torah and the Aristotelian principle of virtue, as a mean between two extremes. Bahya has in mind an ideal of life which combines outward participation in the activities of the world, with an inner detachment from them, which he considers as the true life desired by God. The pious man is in duty bound to accept life in this world as a task, but he must remain inwardly detached from it, seeing the true goal of his life in communion with God, and in the preparation for the world to come, for which he is destined." Guttmann, *Philosophies of Judaism: The History of Jewish Philosophy from Biblical Times to Franz Rosenzweig* (New York: Schocken Books, 1964), 123–24.

12. See Lev. 26:3–10; Deut. 11:13–15.

13. Rashi's commentary to Deut. 16:11 echoes this midrash.

14. The word "tithe" (*aseir*) and the word "rich" (*ashir*) are spelled the same and, although not pronounced the same, sound similar.

15. "Scatter" is here understood to mean giving money to poor people: "spreading the wealth."

16. Tawney, *Acquisitive Society*, 38–39.

17. Paul L. Wachtel, *The Poverty of Affluence: A Psychological Portrait of the American Way of Life* (New York: Free Press, 1983).

18. In a twist of irony, Marsha Richins, professor of marketing at the University of Missouri, studied consumers' levels of materialism and their emotional states before and after making a purchase. She found that more materialistic people experience more positive emotions prior to the purchase than after they have acquired the item, leading to the conclusion that we are happier imagining owning an item than actually possessing it. See Richins, "When Wanting Is Better Than Having: Materialism, Transformation Expectations, and Product-Evoked Emotions in the Purchase Process," *Journal of Consumer Research* 40, no. 1 (June 2013): 1–18.

4

DOES WEALTH AUTOMATICALLY
COARSEN THE SOUL?

Rabbi Neal Gold

In the final chapters of the Book of Numbers, the Israelites' wilderness journey from Egypt to Canaan is coming to an end. After forty years, the children of freed slaves are finally standing on the precipice of the Promised Land. At this dramatic moment, the tribes of Reuben, Gad, and Manasseh approach Moses with a request. The text explains that these tribes "owned cattle in very great numbers" (Num. 32:1), and they saw how the steppes of Moab were perfect for pasturing their animals. They tell Moses, "It would be a favor for us if this land were given to your servants as a holding; do not move us across the Jordan" (Num. 32:5).

The tribes realize that they are comfortable right where they are, preferring the fertile plains to whatever the Promised Land has to offer. We can feel the disappointment in Moses's response: "Are your brothers to go to war while you stay here?" (Num. 32:6).

Still, Reuben and Gad are persistent. They propose an arrangement: "We will build here sheepfolds for our flocks and towns for our children. And we will hasten as shock-troops in front of the Israelites" (Num. 32:16–17). Moses considers their proposal and agrees to their terms. If they fulfill their duty to their people, fighting alongside them, they can return to this far side of the Jordan River to "build towns for your children and sheepfolds for your flocks" (Num. 32:24).

As if this story were not startling enough—after the Exodus, Sinai, and miracles of the wilderness, a group of Israelites would choose their own comfort over the Land of Israel!—Rashi, the great Torah commentator, heard something more. He detected a subtle rebuke in Moses's words. The tribes initially spoke of their "sheepfolds for our flocks" and only second "towns for our children," implying that their flocks/wealth were their priority. In Moses's response, he reverses the sequence, "towns for your children and sheepfolds for your flocks," as if to say that their priorities were backward.[1] They had been seduced by their affluence and were neglecting their responsibility to their community and their families. It is a temptation that has enticed many who have tasted wealth for the first time.

Does this Torah story represent the normative Jewish view of wealth—that it will inevitably cause individuals to abandon their people and their heritage? Much of the Rabbinic tradition is concerned that money has a harmful effect of coarsening the soul. The rich person, according to this view, claims, "I am entitled to all this"—and, by the same logic, the poor person must deserve his lot due to some shortcoming of his own. Citing a handful of Torah verses, the Talmud remarks, "A full stomach is a specific kind of evil" (BT *B'rachot* 32a).

When it comes to money, most of us, of course, would prefer more of it, for the security, safety, and pleasures it can bring to our lives. And our tradition validates that instinct. For instance, a blessing recited weekly at *Havdalah* requests that "our descendants and our money increase like the grains of sand and the stars in the night."

At the same time, most of us know that the pursuit of wealth should not be the defining feature of our existence. Basic ethics tell us that greed and coarse materialism are wrong. Nonetheless, there are spiritual traditions in the world that find godliness in poverty and asceticism. Is Judaism among them?

The Challenges of Poverty

Classical Jewish texts show little nostalgia for poverty. Our tradition understands—through hard-earned experience—that poverty often entails hunger, illness, vulnerability to predatory creditors, and more:

> Nothing is harder in life than poverty; it is harder than all the other afflictions in the world. Our Rabbis said: Were all the afflictions in the world gathered on one side and poverty on the other, poverty would outweigh them all. (*Sh'mot Rabbah* 31:12)

Destitution is something to be relieved and averted, not romanticized.

Living in poverty presents genuine spiritual challenges. When a person is perpetually vulnerable, the fulfillment of mitzvot—the primary Jewish religious obligation—becomes much more difficult. Many Jewish rituals require money: wine for *Kiddush*, candles for Shabbat and holidays, tallit and *t'fillin*, books to study, and so on. Jewish folklore is full of stories about simple Jews who saved and scrambled to buy four cups of wine for the Pesach seder or a beautiful *etrog* for Sukkot. Our history books are full of the sagas of Jewish immigrants who came to America and, because of desperate need, often had to forgo Shabbat, working on Saturdays. As people who express holiness through ritual mitzvot, poverty is a major obstacle to religious living. Long ago, Rabbi Yochanan recognized this sad truth: "All the parts of the body depend on the heart—but the heart depends on the pocket" (JT *T'rumot* 8:4).

The Challenges of Wealth

At first blush, it may seem that wealth is a sign of God's favor. Many of the Torah's heroes were prosperous. Abraham amassed many flocks (Gen. 13:2), Isaac was "very wealthy" (Gen. 26:13), and Jacob returned home to Canaan a rich man (Gen. 32:6). Likewise, the Rabbis respected wealth: "The *Shechinah* rests upon one who is wise, strong, wealthy, and tall" (BT *Shabbat* 92a).

However, much of the Torah takes a more skeptical view.

In Deuteronomy in particular, there is a sense that wealth almost inevitably snowballs into self-worship. For instance, at the end of his life, Moses recites a lengthy poem known as the "Song of Moses." In the Song, Moses surveys the people's history and anticipates its future. He predicts that when the Israelites cross over the Jordan and set up their habitations in the Promised Land—when their dreams come true—they will forget God and come to believe that they made their own success:

> [God] set them atop the highlands,
>   to feast on the yield of the earth;
> Nursing them with honey from the crag,
>   and oil from the flinty rock. . . .
> So Jeshurun grew fat and kicked—
>   you grew fat and gross and coarse—
> They forsook the God who made them
>   and spurned the Rock of their support. . . .
> You neglected the Rock that begot you,
>   forgot the God who labored to bring you forth.
>
> (Deut. 32:13, 32:15, 32:18)

This theme of "you grew fat and forgot God" appears often. Deuteronomy seems to have a grave understanding of human nature: that it is our instinct to say, when we achieve success, "I built this all by myself," without any acknowledgment of God's beneficence or partnership.

The problem is that a taste of wealth breeds a desire to accumulate more: "Rabbi Yudan said in the name of Rabbi Aibo: If they have one hundred, they want two hundred, and if they have two hundred, they want four hundred!" (*Kohelet Rabbah* 3:12).

Financial success tends to create momentum that says more is *never enough*, which becomes an ethical whirlpool. To challenge this impulse, *Birkat HaMazon*, the Blessing after Meals, quotes a key verse from the Torah:

As it is written: "You shall eat [*v'achalta*], and be satisfied [*v'savata*], and bless [*uveirachta*] the Eternal your God for the good land that God has given you" (Deut. 8:10).

The three verbs in this verse form a progression: eat→be satisfied→bless. The first and third are easy enough; we eat and blessings fall from our lips. But the real challenge is the middle verb, "be satisfied." That part is tricky. *Birkat HaMazon* encourages us to express gratitude and awareness that we already have what we truly need.

The Sages worried that too much wealth leads people to think that they are *entitled* to their possessions—and, conversely, that those who have not found success simply must not be working hard enough. This perspective has enabled entire societies to rationalize draconian policies where the wealthy justify their own meritocracy and neglect the needs of the poor—"for their own good." The Rabbis were appalled that any society could be based on such heartless policies, such as those of their Roman tormentors:

> For an example of the sinfulness of the people of our generation: When Rabbi Y'hoshua ben Levi went to Rome, he saw marble pillars covered with sheets so they wouldn't crack from the heat nor freeze from the cold. He also saw a poor man with only a reed mat underneath him and another one upon his back [to protect him from the elements]. (*P'sikta D'Rav Kahana* 9:1)

What a condemnation of a society whose values are all wrong! And yet, how different is it from our own cities where men and women sleep in cardboard boxes in front of fancy storefronts, or our suburbs where gated communities protect residents from ever having to look poverty in the eye?

The sources persistently remind us that all our success contains elements of randomness and luck. That is not to say that the Rabbis did not value a strong work ethic; quite the opposite. The Talmud emphasizes that the Rabbis labored at "day jobs," and they placed a great emphasis on the value of work.[2] Still, even among the greatest of sages, some found financial reward and prosperity in this world, and others did not. There was no correlation between righteousness and wealth.[3] Success was a wheel, where a person could be rich or destitute according to the whims of fate:

> Rabbi Elazar HaKappar says: A person should always pray for God's mercy concerning poverty, for if he does not come into it, his children may; if his children do not come into it, then his grandchildren may. As it is written: "Give [to the needy person] readily and have no regrets when you do so, for in return the Eternal your God will bless you" (Deut. 15:10). According to the school of Rabbi Yishmael, the word *biglal* [for in return] indicates that poverty is a *galgal* [wheel] that goes around and around in this world. (BT *Shabbat* 151b)[4]

Having money is no indicator of moral grandeur, and poverty is not something that is deserved. If one is fortunate enough to be successful, one should be (a) grateful for God's blessings, (b) increasingly generous and empathetic to those in need, and (c) aware of cultivating a disposition of *tz'niut*, "modesty."

Living a Life of *Tzni'ut*

Perhaps of all the virtuous character traits in Jewish ethics, *tz'niut* is the most alien to the American condition. When we have money, there is a tendency to spend it accordingly—to build bigger houses, drive fancier cars, and wear pricier cloths. "If I can afford it, why shouldn't I splurge?" goes the argument. "And as long as I donate money when I'm asked, what harm does it do?"

In fact, exorbitant spending *does* cause harm. Sometimes it is devastating. For instance, when one family in a community spends a fortune on a celebration, it places unspoken pressure on every other family; the expectation of the whole community for what constitutes "acceptable" expenses increases. Families have gone into debt to pay for weddings or bar/bat mitzvah celebrations because of what they thought was expected of them. The result is the current spiritual carnage of our landscape, where money is poured into ever-vaster displays of consumption simply because that is what is considered "the standard" of our celebrations. *Tz'niut* is hardly a communal value in current American Jewish life.

This is not new. It seems as if Jewish communities always have wrestled with the spiraling price tags for life-cycle events and sought ways to limit excessive spending. Sometimes restrictions were enacted out of fear that brazenness would attract the unwanted attention of antisemitic neighbors and authorities. At other times, rules were put into place for the community's *moral* well-being.

There have been many times when Jewish communities enacted sumptuary laws. Throughout the ages, Jewish leaders recognized that behavior of the rich could cause pressure and pain on others in all sorts of ways, and they enacted limitations (*takanot*) on excessive spending. For instance, the Mishnah describes a joyful summer holiday, Tu B'Av, when single women would go out into the vineyards around Jerusalem dressed in white, and they would dance to attract the attention of young men. All of these young women, no matter what their social status, wore white garments that were borrowed from one another, "so as not to humiliate anyone who lacked one of her own" (*Mishnah Taanit* 4:8). (Can we imagine today's young people operating on some similar sort of principle, say, at their high school proms?)

Similarly, in Temple times people were instructed to burn a *pesach* offering that had become ritually impure outside of the Temple precinct. However, the Talmud specifically indicates that people were not allowed to use their own wood to burn their offering; they had to use wood that was arranged by the Temple specifically for this purpose. Why? Rav Yosef explained: In order not to humiliate one who could not afford to provide his own wood (BT *P'sachim* 82a).

In Talmudic times, the high cost of Jewish funerals had the potential to devastate families. In a courageous act of leadership, Rabban Gamliel, the chief authority of the Jewish community in the first century BCE, instructed that he should be buried in a simple white shroud, and the Jews after him followed suit. Pocketless shrouds symbolize that wealth does not accompany us out of this world. But more practically, shrouds and simple burial caskets were acts of economic justice: no one should be bankrupted because of ostentatious pressures from others in the community.[5]

Many examples of Jewish sumptuary laws come from medieval and early modern times. In thirteenth-century Germany, the community declared that feasts should be prepared only in the context of religious obligations (e.g., holidays, life-cycle events) and not for secular purposes. In Poland from the sixteenth through the eighteenth centuries, the Council of Four Lands[6] passed an enactment limiting the size of celebrations and the amount that could be spent on them. In a remarkably egalitarian statement (and a smackdown to rich elitists), the council insisted that at any bris celebration, "Every ten invitees must include at least one poor person"![7]

Practices like white shrouds and the "plain pine box" are still widely observed. They teach us that the choices we make set moral expectations for the communities of which we are a part. We might ask: What would it look like if today's Jewish community created self-imposed limits for the sake of modesty, tastefulness, and their impact on our neighbors?

The "Ambivalent Embrace"

The Jewish community is one of the great immigrant success stories of the United States. Certainly, there are Jews living in poverty here (and the number is rising[8]), but the relative affluence of Jews as a group is an American phenomenon.

Yet the blessings of success have not always been perceived as blessings. Cautious leaders considered upward mobility to be a serious challenge to the community's integrity. Historian Rachel Kranson has described the post–World War II migration of Jews from cities to suburbs as an "ambivalent embrace."[9] That is to say, as American Jews moved to grassier environs, some expressed trepidation that in their exodus there were losses alongside the considerable gains.

One concern was social. The tight-knit, multigenerational communities that marked the urban settlements where first-generation
immigrants lived were sacrificed for larger homes and more spacious
property. Lost, too, were the intimacies that were fostered in religious
communities.[10]

Furthermore, newfound prosperity carried religious implications.
Suburban synagogues in the postwar period, like their neighboring
churches, were perceived to reflect the conformist values of the suburbs. Certainly, this is painting with a broad brush, but the stereotyped
sensibility of people living in the postwar suburbs was not to make
waves and not to jeopardize their cozy lifestyles. Kranson cites an
observation of Albert Vorspan, a preeminent social justice leader of
Reform Judaism:

> When Vorspan reported on the activities of a group of rabbis
> who traveled to St. Augustine, Florida, to participate in a civil
> rights sit-in, he mentioned that the rabbis had been drawn south
> partly out of "escapism" from the "antiseptic middle-class estab-
> lishment of synagogue life." In Vorspan's estimation, these rabbis
> had wanted to participate directly in the civil rights struggle *rather
> than preach to cautious board members and congregants who . . . seemed
> reluctant to make sacrifices or change their behavior in order to bring
> it about.*[11]

In a similar vein, Rabbi Arnold Jacob Wolf of Chicago, one of the most
powerful religious voices in the postwar period, fretted about what the
abandonment of the cities meant for the spiritual integrity of the Jews.
In his synagogue bulletin, he provocatively asked, "Can we escape the
conclusion [that a typical Jew in our community] is likely to be a rich,
important, liberal—hypocrite?"[12]

These are a few of many voices of the era, but it wasn't only
social justice leaders and rabbis who felt ambivalent about upward
mobility. Many migrating Jews instinctively felt something was being
lost. As American Jews moved toward the suburbs in the 1950s and
1960s, there was a wave of sentimentality for the "pristine virtues" of
the shtetl and the tenements. This was the era that produced *Fiddler*

on the Roof and the photo-essays of Roman Vishniac, both of which nurtured nostalgia for the "authentic" values of a lost world. The fact that this world was largely mythical—the shtetl had more than its share of misery, hopelessness, and corruption—was unimportant to a community that was ambivalent about what success said about itself and its values. These cultural artifacts, awash in romanticism, indicate an awareness that with success, certain essential values were imperiled.

The ambivalent embrace was a reflex understanding that material gains do not necessarily correspond to spiritual ones. That ambivalence, it seems to me, is quintessentially Jewish.

The question for subsequent generations—those who grew up with suburban comforts—is whether these reflexes even exist anymore. The chasm between the wealthiest and neediest Americans is wider now than it has ever been, more pronounced than at any other time or place in human history. Social psychologists have demonstrated that poor people are likely to be far more generous in their giving than rich people—one extraordinary irony of American wealth.[13] Living in increasingly sprawling suburbs, it becomes all too easy to avoid confronting poverty or suffering if one so chooses.

Perhaps even the ambivalent embrace is now a thing of the past. As the final walls of segregation against Jews —"exclusive" neighborhoods and clubs, university quotas, exclusion from corporate leadership, etc.—have disappeared, many have enthusiastically embraced affluence and its trappings. Jewish organizations host annual banquets that fete multimillionaire donors. Jewish day schools have tuitions, campuses, and admissions policies that reflect the toniest private schools. This is not to say that synagogues, nonprofits, Federations, and day schools do not have real costs or that that their missions are anything less than vital. But perhaps someday we can have an honest conversation about the role that money and power play in these institutions and to what degree the perpetual pursuit of millionaire donors is a troublesome reflection on the community's values.

Can We Avoid the Trap?

Where does this leave us? Is the conundrum unresolvable—does prosperity inevitably lead to a coarsening of the spirit and an erosion of empathy? Upward mobility is, in and of itself, nothing to be ashamed of. Quite the opposite: The United States was the first nation in the world to offer Jews full civil rights, and our success here can be directly attributed to those freedoms. No one would want to relinquish the freedoms that previous generations worked so hard to attain. The question is what success means and how it can be used in the service of God.

As we have seen, Judaism hardly embraces asceticism and does not find nobility in poverty. But how can we avoid the pitfalls that come with having our dreams come true?

Jewish tradition strives to create a religious system that helps us avoid these traps. For instance:

- **Shabbat** teaches us that our lives cannot be solely devoted to acquisition and achievement. For twenty-five hours each week, we can focus on the greater meaning of life and love, without competition and consumerism. Without the weekly oasis of Shabbat, we are doomed to ever-expanding hours of work, school, and the pursuit of so-called achievement.
- *Tzedakah* instructs us that a percentage of what we thought we owned simply does not belong to us; it *belongs* to those in our world who need it more desperately than we do. *Tzedakah* is not defined by a hazy sense of "giving"; it is very clearly defined in Jewish sources as 10 to 20 percent of our money that we are expected to give away (and the 20 percent upper limit is removed for wealthy people, who are in no danger of impoverishing themselves).[14]
- *B'rachot*—reciting blessings—teach us that we are surrounded by gifts from God that we surely do not deserve. Judaism encourages

us to pause to express gratitude and wonder before eating, before wearing new clothes, and upon using a new tool (like a new computer, phone, or automobile) for the first time. The Jewish structure of daily prayer and reciting blessings is meant to inculcate in us a sense of constant gratitude, humility, and awe.

- **Torah study**, especially about money, consumption, and traits such as *tz'niut* will help us refine these values further and apply their lessons to our own lives.

In these ways and more, Judaism builds a spiritual infrastructure that aims to draw us nearer to God.

Since antiquity, Jewish tradition has recognized that there is a spiritual challenge attached to money. Ultimately, both poverty and wealth are religious trials. Thousands of years ago, an enigmatic sage named Agur son of Jakeh in the Book of Proverbs expressed the dilemma this way:

> Two things I ask of you;
> Do not deny them to me before I die:
> Keep lies and false words far from me;
> Give me neither poverty nor riches,
> But provide me with my daily bread,
> Lest, being sated, I renounce, saying,
> "Who is the Eternal?"
> Or, being impoverished, I take to theft
> And profane the name of my God.
>
> (Proverbs 30:7–9)

In other words, given a theoretical choice, he asks to be neither rich nor poor, but to have enough sustenance to survive without worry. Too much wealth, the sage assumes, will lead to the worship of the self that is at the heart of all idolatry. Poverty, on the other hand, will lead to despondency and desperate, ungodly measures. Better to walk the middle road.

Of course, we generally do not get to choose which path destiny has in store for us. Most of us would agree: given the choice, may God test us with the challenge of wealth! Our task is to recognize the spiritual trial that money brings with it and to grasp the tools our tradition provides to navigate the challenge with grace and generosity.

NOTES

1. Rashi, comment to Num. 32:16.
2. See Proverbs 6:6–11; BT *N'darim* 49b; BT *M'gillah* 6a; BT *P'sachim* 113a; *Avot D'Rabbi Natan* 11; and Maimonides, *Mishneh Torah, Hilchot Mat'not Aniyim* 10:18 for examples.
3. See BT *Mo-eid Katan* 28a.
4. For a similar idea, see *Sh'mot Rabbah* 31:3.
5. For a fuller discussion on the meaning of Rabban Gamliel's revolutionary reforms, see Garry, p. 311 in this volume.
6. The Vaad Arba Aratzot, an assembly of Jewish representatives from Greater Poland, Little Poland, Ruthenia, and Volhynia that coordinated Jewish affairs for several centuries until 1764.
7. Meir Tamari, *With All Your Possessions: Jewish Ethics and Economic Life* (Northvale, NJ: Jason Aronson, 1998), 58.
8. "New Report Reveals Dramatic Rise in Poverty in Jewish Community," UJA-Federation of New York, June 6, 2013, https://www.ujafedny.org/news/new-report-reveals-dramatic-rise-in-poverty-in-jewish-community/.
9. Rachel Kranson, *Ambivalent Embrace: Jewish Upward Mobility in Postwar America* (Chapel Hill: University of North Carolina Press, 2017).
10. For instance, the Conservative Movement's decision from 1950 to permit driving to synagogue on Shabbat is a direct reflection of adjusting religious norms to the needs of suburban Jews. See Nacha Cattan, "Conservative Head Calls Sabbath Driving Rule a 'Mistake,'" *Forward*, November 7, 2003, https://forward.com/news/6998/conservative-head-calls-sabbath-driving-rule-a/.
11. Kranson, *Ambivalent Embrace*, 59; emphasis mine.
12. Kranson, *Ambivalent Embrace*, 58.
13. Paul K. Piff et al., "Having Less, Giving More: The Influence of Social Class on Prosocial Behavior," *Journal of Personality and Social Psychology* 99, no. 5 (November 2010): 771–84.

14. For specifics, see my essay "Tzedakah," in *Navigating the Journey: The Essential Guide to the Jewish Life Cycle*, ed. Peter S. Knobel (New York: CCAR Press, 2018), 149–54.

5

THE ECONOMIC THEOLOGY
OF THE TEN COMMANDMENTS

Rabbi Max Chaiken

The Ten Commandments have always held a special place in Jewish thought and law. They often serve as a microcosm for Torah as a whole, representing the essential ethical tenets contained in our holy texts. What is less well-known about their wide-ranging symbolic content, which addresses our human relationship with the Divine, with ourselves, and with one another, is that they also hold an economic message for us today.

The Decalogue does not explicitly mention money or financial transactions. Yet when read through an economic frame, these ten statements present a unique perspective that comprises the essence of Jewish law concerning money, wealth, and economics. In the words of Seymour Siegel, they convey an "economic theology"—that is, a "general view of the world that [undergirds] the activity of buying, selling, producing, and inventing."[1]

This chapter presents a reading of the economic theology embedded within the Ten Commandments, detailing how this iconic text can be understood as illuminating a "general view of the world" with respect to economic activity.[2] Importantly, in this context I use the term "economics" to refer to the full range of activities by which we produce, distribute, and consume the goods and services that sustain human life.[3] While other definitions may seek to incorporate concepts like scarcity, incentives, or money, this broad approach allows us to glean an economic theology from Jewish holy texts that do not aim to explicitly outline a systematic economic theory. By focusing on production, distribution, and consumption, we can apply the economic values embedded in our sacred laws and stories to our process of ethical decision-making in the contemporary world.

Economic activity always takes place within a legal context.[4] Laws inform economic choices (consider the act of buying an apple versus stealing it), and legal systems help to generate economic theologies and ethics. However, we rely on narrative to make sense of law. American legal scholar Robert Cover puts it this way: "No set of legal institutions or prescriptions exists apart from the narratives that locate it and give it meaning. For every constitution there is an epic, for each decalogue a scripture."[5]

This holds in our discussion of *the* Decalogue as well. The economic components of the Ten Commandments gain staying power in the broader system of Jewish law because of their place in the greater story of our people. Newly freed from four hundred years of slavery, the Children of Israel arrive at Sinai, one of the first stops on their journey back to their ancestral land. There, God descends upon the mountain in thunder and lightning, meeting the entire nation as we stand at the foot of the mountain (Exod. 19:16–17). The Ten Commandments follow as the first instructions that Moses transmits to the people on behalf of God (Exod. 19:25–20:1).

The economic message begins immediately, reinforcing the importance of the narrative context: "I am the Eternal, your God, who brought you out from the land of Egypt, from the house of slavery" (Exod. 20:2).[6] Traditionally, commentators have understood this commandment to represent a statement of belief.[7] Yet the text also situates the relationship to God as intricately bound to the economic narrative of the people of Israel. Instead of being slaves to the Egyptians, the

Children of Israel become servants only to God.[8] Instead of enduring harsh labor, which threatens their very lives, they now have the
freedom to sustain and protect their lives through their labor.

God's gift of economic freedom, however, comes with strings
attached. As Redeemer from Egyptian bondage, God becomes a partner in any wealth that the Children of Israel come to create or possess.
Their freedom exists alongside the privilege of being co-sustainers of
human life with the Divine. Several scholars fully explore this component of the Jewish economic theology,[9] but we can deduce it ourselves
from this careful reading of the first of the Ten Commandments: a
people who once suffered through slavery now have freedom, thanks
to their relationship with the Divine, who allows their work to support
their own sustenance.

This principle also contributes to anti-ascetic thinking in Jewish
law.[10] Unlike other ancient traditions, the Hebrew Bible does not laud
poverty nor show any disdain for the physical satisfaction of material
needs. Since living and acting in response to our physical needs represents a fulfillment of a partnership with the Divine, material success
and bounty represent God's blessing.[11]

The ensuing nine commandments help to generate additional pillars
of this economic theology. Rodney Wilson begins his exploration of
Jewish economic thought by turning to three of the ten in particular:
the commandment to refrain from work on Shabbat and the respective
prohibitions on stealing and coveting your neighbor's possessions.[12]
Indeed, these three quite directly address economic topics, but as we
have just seen, their context adds gravity to their message. Take first
the prohibition of labor on Shabbat:

> Remember the Sabbath day for its holiness. Six days you shall labor
> and do all of your work, but the seventh day is a Shabbat for the
> Eternal your God—do not do any work; neither you, nor your son
> or daughter, your male or female servant, nor your cattle nor the
> stranger within your gates. For in six days the Eternal made the
> heavens and the earth . . . and rested on the seventh day, therefore
> the Eternal blessed the Shabbat and made it holy. (Exod. 20:8–11)

Jewish law traditionally understands this commandment to contain both a positive and a negative element. Positively, the people Israel are encouraged to work for six days.[13] Jewish thought has always placed a great value on work and providing for the material needs of life. Work brings honor to the laborers, helping them fulfill their new role as free, co-creators with the Divine. Negatively, one must refrain from work on Shabbat and allow others to do the same (including, ironically or not, any of the newly freed slaves' own servants). Ceasing productive activity generates a pause in the routines of material life to allow time for focus on one's spiritual life.

The economic philosopher Tomáš Sedláček argues that the Sabbath represents one of the lasting economic contributions of the Hebrew Bible, because it exemplifies a part of life "in which it is not allowed to economize, rationalize, or maximize efficiency."[14] He continues:

> The observance of the Sabbath bears the message that the *purpose of creation was not just creating* but that it had an *end*, a *goal*. . . . The whole Being was created so that we may find in it rest, accomplishment, joy.[15]

This parallels the reasoning given in the text itself: that God rested on the seventh day and blessed it, commanding the Israelites to do likewise. Torah doesn't always give reasons for observing a given commandment, but here the text explicitly posits the theological precept of *imitatio Dei*, the goal of emulating God, in its reasoning for Sabbath rest. In turn, *imitatio Dei* returns time and again in the efforts to understand economic theory and ethics within the scope of traditional Jewish law.[16] Curiously, Deuteronomy offers different reasoning for the commandment to refrain from work on Shabbat in its rendition of the Decalogue:

> Remember that you were a slave in the land of Egypt and the Eternal your God brought you out of there with a strong hand and an outstretched arm, therefore the Eternal Your God commanded you to make the Sabbath day. (Deut. 5:15)

Here Torah enjoins the Jewish people to recall their very story as they limit their production in observing Shabbat. The weekly pause in labor reminds the Israelite of her former enslavement; it serves as a warning not to allow anyone to become economically enslaved to his own material growth. Like the iteration in Exodus, the requirement of rest on the seventh day in Deuteronomy applies to sons, daughters, laborers, and farm animals. None are exempt, because none should be objectified as mere means of production.

The warning not to steal (commandment eight) highlights the importance of property rights, which in turn serve as a prerequisite for market activity.[17] In order for markets to function properly, people must be able to own property with some degree of security. They must then be able to use their property and dispose of it according to their own choices. Economists call this responding to incentives, price or otherwise. Property rights have never been absolute in Jewish law, but they do represent a bedrock principle. The prohibition of theft in the Ten Commandments helps to ensure as much.[18]

Then the final commandment of the Decalogue warns as follows: "Do not covet your neighbor's house. Do not covet your neighbor's wife, servant, ox, donkey, or anything that belongs to your neighbor" (Exod. 20:14).[19] This extends beyond prohibiting an action (theft) to attempting to curb a thought—namely, desire itself, or greed.[20] The reminder not to lust[21] after that which belongs to others thus further constrains the Israelites' newfound economic freedom, because it addresses the broad category of demand. While their newfound freedom enables the production and consumption that sustain their lives, the Israelites must be careful to find ways to curb their demands. Unlimited consumption has no place in Israelite society. We must place limits on our constant desire for "more."[22]

In fact, reading carefully, we find that every commandment of the Decalogue can be understood as contributing to the economic message—not merely those that address the Israelites' economic history or the themes of work, property, and desire. The injunctions not to worship *other* gods and not to bow down to idols (second commandment) state that the Israelites "must not bow down to them or *serve* them" (Exod. 20:5). The Hebrew word for "serve" stems from the same etymological root as the word for "work" or "worship," which is also the same root as the word for "bondage/slavery" from which the Israelites were freed. God liberated the people, giving them a first taste of economic freedom and the hope of prosperity. Worshiping idols or other "gods," literally *working* for them, would then presumably attribute that economic freedom to them, rather than to God. Money itself can be understood as one such idol, and our story proceeds with an explicit example in the Israelite apostasy of the Golden Calf. Afraid for Moses's well-being, Aaron and the Israelites create a calf made of gold and declare it to be the god "who brought them out of Egypt" (Exod. 32:1–8). In other words, in a moment of uncertainty for their future, the Israelites' greatest sin stems from their worship of a form of money as god.

While there may be many reasons to honor one's father and mother (fifth commandment), parents have a direct impact on one's ability to learn, grow, and eventually earn one's own livelihood. The biblical text supports such a reading when it stipulates that this commandment be followed "in order to lengthen one's days" (Exod. 20:12). Prohibited by the sixth commandment, murder, too, impacts economic activity, since in addition to the horrible grief or trauma inflicted on victims' families, the loss of life represents the loss of productive potential. Even the prohibitions against taking God's name in vain and speaking falsely against one's neighbor (commandments three and nine) relate the importance of speech and honesty. Vows and words make a difference and impact market activity in numerous ways.

Collectively, this reading posits that the Ten Commandments illustrate the foundational principles of Jewish economic theology. These core values may seem to exist in tension with one another, particularly when we return to the frame of consumption, production, and distribution of goods. With regard to consumption, we are encouraged to satisfy our material desires and to lengthen our days, but not to allow our desires to go unchecked. We must find a way to be "happy with our lot, or: *s'meichim b'chelkeinu*," if we truly want to appreciate any material wealth or riches we might generate.[23] Our work, our production as free people, can and must sustain our lives, but we are forbidden from letting it become an end in itself. Shabbat serves as our weekly reminder that we, and those around us, exist as more than mere producers. Even with respect to distribution of goods, we observe this tension here as well. We are permitted private property but are reminded that God exists as partner and co-owner in the creation of wealth. By incorporating both elements, the Decalogue sets the stage for later laws and stories that require all Israelites to have access to the goods that sustain their lives.

In turn, we see how these pillars might inform and guide our choices in the economic realm. Those choices should always recall our story as we strive to live in covenant with "the Eternal, our God, who brought us from the land of Egypt, from the house of slavery" (Exod. 20:2). Yet navigating these tensions thoughtfully also requires us to accept the possibility of ethical pluralism, wherein different applications of these values might lead to different "right answers" on any given question of economic ethics. Two different individuals may have very different understandings of the balance between appreciating material wealth and allowing our material desires to rule over us. One person's definition of hard work may strike another as a neglect of the importance of Sabbath rest. While this approach eludes easy answers, offering a matrix of values rather than well-defined ethical actions, reading the Ten Commandments this way helps us give our holy narratives and laws a voice as we seek to navigate our daily economic choices.

NOTES

1. Seymour Siegel, "A Jewish View of Economic Justice," in *Contemporary Jewish Ethics and Morality*, ed. Elliot N. Dorff and Louis E. Newman (New York: Oxford University Press, 1995), 338.

2. The Ten Commandments appear twice in the Torah, first in Exodus 20, and later in Deuteronomy 5. I address minor differences between the two below but will default to the Exodus version of the text throughout the rest of this chapter. Despite these variations, however, I must note that the traditional framework of Jewish law understands these to represent *one* revelation. This analysis does not preclude such a reading, and in fact, understanding the text in this way serves to strengthen the economic theology therein.

3. E. Ray Canterbery, *A Brief History of Economics: Artful Approaches to the Dismal Science*, 2nd ed. (Hackensack, NJ: World Scientific, 2011), 6.

4. Rodney Wilson, *Economics, Ethics and Religion: Jewish, Christian and Muslim Economic Thought* (New York: New York University Press, 1997), 5–6; also cf. Canterbery, *A Brief History of Economics*, 6.

5. Robert Cover, "Nomos and Narrative," in *Narrative, Violence, and the Law: The Essays of Robert Cover*, ed. Martha Minow, Michael Ryan, and Austin Sarat, 95–172 (Ann Arbor: University of Michigan Press, 1993), 95–96.

6. All translations are those of the author unless otherwise noted.

7. See, for instance, Maimonides, *Mishneh Torah, Sefer HaMada*, chap. 1, *halachah* 1.

8. For more on the transition from serving Pharaoh to serving God, see Jill Jacobs, *There Shall Be No Needy: Pursuing Social Justice through Jewish Law & Tradition* (Woodstock, VT: Jewish Lights, 2009); or Aryeh Cohen, *Justice in the City: An Argument from the Sources of Rabbinic Judaism* (Boston: Academic Studies Press, 2012). Jacobs titles her chapter on labor law "Servants to Servants or Servants to God: Workers, Employers, and Unions" (*There Shall Be No Needy*, 97–131), and Cohen's first chapter is called "Acting Like Pharaoh or Acting Like God" (*Justice in the City*, 27–38).

9. Wilson, *Economics, Ethics and Religion*, 27–32; also cf. Meir Tamari, *With All Your Possessions: Jewish Ethics and Economic Life* (Northvale, NJ: Jason Aronson, 1987), 36; Meir Tamari, *The Challenge of Wealth: A Jewish Perspective on Earning and Spending Money* (Northvale, NJ: Jason Aronson, 1995), xxii; Jacob Neusner, *The Economics of the Mishnah* (Chicago: University of Chicago Press, 1990), 117–18. Tamari goes so far as claiming that "the Divine origin of wealth is the central principle of Jewish economic philosophy" (*With All Your Possessions*, 36).

10. Tomas Sedlacek, *Economics of Good and Evil: The Quest for Economic Meaning from Gilgamesh to Wall Street* (New York: Oxford University Press, 2011), 49–52.

11. Jacobs, *There Shall Be No Needy*, 55–59; Tamari, *With All Your Possessions*, 30–31.

12. Wilson, *Economics, Ethics and Religion*, 25–27.

13. Whether we are *commanded* to work or not seems open to interpretation. Ibn Ezra's commentary on the verse (Exod. 20:8) explicitly stipulates, "It is permitted to work, and it is not a mitzvah/commandment." He uses language of permission, and many classical commentators seem happy to oblige his understanding.

14. Sedlacek, *Economics of Good and Evil*, 88.

15. Sedlacek, *Economics of Good and Evil*, 89.

16. Both Tamari and Levine present extensive discussions of *imitatio Dei* and its role in guiding economic ethics within classical Jewish law. Tamari (*With All Your Possessions*, 243) includes it as part of the "conceptual framework of the Jewish welfare system" and references it again in his chapter on economic obligations to others and to society at large (*Challenge of Wealth*, 150–51). Aaron Levine goes so far as to call *imitatio Dei* the "guidepost for economic public policy in the Torah society" (Aaron Levine, *Economic Public Policy and Jewish Law* [New York: Yeshiva University Press, 1993], 12).

17. The definition of property rights, along with an understanding of how they operate in any given society, serves as a prerequisite for *any* economic activity, not just market-based economies. A full exploration of this principle falls beyond the scope of this chapter, but the impact of property rights (or lack thereof) on economic activity lies at the heart of any study of law and economics.

18. See Tamari, *With All Your Possessions*, 51–53, for further discussion of the limitations on property rights.

19. In both instances of the Decalogue, the neighbor's wife is listed alongside his possessions in this injunction. The intersection of gender and economic theory within Jewish law represents an area for further exploration and analysis. Ample scholarship exists on the treatment of women as property in ancient society and in classical Jewish law. Here, I assume that the underlying economic theology can be applied in an egalitarian fashion and, in fact, must be applied in such a fashion to maintain any normative consequences for economic ethics today.

20. Wilson, *Economics, Ethics and Religion*, 26–27.

21. The Deuteronomic code uses a different verb in its rendition (Deut. 5:18) than the verb traditionally rendered as "covet." There it states, *Lo titaveh beit rei-echa*, "You should not *lust* after [or *crave*] your neighbor's home." The lexical range of the verb *titaveh* conveys a stronger and more forceful desire—a desire for boundless consumption, or perhaps for the endless satiation of physical needs (see Num. 11:4). Accordingly, I translate here using the word "lust" rather than "covet."

22. Tamari calls this concept an "economics of enough" and argues that it helps to ensure the ethical use of wealth (*Challenge of Wealth*, xxiv, 127–45).

23. The quote plays on *Mishnah Avot* 4:1, which asks, "Who is rich? One who is happy with their lot." This should not be taken to insinuate that such maxims of wisdom represent systematic statements of economic values. Rather, they do occasionally illustrate quite well the broader principles within the economic theory at work in classical Jewish legal texts like the Ten Commandments.

This chapter has been adapted for this volume from the author's rabbinic thesis, "Telling a New Story: A Model for Economic Ethics in Jewish Law" (Hebrew Union College–Jewish Institute of Religion, Los Angeles, 2018).

ETHICS IN FOCUS

When Donors Behave Badly:
Guiding Principles for Jewish Institutions

RABBI A. BRIAN STOLLER

What should a synagogue or Jewish institution do when a donor is known to be involved in illegal or immoral activity? For example, imagine that after a synagogue dedicates a newly renovated sanctuary, the beloved community elder who gave more than a million dollars toward the project is indicted for embezzling money from her employer. Or suppose that a prominent nursing-home proprietor, whose facilities have a reputation for unclean conditions and abusive treatment of residents, offers to provide scholarships for needy kids to go to summer camp. As Jews, we seek to be guided in our response to these situations by the moral voice of our tradition. While there are few clear-cut answers, our texts provide certain principles that can inform our decision-making.

What Happens When Two Moral Obligations Conflict with Each Other?

A CCAR responsum on the case of a synagogue contribution by a criminal points out that it is a mitzvah incumbent upon every Jew to support the synagogue financially.[1] Similarly, the mitzvah of *tzedakah* obligates each individual to support Jewish communal institutions. The

Reform Movement has said that synagogues (and communal organizations) should not refuse a donation from a person of questionable character, because we do not have the right to prevent someone from fulfilling his religious obligations.[2] Moreover, denying the would-be giver the opportunity to do a mitzvah would further alienate him from the righteous path. As Maimonides says, "We do not tell a wicked person: 'Increase your wickedness by failing to perform mitzvot.'"[3]

At the same time, accepting the donation may violate a different mitzvah, namely the prohibition against placing a stumbling block before the blind. As Jewish business-ethicist Meir Tamari suggests, a criminal or person of ill-repute may be "blind, so to speak, to the moral consequences of his actions."[4] Accepting *his* donation might well send the message that his behavior is not all that problematic in the eyes of the Jewish community either. Any honor or gratitude given to someone in acknowledgment of a contribution would only strengthen that message. By accepting the gift, therefore, we might inadvertently encourage the donor to continue in these errant ways and cause the donor to stumble further.

Clearly these conflicting moral obligations cannot both be operative at the same time, but the sources suggest that there are circumstances in which one or the other should take precedence.

What Causes Money to Become "Dirty"?

According to Deuteronomy 23:19,[5] anything paid to a harlot for prostitution (which is forbidden by the Torah) and the monetary value of dogs used by hunters and watchmen to intimidate the public (which are lawful but unseemly activities[6]) are unacceptable as donations to the Holy Temple.[7] Similarly, Maimonides rules that "when one steals or obtains an object through robbery and offers it as a sacrifice, it is invalid and the Holy One hates it."[8] Though these laws technically apply only to the *Beit HaMikdash*, their core principle is just as relevant to our synagogues and Jewish organizations today. That principle suggests that the Torah regards money and anything else acquired through illegal and immoral means as "dirty" and unfit as an offering. Therefore, should someone seek to make such a donation, the synagogue or communal entity should refuse to accept it, even though doing so would prevent the person from fulfilling his obligation to support the community.

But if money gained through illegal or immoral activity is "dirty," what about money that is earned on the up-and-up by someone who behaves immorally in other areas of her life? To wit, is there a difference between a donation from Bernie Madoff, who acquired his wealth through theft and fraud, and a donation from Harvey Weinstein, who earned his money legitimately but sexually harassed and manipulated countless women? In a relevant discussion about *kohanim* (priests), Maimonides holds that a *kohein* is not disqualified from performing his religious duty on account of immoral behavior in his non-priestly life *unless* he commits one of the three cardinal sins of Rabbinic Judaism (i.e., idolatry, illicit sex, and murder).[9] Following this reasoning, could modern Jewish institutions say that immoral behavior unrelated to how one's money is gotten should not disqualify a donor from carrying out her religious duty *unless* she commits an act that the modern Jewish community regards as a cardinal sin? If so, what actions would rise to that level?

Should the Donor Be Acknowledged Publicly?

The sources raise two key concerns about publicly honoring a donor of dubious character. One is that a plaque or other form of acknowledgment bearing the giver's name will draw constant, unwanted attention to this sinful behavior. The other is that people of ill-repute will "utilize a gift to the synagogue [or other Jewish institution] as a means of purchasing a good name"[10] and atoning for their sins.[11] In order to avoid these undesirable outcomes, the Reform Movement recommends that congregations (and other organizations) accept the donation but not publicly acknowledge the donor unless and until he does *t'shuvah* and abandons this immoral behavior.

In sum, the sources suggest that synagogues and organizations should not accept donations of funds or items that are known with certainty to have been gotten illegally. Beyond this, the guiding principles outlined here leave room for professional and lay leaders to exercise judgment based on communal values and the nuances of each situation. While decisions will need to be made on a case-by-case basis, institutions would benefit from engaging in intentional conversations about core values and principles that will guide their approach in situations in which donors behave badly.

NOTES

1. CCAR Responsa Committee, "Synagogue Contribution from a Criminal," Central Conference of American Rabbis, accessed September 17, 2018, https://www.ccarnet.org/ccar-responsa/curr-52-55/. Readers should consult this responsum for a thorough analysis of the relevant halachic issues.
2. See the CCAR responsum cited above, as well as Mark Washofsky, *Jewish Living: A Guide to Contemporary Reform Practice* (New York: UAHC Press, 2001), 45.
3. Maimonides, *Mishneh Torah, Hilchot N'siat Kapayim* 15:6. Translation by Rabbi Eliyahu Touger, *Mishneh Torah: Hilchot Tefilah II and Birkat Kohanim* (New York: Moznaim, 2007), 218.
4. Meir Tamari, *The Challenge of Wealth: A Jewish Perspective on Earning and Spending Money* (Northvale, NJ: Jason Aronson, 1995), 32.
5. Deut. 23:19 states: "You shall not bring the fee of a whore or the pay of a dog into the house of the Eternal your God in fulfillment of any vow, for both are abhorrent to the Eternal your God."
6. In his comment to Deut. 23:19, Abraham ibn Ezra explains that "the pay of a dog" refers to activity that, although not forbidden, is "disgraceful" (*derech bizayon*).
7. These explanations of the phrases "the fee of a whore" and "the pay of a dog" are given by Rashi and Nachmanides in their commentaries to the verse.
8. Maimonides, *Mishneh Torah, Hilchot Isurei Mizbei-ach* 5:7. Translation by Rabbi Eliyahu Touger, *Mishneh Torah: Sefer Ha'Avodah* (New York: Moznaim, 2007), 334.
9. Maimonides, *Mishneh Torah, Hilchot N'siat Kapayim* 15:1–6, esp. *halachot* 3 and 6.
10. Washofsky, *Jewish Living*, 45.
11. See Nachmanides's comment to Deut. 23:19.

TALKING ABOUT MONEY

Financial Lessons from My Parents

ELANA ALTZMAN, MD

My parents are downsizing. They are selling their house and moving into an apartment. The house has too many stairs, and my father has tired of the constant maintenance it requires. He would never hire someone to do simple tasks until recently; this is one of the reasons my parents are now in a position to move to a home that will accommodate their current needs.

My parents were in their early forties when we came to the United States from Soviet Russia. They were starting out at an age when most people reach the top of their careers. Right away my father began the search for a job. My mother worked on improving her English skills, taking care of us children and my ailing grandmother, finding a job later. My father is an engineer with a doctorate degree. In Russia, he headed a research lab and had a number of patents, articles, and books. He knew none of it would matter here and did not care. His sole goal was to take care of his family. His professional accomplishments were a means to that end. When my mother worried how they would feed their children in America, he promised her we wouldn't starve. He would find a job, if not in engineering, then in any field allowing him to provide for their family. Leaving Russia for the safety of his Jewish children was a necessity.

We came to the United States with ten suitcases. Two of them contained my father's books—not books he wrote, but the reference books he thought would be useful in his new job in America. One suitcase contained a typewriter. To learn the basics of a job search, he immediately met with the employment counselor at the organization that oversaw refugee absorption. He dove in right away, spending hours at the library looking through the *New York Times* help wanted section. My mother typed the resumes and cover letters; my father started going on interviews. In this, as everything else, they were a team.

The New York Jewish community provided a small amount of money to refugee families for their first three months. My father decided that he would give himself the three months to find an engineering position. If he didn't, he would start driving a taxi—work that could provide the bare minimum for the five of us. Two and a half months later he was offered an entry-level engineering job. It was meant for a college graduate, not a man with twenty years of experience, but my father was overjoyed. It was in his field, and it paid $300 a week. In 1981, it was enough to start.

After a few months, we moved to a larger apartment, still two bedrooms, but no longer above a dry cleaner. My mother, unhappy with the education I was receiving in a yeshivah, took me to look at a top private school in Brooklyn. My parents figured out financial aid forms, and the school gave me a scholarship of $4,000, the maximum their board allowed. I started at the school. My parents could not afford the right clothes or school supplies for me, but they ensured I was getting a top-notch education, and that was paramount. The remaining $800 a year in tuition was a large sum for them, but they managed, knowing they were investing in my future.

My parents quickly learned about saving for retirement, and after two years at his first job, my father found another position, which paid more and offered a generous retirement plan. Then my mother started working. They saved enough to buy a small house and after a few years traded up to a bigger one, a two-family, counting on tenants to defray to cost.

They did not need anyone to teach them how to live frugally. Smart people who grew up with nothing during World War II, they knew how instinctively. They shopped sales, bought most of their furniture secondhand, gratefully accepted hand-me-downs, spent extra on quality, but not brand names. Their home renovations were practical, never luxurious. If an opportunity came along to earn a little extra, they took it. This summarizes my parents' attitude toward money: take the opportunity to earn, spend what you can afford on the best quality and the greatest utility, and above all, do whatever it takes to provide for your family. I learned these lessons well, along with a bit of the insecurity concerning money that comes as part of the legacy. My children, I believe, have absorbed both sides of these lessons, too.

The two-family house is the one my parents are moving out of now. They want me to take as many of their possessions as I can, so they still feel close to their things. And I am happy to have tangible connections to my parents and my history. One item my father convinced me to take is a light fixture. Long ago, he was driving to work and saw a man throwing it out. He pulled over and asked if it worked. The man said it did, and my father took it. It hung in my parents' house for years, my father rejoicing in its looks, an antique, acquired for the right price. It now hangs in my living room, an odd, but appealing piece dubbed Arabian Nights by my children. To me it's symbolic of how much my parents accomplished. I hope my kids don't just see a quirky light fixture. I hope they also learn some of its lessons.

Part Two

The Power of Money:
Tzedakah and *Tzedek*

Applying the lessons learned in part 1, this section explores the good we can do with our money through philanthropy, investing, and social justice work. Judaism does not want us to be controlled by our lust for money, seeing acquisition as a goal unto itself. Rather, we are instructed to use our wealth to shape the world around us to create justice, to repair what is broken. In this manner, our money can have power, positive power, especially when guided by Jewish ethics.

"Economic Justice Is the Foundation of All Justice," by Rabbi Seth M. Limmer, DHL, creates a bridge between the material in parts 1 and 2, offering a compelling argument, girded by strong biblical and Rabbinic textual references, for poverty as "the most fundamental source of injustice." Rabbi Limmer links Jewish attitudes toward poverty to the imperative to work in our own time to counterbalance the economic imbalance reflected in so many social problems. His chapter informs the rest of this part of the book.

Rabbi Ruth Adar provides a guide as how to give money in her "*Tzedakah*: How We Choose Where We Give." This chapter offers important practical teachings needed as we each determine how much to donate and to which individuals or organizations. Interestingly,

Rabbi Adar's chapter is referenced by several of the other chapters in this book, revealing the intertwined nature of the subjects presented throughout the chapters.

Socially responsible investing (SRI) is not a new approach to personal investing, but rather it is an evolving finance vehicle. Michael A. Kimmel and Rabbi Howard Shapiro's "Socially Responsible Investing" traces the history of these types of investment and their changes over time. They also share the history of the Reform Movement's Reform Pension Board's decision to launch the Reform Jewish Values Fund. As Kimmel and Shapiro present positive and negative screens for investments, they discuss the interaction of the ethics-screened investment approach with the Boycott, Divestment, and Sanctions (BDS) movement. This section of their article provides an interesting application of the material that Rabbi Joshua Weinberg explores in his chapter "Financing Zion: Looking Back to Shape Today" in part 3.

While Kimmel and Shapiro focus on positively impacting the world through one's investments, Rabbi Joel M. Mosbacher writes of a social justice initiative to halt gun violence by leveraging the lobby of gun buyers in law enforcement. In "Guns: Leveraging the Power of Money for Justice," Rabbi Mosbacher describes his personal connection to gun violence, the challenges of confronting the gun industry and gun lobby, the complacency of our elected officials, and a newer effort to leverage law enforcement gun purchasers and investor power to encourage the gun companies to reduce gun violence. This is a brilliant example that money is not innately evil. Using the influence of money, good can right wrong.

Complementing Rabbi Adar's chapter on how to give *tzedakah*, Rabbi Leah Rachel Berkowitz provides a guided tour of many of the ancient and modern vehicles for donating money and items in "Structures of Jewish Giving: A Virtual *Tzedakah* Tour." As giving *tzedakah* is such a lauded value within Judaism, it is not surprising to find such a variety of methods for donating. While Rabbi Berkowitz writes of the vehicles of *tzedakah* within Jewish communities from ancient to modern times, Andrés Spokoiny and Dov Ben-Shimon present two different views of the meta-question of what philanthropy should look like within the contemporary Jewish community. In "The Changing Face of Jewish Philanthropy," Spokoiny, president and CEO of the Jewish Funder's Network, reflects on the changes to Jewish philanthropy, with contemporary donors seeking an unmediated, high-impact way of giving, which is often devoid of the traditional structures and obligations of the Jewish community. In "My Jewish Federation: Legacy and Change," Dov Ben-Shimon, executive vice president and CEO of the Jewish Federation of Greater MetroWest New Jersey, talks of the challenges facing legacy institutions, the ways his organization's approach to philanthropy is evolving, and the timeless need for Jewish Federations for both the local and global Jewish community. These authors present very different points of view, yet find much common ground in recognizing that challenges abound and in their passion for Jewish values and Jewish philanthropy.

Returning to a more finite question of *tzedakah*, Rabbi Nicole Auerbach tackles the uncomfortable scenario that happens daily in her "Ethics in Focus: Giving Money to Panhandlers?" In "Talking about Money: In Praise of Beautiful, Bold *Tzedakah* Boxes," Rabbi Zoë Klein Miles offers a poetic meditation on and new meaning for this central ritual object found in almost every Jewish home.

6

ECONOMIC JUSTICE IS
THE FOUNDATION OF ALL JUSTICE

Rabbi Seth M. Limmer, DHL

> There is nothing in the world more difficult than poverty, for
> poverty is more difficult than all the afflictions in the world.
>
> Our Rabbis said: If all the afflictions in the world were placed
> on one side, and poverty on the other . . . poverty remains
> more difficult than all those afflictions.[1]
>
> *Sh'mot Rabbah 31:12*

On the one hand it seems tautological that economic justice is the foundation of all justice. In elementary school we are taught that the basic human needs are food, clothing, and shelter; since antiquity these fundamental necessities have been acquired through economic means. Our nation has long equated justice with financial parity: the great American programs of social welfare are all economic at their core. In the Great Depression, the work of the WPA was creating meaningful employment, while the program guaranteeing financial stability to the retired workforce was called "Social Security." During the civil rights heyday of the sixties, urban renewal projects—which we now see as misguided—sought to provide stable housing at *reasonable pricing*. In recent years, the very program to provide health care to every American was coined in economic terms: the *Affordable* Care Act. While some might say money is the root of all evil, the moral decency of any society is determined by how evenly its financial resources are distributed. A nation that oppresses its poor is a nation without justice; the Jewish ideal for society has always been to see to the security of the most vulnerable.[2] In Judaism, there is no security that does not include economic security.

The Hebrew word *oni*, translated as "poverty," at its root means "oppression."[3] In the Bible, poverty is the paradigm of oppression: to be poor *is* to be oppressed. To the Jewish mind, the scourge of material need is the foundational injustice. Thus, the Rabbis saw the lexicon of biblical terms for poverty as a catalogue of suffering. In the midrash below, formatted to accentuate the manifold experiences of being poor, the Sages employ Moses's metaphorical language about poverty "laying low" an individual and they expand our sense of the many deprivations of poverty by scouring the Bible for as many different such metaphors as possible:

> There are eight names for a poor person: *ani, evyon, miskein, rash, dal, dach, mach, heilech.*

- *Ani*: according to its meaning [namely, "oppressed"].

- *Evyon*: because they desire [*mi-taev*] everything.

- *Miskein*: because they are despised by all, as it says, "The wisdom of the poor [*miskein*] is despised" (Ecclesiastes 9:16).

- *Rash*: dispossessed [*mitrosheish*] of property.

- *Dal*: detached [*m'duldal*] from property.

- *Dach*: crushed [*m'duchdach*] because they see something and are unable to eat, they see something and are unable to taste or to drink.

- *Mach*: they are low [*mach*] before everyone, they are trod on like the lowest rung.

- *Heilech*: [inferring, I believe, from the above terms "crushed" and "low,"] weak.

Thus, Moses speaks [and subsequently provides legal recourse in Leviticus 25:25]: "When your kinfolk is laid low in poverty." (*Vayikra Rabbah* 34:6)

This midrash describes poverty as the physical state of deprivation paired with the emotional pain of being the lowest rung on society's ladder. Our Rabbis might say poverty is the most fundamental source of injustice. Therefore, if we want to bring the fullness of justice to our world, the foundation of our task will be in establishing economic justice.

Economic justice is at the core of countless Jewish principles and practices. Here we will examine how central Jewish texts respond to the problem of poverty. In turn, we will see how the Torah lays down laws to establish economic justice, how the prophets create a moral language protesting poverty, and how the Rabbis react to the oppression of poverty in theological terms. Thus, we will see that legally, morally, and theologically, economic justice is the foundation of justice, defined Jewishly.

The Torah: Laws Preventing Poverty

Judaism aspires for the day when economic justice will exist; until the arrival of that messianic day, the Torah prescribes practices to mitigate the effects of poverty. Nowhere is the balance of the ideal hopes and realistic laws seen more clearly than in Deuteronomy 15. "Never shall there be among you those in want" is the utopian promise that begins the chapter (Deut. 15:4).[4] Since that hope is as yet unfulfilled, we are given this specific command:

When there is in your midst a person in want . . . you shall neither harden your heart nor remove your hand from your kinsfolk, the one who wants. Instead, you shall certainly open your hand to that person, and shall certainly provide for them enough to satisfy their needs, in accord with that which they need. (Deut. 15:7–8)

Deuteronomy looks toward the day when poverty is eradicated but knows that—until that day comes—Judaism demands physical and (as we will soon see) psychological provisions for the poor. Today's injustices of financial distribution require remediation in the here and now when people suffer the perils of poverty.

Programs of social justice—specifically those that seek to maintain economic equity—are prescribed in the Bible's priestly material. The Holiness Code in Leviticus defines the parameters of behavior in matters ranging from treatment of elders to the proper manufacture of garments. This chapter is foundational in its discussion of *pei-ah*, in which landowning farmers refrain from harvesting the edges of their fields and leave what remains unpicked for the poor and the stranger (Lev. 19:9–10).[5] Such a practice—in kinship with Deuteronomy—sees to the physical and emotional sustenance of people in need. The harvest itself provides nourishment for their bodies, and their ability to approach from outside the edges of the field—and thus retain their anonymity—prevents potential embarrassment or social degradation.

One more biblical paradigm to consider, Leviticus 25, outlines the calendrical guarantee of economic justice in society: the cycle of Sabbatical and Jubilee years. In the fiftieth Jubilee year, we are called to "proclaim liberty throughout the land to all the inhabitants thereof" and restore every soul sunken into debt servitude to their landholdings (Lev. 25:10), thereby eradicating their poverty by returning to them the primary ancient resources for economic prosperity.[6] While these biblical cycles of release are connected to concepts of divine dominion over land—"For the earth is Mine!" says God (Lev. 25:23)—they are also explicitly linked to poverty through the chapter.[7] Most compellingly, the text commands, "When your brother is in straits [of poverty], and stretches out his hand amongst you, you shall strengthen him, whether stranger or alien; let him live with you!" (Lev. 25:35).[8] Like Deuteronomy, the Sabbatical and Jubilee programs of Leviticus blend the ideal with the real: while the Jubilee year is intended to eradicate poverty, we are commanded in all other years to ensure that we strengthen those in need, and the Torah tells us how to do so.

The Prophets: Moral Protest against Economic Oppression

The laws of Torah demand engagement in the work of economic justice. The words of the prophets provide the explicit morality behind these commands. Amos lived in the eighth century BCE, the so-called silver age of the Israelite monarchal period, in which the Northern Kingdom, especially, enjoyed great economic success.[9] The first of our literary prophets, Amos bore witness to the moral failings of a wealthy Israel during a period of relative peace. He predicted powerful punishment for sins that included the following failures:

> They sold for silver the righteous; the needy for a pair of sandals.
> They trod the dust of the earth on the head of the poor. . . .
> They incline on garments pawned in pledge.
>
> (Amos 2:6–8)

Amos decried the devaluation of those in need; they were treated as a cheap commodity, trod upon by the very shoes whose price was more important than were they. Those who needed to pawn their belongings likewise had their few material resources abused; such garments were treated not as bailed property to be protected—which is what the Torah demands—but rather were used as picnic blankets for idolatrous festivals. Importantly, Amos sees this devaluation of the poor as the result of the overvaluation of personal prosperity. In the prophet's estimation, it was the immense and disproportionate riches enjoyed by the wealthy class that led first to a societal divide and then to deviant behavior. When he admonishes those who "financially oppress the poor and crush those in need," he refers to them as "cows of Bashan" (Amos 4:1), likening the idle wealthy of Samaria to overstuffed livestock who loll all day in fields of green. This demeaning moniker resonates with another biblical description of how quickly the rich can lose their moral compass: "Jeshurun became fat, and kicked [rebelliously]; you got fat, you became obese, you were covered [in fat], and thus did you forget the very God who made you" (Deut. 32:15).[10]

Amos sets the moral tone for the prophets who followed: a massive divide between the rich and the poor is unjust; the existence of a wealth gap that stratifies society, which we might call economic injustice, is simply a sin. A quick compilation of quotes from subsequent prophets proves Amos's influence and demonstrates their commitment as the joint moral voice of Israel to plead the cause of the poor:

- *Micah 2:2:* They covet fields and seize them violently; houses and carry them away. Thus they impoverish every man and his house, every man and his inheritance.
- *Isaiah 3:13–15:* The Eternal stands up to accuse, rises to judge the people. The Eternal enters into judgment with the elders of God's people and its ministers. "It is you who have consumed the vineyard! The spoil of the poor is in your houses. What do you mean that you crush My people, and grind the face of the poor?" says the God of heaven's host.
- *Ezekiel 22:29:* The people of the land have oppressed oppressively, and most violently seized; they have wronged the poor and in need, and the stranger have unlawfully oppressed.
- *Proverbs 31:9:* Open your mouth, judge righteously, and plead the cause of the poor and the needy.[11]

Economic injustice was a moral problem for the prophets. And while prophets preached pronouncements more than they proposed policy, their vision of a world with economic justice is best seen in the words of Micah. This prophet of the eighth century BCE understood that to be poor is to be constantly afraid, to be filled with worries about the next meal and a place to sleep, along with the concern as to how long this struggle must be endured. Micah also knew that the real end to poverty is self-sufficiency, which in his age meant owning land and farming it successfully. Thus we can understand the beauty of Micah's vision for a future of widespread financial security, of economic justice: "Then all people shall sit under their own vine and their own fig tree, and there will be nothing to make anyone afraid" (Micah 4:4). A moral world, for our prophets, is not one divided into the idle wealthy and the suffering poor, but rather a society in which all are able to be self-sufficient.

The Rabbis: A Theology against Poverty

Our Rabbis, spiritual inheritors of the prophetic tradition, also saw economic justice as fundamental to Judaism. Like the prophets before them, the Rabbis are troubled by how easily people forget the dignity, the value, and inherent worth of those who live in abject need. Pursuing the troubling trajectory of human behavior, the Rabbis explain how that devaluation leads to dehumanization, and thus a desecration of the Divine.

We are led down this logical path by a relatively obscure sage, Rav Natan bar Abba. After citing in his name an explication of an obscure term, the Talmud continues to quote a few more statements attributed to this scholar occupied with the experience of poverty. His first teaching resonates with the rhetoric of Amos, as he condemns the wealthy Jews of Babylonia to a metaphorical hell:

> Rav Natan bar Abba said that Rav said: The wealthy Jews of Babylonia will descend to hell because they do not have compassion on others. This is illustrated by incidents such as when Shabbetai bar Marinus came to Babylonia. He requested their participation in a business venture [to lend him money and receive half the profits in return], and they did not give it to him. Furthermore, when he asked them to sustain him with food, they likewise refused to sustain him. (BT *Beitzah* 32a)[12]

Here, it is not oppression of the poor that is the crime, but simply having wealth without compassion. The terrible reception Shabbetai bar Marinus received in Babylonia, which included the refusal either of a business loan or any immediate aid, is judged as almost inhuman.

Such shunning of the poor earned the entire elite of Babylonian Jewry eternal damnation. If Rav Natan's first teaching decries the deeds of the wealthy, he next turns his attention to the experience of those who are in need:

> Rav Natan bar Abba said that Rav said: All those who look expectantly at the table of others, the world is dark for them. For it is said [Job 15:23]: "He wanders far and wide for bread; where is it? He knows that ready at his hand is the day of darkness [namely death]." (BT *Beitzah* 32a)

This lesser-known student of the great sage Rav understands how dire is the experience of hunger, the pain of abject need. To be hungry is like living in a dark world, sensing that death is near at hand. This nexus of poverty and death is explored immediately after Rav Natan's lesson, when we encounter a horrifying teaching in the unified name of the Sages:

> Our Rabbis taught: There are [three] whose lives are not lives. These are they: the one who looks expectantly at the table of his friend, the one whose woman dominates him, and the one whose afflictions dominate him and his body. And there are some who say: even the one who only has a single garment. (BT *Beitzah* 32a)

The powerful, troubling insight here is that the life of a poor person might not even be considered a life. Where Rav Natan bar Abba sees a world of darkness for those struggling in poverty, his colleagues come to the conclusion that such a life is not really living. Here, the comparisons [although sexist] are important: those whose lives cannot be called "living" are those whose existence is dominated by others. To be without food or without clothing is to be dominated by the search to bring an end to deprivation, an all-consuming quest to find the light that will cast aside the darkness of poverty. The Rabbis question whether sufferings such as these can even be called "living."

Some sages go even further than this. We read elsewhere in the Talmud: "Four are considered as if they are dead: the poor, the leper, the blind, and the one who has no children" (BT *N'darim* 64b).[12] Here, the Sages' assertion is even stronger than what we previously witnessed: it is not just that the life of a poor person cannot be called a life, but also that such a person should be deemed as dead! Although speaking in startling terms, the Rabbis make clear a mundane truth: to be poor is often to be dehumanized. Poverty dehumanizes in two ways. First—in this extreme portrayal of the Sages—this state of utter deprivation has the power to reduce the beauty and depth of human life almost exclusively to animalistic concerns of sustenance and shelter. Second, the materialistic societies that create the imbalances of poverty often punish the very people their insatiable venality impoverishes: as a group, the poor are massed into ghettoes and slums; as individuals, the poor are shunned and ignored even as they ask for assistance. Our Sages of the Talmud know what many in poverty still experience today: to be poor is to be dehumanized.

This crime of dehumanization is even worse in our Jewish world-view, because any sin against humanity becomes a crime against God. As a tradition built upon the bedrock of Genesis's assertion that every human being is created in the divine image, we know that to deny a person's humanity is also to deny their *divinity*. A society that impoverishes people devalues the divine capacity of its citizens. Less kindly put: gross disparities of wealth are not just an offense *before* God, they are an offense *upon* God. This important distinction undergirds the laws of the Torah and the morality of the prophets: God assumes the plight of the poor because when people are forced to live in poverty, so is God. Since the days of the Flood, God demands a reckoning for any human blood spilled by the hands of another person (Gen. 9:6). Thus our tradition dreams of the ultimate eradication of poverty, including the divine punishment of those who benefit from the suffering of others:

> "The tillage of the poor yields much food, but substance is swept away for lack of moderation" [Prov. 13:23]. Rabbi Shimon ben Yochai said: In this world the rich eat the poor; but in the

world-to-come God will demand [recompense] of them, as it is said [Ps. 12:6]: "Because of the plundering of the poor and the groans of the needy, I will now rise [to act], says the Eternal." God will say, "The time has come for Me to demand from you *because of the plundering of the poor and the groans of the needy*: that which you have seized in violence, and that with which you caused them such distress." (*Midrash Mishlei* 13 on Prov. 13:23)

In this world, the rich oppress the poor, the rich consume the poor, and thereby the rich commit violence upon God. In the future, however, the Divine will exercise judgment upon those who benefit from vast disparities of wealth and thereby oppress not only the poor, but God as well. With this, the Rabbis expand poverty from a moral failing to a theological problem. In normative Judaism, theology, morality, and law all demand economic justice.

Conclusions

Poverty, in Judaism, is the most fundamental source of injustice. If we think about the issues of social justice prevalent in our day, even those matters not overtly defined by poverty are linked to economic justice: disability protections, bail reform, affordable housing, quality child care, voting rights, immigration reform, and women's health, to name but a few. More obviously, major concerns around living wage, hunger, homelessness, gender pay equity, and the social safety net are squarely in the arena of economic justice. So much of the instability of our world stems from economic imbalance, from literally unbearable gaps between the wealthy and the poor. Jewish tradition—from Torah's law through prophetic morality to Talmudic theology—consistently teaches that we are to right this most fundamental of wrongs. In order to bring justice to our world, we must build that world upon a foundation of economic justice.

NOTES

1. This translation and all others (unless otherwise noted) are my own.
2. The Bible frequently adjures the community to see to the protection of "the stranger, the orphan, and the widow." While much has been written about the reasons for these three groups as being paradigms of biblical vulnerability, in this context we should note that the stranger might be outside of the economic system, while the orphan and widow likely lack an earner (either father or husband) who might see to their financial security. See David Saperstein, introduction to *Moral Resistance and Spiritual Authority* (New York: CCAR Press, 2018).
3. The basic Hebrew word for "poor person" is *oni*. *Oni* is from the same linguistic root as the regular terms for "oppression." Exod. 1:11 refers to the oppression Pharaoh imposed on the Israelites; Lev. 23:27 describes the requirement for self-affliction (today, fasting) on Yom Kippur.
4. The Hebrew here for a poor person is *evyon*, as we saw above, one who is in want of everything.
5. The Hebrew here for a poor person is *oni*, "the oppressed."
6. The translation here is *not* my own, but that of the King James Version famously engraved on the Liberty Bell.
7. Lev. 25:23 expresses these words in God's voice: "The land shall not be sold beyond reclaim, for the earth is Mine; for strangers and aliens are you in My midst."
8. Poverty is the subject matter of much of the continuation of the chapter and is explicitly mentioned in Lev. 25:39 and 25:47.
9. Shalom Paul, *Amos: A Commentary on the Book of Amos* (Minneapolis: Fortress Press, 1991).
10. Most scholars agree that this text is from the sixth century BCE, and thus later than the words of Amos, which indicates that this particular imprecation of Deuteronomy was likely build upon Amos's famous indictment of Samaria (which is specifically mentioned in the previous verse in Deuteronomy). Regardless of how one reads, the notion that the excess of wealth—here seen through the metaphor of "fat"—perverts social norms was likely a centuries-long refrain in ancient Israel.
11. While all these verses are biblical (as cited), they are all found on the pages of *The Way of the Upright: A Jewish View of Economic Justice*, by Rabbi Richard G. Hirsch (New York: UAHC Press for the Commission on Social Action, 1973), 4–6. This volume is one of myriad compendia that list many verses in which we see the prophets committed to the cause of the poor.
12. The bracketed speculation about the specifics of the refused business venture follows Rashi's commentary on this passage.

13. The Hebrew here for a poor person is *oni*. The immediate context of this anonymous baraita is a teaching of Rabbi Y'hoshua ben Levi stating that a person who does not have children is considered like a dead person.

7

TZEDAKAH

How We Choose Where We Give

RABBI RUTH ADAR

It is a positive mitzvah to give *tzedakah* when one has the means in hand. And a person needs to be very, very careful about it, more than all the positive mitzvot, because it might be a matter of life and death for the recipient.

Arbaah Turim, Yoreh Dei-ah, Hilchot Tzedakah, 247

It is, of course, a monumental undertaking to eradicate poverty or other social ills. Our communal as well as personal resources are limited, and this means that we must make difficult choices concerning the proper allocation of our *tzedakah* funds.

Mark Washofsky, Jewish Living:
A Guide to Contemporary Reform Practice

What Is *Tzedakah*?

Tzedakah is Torah's answer to the problem of poverty.[1] A gift of money or goods for the relief of suffering, *tzedakah* is a mitzvah incumbent upon every Jew. The word *tzedakah* is related to the word *tzedek*, "justice." "Charity," from the Latin *caritas* (love), implies a gift given from a feeling of love. "Philanthropy," from the Greek for "love" and "humanity," also suggests an emotion. Both charity and philanthropy are voluntary acts; *tzedakah* is mandatory. *Tzedakah* is a duty, something owed regardless of one's inclination toward the recipient—or indeed toward the act of giving itself. It should be noted that volunteer work is a separate mitzvah, *g'milut chasadim*, "deeds of loving-kindness."

Sources in Torah

The primary source for the mitzvah of *tzedakah* in Torah is Deuteronomy 15:7–8:

> If . . . there is a needy person among you, one of your kin in any of your settlements in the land that the Eternal your God is giving you, do not harden your heart and shut your hand against your needy kin. Rather, you must open your hand and lend whatever is sufficient to meet the need.

Support of needy relatives is included in the concept of *tzedakah*:

> If your kin, being in straits, come under your authority, and are held by you as though resident aliens, let them live by your side: do not exact advance or accrued interest, but fear your God. Let your kin live by your side as such. (Lev. 25:35–36)

Support of the needy by farmers in the Land of Israel is directly commanded:

> When you reap the harvest of your land, you shall not reap all the way to the edges of your field or gather the gleanings of your harvest. You shall not pick your vineyard bare, or gather the fallen fruit of your vineyard; you shall leave them for the poor and the stranger: I the Eternal am your God. (Lev. 19:9–10)

Even though some of the biblical commandments about support of the needy were specific to agriculture in the Land of Israel, our teachers have used them to develop a deeper understanding of *tzedakah*. For instance, in the Talmud, Rabbi Shimon teaches that the mitzvah of leaving the corners of the field for the poor prevents "theft from the poor" (BT *Shabbat* 23a). His use of the word "theft" underlines that the food in the corners of the field belongs to the poor. The poor have a right to our support.

How Is the Mitzvah of *Tzedakah* Properly Carried Out?

Tzedakah is the sacred duty of every Jew. The tradition guides us as to the amount but leaves us many choices in our giving. Every Jew should give, but every giver has the right to choose how to divide their *tzedakah* among those entitled to receive it.[2]

Once one has verbalized a commitment to give *tzedakah*, that commitment must be acted upon as quickly as possible, either paying out the funds or setting them aside for later payment, so as not to violate the mitzvah *bal t'acheir*, "do not delay."

How Much Should an Individual Give for *Tzedakah*?

Traditionally the target for giving *tzedakah* is 10 percent of income after taxes. The *Shulchan Aruch* specifies an upper limit of 20 percent of income for the money for *tzedakah*, lest the giver fall destitute and in need of *tzedakah* himself.[3]

The needy are not exempt from the obligation of *tzedakah*. No matter how low a person's income, all are required to participate.[4] Even the person who is a recipient of *tzedakah* should contribute to the relief of others. However, the amount given need not be large, and many expenditures count as *tzedakah*, including financial assistance given to relatives. The *Shulchan Aruch* sets a minimum of one-third of a shekel per year.[5] Sources disagree as to the exact amount of modern cash equivalent to one-third shekel, but it appears to be a very small amount.

One way of fulfilling the mitzvah is to set aside a personal *tzedakah* fund or budget, out of which payments can be made as opportunities present themselves.

How Should *Tzedakah* Be Given?

Maimonides has given us his famous "ladder":

1. The highest form of giving is to give the means to independence via a partnership or loan.
2. Giving *tzedakah* anonymously to an unknown recipient. Communal organizations can facilitate this.
3. Giving *tzedakah* anonymously to a known recipient.
4. Giving *tzedakah* publicly to an unknown recipient.
5. Giving *tzedakah* before being asked.
6. Giving *tzedakah* after being asked.
7. Giving less than one should but giving cheerfully.
8. Giving unwillingly.[6]

Even the lowest rung on the ladder fulfills the mitzvah of *tzedakah*, but Maimonides makes the point that there are more and less meritorious ways to do so.

Notice that while it is a common saying that "the highest form of giving is a loan," that is not what Maimonides says. Rather, it is to give another person the means to independence, which *might* take the form of a loan, which, according to the rules of lending to fellow Jews, would be a no-interest loan. The ladder moves downward from that high level, where the parties are known to each another but in a partnership of some kind, through anonymity on both sides, to anonymity by the giver, to anonymity of the receiver, to descending attitudes about giving. The person who is forced to give (by peer pressure or perhaps shaming) still fulfills the mitzvah but does so only minimally.

Limited Funds, Unlimited Needs: Making *Tzedakah* Choices

The goal of *tzedakah* as expressed in the Torah is that there shall be no one in need in the community, although Deuteronomy 15:11 admits "there will never cease to be needy ones in your land." Those words have proved true in more ways than one: the individual who wishes to give *tzedakah* today is faced with many outstretched hands and the certainty that in choosing one person or organization to support, others must be turned away. How, then, are we to make our choices?

Need: A Core Concept for *Tzedakah* Decisions

The Torah texts prioritize the most basic human needs: food and shelter. A more modern source, Maslow's "Hierarchy of Needs," offers one alternative for thinking about needs, from the most urgent to the least urgent:[7]

1. Physical needs: air, food, water, sleep, waste disposal.
2. Safety needs: physical safety, employment security, income security, health security.
3. Social needs: friendship, sexual intimacy, family.
4. Esteem: self-respect and the respect of others.
5. Self-actualization and spiritual needs.

A different model for thinking about needs is that of Viktor Frankl, whose experience in the Shoah led him to theorize a priority of needs opposite to Maslow's. Frankl argues persuasively that humanity's deepest need is for a sense of meaning and purpose in life. For Frankl, educational and communal opportunities outweigh food and shelter.[8]

There are also specifically Jewish needs to take into consideration, which would be at the top of Frankl's priorities. Jews are commanded to provide Torah education for their children (BT *Kiddushin* 29a). There are other requirements for participation in the Jewish community as well (e.g., holiday meals, membership in a minyan for prayer, the acquisition and maintenance of Torah scrolls). Education for adults, as well as for teachers and rabbis, is a necessity in Jewish life. Communal funds for these purposes have been a feature of Jewish life for centuries.[9] Very few families could afford to pay the cost of all their Jewish education and mitzvot without the communal pooling of resources.

Ultimately it is up to the giver to decide upon a definition of need. The general principle is that gifts must relieve the burdens of the needy to qualify as *tzedakah*.[10]

How Can We Prioritize Needs?

Maimonides teaches us another ladder, this time a ladder of priorities in choosing the recipients of *tzedakah*.[11] He orders them from highest priority to lowest:

1. *Pidyon sh'vuyim*, "the ransom of captives": This was a constant issue in medieval Jewish communities, because outsiders had learned that Jews would do their best to ransom a kidnapped member of their community, especially a Torah scholar. Today it is a difficult strategic issue for the Israeli government, which must balance the desire to ransom captives and bring home bodies for burial against the fact that such ransoms or captive exchanges endanger Israeli troops. In the United States, the bail bond system leaves many individuals captive, awaiting trial; assisting with bail is another way to "free the captive."

2. Keeping oneself out of poverty: Jewish tradition frowns on excess, including excess in *tzedakah*. One's first responsibility (after freeing a captive, which may be a matter of life and death) is to care for oneself. This value will be discussed later in more detail.

3. Close relatives who need assistance, in order of closeness: Paying for rent or food for a relative who cannot work or who cannot find work fulfills the mitzvah. Also, the *Shulchan Aruch* is explicit that money given to an adult child for education or to "keep them on the right path" qualifies as this kind of *tzedakah*.[12]

4. Poor members of one's household, including servants: We should pay those who work for us a sufficient wage; that is not *tzedakah*. However, we should also be sensitive to the misfortunes and illnesses of the persons connected with our household and assist as we are able.

5. The needy who live nearby, in order of closeness: We can support the local food bank and organizations that serve the poor.

6. The needy who live farther away: This is a relative concept, but in general Maimonides seems to suggest that while the faraway poor should be supported by *tzedakah* from their own area, when those resources are overburdened (as in a time of disaster) those farther away must step up and help. The *Shulchan Aruch* specifies that the poor of the Land of Israel take precedence over the poor of any other land.[13]

There are also strong traditions for the support of needy Torah scholars,[14] for Torah education, and for the needy in the Land of Israel, giving to any of which qualifies as *tzedakah*.[15] Other texts suggest priorities according to vulnerability, intensity of need, or even level of education. If we learn from Frankl that the need for meaning and for nourishment of the spirit is actually a survival need, then the support of Torah learning and Torah scholars fits every level of priority. In balancing these concerns, we can look to the words of the prophets. In their words, care for the poor takes precedence over sacrifices and ritual requirements, and neglect of the poor is a breach of the covenant (e.g., Isa. 1:11–19).

One element that did not enter the equation in the times of the prophets or Maimonides is the question of supporting organizations that work for long-term systemic change. Classically, *tzedakah* addresses immediate need. However, if the highest form of giving is the gift of long-term independence, then may we not count the gift of release from a systemic illness or abuse as *tzedakah*? And if the highest priority is to "free the captive," then surely the freeing of captives of systemic racism, sexism, or poverty should qualify, as should contributions toward prison and bail reform.

The tradition insists on the priority of the preservation of life and the freeing of captives. After that, it is a matter of individual conscience and choice. The contemporary Orthodox scholar Cyril Domb cites a commentary on the *Shulchan Aruch* as teaching that the strict rules of priority are for organizations, but that personal *tzedakah* is up to the discretion of the donor.[16] An individual Jew is free to allocate *tzedakah* as one sees fit.

Tzedakah Given to Individuals: Considerations

Tzedakah may be extended to an individual, or it may be given via a communal agency. Recipients need not be Jewish; the codes specify that everyone who asks for bread should be given food, whether Jewish or not.[17]

Some questions to consider in giving to individuals:

1. How immediate is the need? What do I believe could happen if they do not receive my *tzedakah* now? Is a life at stake?
2. What other sources of help are available to them? How quickly can they be depended upon to act?
3. How do their needs compare to other requests currently before me?
4. Do my feelings about them influence me for or against them? If so, I should consider consulting with someone whose judgment I trust.
5. How can I help them while preserving their dignity?
6. Can I help them in such a way that they will achieve independence and not need help again?
7. Maimonides praises the giver who does not wait to be asked. In dealing with people near to us (family, members of the household including people who work for us, etc.), part of the mitzvah of *tzedakah* is keeping our eyes open for need.

It is important, too, to think through our behavior in saying no to an applicant. We may feel that a person is undeserving or that they are annoying, or we may simply be uncomfortable saying no. Our tradition teaches that saying no as kindly as possible is part of the mitzvah of *tzedakah* in all cases.[18]

Tzedakah and the Self

We have already seen that the first *tzedakah* obligation of an individual after freeing captives is to keep themselves out of poverty. This is not selfishness; it is an acknowledgment that anyone can have a reversal of fortune and that the *tzedakah* resources in any community are limited. The codes are unambiguous on the subject, insisting that we are obligated to give our own *parnasah* (sustenance) priority over that of any other person.[19] We should not endanger our ability to live and earn a living by giving (or living) beyond our means.

Jacob ben Asher, author of the *Tur*, wrote in the name of Saadyah Gaon, "A man is obligated to give his own sustenance priority over that of any other person."[20]

For this reason, savings and investment against misfortune and for old age might properly be considered part of *tzedakah* planning, especially for those with limited incomes. Some measure of *tzedakah* should be given to another recipient, though, since we may not give all our *tzedakah* funds to a single recipient.[21]

Tzedakah Given through Organizations: Considerations

There are many appropriate communal organizations to facilitate the giving of *tzedakah*—a rabbi's discretionary fund, an organizational fund for relief of the unfortunate, or the Hebrew Free Loan Society, among others. Given that recipients may be Jewish or non-Jewish, the local community food bank or kitchen might be an excellent choice.

Considerations in considering communal organizations:

1. Whom does the organization serve?
2. While it may be tempting to choose organizations that say "Every penny goes to the needy," in fact a well-run organization needs transparent management and accounting. It is reasonable to ask how funds are spent. Two good resources for this research are CharityNavigator.org and CharityWatch.org.

3. Does the organization embody the values it claims? Are employees treated with respect and paid properly for their work? Is the compensation of management in line with other similar organizations? How diverse are the board and leadership?

4. Does the organization treat applicants and grantees respectfully? Does it ask for only the personal information it needs to make decisions? Is the application process demeaning? There is an extended discussion among the Rabbis in the Talmud (BT *Bava Batra* 9a) about the inquiries that may and may not be made of applicants and of eligibility for assistance.

5. How does the organization treat applicants whom it turns down? Since the intent of *tzedakah* is to reduce the distress of the disadvantaged, it is doubly important to handle the process of decision-making in such a way that disappointment and embarrassment are held to an absolute minimum. A no, when it is necessary, must be compassionate, prompt, and private, whether it comes from an individual or from a communal institution.

6. Institutions in the State of Israel should be subject to the same scrutiny as other communal institutions.

Crowdfunding and *Tzedakah*

The advent of the internet and social networks has brought crowdfunding, a new mode of asking for *tzedakah*. GoFundMe.com, Fundly.com, and GiveForward.com are all examples of crowdfunding websites. Individuals announce their need for funds and donors contribute. This cuts out the middle, so to speak, with mixed results. On the one hand, it is extremely efficient, with low administrative costs (generally a small percentage to the website). On the other hand, donors have responsibility for assessing the need. A responsible donor will want to ask: What happens if there are excess funds? To whom will those go?

"New Philanthropy" and *Tzedakah*

Since the 1990s there has been a revolution in thinking about philanthropy. Donors have brought investment-like thinking to philanthropy, talking about "return on investment" and "investing" in causes. There has also been an interest by donors in retaining more control of gifts. While this may be appropriate for philanthropy, it is important to remember the core principles of *tzedakah*.

Our tradition values anonymity in *tzedakah*. It values a relinquishing of control, as in the example of the corners of the field, *pei-ah*. A farmer could not reserve *pei-ah* for only the poor he deemed "deserving." He could not designate it for certain poor friends. When food and therefore survival are concerned, we may not question the request at all.[22]

A donor may meet the requirements of *tzedakah* with unrestricted gifts to appropriate individuals or organizations and then be more restrictive or investment-minded in additional gifts.

Conclusion

Certainly, it is possible to fulfill the letter of the law of *tzedakah* by setting aside cash and then giving it away to at least two people or organizations. Doing so carelessly, however, carries the possibility of doing harm rather than good. In giving *tzedakah*, the thoughtful Jew will want to consider to whom the funds will be given and how that giving will be carried out. If the recipients are organizations that will be acting as agents of the donor, they should be well-run and treat their clients with the same respect required of an individual donor. If the recipients are individuals, then great care should be taken to make matters better, not worse, for them and to treat them with the respect due a fellow human being.

A successful process of *tzedakah* will take the world one step closer to the vision of a world redeemed, of a community in which no one is in need. Moving through that process with care for the ethical issues involved will help to ensure that we do good, not harm, with the mitzvah.

> Give readily and have no regrets when you do so, for in return the Eternal your God will bless you in all your efforts and in all your undertakings. (Deut. 15:10)

NOTES

1. This chapter is an updated version of "Ethical Priorities in Giving Tzedakah," *CCAR Journal: The Reform Jewish Quarterly* 56, no. 2 (Spring 2010), 69–78.
2. Cyril Domb, ed., *Ma'aser Kesafim: On Giving a Tenth to Charity* (New York: Feldheim, 1980), 105.
3. Josef Karo, *Shulchan Aruch, Yoreh Dei-ah* 249:1–2. The 20 percent limit, lest the giver bankrupt himself, is in the *Mapah*, the gloss on the text by Moses Isserles.
4. Mark Washofsky, *Jewish Living: A Guide to Contemporary Reform Practice* (New York: UAHC Press, 2001), 298; also *Shulchan Aruch, Yoreh Dei-ah* 249:2.
5. Washofsky, *Jewish Living*, 298.
6. Maimonides, *Mishneh Torah, Hilchot Mat'not Aniyim* 10:7.
7. A. H. Maslow, "A Theory of Human Motivation," *Psychological Review* 50 (1943): 370–96.
8. Victor E. Frankl, *Man's Search for Meaning* (New York: Pocket Books, 1959).
9. Byron L. Sherwin and Seymour J. Cohen, *Creating an Ethical Jewish Life: A Practical Introduction on Classic Teachings on How to Be a Jew* (Woodstock, VT: Jewish Lights, 2001), 225.
10. Washofsky, *Jewish Living*, 209.
11. Maimonides, *Mishneh Torah, Hilchot Mat'not Aniyim* 7:13, 8:10.
12. *Shulchan Aruch, Yoreh Dei-ah* 251:3.
13. *Shulchan Aruch, Yoreh Dei-ah* 251:3.
14. *Kitzur Shulchan Aruch* 34:14.
15. Nathaniel Katsburg, "Halukkah," *Encyclopaedia Judaica* (Jerusalem: Keter, 1971), 1207–16.
16. Domb, *Ma'aser Kesafim*, 105.

17. *Shulchan Aruch, Yoreh Dei-ah* 251:13.
18. Maimonides, *Mishneh Torah, Hilchot Mat'not Aniyim* 10:5; also BT *Shabbat* 23a.
19. *Tur, Yoreh Dei-ah* 251, cited in Rovner, in *Ma'aser Kesafim*, ed. Domb, 38; also Maimonides, *Mishneh Torah, Hilchot Arachim V'Charamim* 8:13.
20. *Arbaah Turim, Yoreh Dei-ah* 250.
21. *Shulchan Aruch, Yoreh Deah* 257:9.
22. *Aruch HaShulchan* 251:12.

8

SOCIALLY RESPONSIBLE INVESTING

MICHAEL A. KIMMEL
AND RABBI HOWARD SHAPIRO

Not long after the Flood, Genesis continues the narrative of the earth's repopulation, telling us that everyone on earth had the same language and the same words when they settle in the Valley of Shinar. It is there they decide to build a city with a tower reaching as high as the heavens (Gen. 11:1–4). The problem with the tower was not its height or its architecture; it was its builders' use of their resources. The modern biblical scholar Rabbi Benno Jacob taught that the people used much raw material and developed new skills to build the tower. However, rather than using their resources and talent to help improve the lives of the poor, sick, and aged, they focused on building a tower, higher than any other.[1] The story culminating with God's scattering of the people as punishment underscores the basic Jewish value that the privilege of living is bound to the mitzvah of "doing good." We are souls on a journey toward purpose.

And so it is with money. Our Jewish tradition imagines that when we stand before God at the gates of heaven, we will be asked several questions, including whether we looked to the future and whether we were fair and ethical in our business dealings (Babylonian Talmud, *Shabbat* 31a). Our role on earth is to increase the level of holiness and to use our resources, our wealth, as instruments to do *tikkun olam*, repair the world for all.

The goal of this chapter is to familiarize you with ways to translate the value of *tikkun olam* into the financial investment arena. We will also offer as a model the Reform Pension Board, the retirement plan for many of the Reform Movement's professionals, and its work to create the Reform Jewish Values Fund, a fund designed to specifically reflect Reform Jewish values.

Socially responsible investing (SRI) enables investors to express their values through their financial investments. These types of investments are designed not only to generate earnings, but also to "do good" and/or "not cause harm" using the values lens of the investor. There are many terms that we will use: socially responsible investing, impact investing, negative screens, and positive tilts. They refer to values-based methods through which different faith traditions have looked at money over time. It is our hope that these diverse positions will expose you to the many investment paths you can take as you seek to live your values.

Socially Responsible Investing Born in Faith Traditions

Rooted in many faith traditions, SRI has evolved into a full-fledged industry, including financial instruments that enable just about anyone to invest based on their values. In almost all the religious traditions, the concept of ownership carries rights and responsibilities; one of the most fundamental values is "do no harm." This, in fact, is at the core of traditional faith-based investing and to a large degree traditional SRI overall: avoid investing in products or industries that conflict with a set of moral values. We will explore the history of some of those religious traditions here.

According to Islamic standards, investments must follow three Shariah-compliant principles. The first is the absence of interest, *riba*, in the investment, as Islam has a strict prohibition on interest.[2] The second prohibits investments from promoting behaviors prohibited by Islam, including alcohol, banks and insurance companies that are non-Shariah compliant, gambling, pornography, pork, weapons manufacturing, non-Shariah compliant animal slaughter, and tobacco. The third principle states that contracts must be in writing and completely transparent. All three basic principles listed are rooted in Islam's central holy text, the Qur'an, which dates to the sixth century CE, and are commonplace today in Islamic values-aligned investments.[3]

Fast-forward to the eighteenth century. Under the leadership of John Wesley, the Methodist Church renounced the slave trade, smuggling, and conspicuous consumption and avoided investments in companies manufacturing liquor or tobacco products, weapons, and gambling. In his sermon "The Use of Money," Wesley essentially established the concept of social investment screens.[4] During the same period, the Quakers, at their national annual meetings, prohibited members from participating in the slave trade—buying or selling humans. This concept carried forward to the modern day.[5] The Quakers were one of the first religious or secular groups to offer a socially screened investment solution.

The Secular World Joins the Cause

The 1960s and '70s, with the rise of the anti-war and racial equality movements and the growing focus on women's rights, safeguarding consumer protections, and protecting the environment, found the secular world not only embracing traditional faith-based SRI, but also taking it to a new level. Vietnam War protesters demanded the divestment from defense contractors by university endowments. In 1971, the Pax World Balance Fund was launched for those investors seeking to avoid direct investment in the supply chains for one of the most toxic chemicals, Agent Orange.[6]

Something else happened in 1971. Reverend Leon Sullivan (at the time a board member of General Motors) drafted a code of conduct for businesses operating in South Africa to lessen discrimination. This code later became the Global Sullivan Principles. These principles were the basis for the divestment activities, promulgated across the United States and beyond, against those companies doing business in South Africa, with the goal of ending apartheid. These efforts did not singularly bring down apartheid, but they did draw international attention to the issue, contributing to its undoing.[7]

Other funds followed, but since its early days in the 1970s, SRI principles and practices have matured in a number of ways. Organizations such as the Interfaith Center for Corporate Responsibility were founded to bring together coalitions of faith-based investors, pioneering the use of shareholder advocacy (and sometimes activism) to press corporations on environmental, social, and corporate governance (ESG) issues. The idea is to hold publicly traded corporations responsible for their business practices and to press for change by being part of the company as investors. Efforts include initiating conversations with corporate management or the boards of directors on issues of concern, as well as submitting and voting proxy resolutions.

The Industry Matures and Changes

In the 1980s and '90s, the SRI industry continued to develop. Instead of simply screening out those investments anathema to one's moral or ethical values, investors recognized that positive screening, or intentionally investing in corporations that demonstrate beneficial environmental, social, or governance (ESG) practices, might generate better long-term investment performance than those that do not. Today, ESG investing uses these factors (similar to factors used to screen out investments) to measure the sustainability and ethical impact of an investment. Environmental factor examples include pollution, climate change, and environmental management; social factor examples include pornography and other adult entertainment, tobacco, alcohol, human rights, and sexual orientation; and governance factor examples include board accountability, board diversity, and CEO compensation.

SRI has continued to evolve in the twenty-first century. A new approach turns negative screening on its head by purposely investing in those companies producing products antithetical to one's values with the aim of effecting change as an activist investor. The goal is simple—if you own the stock, you have a voice. Guns are a controversial example. An investor may be inclined not to own stock in American Outdoor Brands, the maker of semi-automatic rifles, including the ones used in several recent mass shootings. However, if one wants to lobby the company to change its policies or products that would lead to greater gun safety, it is more effective to be a stock owner and vote one's shares through proxy voting or through shareholder advocacy. This is not a simple decision for investors, especially faith-based investors, to decide to seek companies that build or sell things that counter to their values when shareholder activism may make a difference, since this SRI approach makes the investor part of the ownership.

The most recent term to come into this SRI world is "impact investing." While positive investing/screening focuses on investing in the stock of a corporation, impact investing targets private companies by making direct investments based on specific objectives, alongside financial return. This provides businesses whose mission it is to do "good" access to capital that philanthropy may not be able to provide. Examples include investments in microfinance, community development finance, and clean technology. Rooted in the venture capital community, investors often take active roles in helping the companies succeed. This type of direct investing enables investors to create a greater social impact than they would have if they simply owned the stock.

SRI and Israel

As they consider their investments, Jewish investors should be aware of the BDS (Boycott, Divestment, Sanctions) movement. Among other things, BDS calls for the divestment of companies either domiciled in Israel or non-Israeli companies conducting business in Israel or the disputed territories. Jewish investors should be aware as they research SRI- or ESG-themed investments that some funds may be influenced by BDS. In its 2005 resolution, the Union for Reform Judaism (URJ) took the position to

> oppose efforts to impose economic sanctions on Israel or on companies working in or doing business with Israel; urge religious, civic, labor, academic and other institutions to oppose divestment and other economic sanctions against Israel as tools to address the Israeli-Palestinian conflict and to support efforts to change such policies where they have been adopted; encourage those seeking peace to focus their efforts on reconciliation, including the many meaningful coexistence programs that are necessary to foster a generation of Israelis and Palestinians who will work and live side by side and move beyond the teaching of hate and violence.

The Reform Movement argues that using economic sanctions against Israel are more likely to hinder rather than advance the peace process that leads to a resolution of the Israeli-Palestinian conflict, which the URJ is deeply committed to supporting.[8] For Zionists, investing in a company that is domiciled or operates in Israel can be a positive screen, as this type of investment promotes the development of the Jewish homeland. One can call it ESGI, adding Israel as an additional positive factor in making investment-related decisions.

Investing with Jewish Values

From the commandment in Leviticus to leave a portion of your field to those in need so they may harvest with dignity (Lev. 19:9–10) to the injunction to conduct your business dealings with fairness and integrity (Lev. 25:14), our earliest sources underscore our commitment to *tikkun olam*. One of the most familiar of Maimonides's teachings is that the highest form of charity is to provide those in need with a job, so that they can support themselves. This may include entering into a partnership, loaning money, or as a last resort, giving a gift. The goal, according to Maimonides, is to "strengthen his hand until he does not need to ask others for help."[9]

Efforts in recent years in the Jewish values-based SRI/impact investing world are notable. For example, JLens Investor Network was formed in 2012 to educate, advocate, and advise Jewish investors on values-aligned impact investing concepts. Among other things, they conduct shareholder advocacy on behalf of its investors with public companies on subjects important to its network.

And in the spirit of *tikkun olam*, the Union of American Hebrew Congregations (UAHC), since renamed Union for Reform Judaism (URJ), adopted a resolution on socially responsible investment that established the Chai Investment Program (CHIP) in 1997. It called for all Reform Movement institutions and congregations to invest 1.8 percent of their investment funds in community development vehicles, such as local credit unions and loan funds whose mission was to increase access to credit for those in generally depressed communities across the United States who would otherwise not have the financial resources necessary for economic development.[10] This resolution was one of many Reform Movement resolutions and actions regarding discrimination in matters of economic investment and responsible business dealings over the past thirty years.

The Reform Pension Board: A Goal and a Timeline

The Reform Pension Board (RPB) has been on a long but steady road to bring the concepts of SRI, ESG, negative and positive screens, and impact investing to the financial halls of the Reform Jewish world. It is a case study in patience and progress. The timeline below gives a sense of the steady but cautious path it has taken, and is offered in the context of this chapter to show how the RPB has arrived where it is today:

1986: Divests from companies doing business in South Africa per the Global Sullivan Principles

1990: Forms its Socially Responsible Investment Committee

1992: Joins the Interfaith Center for Corporate Responsibility (ICCR)

1993: Rescinds restrictions on investing in South Africa

1994: Implements negative screen on tobacco companies

1994: Endorses the CERES Principles (set of guidelines for businesses that were created by an independent body to ensure the embrace of unified standards to safeguard the environment)

1995: Makes four $50,000 investments in certificates of deposit in community development banks with RPB administrative reserve funds

1997–99: URJ (UAHC) passes resolution on socially responsible investing, which led to development of the Chai Investment program (CHIP); 1.8 percent of assets invested in community development agency bonds

2003: Engages Institutional Shareholder Services, a company that specializes in voting proxies, to vote the proxies on its behalf

2006: Develops custom proxy voting policy reflecting Reform Jewish values

2007: Implements negative screen on companies that conduct business with the Sudanese government per the Sudanese Divestment Taskforce

2014: Formalizes and documents approach to SRI through the adoption of RPB's Jewish Values Investing Policy[11]

2018: Launches Reform Jewish Values Fund

RPB's Reform Jewish Values Fund, available to both participants in RPB's retirement plan and to URJ-affiliated congregations to invest their own institution's money, was built on the foundation listed above. The fund is designed to provide an investment vehicle that tracks a global stock benchmark but is also guided by the values as defined by the resolutions of the CCAR, the URJ, and the Commission on Social

Action of Reform Judaism. It is a living fund designed to be reexamined at appropriate intervals, with its guidelines accommodated to the values of the Reform Movement. The fund currently avoids companies that are involved with predatory lending, civilian firearms, land mines, and cluster munitions. It shuns tobacco and coal manufacturers, as well as companies that conduct business with the Sudanese government. And the fund places greater emphasis on companies with better-performing ESG practices, with positive impact on the environment, and with business ties to Israel. As stated earlier, the decision to own or not own shares of a company based on one's values is complex. There are arguments for and against ownership. In deciding to screen out certain kinds of companies, the basic principle RPB used was that it did not want this new fund to own the stock of companies whose core business conflicts with the principles as defined by the Reform Movement's resolutions.

What This Means for All of Us

"You shall love the Eternal your God with all your heart, with all your soul, with all *m'odecha*" (Deut. 6:5). While this last word is commonly translated as "your might," many in our tradition read it to mean "your means."[12] We are given the challenge of loving God by using our wealth for the betterment of all. We are commanded to love by sharing, by caring, by creating, and by actively creating opportunities where our assets help us fulfill our mission of stewardship for the world we have been gifted. We are, in fact, summoned to live our values in every way possible. Investing in a values-based fund is one of the many ways that we can live these words of Torah.

NOTES

1. Harvey J. Fields, *A Torah Commentary for Our Times*, vol. 1, *Genesis* (New York: UAHC Press, 1990), 33.

2. To learn about Judaism's understanding of interest, see Elkin, p. 195 in this volume.

3. "Shariah-Compliant Investments," UBL Funds, accessed September 16, 2018, http://www.ublfunds.com.pk/international/resources-tools/ learning-center/shariah-compliant-investments/#What%20is%20a%20 Shariah-compliant%20investment.

4. John Wesley, "The Use of Money," Global Ministries, the United Methodist Church, accessed September 16, 2018, https:// www.umcmission.org/Find-Resources/John-Wesley-Sermons/ Sermon-50-The-Use-of-Money.

5. "Eliminating Slavery amongst Quakers," Quakers in the World, accessed September 16, 2018, http://www.quakersintheworld.org/ quakers-in-action/58.

6. Blaine Townsend, *From SRI to ESG: The Origins of Socially Responsible and Sustainable Investing*, Bailard Thought Series (Foster City, CA: Bailard Wealth Management, 2017), http://www.bailard.com/wp-con-tent/uploads/2017/06/Socially-Responsible-Investing-History-Bailard-White-Paper-FNL.pdf.

7. Molly Roth, "Sullivan Principles," *Encyclopedia of Greater Philadelphia*, 2013, http://philadelphiaencyclopedia.org/archive/sullivan-principles/.

8. "Resolution: Divestment and Other Economic Actions as Obstacles to the Advancement of Middle East Peace," Union for Reform Judaism, adopted 2005, https://urj.org/what-we-believe/resolutions/divestment-and-other-economic-actions-obstacles-advancement-middle-east.

9. Maimonides, *Mishneh Torah, Hilchot Mat'not Aniyim* 10:7.

10. "Resolution: Socially Responsible Investment," Union for Reform Judaism, adopted 1997, https://urj.org/what-we-believe/resolutions/ socially-responsible-investment.

11. "About the RPB—Jewish Values Investing," RPB, accessed September 16, 2018, https://rpb.org/about-the-rpb/jewish-values-investing/ ?highlight=Jewish%20Values%20Investing%20Policy.

12. For example, Rashi's comment on Deut. 6:5.

9

GUNS

Leveraging the Power of Money for Justice

RABBI JOEL M. MOSBACHER

It should be enough to be right.

That's what I've thought every day since January 19, 1999, when my father was murdered by gun; it's what I think of every time I hear another story of the thousands of murders that happen each year that *do not* interrupt your regularly scheduled programming and *do not* make even a column inch in the local newspaper.

That's what we thought after Columbine in 1999 and Virginia Tech in 2007. That's what we thought in 2012 after Newtown, Connecticut. That's what we thought in 2018 after Parkland. Surely when it's not safe to go to school, our elected officials will act, because keeping our children safe is the right thing to do.

That's what we thought after we realized that more than thirty thousand Americans were dying by gun each year;[1] after we learned that more Americans had died by gun since 1968 than have died in all of America's wars since 1776.[2]

That's what we thought when we looked once again at Leviticus 19:16, where it is written, "You shall not stand idly by the blood of your neighbor."

It should be enough to be right, to have the evidence, to have the data, to have the moral and religious high ground.

But sadly, it is rarely enough to be right if you want to make change. If you want to make change, you must have power.

When the Industrial Areas Foundation (IAF), the nation's oldest and largest network of community organizing, developed the Do Not Stand Idly By campaign to reduce gun violence, we knew that if we were going to impact the seemingly intractable scourge of gun violence in America, we were going to have to assemble a lot of power.

But how could a bunch of rabbis, ministers, priests, imams, and congregants possibly assemble the power we would need? Who are we to assemble and wield power?

We are leaders who have organized people and organized money on many issues. And we have the audacity to believe that when we organize people and money, we can make grassroots change on important issues.

It is one thing for synagogues, churches, and mosques to organize the people who sit in our pews. Given the right cause, tapping into their sense of morality as well as self-interest, religious leaders can motivate them to march, to make phone calls, to send e-mails and letters, and to sign petitions.

But what about people of faith wielding the power of money? Some might feel squeamish about this, as it is often said that money is the root of all evil. That view could deter us from using the power of money to effect change. But this avoidance, reaching beyond Christian culture in America, stems in part from an oft misquoted passage from the New Testament, in which Timothy teaches, "*The love of money* is the root of all kinds of evil*" (I Timothy 6:10). In fact, money itself is morally neutral. Our attitude toward it, and how we use it, determines the effect that money has on us and the world in which we live.[3]

When it comes to the issue of gun violence, we know that there are powerful monetary forces at play; the National Rifle Association and the gun manufacturers who bankroll that powerful lobby unabashedly use money to influence policy and the politicians who make policy. It is clear that if we want to reduce gun violence, we will need to wield the power of money to do so.

The Talmud (BT *K'tubot* 68a) teaches, "Rabbi Chiyya bar Rav from Dipthi taught that Rabbi Y'hoshua ben Korchah said: Anyone who closes his eyes from *tzedakah* is as if he serves idols." The text makes the case that when we fail to act on justice when we have the ability to do so, we are, in a sense, complicit in the injustice. When we close our eyes to the power money plays in the story of gun violence, and when we fail to use the power of money that we can wield, we are complicit in permitting the violence to continue. Sermons, public statements, and petitions have their place, but it is simply not enough to hold the moral high ground when we wish to make an impact on the fundamental injustices of our world. We must organize powerfully, and that powerful organizing often involves money.

After the Newtown, Connecticut, mass shooting, leaders across IAF decided that we could stand idly by no longer as our neighbors' blood was shed, as it has been for decades in cities across America. Newtown was, of course, not the first shooting of its kind, but it was a wake-up call to millions of Americans who thought, perhaps, that they were immune to the scourge, who thought that gun violence, while deplorable, was something that only happened in communities of color.

But what could we do, we asked ourselves? Who has the power to reduce gun violence in America, and how can we possibly convince them to use that power?

Congress and the president have the power to reduce gun violence; they could pass and sign legislation that will make it more difficult for people who should not have access to guns to acquire them. Closing the so-called gun show loophole, requiring universal background checks and training for those who purchase weapons, and legally reducing the size of ammunition clips, thereby limiting the easy killing power of guns, are but a few things that the legislative and executive branch could do that would dramatically reduce the scourge of gun violence in America. But they have not done these things or anything like them.

After each mass shooting, much is made in the media about the impact that legislation could have on this problem. And then, the news cycle turns to the next crisis, and Congress and the president fail once again to act. Again and again, our elected officials have stood idly by while their neighbors bleed. These officials have not *forgotten* to pass any meaningful laws to reduce gun violence in America. They have actively *decided*, influenced no doubt by the power of the money given to them as campaign contributions by lobbyists like the National Rifle Association, to do nothing at all.

I am reminded of the following passage from the Talmud:

> When the community is immersed in suffering, a person may not say: I will go to my home and I will eat and drink, and peace be upon you, my soul. And if he does so, the verse says about him: "And behold joy and gladness, slaying oxen and killing sheep, eating flesh and drinking wine; let us eat and drink, for tomorrow we shall die" (Isaiah 22:13). And the prophecy continues with what is written afterward, in the following verse: "And the God of hosts was revealed in my ears: Surely this iniquity shall not be expiated by you until you die" (Isaiah 22:14). (BT *Taanit* 11a)

When public officials decide to do nothing in the face of such suffering in our country, we should hold them accountable. We should either convince them to act or vote in other citizens who will act. And many gun violence prevention organizations are doing that work intensively. Groups like Everytown for Gun Safety, Moms Demand Action, the Brady Campaign, and Giffords's Law Center are working tirelessly on legislation that will effect change, electing the officials who will support needed legislation.

When IAF decided to act on this issue, we knew that there were already incredible organizations working the legislative angle. We wondered: besides Congress and the president, who else, if anyone, has power to reduce gun violence?

We asked mayors, police chiefs, sheriffs, and other public officials with whom we had been in relationship around other issues in the past. And after some months of research, we realized that there was a whole other group of people who were, in the language of the above Talmud text, going home to eat and drink while Americans were suffering death after death by gun: the CEOs of the major gun manufacturers.

After Columbine, Newtown, Oak Creek, Las Vegas, Parkland—there were names you never heard in the news but should have. No one was speaking about Gaston Glock, Ugo Beretta, Christopher Killroy, and James Debney.

It would be no surprise if you, the reader, did not know their names, their faces, or their stories; they want it that way. These four men, and the companies they lead, are the manufacturers of the vast majority of the more than three hundred million guns that exist in this country.[4] Glock, Beretta, Sig Sauer, and American Outdoor Brands (formerly Smith and Wesson) are satisfied to make weapons of mass destruction, fill the coffers of elected officials to ensure that their industry is the most coddled industry in America, and then say, "Peace be upon you."

It is time that these industry leaders played their part in reducing gun violence. And they could begin today. They could do two essential things that would make a dramatic impact on the issue of gun violence: they could control their worst dealers, and they could innovate in safer gun technology.

The vast majority of gun dealers in America are responsible dealers: they follow local and state laws; they train their employees to recognize straw purchasers who buy guns for others who cannot legally purchase a weapon; they track their inventory responsibly. These "good" gun stores almost never have a crime gun traced to their store.

On the other hand, according to statistics from the Bureau of Alcohol, Tobacco and Firearms, an astounding 60 percent of guns that turn up at crime scenes can be traced to 1 percent of gun stores, and nearly all crime guns can be traced to just 5 percent of gun stores.[5]

Gun manufacturers, like the makers of any product, decide which stores they are going to deal with. If gun manufacturers decided either to stop doing business with those 5 percent of stores or to hold them accountable for their irresponsible practices, they could choke the flow of crime guns that massacre more Americans every two years than were killed in the Vietnam War.

And second, gun companies could invest in research and development in safer gun technology. "Smart guns" are guns that can be fired only by authorized users. Innovators in this area have experimented with RFD chips, biometrics, and other technologies that would make it impossible for children to accidentally shoot their playmates and for people in mental distress to use someone else's gun to harm themselves or others. Smart guns could prevent police-involved shootings as well. If any of the big-four manufacturers invested in this technology, they could help keep Americans safer (and make money in the process).

But they are not going to act just because we are in the right. It is obvious that they are not going to act simply because thirty thousand Americans are dying by gun each year. They are not going to act because Leviticus obligates people of faith to act. They will act only if it is in their financial self-interest.

So how do a group of rabbis, ministers, imams, and other organized faith leaders incentivize gun companies to play their part in reducing gun violence? By leveraging the power of money.

We found that 40 percent of the guns sold in this country each year are purchased with *our* tax dollars by *our* police departments and *our* armed forces.[6] The theory is that if we could marshal the purchasing power of 40 percent of the gun market share—our cities, states, and the federal government—gun manufacturers would respond to their demands for reliable dealer networks and safer technology. And further, if the banks and major investment houses pressured gun companies for corporate responsibility by using their investment power, rather than divesting, we believe this would influence these companies to help reduce gun trafficking and increase safety even with their deadly products.

Thus was born the Do Not Stand Idly By campaign to reduce gun violence.[7]

In the last five years, we have gotten 125 public purchasers of weapons to commit to using their purchasing power to press Gaston Glock, Ugo Beretta, Christopher Killroy, and James Debney to control their worst dealers and innovate safer gun technology. And we have also worked with organizations like the Interfaith Center for Corporate

Responsibility[8] to leverage investor power to press gun companies to help reduce gun violence.

The Talmud teaches, "Rabbi Elai said: In three matters a person's true character is ascertained: in his cup, in his pocket, and in his anger" (BT *Eiruvin* 65b). We will leave aside for this chapter the issue of the cup.

But we citizens, we Americans, we people of faith, are angry. We are angry about the seemingly relentless scourge of gun violence and the relentless silence of our public officials and the corporations that have the power to keep us safer. And because we know we will be judged based on how we handle that anger, we have decided to focus our anger on powerful action. And we have concluded that "the pocket" is the key to unlocking this issue.

As discussed above, money is not the root of all evil. In this case, the power of organized money can force the gun industry, which has been protected since the Bill of Rights was passed in December 1791, to step up, play its part, and help keep Americans safer.

It is long past time. We are right. And we are powerful, because we can leverage the power of money. And we will win.

NOTES

1. Christopher Ingraham, "This Is What One Year of Gun Deaths in America Looks Like," *Washington Post*, October 2, 2015, https://www.washingtonpost.com/news/wonk/wp/2015/10/02/this-is-what-one-year-of-gun-deaths-in-america-looks-like/?noredirect=on&utm_term=.6458b0a7e86d.
2. Nicholas Kristof, "Lessons from the Virginia Shooting," *New York Times*, August 26, 2015, https://www.nytimes.com/2015/08/27/opinion/lessons-from-the-murders-of-tv-journalists-in-the-virginia-shooting.html?smid=fb-share&_r=1.
3. The Jewish view of the neutral nature of money is explored thoroughly in other chapters in this volume; however it is important to note the misunderstanding of the Timothy text, as this work includes Christian

leaders and activists. The Christian influence on our greater America culture is also noteworthy.

4. William J. Krouse, *Gun Control Legislation*, Congressional Research Service, November 14, 2012, https://fas.org/sgp/crs/misc/RL32842.pdf.

5. Bureau of Alcohol, Tobacco and Firearms, *Commerce in Firearms in the United States* (Washington, DC: U.S. Department of the Treasury, February 2000).

6. Nima Samadi, *Gun and Ammunition Manufacturing in the US*, IBIS-World Industry Report 33229a, October 2012, http://bloximages. newyork1.vip.townnews.com/galvnews.com/content/tncms/assets/v3/ editorial/a/8f/a8f655e4-75cb-11e3-a8d0-001a4bcf6878/52c8f03bf155c.pdf. pdf.

7. Do Not Stand Idly By, http://donotstandidlyby.org/.

8. Interfaith Center on Corporate Responsibility, https://www.iccr.org/.

10

STRUCTURES OF JEWISH GIVING

A Virtual *Tzedakah* Tour

RABBI LEAH RACHEL BERKOWITZ

At the core of the Bible's conversations about wealth is the message that it doesn't belong to us. Our good fortune is a result of God's blessings, and those blessings are contingent on our adherence to our sacred covenant. And at the heart of this covenant is the commandment to care for the vulnerable. In the Holiness Code, the Israelites are commanded:

> You shall be holy, for I, the Eternal your God, am holy. . . . When you reap the harvest of your land, you shall not reap all the way to the edges of your field, or gather the gleanings of your harvest. You shall not pick your vineyard bare, or gather the fallen fruit of your vineyard; you shall leave them for the poor and the stranger: I the Eternal am your God. (Lev. 19:2, 19:9–11)

In addition to this commandment to share the bounty of our harvest, the Bible and the Talmud provide us with models for caring for the stranger, the orphan, the widow, the poor, and even the Levite (the original underpaid Jewish professional), which emphasize the following:

1. Poverty is cyclical: There is neither a permanent wealthy class who gives nor a permanent underclass who receives. Anyone could be in either position at any time.

2. *Tzedakah*'s goal is human dignity and self-reliance: The assistance we give is meant to set our community's poor on their feet so that they can ultimately support themselves.
3. We are responsible for our own kin: Though we are frequently commanded to help the stranger, our primary obligation is to assist our family and our community, however that is defined in a given time and place.

Tzedakah in the Bible: The Corners of Your Fields

The laws of the Torah are grounded in an agrarian society. Therefore, most types of giving have to do with the redistribution of produce during various harvests. One of these was a tithe called *maaseir ani*, a tenth of one's harvest, which was set aside every third year for the stranger, the orphan, the widow. These contributions also supported the Levites, who, despite their auspicious position in Israelite society, did not have an ancestral landholding on which to grow food (Deut. 14:27–29, 26:12).

While the Levite might have been able to subsist entirely on the offerings that farmers brought to the Temple, the remaining vulnerable groups also relied on contributions in the form of produce left in the field or on the vine. The Israelite was commanded to leave the corners of the grain field, *pei-ah*, unharvested, as well as leaving behind any dropped grain, or gleanings, *leket*. They were not to go back for any grain they might have forgotten, *shich'chah*. Similarly, they were to leave some grapes on the vine, *ol'lot*, and not pick up any grapes that were dropped during the harvest, *peret*. All of these are to be left behind for vulnerable groups: the poor, the stranger, the widow, and the orphan (Lev. 19:9–10; Deut. 24:19–21).

The most notable example of the act of gleaning appears in the Book of Ruth. Ruth is a Moabite, who comes to Bethlehem with her mother-in-law after both of them have been widowed. Without the means to support herself and her mother-in-law, Ruth gleans in Boaz's fields during the barley harvest. Boaz's adherence to this biblical commandment—and his great kindness toward Ruth—ultimately result in their marriage. Ruth and Boaz become the great-grandparents of King David, thought to be the progenitor of the Messiah.

From this, the third-century Palestinian rabbi Zeira extrapolates that the whole Book of Ruth is meant to teach us "the greatness of the reward for acts of loving-kindness," that is, the lineage of the ultimate redeemer (*Ruth Rabbah* 2:14). The implication is that through observing the commandment to care for the vulnerable, we, too, might bring about the ultimate redemption.

Today, there are many organizations—Jewish and not—that continue this practice by redistributing unharvested or unsold produce from farms and farmers markets to feed the hungry. One of these is Leket Israel, an Israeli national food bank that gathers the unharvested produce of farmers, surplus foods from manufacturers, and leftovers from restaurants and event spaces. These are then redistributed to nonprofit organizations that serve those in need.[1]

Rabbinic Approaches to *Tzedakah:* Community Collections

Following the destruction of the Temple in 70 CE, many of the agricultural models in the Bible became obsolete, especially for those living in the Diaspora and those living in more urban settings. In the Mishnah (second century CE) and the Babylonian Talmud (sixth century CE), we begin to see the Rabbis developing new structures by which both rural and urban communities could support the poor. One of these was the *tamchui*, a proto-food bank consisting of voluntary donations of foodstuffs, collected and distributed daily by three trustees appointed by the community.[2]

The Rabbis also established the *kupah*, a community fund that collected money to be distributed on a weekly basis. In this system, a group of two trustees went door-to-door throughout the week, encouraging members of the community to give an appropriate amount. On Fridays, a group of three trustees—similar to a *beit din* or rabbinic court—would preside over cases of people in need and allocate the funds necessary for each person or family to eat for the coming week.[3]

One need not have been a long-standing member of the community to apply for assistance. Rather, the community took responsibility for the immediate needs of all. Then, as a person became more settled in a community, they became eligible for a higher level of assistance. In the Mishnah, we learn that an *ani ha-oveir*, a wandering poor person, was entitled to a loaf of bread. One who stayed overnight was given lodging; one who stayed for the Sabbath received enough food for three meals (during this time period, it was customary to eat two meals on a regular day and three on Shabbat). One who stayed longer might qualify for *tamchui*—provisions for the day's two meals—and *kupah*—funds to buy fourteen meals for the coming week (*Mishnah Pei-ah* 8:7).

Just as one qualified for assistance based on how long they were in town, one who moved to a new town soon became responsible for assisting others, as we see in the Babylonian Talmud:

> [One must reside in a town] thirty days to become liable for contributing to the *tamchui*, three months for the *kupah*, six months for the clothing fund, nine months for the burial fund, and twelve months for contributing to the repair of the town walls. (BT *Bava Batra* 8a)

Today, many communities have formed *tzedakah* collectives that draw upon the model of the *kupah* and the *tamchui*. Each year around Purim—a time when it is customary to make gifts to the poor—the Rashi School in Dedham, Massachusetts, conducts its Purim Tamchui Project. Students and their families at this Reform Jewish day school make donations to the collective *tamchui*. Students hear from representatives of five different charities, then allocate the collected funds to each of these organizations using poker chips.[4] As such, they become the trustees of their own charitable fund.

Another example of a modern-day *kupah* is the Ziv Tzedakah Fund, founded by activist Danny Siegel in 1981. Building on the tradition of giving *tzedakah* when one travels to Israel—to ensure a safe journey—Siegel began seeking out "mitzvah heroes" in Israel to whom he could distribute the contributions he collected before each trip, then reported on the projects he had donated to upon his return home. His aim was to support "small-scale projects that transformed people's lives in meaningful ways."[5] What began as less than a thousand dollars in contributions ultimately became a fund that distributed tens of millions of dollars by the time it closed in 2008.[6]

Maimonides's Highest Degree: *G'machim, Landsmanshaften,* and Free Loan Societies

The twelfth-century Jewish philosopher Maimonides is perhaps best known for his eight degrees of *tzedakah*, which prioritize the attitude of the giver, the dignity of the recipient, and, of course, giving an appropriate amount. According to Maimonides, the highest level of giving is to empower a fellow Jew to become self-sufficient through a gift, a loan, a business partnership, or a job opportunity.[7]

Over the course of Jewish history, these loans took on many shapes and forms, but in all cases were interest-free—at least when performed for the purpose of *tzedakah*. Such loans were aimed at preserving the dignity of one's fellow and moving them toward financial independence.

The earliest form of interest-free loan was the *g'mach*, an acronym for *g'milut chasadim*, acts of loving-kindness. The *g'mach* was a community-based source of interest-free, no-fee, short-term loans to help individuals and families navigate through difficult times.

Because these loans were administered within the context of a community, there was an expectation that the community would be repaid even without financial disincentives like fees, interest, and debt collectors. Even as the *g'mach* protected the privacy of the borrower, the borrower likely held some relationship with the administrators of the *g'mach*, as well as an awareness that the funds or items borrowed might soon be needed by others in their community.

Over the years, the model of the *g'mach* expanded to include collections of items that were needed only on a temporary basis: a crib, a wedding dress, or extra chairs for a party. In recent years, they have also included laptops and video games for children in the hospital.[8] There are now also *g'machim* for moving supplies, breast milk, and wigs for patients undergoing chemotherapy.[9]

A similar lending philosophy undergirds the concept of the *landsmanshaften* and the free loan society, which were *tzedakah* structures that evolved to meet the needs of a changing Jewish landscape. Until the late eighteenth century, many Jewish communities had been insular, tight-knit, and often self-governed, making the collection and distribution of *tzedakah* a neighborhood affair. As Jews were emancipated in several countries across Europe—or immigrated to the United States—Jewish communities developed new structures for sustaining their fellow Jews and new definitions of what constituted a community.

While much *tzedakah* was still practiced in the context of synagogues and neighborhoods, many Jewish communities also began to form philanthropic organizations to address the social problems of their day on a local, national, and global level. Rather than address the needs of individuals within one small community, many of these institutions were formed to address particular issues such as promoting public health, helping people with disabilities, providing vocational training, and establishing settlement houses for new immigrants. Many of these organizations later came under the auspices of the first Jewish Federations, which began to emerge at the end of the nineteenth century in order to consolidate social services. Funds could be collected by these umbrella organizations, and then distributed to a variety of recipients, similar to how it was done through the *kupah* of the Rabbinic era.[10]

In the late nineteenth century, a large influx of Eastern European Jewish immigrants settled in the United States. Although many of them benefited from these existing philanthropic organizations, some were reluctant to accept charity from their more established German Jewish neighbors. Instead, Eastern European Jews established collectives to help new immigrants to become self-sufficient while simultaneously maintaining their dignity. These *landsmanshaften* were societies centered not around one's neighborhood in New York City, but around one's city or town of origin. They provided insurance and sick benefits, cemetery rights, and burial services, as well as interest-free loans.[11] They even provided funds for new immigrants to come over from their towns of origin.[12] Some of these organizations were founded in synagogues; others began as freestanding funds to meet the basic needs of the community and later evolved to become houses of worship and learning. Others remained as secular support networks.

According to Rabbi David Rosenn, the executive director of the Hebrew Free Loan Society, free loans were—and continue to be—rooted in "social capital rather than financial capital." Rather than asking the borrower to put up collateral—something a new immigrant might not have—the borrower was asked to provide a family member or friend as guarantor, in hopes that the "powerful motivation not to disappoint" one's guarantors would ensure the repayment of the loan.[13]

At the inception of the Hebrew Free Loan Society in 1892, a loan might be the means of providing an aspiring peddler with a pushcart and one's first set of merchandise. Today, free loans provide many other ways of helping borrowers get on their feet financially, such as loans for education and vocational training, housing loans to prevent foreclosure, and family loans to subsidize fertility treatments or adoption services. There is also a growing need to help individuals and families suffering from addiction, by subsidizing treatment and rehabilitation, as well as covering the costs of their time off from work.[14] While the recipients of these loans were never limited to the Jewish community, the mode of giving hearkens back to Deuteronomy, where we are commanded to lend to our fellow "sufficient for whatever they need" (Deut. 15:8).

Giving Today: How Do We Share Our Abundance?

Though the Jewish tradition teaches us to care for the vulnerable in front of us during times of scarcity, many segments of the Jewish community today grapple with the responsibilities of abundance and even affluence. We still have many structures within our society to care for our own, whether at home or abroad, but we have also turned our attention to causes beyond the Jewish community and our "kin."

This expansion of our definition of community is in part because we have more financial resources at our disposal and in part because new technologies enable us to give to others anywhere in the world with the touch of a button. Individuals and small groups can now raise money using social media and crowdfunding sites, whether they are seeking support for a personal project or fundraising for an established nonprofit organization.

While there are many organizations that provide assistance for the vulnerable through a Jewish lens, the synagogue is still a major locus of charitable giving. Many synagogues have discretionary funds for their clergy, education director, or other senior staff. While these discretionary funds might be used to subsidize synagogue programming and professional expenses, they also provide the resources for leaders of the synagogue to give to those in need. Clergy and professionals can use these funds to make contributions to nonprofit organizations or to provide confidential assistance to individual persons, both within and outside of the synagogue community. These funds are maintained through contributions by members of the community, in honor of special occasions or as honoraria to the synagogue leaders.[15]

Another recent development in the realm of Jewish giving has been the mitzvah project undertaken by bar/bat mitzvah students. In modern times, there has been an effort to balance the conspicuous consumption of *b'nei mitzvah* celebrations and to ground the experience in Jewish values. Many communities do this by encouraging *b'nei mitzvah* to perform an act of *tzedakah* in conjunction with this rite of passage.

While we don't know exactly when or how this custom began, Danny Siegel, the *tzedakah* activist mentioned above, believes that the first mitzvah projects began in the 1970s. Some of the earliest efforts to integrate *tzedakah* into *b'nei mitzvah* centered around the plight of Soviet Jewry. *B'nei mitzvah* "twinned" with Soviet Jews, donating to their cause and sometimes corresponding with them.[16] While many attribute the rise of the mitzvah project to Siegel himself, who helped to popularize the idea, Siegel believes one of the pioneers of this custom was Rabbi Bernard King of Newport Beach, California. Rabbi King's sons each staged large-scale charitable events in conjunction with their *b'nei mitzvah* celebrations in the mid-1980s: the older, a concert by a band that featured mentally challenged musicians; the younger, a trip to a baseball game for the residents of a local homeless shelter.[17]

A mitzvah project can be as simple as allocating a portion of the monetary gifts received to a charitable cause, since, as Siegel points out, "the gifts are not 'their hard-earned money.'"[18] Students might also choose a cause for which they can raise money, collect resources, or volunteer in the months leading up to their *b'nei mitzvah*. Sometimes the cause is incorporated into the celebration itself: items collected for a nonprofit—such as children's books, pet supplies, or canned goods— might be crafted into centerpieces or used in place of bimah flowers. In addition, leftover food or flowers from the celebration might be donated to a shelter or hospital.[19]

The Jewish Federation of Durham and Chapel Hill in North Carolina ensures that *b'nei mitzvah* celebrations will include a charitable contribution through their *"Tzedakah* in Bloom" program. The Federation rents out silk flower arrangements to *b'nei mitzvah* families to use on the bimah or as party centerpieces, in exchange for a donation to the Jewish Family Services.[20]

The nonprofit organization Mazon: A Jewish Response to Hunger encourages families to donate 3 percent of what they spend on their *simchah*—*b'nei mitzvah*, weddings, and child-welcoming ceremonies— to fight hunger.[21] This is a modern take on the ancient Jewish custom of inviting people in need within the community into one's celebration.

Conclusion: Making *Tzedakah* Priorities

In our modern world, giving *tzedakah* has become both easier and more complicated. While we have more resources and tools at our disposal than ever before, we also have more information about scarcity and suffering around the world. This can lead to difficult choices about where to allocate our resources. For help in making these decisions, we can return to our guiding principles: sharing our abundance with the most vulnerable, preserving the dignity of the recipients of *tzedakah*, empowering those in need to become self-sufficient, and prioritizing the needs of those in our own community, however we define it. In this way, we can ensure that we make the best use of the abundance with which we have been blessed.

NOTES

1. Leket Israel, https://www.leket.org.
2. Maimonides, *Mishneh Torah, Hilchot Mat'not Aniyim* 9:2, 9:5.
3. Maimonides, *Mishneh Torah, Hilchot Mat'not Aniyim* 9:1, 9:3, 9:5.
4. Susan Jacobs, "Nurturing Educated Philanthropists," *Jewish Journal*, March 27, 2014.
5. Conversation with Rabbi Neal Gold, May 31, 2018.
6. "Danny Siegel," The Heart of the Covenant Foundation Awards Program, 1993, https://www.covenantfn.org/award-person/danny-siegel/; Meredith Kesner Lewis, "Ziv Tzedakah Fund to Close," My Jewish Learning, December 27, 2007, https://www.myjewishlearning.com/mixed-multitudes/ziv-tzedakah-fund-to-close/.
7. Maimonides, *Mishneh Torah, Hilchot Mat'not Aniyim* 10:8–15.
8. Beth Pollak, "The *Gemach*," My Jewish Learning, accessed September 17, 2018, https://www.myjewishlearning.com/article/the-gemach/.
9. Samuel G. Freedman, "Loans without Profit Help Relieve Economic Pain," *New York Times*, December 2, 2011.
10. "Charity throughout Jewish History," in *Encyclopaedia Judaica* (Farmington Hills, MI: Gale, 2008).
11. Moses Rischin, "Germans Versus Russians," in *The American Jewish Experience*, 2nd ed., ed. Jonathan D. Sarna (New York: Holmes & Meier, 1997), 145.

12. "Landsmannschaften," Jewish Virtual Library, accessed September 17, 2018, https://www.jewishvirtuallibrary.org/landsmannschaften.
13. Interview with Rabbi David Rosenn, June 15, 2018.
14. Interview with Rabbi David Rosenn, June 15, 2018.
15. "Guidelines for Rabbis' Discretionary Funds," Central Conference of American Rabbis, accessed September 17, 2018, www.ccarnet.org.
16. Danny Siegel, "Bar and Bat Mitzvah Mitzvah Projects, Part One," Times of Israel, February 7, 2016, http://blogs.timesofisrael.com/bar-and-bat-mitzvah-mitzvah-projects-part-one/.
17. Danny Siegel, "Bar and Bat Mitzvah Mitzvah Projects, Part One."
18. Danny Siegel, "Bar and Bat Mitzvah Mitzvah Projects, Part Two," Times of Israel, February 14, 2016, https://blogs.timesofisrael.com/bar-and-bat-mitzvah-mitzvah-projects-part-two/.
19. Suzanne Borden, "Putting the 'Mitzvah' Back in Bar and Bat Mitzvah," in *Jewish Family and Life: Traditions, Holidays, and Values for Today's Parents and Children*, ed. Yosef I. Abramowitz and Rabbi Susan Silverman (New York: Golden Books, 1997), 89–94.
20. "Tzedakah in Bloom," Jewish Federation of Durham–Chapel Hill, accessed September 17, 2018, https://www.shalomdch.org/explore-federation/about-us/who-we-are/jewish-family-services/tzedakah-in-bloom/.
21. "Include Mazon in Your Simcha," Mazon, accessed September 17, 2018, https://mazon.org/ways-to-give/include-mazon-in-your-simcha.

11

THE CHANGING FACE
OF JEWISH PHILANTHROPY

ANDRÉS SPOKOINY

To understand changes in Jewish philanthropy, let's talk about baby strollers.

Not because philanthropist behave like infants, but because baby strollers tell us a lot about society in this early twenty-first century, and philanthropy is locked in co-evolution with broader societal trends.

Until the 1960s, baby strollers were built with the child facing the mother or father. But at the end of that decade, something started to change. Today, virtually all strollers are designed with the baby facing ahead, with his back to the parent. Our young, from a very early age, interact directly with the world, without intermediation. In the past, the baby didn't look directly at the world. A grown-up filtered, interpreted, and explained the world to her. A little human had no relation with the world as such, but with a version of the world curated by the parent.

I find the baby stroller to be a powerful metaphor for our world today, for we are in a relentless quest to eliminate intermediation between the individual and the world. In every aspect of life, we are "cutting out the middleman," and this spells doom for a host of social actors, from the travel agent to even the rabbi.

The modern human is a "self-made" person, in the sense that she will build her identity in an autonomous fashion, relatively free from the dictates of ingrained societal mores, religious taboos, or hierarchical control. In the baby stroller metaphor, the two main characteristics of our society come into play: the sovereign individual and the disintermediation of the world. These two are having a direct impact on philanthropy now and will continue to shape what it will look like into the future.

The Emancipation of the Individual

The twenty-first century sees the completion of a process started with the Enlightenment: the liberation of the individual and his coronation as the center of the social order (see the works of Marcel Gauchet, Olivier Rey, and Alain Ehrenberg).

We take as a given today that the goal of social organization is to promote the freedom, creativity, critical spirit, autonomy, and originality of each individual. But we fail to realize how new and revolutionary these objectives are. In the traditional world, originality was punished, not encouraged; autonomy was condemned, not promoted, and the individual had no intrinsic value beyond his or her place in the social structure. What people needed to know most was not how to "be themselves," but what was expected of them in the social order.

The process of liberation of the individual was gradual. In the nineteenth and twentieth centuries, people being newly freed from coercive powers of absolutism and religious control could choose to organize their lives in accordance with ideologies of their choosing (be they secular or religious). But they were still picking from existing options, selecting a "meta-narrative" that would mediate between them and the world and organize their understanding of society and humanity. You could choose, say, socialism, and that would come as a package with other ideas such as historical materialism. However, since World War II, we have developed what Jean-François Lyotard, in *The*

Postmodern Condition, called "skepticism towards meta-narratives."[1] In other words, the process of individual liberation was taken to its logical conclusion: we don't just choose between existing paths, but *we build our own*. The new technologies of the twenty-first century are accelerating these processes exponentially and empowering the individual to an unprecedented degree. If the twentieth century saw the emergence of the "emancipated individual," the twenty-first gave us the "hyper-empowered individual."

This change brings freedom but also places an enormous burden on the individual: she faces an infinity of choices that were hitherto made for her by society. Deciding "who to be" is a fraught exercise, full of self-doubt, anxieties, and opportunity costs. It engenders a deep feeling of existential solitude. The full implications of this empowerment for our sense of meaning and happiness are complicated and exceed the scope of this chapter, but the change is here to stay: the "individual sovereign" has replaced the collective as the organizing principle of society.

The Jewish community and Jewish philanthropy are not immune.

Three Interlocking Revolutions

This *coronation of the individual* creates three different, yet interlocking, revolutions in Jewish communities. These are major upheavals that are part crisis and part opportunity.

A Revolution of Meaning

Individual Jews, like all human beings, are on a quest for meaning. But hyper-empowered individuals of the twenty-first century no longer quest toward the traditional sources of meaning on which Jews used to rely. "Skepticism towards meta-narratives" has affected all Jewish religious and secular ideologies, and the Jewish world has been slow to adapt. By and large, our ideological landscape is the one we created in the late nineteenth and early twentieth centuries in response to a different set of circumstances. Unlike the era in which these institutions were created, identity and ideology are not acquired whole by belonging to a group, but are developed by a personal process of identity building. "Radical free choice" affects the spiritual realm, and today's ideologies are assembled by the individual as a collage of disparate elements. The disintermediation of the world profoundly affects ideologies, and because ideologies organize our perceptions of reality, it effectively changes reality itself.

My own life can illustrate this shift. In the past, I probably would have defined myself as a Conservative Jew. Today, I don't ascribe to any ideology wholesale. I pick and choose from different Jewish movements and build a collage that makes sense only to me. And I'm not alone. Many Jews see no contradiction in driving to a Chabad synagogue on Shabbat; others may feel most comfortable with the aesthetics and accessibility of a Reform service, even while espousing some values contrary to the ethics espoused by the Reform Movement's official bodies.

A Revolution of Community

A society with the individual at its center begets a reevaluation of the concept of community. The modern individual will not be comfortable with communities that feel constraining. Communities require boundaries; thus, even the most progressive of communities include exclusionary elements that are anathema to modern individuals. The traditional community rests on concepts like belonging and loyalty, and therefore Jewishness is traditionally meant to be a lifelong affiliation. All those concepts are being challenged by the modern individual who wants to chart his or her own course, retaining the option to shift between affiliations and loyalties. Moreover, traditional communities are organized so that the individual is subservient to the collective. We have yet to reinvent the collective in a way that places the individual at the center. Disintermediation affects our concept of community as well. If I can curate and interact with a customized set of peers directly (as on social media), I can "cut out the middleman" of community.

A Revolution of Organizational Structures

Jewish communal organizations are, for the most part, a product of the early twentieth century. They follow the paradigm of the industrial era: centralization, efficiency, unity of command, vertical information flow. This organizational model is ill-equipped to serve the hyper-empowered individual who is both the client and the worker of those organizations. Most organizations still see themselves as traditional providers of programs and services rather than as platforms where individuals can deploy their creativity. Most organizations are pyramids instead of networks. They treat information as proprietary rather than "open source," and they have centralized rather than distributive leadership. They are territorial and still rely on a paradigm of "command and control" instead of "collaborate and connect." Happily, some Jewish organizations are beginning to break this mold. My own organization, Jewish Funders Network, is a diverse community of philanthropists growing the size and impact of Jewish philanthropy as a whole without any centralized plan for how to do that. Community-building nonprofits like Moishe House and OneTable also offer models of building flexible platforms for bottom-up creativity and variety. Many Jewish Federations, such as those in Detroit, Atlanta, and San Francisco, are also taking positive steps in this direction.

Jewish philanthropy is at the center of these three revolutions. Current philanthropic trends are both a product and a cause of these upheavals and respond to the larger social trends described above.

Disintermediation

Like everything else in society, philanthropy is being disintermediated. In the past, funders were comfortable with Federations and other communal organizations organizing their philanthropy for them. Donors contributed to a central *kupah* (charitable fund) and trusted that central body to make philanthropic decisions for them. This approach doesn't suit the hyper-empowered individual who is not willing to outsource these decisions to others.

Funders want to decide for themselves where the money goes. Instead of seeing "intermediaries" as vehicles for connecting with the issues they care about, donors view them as unnecessary expenses and infringements on freedom of action—barriers between the donor and the grantee, hurdles to overcome.

These "intermediaries" actually serve an important need. They have the capacity to assess needs professionally rather than emotionally; they can establish priorities and identify gaps. They also have a "bird's-eye view" of the entire system rather than being focused on a specific issue. But that intrinsic value of central organizations is frequently not perceived by donors.

Today's funders seek to relate directly with the causes they care about.

Two responses to this new frame can be seen in the growth of donor advised funds (DAF) and private foundations. DAF (some of which are held by Federations) allow funders to direct their giving, providing a cheap and efficient way for a relatively small funder to enjoy independence similar to that of a private foundation, but without needing to worry about running a board of trustees, handling IRS reporting, or other administrative requirements for a foundation. At the same time, the number of private foundations has skyrocketed, both in the Jewish community and in general society. Private foundations offer more freedom of action to the funder than DAFs do. They allow the funder to invest in a wider range of causes and organizations, but they also demand more governance and administration, from setting a board of trustees to IRS reporting. The DAF offers slightly less flexibility, but the donor completely outsources the administration to the fund. At any rate the main appeal of these two philanthropic vehicles is that they offer donors a large degree of freedom and control over their philanthropy.

Out with Loyalty, In with Impact

The "end of loyalty" affects philanthropy in significant ways. In my experience at Jewish Funders Network, I've found that fewer and fewer funders give out of a sense of loyalty or responsibility to institutions. Previous attachment to an organization is not reason enough for donors to keep giving. In the past, family tradition, inertia, and a deeply ingrained sense of communal responsibility drove giving to central organizations. Today, the main driver of giving is impact. Individual funders want to know what *their* gift is achieving. They want to be able to tie their contribution to specific outcomes, and they'll select organizations that maximize their impact. That means that the relationship between funders and grantees is virtually inverted. In the past, nonprofits would regard donors as their tools for doing good. Today, the opposite is true: funders regard nonprofits as their tools and shop around to find the best vehicle for their philanthropy. Relationships count, as always, but the relationship is now one based on a *partnership for impact*.

Of course, funders still have loyalty. They aren't fickle regarding their values and interests, but loyalty to values doesn't translate into loyalty to organizations. In fact, it encourages donors to migrate between organizations based on perceptions of effectiveness and impact.

Hands-On Partnership

A corollary to funders' desire to see and feel their impact is their demand to be engaged "hands-on" with their grantee. Funders want to contribute their holistic value (expertise, resources, commitment, etc.) rather than just money. This is often seen as a problem for nonprofits, because most see development as "sales." In fact, it is an opportunity to reimagine and redesign development as a process of long-term engagement and partnership.

Multiple Interests and Synergies

Funders today, more than ever, are eclectic in the causes they support. Gone are the days when funders had one major cause they supported. Today's Jewish funders give to many causes, both general and Jewish. In fact, just 4 percent of Jewish funders give only to Jewish causes. Many of us are tempted to guilt-trip Jewish donors into giving more Jewishly, but that never works. Donors demand that communal leaders embrace rather than condemn their multiple interests. They are open to an integrative approach that does not put Jewish giving into silos and that opens possibilities of synergies between Jewish and non-Jewish causes.

At the same time, it's important to notice that consistency is not a postmodern trait; funders can be conservative and hawkish on, say, Israel, and progressive on domestic issues. The weakening of ideologies implies that donors—like other individual Jews—will see no need to "buy the entire package" of a given denomination. Each funder is unique, and knowing their particular mix of interests is key to a productive philanthropic partnership.

The Overhead Malaise

This is a challenge. As donors focus on specific programs, they tend to disregard capacity building at the organizational and communal level. Their drive toward impact and efficiency makes them reluctant to fund what they perceive as wasteful expenses. Thus, funders implement arbitrary limits on "overhead" and inadvertently starve nonprofits of the resources they need to operate. The desire to gift to specific programs causes the core infrastructure of organizations to be underfunded. This "nonprofit starvation cycle" is proving to be a serious problem in both Jewish and general philanthropy.

New Philanthropic Vehicles

Funders are seeking new philanthropic vehicles that give them more control and maximize impact. Furthermore, funders today don't relate to traditional sectors as silos. In the past, the business sector, the government sector, and the philanthropic sector were seen as having very different values and missions. Professional theory cautioned against breaking the barriers between them. But recently, more and more funders are using business tools, from social enterprises to impact investment to social impact bonds, to achieve their missions. At the same time, funders are open to partnerships with government as a way to bring their ideas to scale.

Simultaneously, technology provides new tools for directing and managing one's giving. From crowdfunding to tools that allow donors to connect directly to grantees and to each other, technology is reshaping the way philanthropists operate.

The fact that traditional collective philanthropy is in crisis doesn't mean that funders are inherently opposed to collective giving. In fact, networked giving—giving with small groups of peers, as in giving circles, or formal coalitions of funders—have gained in popularity in recent decades. These vehicles offer the "best of both worlds." Funders can pool their resources and work with peers, while at the same time maintaining a high degree of control over their allocations. They can do collective giving without sacrificing their autonomy.

Good or Bad for the Jews?

The impact of these philanthropic revolutions on the Jewish community is widespread and complex.

On one hand, the emergence of independent philanthropy has sparked a wave of communal innovation and creativity. Once unleashed, the individual entrepreneurial spirit in philanthropy has created the most remarkable communal innovations of the last few decades. From Birthright Israel to PJ Library, from One Table to Moishe House, transformational programs can be tracked to the visions of independent funders. Most probably, none of these innovations could have come out of Federations—not because Federations are incapable of creative thinking, but because there's a built-in (and necessary) risk aversion in communal bodies. A Federation board has a fiduciary responsibility to thousands of donors. It would be borderline unethical to dedicate resources to unproven, risky endeavors. This is not to say that Federations don't take risks—they do, just as governments do invest in breakthrough research—but at relatively lower levels; private foundations have a much larger capacity to absorb risk than communal bodies.

When that is understood by both philanthropists and organizations, interesting partnerships can emerge. Communal organizations (as well as governments) can lean on independent funders to generate and test innovative ideas, and funders can partner with communal organizations (and governments) to reach scale once models are proven.

Naturally, the emergence of independent philanthropy has created a drive toward an ethos of "do it yourself and do it alone." There's little patience with process and a reluctance to be "outvoted" when working in communal settings. The collective dimension was, of course, weakened and the relative weight of communal philanthropy diminished. Even when annual campaigns remain stable, they represent a smaller proportion of total Jewish giving. At the same time, "flexible" or "autonomous" vehicles like donor advised funds are growing exponentially.

But funders are also realizing that "doing what you want" may be easy, but achieving impact is not. Systemic impact demands some sort of collective action. "My" program can be effective in and of itself, but it may fail to "move the needle" in relation to the bigger social problem I'm trying to solve. Systemic impact demands a systemic vision of an entire field and the deployment of tools that are generally beyond the reach of a single funder. Yet going back to the "good old days" of communal giving is not really an option.

Therefore, the main challenge of the community in terms of philanthropy is the creation of new collective frameworks that don't drown the individuality or the entrepreneurial spirit of the "individual-sovereign" but allow for the creation of networks, coalitions, and communal actions that maximize impact and solve problems. My own organization, the Jewish Funders Network, is but one attempt to create a bridge between the individual and the collective.

Finally, and certainly no less important, are the ethical consequences of these changes to the philanthropic field.

In the secular space, big funders find themselves impacting communal policy without having been elected to do so. It's meritorious of Mark Zuckerberg to invest $100 million in the Newark school system and bring his entrepreneurial drive to that problematic arena, but is that legitimate? Shouldn't members of the affected community have a say?

In the Jewish space, too, the emergence of mega-donors who act outside of the communal frameworks poses the same questions. Who gets to set communal priorities? How do large gifts skew organizational and communal agendas? How do we make sure that big contributions by major funders don't become a disincentive for communal partnership and grassroots ownership of programs and institutions? How do funders use and misuse their newly acquired power in the community?

These questions need to be the basis for a community-wide conversation. Funders will need to be willing to self-regulate their power, and communities will need to be find ways to accommodate and work with individuals that are radically different from the ones that created their own structures a century and more ago.

At its core, philanthropy will continue to be what it has always been: a way of expressing generosity and care; a desire to right wrongs and leave a legacy in the world; a drive to make the world a better place and make a positive impact on the lives of others. In the Jewish case, philanthropy is also informed by a multi-millenary tradition, by the central place of peoplehood and mutual responsibility (*K'lal Yisrael*) in the Jewish ethos, and by a relentless quest for a more just and compassionate world. Values can and should remain constant, even if the expression of those values needs to adapt to a changing set of historical circumstances.

It's our collective task to make sure that the Jewish philanthropy of the twenty-first century and beyond lives up to its values, promise, and potential.

NOTE

1. Lyotard, Jean-François, *The Postmodern Condition: A Report on Knowledge*, Trans. Geoff Bennington and Brian Massumi, U. of Minnesota Press (Translation published in 1984; original French work in 1979), page xxiv.

12

MY JEWISH FEDERATION

Legacy and Change

DOV BEN-SHIMON

There I was, in the middle of a heated conversation with a volunteer. "How *dare* you?" she said. "Do you even *know* what made our Federation great? It was the fact that we raised *millions* of dollars, every year, to give it away to our agencies. Do you *understand* that? Why would you try to *change* it?"

She was right.

Not only do we raise money to give it away, it's basically written into our name—we're a Federation, meaning agencies federated together to create a united Jewish fund in the community. We raise money to give it away. And it has been a tremendously successful model for decades.

But she was also right that we're changing. Our approach to philanthropy as a legacy institution has been evolving, while we continue our important role in the Jewish community.

I'm the CEO of one of the largest Jewish Federations in North America. Therefore, my view is neither academic, nor is it an attempt to represent the amorphously grouped "Jewish legacy institutions." But the following is my understanding of how we at Federation approach philanthropy today in order to fulfill our vital mission.

A Changing Jewish Community

Death, migration, competition, and generational priority shifts are facing Jewish organizations. As discussed widely, today's Jews do not feel obliged to join or fund the traditional structures of their communities. The challenge for us—Federations, synagogues, agencies, and organizations—is that we're not relevant to many in the North American Jewish community. So, Federation, as a legacy institution, is now laying the groundwork to be relevant, engaging, attractive, and meaningful to the leaders and donors of tomorrow. Does it mean alienating today's donors? Absolutely not—it's not a zero-sum game: a strong, clear vision of expanding our engagement with the next generation boosts our conversation with our current leaders. They want to know that someone is coming up after them, to continue their work and to sustain timeless Jewish values.

In my community we tell a story (possibly true, possibly apocryphal) about two volunteer leaders arguing about which was better for our Federation—to have one $100,000 donor (to raise funds efficiently to have an impact on the community, to help our agencies and Israel) or to have a thousand donors, each giving $100? No matter the source of the story, it's taken us many years to realize that it's better for us to have thousands and thousands of donors at the $100 level than a small group of donors giving very large gifts. A community organization can't survive long-term on a limited, but generous, major-gift donor base alone. Would I say no to more $100,000 donors? Of course not. But this shift in fundraising is really a shift in engagement, because Jewish Federations are *not innately fundraising organizations*. Fundraising helps us fulfill our mission, but it doesn't define who we are. Being able to engage with thousands of donors allows many to be part of this mission, steeped in Jewish values, building the Jewish community.

This shift in fundraising is also in reaction to feedback. We keep hearing that legacy institutions overemphasize solicitation at the expense of building relationships. We've heard that we haven't built meaningful relationships with non-major givers. And this has led to community members having a less than favorable impression of Federation, even when they like our programs without realizing our role in them. Reflecting our mandate to engage all in our community, every day my Federation sends chaplains to visit the sick, PJ Library books to kids and families, and *sh'lichim* (Israeli emissaries) to schools, synagogues, and agencies. We also connect volunteers to awe-inspiring social service opportunities, baking challah for those in need, spending time with our elderly, or taking part in Diller and other terrific teen programs.

People Give Differently Than They Used To

Federations have incredible achievements under our belts. We also have excellent professional staff, nationally and internationally recognized Israel programming, a strong culture of fundraising, dedicated and smart lay leadership, and more.

As discussed in other chapters in this book, there's been a shift in philanthropy throughout our greater society. In many ways, Federation and its mission find it hard sometimes to compete against the single-issue sexiness of the hospitals, the universities, the children's causes, or the elite IDF unit, which all vie for donors' attention. Like me, you've probably heard an assumption that with fewer affiliated Jews and fewer people giving to charity, the easy answer is to say, "Let's scrap the whole thing. It's a dinosaur. Federations and similar legacy institutions are going to slowly dwindle and die." I've heard this argument over and over for the last twenty years. Every few years (or months), some passionate writer predicts the death of the Federation system. And yet, to paraphrase the Monty Python sketch, we are not dead yet. And the five reasons for this continued survival tells you everything you need to know about why we're necessary, not only for the vulnerable of the Jewish world, but also for you and *your* local Jewish community.

First, *no one else can do what an effective Jewish Federation is able to do*. No one cares for those in need, builds Jewish community, and initiates rescue programs with just twenty-four hours' notice. All the amazing things that make you proud—pulling Jews out of evil and dangerous places, sending emergency funds to Israeli hospitals and kids at risk under missile attack, supplying immediate support, while lobbying and securing funds for Holocaust survivors—none of these happen without a Federation infrastructure behind them. We offer security consultations, expertise, and guidance for our synagogues and agencies; we provide human resources support, training programs, and scholarships for summer camps, funding for day schools, Israeli educators for religious and day schools, and much more. Could these things be done without Federations? Sure. But we are the community hub that makes all these tasks our daily work, fueled by unmatched experience and expertise.

Second, *we help build leaders for the entire community*. Studies have continually shown that community and philanthropy are cumulative, not exclusive. If you participate in four things in your Jewish community, chances are you'll engage in five or six. Jewish communal participation is an existential good for everyone, including, most importantly, the participants themselves. But if you do only one thing—if you only sit on your synagogue board, or serve on one agency committee, or support one philanthropic cause—it will probably not last for you. And it won't be great for that one group you support either. You won't learn how to compare and contrast, to argue, to look at 990s and audits and budgets. You won't learn how to ask tough questions, to check the CEO's activities, or to debate. And you won't understand what philanthropy really means as a communal enterprise. Today's Federation engages individuals in the work of the entire community and creates connections among synagogues and agencies. We provide training that enriches all institutions. The resulting synergy creates more volunteerism and philanthropy throughout the entire community.

The vast majority of leaders in our community come through Jewish Federations' Young Leadership Cabinet, an enrichment program run and funded by Federation. In fact, in my Federation, we have a full-time professional who works on a "pipeline" of leadership opportunities for all our synagogues, agencies, and organizations. We know that if you're a Federation budget chair today, you could be a synagogue president in four years. And maybe a national agency chair in eight years. We consider what courses, classes, mentorships, and experiences we need to start providing you with today to help develop you as a leader. Only a Federation can guide your leadership potential from a social service agency to a synagogue to an advocacy program.

Third, *there are issues and concerns that only a Jewish Federation can and should touch.* Don't misunderstand me—I admire, respect, and value the role and participation of single-issue agencies, synagogues, and family foundations. They are crucial partners in building a healthy, vibrant, and diverse Jewish community. Yet, I have seen again and again the irreplaceable role that *only* an effective Federation can play in a community.

For example, if a hostile attacker walks down one of our heavily Jewish neighborhoods with evil intent, who notifies the school three blocks down the road to go into lockdown when the perpetrator is at the Judaica store up the road? It happened in our community. That's why we created a Community Security Platform to connect Homeland Security, state police, dozens of local police departments, and county prosecutors to the institutions that constitute our community. Federation has the unique role of uniting all the individual institutions in our community to be able to create one interface with our state and federal agencies to create the best ongoing security response possible. This is facilitated by Jewish community professionals who work on these issues all the time, investing in sustained relationships with both the individual Jewish institutions and our government agencies. That is what many expect and need in their Federation.

Fourth, *Federations are there to ensure the needs of the community are covered, even when short-term funding evaporates.* I've lost count of the number of people who say to me "Federations aren't innovative." It's sometimes true and that's okay. There are smaller philanthropic institutions that are innovative, focused on single issues. And that's a good thing. However, when the attention moves to the next popular cause, it's the Federation that will address the perennial needs. Not always perfectly, but Federation focuses on the community's long-term needs and goals, finding the funding to address them. Our best practices include the requirement for matching funds, appropriate staffing, and ongoing evaluation, and we fine-tune these standards continually to ensure community priorities can continue even if the original funders walk away.

And finally, *Federation provides vital vetting for new ideas*. When new philanthropic initiatives are presented, it's all too easy to forget the ongoing needs of elderly Holocaust survivors, our social services agencies, or our neglected cemeteries. Bold, radical visions *should* be questioned, held up in the marketplace of Jewish philanthropic ideas, not just for the innovative nature of their proposals, but also for their appropriateness and their rootedness in Jewish values. Federations do this vetting every day. They debate. They argue. If you believe that your program deserves to be listened to, then in our Federation you have to persuade and negotiate. This approach has worked well for the Jewish community and will continue to do so. It makes us excellent stewards of the community's money and mission.

At Federation *Tzedakah* Equals Jewish Values, Living Lives of Meaning

Why do Jewish Federations focus on *tzedakah* and solicit donations? Quite simply because our view of philanthropy is based on a vision of social justice and communal action. When we solicit gifts, we give existential meaning to our supporters and to our community. When a Federation fundraiser asks you for a UJA gift, she's not just asking for the elderly Holocaust survivor on the fifth-floor walkup in the

Belarussian village or the at-risk kid in the Israeli peripheral town. She's asking for *you*. What you do with your *tzedakah* reflects the kind of Jew you are. What makes you proud, inspired, moved? What will allow you to look in the mirror tonight, at two o'clock in the morning, and feel good about what you see looking back at you? We're more than a channel of giving money away.

So how are we approaching philanthropy today? In four ways.

First, *we're upholding the best of our philanthropic tradition.* As the Jewish community debates our communal future, there are still Jews at home and around the world who are in immediate need of hope, rescue, and care. If we walk away from whom we have been just to become something new, then we don't deserve to call ourselves a Jewish community. It's that simple.

Second, *we're protecting Jewish communal philanthropy and professionalism.* As our Jewish community strives to ensure safe, respectful spaces for all, it's the legacy institutions that can stand up for the vulnerable, protect against sexual harassers and abusers, and encourage professional and lay leadership development to ensure our community is a place of equal opportunity and safety. Federation should partner with worthy specialists, but this important work won't get done solely by single-issue nonprofits. There are too many gaps between organizations and too many needs not to utilize the unique position and experience we hold. We're the glue bringing together the community, and we have the needed infrastructure and staff.

Third, *we're providing a successful and relevant philanthropic model.* At the end of the day, legacy institutions like Jewish Federations have survived so long because they represent a decent working model that allows philanthropists, community leaders, supporters, rabbis, and institutions to create something better. The model will always evolve, continuing to be a reflection of our best and worst moments. Organizations from outside the Federation world will increasingly look to us for best practices, and many of those that insist how radically innovative and trendy they are will fall by the wayside, leaving us to continue with our tried-and-true model.

And finally, *we're the philanthropic "someone else."* The "someone else" are the ones who stand up when needed. Time and again in our North American Jewish communities, I've heard leaders and philanthropists abnegating responsibility, claiming, "It's not our mandate," when Jews were starving or were in need of rescue or protection. The expectation was the same: "someone else" would clearly step up to the plate to care, to build, or to save. Federations have always been the someone else.

One last thought: On the night of February 11, 2015, in the middle of intensive artillery bombardment, three buses left the city of Donetsk in East Ukraine, filled with 130 Jewish elderly, families, children. In a carefully negotiated ceasefire, they were brought to the safety of the city of Dnepropetrovsk, away from the fighting. Their lives were saved.

Federations, those allegedly lumbering slow dinosaurs, are the ones that funded local partners on the ground, building up their local capacity and credibility to negotiate a ceasefire and to run a fast evacuation with all the support services around it.

But even more importantly, it was the Federation Annual Campaign reserve funds, the community mobilizations, the commitment to long-standing support and partnerships, and the ability to turn to partners, saying, "Go for it, we've got your back," that made all the difference.

In the middle of the fighting, in an emergency, in a war, it's the Federation system that has always stepped up to uphold our values. Close to home, in Israel, or thousands of miles away in places that many of us have never even heard of. For the rescue efforts and for the daily support for hundreds of thousands who have no one, the Federation system truly believes no one should be left behind.

We are ready, at a moment's notice, to fund a rescue mission, quietly, carefully, to save Jews. Anywhere. That's saving the world. That's philanthropy.

ETHICS IN FOCUS

Giving Money to Panhandlers?

RABBI NICOLE AUERBACH

Imagine you are riding the subway.[1] A man boards, holding a sign that says: "Please help. I need $20 to pay for a place to sleep tonight. God bless you." You have $20 on you, and you could afford to give it to him without causing financial hardship. A public service announcement posted on the train asks riders not to give money to panhandlers. How should you respond?

This is hardly a hypothetical scenario. In America, it is a rare day when we do not see someone sitting on the street, standing at the freeway exit, or waiting on the subway platform holding a cardboard sign, asking for help. Ask any city-dweller and they will be able to share their particular strategy for navigating this situation. Some offer food, to avoid giving money to someone who might spend it on drugs. Others are adamant that it is better not to give, citing public service announcements that exhort us to give instead to organizations that address the root causes of poverty. Many of us, when faced with seemingly limitless need, simply avert our eyes.

These are understandable human responses, which transcend ethnic or religious affiliation. But how are we to respond *as Jews*? The Torah famously admonishes us:

> If . . . there is a needy person among you, one of your kin in any of your settlements in the land that the Eternal your God is giving you, do not harden your heart and shut your hand against your needy kin. Rather, you must open your hand and lend whatever is sufficient to meet the need. (Deut. 15:7–8)

But what does our tradition demand of us when faced with seemingly endless requests for help? As a Jew, how should you respond to the man on the subway? By giving nothing, as suggested by the PSA? By giving food? By giving him the full $20? By offering him $1, knowing that he will also be collecting from others?

This is not a new dilemma. Indeed, it was quite a familiar one for the medieval scholar Maimonides (Spain/Egypt, 1135–1204), who offers helpful guidance regarding our obligations to the poor.

What Should We Give? And to Whom?

In his commentary on the statement that acts of *g'milut chasidim*, acts of loving-kindness, are without limit, Maimonides writes:

> *G'milut Chasadim:* They say here that there is no limit to *g'milut chasidim*. That is to say, acts done with one's body. But there is a limit to acts concerning money: 20 percent [of one's net income]. One is not obligated to give more than 20 percent of one's net income, but can do so out of extreme piety. . . . Here is how I explain this: If a man sees a captive, he must immediately aid him, as God commanded. Or someone who is hungry or naked, he must immediately aid him, providing him with food or clothes, as God said: "And lend whatever is sufficient to meet the need" (Deut. 15:8). This is to say that you should fulfill all of their needs. One is obligated to fulfill all of their needs, as long as they are in need, so long as their need or the cost of their redemption is less than 20 percent. But, if they need more than 20 percent, give them only 20 percent. One does not sin if one avoids fulfilling all of their needs, because it is more than 20 percent. But if you do not give anything, it is humiliating.[2]

Maimonides lived at a time when there was a general welfare fund within the Jewish community. Yet, unlike the PSA in the subway, he does not suggest that one could discharge one's obligation to a particular needy person by contributing only to a general fund. Instead, this text suggests that we are directly obligated to the person in front of us. We must assess what the person needs and fulfill that particular need.[3] In our hypothetical example, the man on the subway said he needed a place to sleep. If he had said he was hungry, you could fulfill your obligation by giving him some food. Instead, he needs a place to stay. And other than offering him a place to sleep, giving money is the only practical way to address that need.

How Much? And What If I Don't Have Cash?

Wait. Would Maimonides really require us to hand over 20 percent of our income to the man on the subway? Thankfully, no. While that might be the case if he were to approach you privately, in this situation, he was publicizing his need to a large community of potential givers. Maimonides suggests that this makes a difference. He writes:

> As for the needy who goes door to door [i.e., asking publicly], you do not have to give him a large amount of money, instead give him a small amount. It is forbidden to turn away one who asks empty-handed, even if you only give him a "small fig." As it is written (Ps. 74:21), "Let not the downtrodden turn away disappointed."[4]

In our subway situation, then, one need not give the full $20. But according to Maimonides, we *must* give something. What if we cannot? Then, at the very least, we must recognize the person and offer a kind word. As Maimonides writes in his well-known "eight levels of *tzedakah*":

> If a poor person asks you for money and you don't have anything to give him, you can give him kind words. It is forbidden to berate him or to yell at him, because his heart is already broken and is

already depressed. Behold he says, "A broken and depressed heart, O God you will not humiliate" (Ps. 51:19), and says, "To give life to the spirit of the humble and to give life the depressed heart" (Isa. 57:15). Woe to him who shames the needy. Do not shun him, rather be for him a father in compassion and speech, as it is written, "I am a father to the poor" (Job 29:16).[5]

Rabbi Isaac of Corbeil (France, thirteenth century) goes even further, stating that "the one who commiserates with a poor person with words is much greater than one who gives *tzedakah*."[6]

From these texts, we learn that fulfilling the commandment of *tzeda-kah* involves more than simply handing out money. Indeed, refusing to "turn our eyes" away from the poor, and instead purposefully engaging with them, is an essential component of fulfilling this religious obligation. The uncomfortable (and inspiring) truth is that our tradition is not satisfied with even generous giving to general charitable funds. Rather, it insists that we examine the person before us carefully enough to ascertain their particular needs and engage them with kindness.

Returning to our man on the subway, we don't need to hand over $20, but we should give what we can. And whether we give or not, when we are confronted with someone in need, our tradition commands that we close our book, take off our headphones, look the person in the eye, and treat them with the compassion they deserve. Doing so can transform the interaction from a routine and annoying transaction to a moment of sacred encounter, in which we are given the opportunity to fulfill our purpose: to make God's justice and compassion manifest in this world. Even on the subway.

NOTES

1. This piece is based on research originally done in collaboration with my friend and colleague, Rabbi Adam Lutz, for a course taught by our teacher and mentor Dr. Alyssa M. Gray. I remain incredibly grateful for both of their wisdom and insight.
2. Maimonides on *Mishnah Pei-ah* 1:1.
3. Similarly, Rabbi Isaac of Corbeil (France, thirteenth century) writes that one does not discharge one's obligation to give *tzedakah* by giving to a communal fund, because that fund may be used for things other than aiding the poor (*Sefer Mitzvot Katan* 248).
4. Maimonides, *Mishneh Torah, Hilchot Mat'not Aniyim* 7:7.
5. Maimonides, *Mishneh Torah, Hilchot Mat'not Aniyim* 10:5.
6. Rabbi Isaac of Corbeil, *Sefer Mitzvot Katan* 248.

TALKING ABOUT MONEY

In Praise of Beautiful, Bold *Tzedakah* Boxes

Rabbi Zoë Klein Miles

Rabbi Dov Peretz Elkins tells a story about a woman guiding the rabbi through her extravagant home, proudly pointing out every lavish detail. In contrast, when the same rabbi visits the woman's elderly mother, the mother points only to her windowsill lined with very simple and plain *tzedakah* boxes. "Now, Rabbi," the mother says proudly, "*this* is interior decorating!"[1] This story makes a distinction between arrogance and modesty, between investing in empty valuables and investing in meaningful values.

The idea of an expensive, ornate *tzedakah* box flies in the face of its very purpose, to be a humble vessel. It should not draw attention to itself. Or should it?

Hidur mitzvah, "beautifying the commandment," is the Jewish concept of enhancing a mitzvah through joy and aesthetics. It is derived from Exodus 15:2, "This is my God whom I will glorify." Rabbi Yishmael commented on this verse saying, "Is it possible for a human being to add glory to the Creator? What this really means is: I shall glorify God in the way I perform mitzvot. I shall prepare before God a beautiful *lulav* and beautiful sukkah."[2]

The Tabernacle was created with the finest material, and its center-piece, the Ark of the Covenant, was overlaid with gold and ornamented with cherubim. Today we place Torah in a beautiful ark. Even the tiny box of the mezuzah is crafted by an artisan. Why not the *tzedakah* box?

You might answer: Because while the ark and mezuzah contain Torah, the *tzedakah* box contains . . . money. We don't associate money with the sacred. However, currency is the current that connects community. It is how we lend support, how we give hope, how we change the present and build the future.

One of our modern challenges is, however, that the home *tzedakah* box is often empty. Or it is filled with coins that are never actually given away. Along with menorahs that have no drippings of wax, Haggadot void of wine stains and crumbs, it becomes part of a nostalgic landscape of decorative Judaica. Museum artifacts rather than beloved instruments of joy and connection.

Times are changing. Donating money today does not come with the satisfying clink of coins in a tin box. Rather, we donate with the soft click of a hyperlink on a website. Or by texting the word "DONATE" to a number on a screen.

For that reason, perhaps today, more than ever, we need *tzedakah* boxes that draw attention to themselves. We need *tzedakah* boxes that are bright, bold symbols to stimulate the spirit into action. Just as one is prompted to throw coins into a beautiful fountain to make a wish, as opposed to a muddy puddle, one may be inspired toward *tzedakah*—the *action answer to wishes*—by a beautiful *tzedakah* box, one we craft ourselves or one we purchase (supporting a Jewish artist).

NOTES

1. Excerpted from Dov Peretz Elkins, *Jewish Stories from Heaven and Earth* (Woodstock, VT: Jewish Lights, 2008).
2. *M'chilta, Shirata*, chap. 3, ed. Lauterbach, 25.

· Part Three ·

Israel

As highlighted by several of the authors, Jews are obligated to support the people of Israel through *tzedakah*. Rabbi Daniel R. Allen, z"l shares his engaging *"Tzedakah* and *Aliyah*: How American Jews Helped Build Israel," revealing the story of Israel through the unusual lens of money. A reflection of the ups and downs of American Zionism, this chapter shares trends, infrequently told stories, and notable characters. Rabbi Joshua Weinberg's "Financing Zion: Looking Back to Shape Today" provides a different point of view, while providing some history not emphasized by Rabbi Allen. His chapter expands the focus to the modern relationship between Israel and Diaspora Jews. Rabbi Weinberg also explores the realities of concentrated mega-donations from specific individuals, as well as the BDS movement. He frames his chapter in a directive for Reform Jews, offering a vision of what progressive Judaism in Israel can be.

Rabbi Noa Sattath, director of the Israel Religious Action Center (IRAC), shares some of her organization's significant efforts to ensure that democracy flourishes in Israel in her chapter "IRAC Builds Democracy through the Power of Money." The cases she describes illustrate both the corrupting force of money and the counterbalance of law and democracy. Like Rabbi Mosbacher's chapter in part 2, this chapter argues that money can be leveraged for good.

As noted in the introduction, Rabbi Edward Elkin's "Full Faith and Credit: Jewish Views on Debt and Bankruptcy" has been placed in this part, as a recognition that the Jewish laws and values related to credit and debit have their roots in biblical Judaism in the Land of Israel. This chapter is cross-referenced by several of the other chapters, when their subjects overlap. Rabbi Elkin's chapter, in particular, provides important background for "Moneylending and Jews: Falsehoods, Stereotypes, and Shame," by Joshua Holo, PhD.

"Ethics in Focus: When You Hire a Rabbi in Israel," by Rabbi Ayala Ronen Samuels, PhD, gives both Diaspora and Israeli Jews a great deal to think about when engaging a rabbi for a life-cycle event. Once again, the power of money is demonstrated in this chapter, which also foreshadows the upcoming part 4, addressing employment ethics. In "Talking about Money: *Etrog* Envy," Rabbi Mary L. Zamore writes of her frustration over buying an *etrog* to use on Sukkot, knowing that her money indirectly funds causes opposing her expression of Judaism.

13

TZEDAKAH AND ALIYAH

How American Jews Helped Build Israel

Rabbi Daniel R. Allen, z"l

"Everyone in Israel must in his heart steadfastly resolve to go to Eretz Yisrael, and remain there. But if he cannot go himself, he should, if his circumstances permit—whether he be a craftsman or a merchant—support some person in that country and so do his part in restoring the holy land which has been laid waste, by maintaining one of its inhabitants."

In the eighteenth century, in the introduction to his siddur, *Siddur Yavetz*, Rabbi Jacob Emden, the leading Talmudist of his day, connected the two mitzvot of *aliyah* and *tzedakah*. Their linkage in the American Jewish community creates a story of doers, donors, and door-openers. It is a story of collective action and individual initiative. It is a story of people, persistence, and passion.

Let's begin with the efforts of the World Zionist Organization (WZO), the driving political force behind the reestablishment of the Jewish State of Israel.

The WZO, called into being by Theodor Herzl in the late 1800s, created the Jewish Agency for Israel (JAFI) as its operating body, as well as two fundraising organizations, Keren Kayemet LeIsrael–Jewish National Fund (KKL-JNF) and Keren Hayesod (KH), which together would become the basis for financial support, both for the Zionist movement and the creation of the State of Israel.

The purpose of KKL-JNF was land acquisition. Its campaign used the now-famous "Blue Box" *pushke*. The idea was based on the methodology of the biblical census where every Jew contributed half a shekel. The hope was that contemporary Jews would do the same to help bring about a sovereign Jewish state. By the time of Israel's Declaration of Independence in 1948, world Jewry through this campaign had legally acquired a vast majority of the land provided for the Jews in the Partition Agreement. The ideology behind the KKL-JNF was that while there could be a sovereign government, the Jewish people as a whole should hold title to the land, and the collective should make decisions.[1]

KH was WZO's general fundraising arm. It operated in the early twentieth century under various names in the United States. During that time, American *tzedakah* focused on local needs—burial societies, educational institutions, synagogues, and welfare. The dynamic between the German and Eastern European Jews often meant two institutions for every function—separate but equal collectives.

In 1912 at a meeting held in New York City's Temple Emanu-El, Henrietta Szold and other Zionist women leaders founded the American Zionist organization, which they named Hadassah to honor Queen Esther, the heroine of the Jewish people in the Purim story. Hadassah's goal was to promote Zionism through education, public health initiatives, and the training of nurses for Palestine. Hadassah became the model for women's Zionist membership organizations. Their focus was on specific projects in line with their particular ideologies, while the KH fundraising was to support state building broadly.[2]

In 1921, the KH campaign was led by Supreme Court justice Louis D. Brandeis. Over time, a disagreement arose between the WZO in Israel and Brandeis. He felt that American Jews should make the decisions on the use of funds they contributed. His point of view eventually became enshrined in Internal Revenue regulations and law on overseas giving by Americans.

Brandeis left as chairman of KH fundraising and established the Palestine Endowment Fund. PEF Israel Endowment Fund continues to operate.[3]

There were many iterations of the KH campaign in America. The United Palestine Appeal was established in 1924 as a joint effort of the Jewish Agency, Hadassah, Hebrew University, JNF, and Mizrachi. In 1939, after Kristallnacht, the United Palestine Appeal (UPA), now a campaign only for the Jewish Agency, and the American Jewish Joint Distribution Committee (JDC), whose campaigns supported Jewish welfare needs around the world, joined together to form the United Jewish Appeal (UJA). UJA was owned 50 percent by the UPA and 50 percent by JDC. The division of revenue was approximately 60 percent JDC and 40 percent UPA.[4]

Refugees and Overseas Needs was established, combining the efforts of the American Jewish Joint Distribution Committee, led by Rabbi Jonah Wise, the United Palestine Appeal, led by Rabbi Abba Hillel Silver, and the National Coordinating Committee Fund, led by William Rosenwald. The three founders, in a joint communication to their constituents, emphasized that funds were needed to support Jews in Europe and Palestine. Their goal was to triple their previous collective total.

The UJA campaign became one of the most successful philanthropic enterprises in America. The UJA even entered American comedy: Three guys are lost on an island. The first says, "We'll never be found." The second says, "We'll build a fire and someone will find us." The third says, "I haven't finished paying my UJA campaign pledge. I'm sure they will find me."

In the early 1940s, with World War II raging, fundraising was not generally successful. Two Israel groups, however, did raise significant funds in America: the Haganah, an arm of the Jewish Agency, and the Irgun. These were the two major Jewish forces in Israel fighting the British for independence.

In the mid- to late 1940s, Haganah fundraising, as well as its efforts to amass material goods, was run by the Sonneborn Institute. Rudolf Sonneborn was a major New York financier and Zionist. The institute established cells of people around the country who were given a specific task. For some, the responsibility was to raise money. Other cells recruited for the Haganah or acquired weapons, blankets, and other needed commodities. In Montana, one family purchased two used U.S. naval vessels for the nascent Israeli navy. Only the small group, known as "The Institute" in New York, knew who was in each cell. These efforts functioned under the radar of the U.S. government. "The Institute" was an example of an individual spearheading a major campaign. Many of its leaders around the country emerged after World War II as the early leadership of the United Jewish Appeal.[5]

UJA's first $100 million campaign was in 1946. JDC received 57 percent of the funds, and UPA 43 percent to help build the *Yishuv*, the Zionist project.[6]

In 1948, at the time of the establishment of Israel, approximately 10 percent of American Jews were members of any Zionist organization. Hadassah, Pioneer Women (which is now Na'amat), Mizrachi Women (which is now Emunah), AMIT, and other Jewish women's groups made up the majority of Zionist membership.

Jewish Welfare Federations continued their work, funding local needs. With the birth of the state, Federations began to approach their local UJA to begin campaign partnerships in order not to have competing major campaigns. This process fully concluded with a merger of the New York UJA and New York Federation of Jewish Philanthropies and UJA in 1985. National UJA remained a separate organization.

In 1952, the government of Israel established State of Israel bonds in order to augment its operating budget. Like U.S. savings bonds, the purchases were an investment and not a donation. These funds provided direct capital for the government of Israel.

Some questioned the need for Diaspora philanthropy once Israel bonds was in place. In 1952, eight men representing the leadership of UJA and Israel gathered in the King David Hotel in Jerusalem. The proposal was made to close the UJA and only request support for Israel bonds. The final vote was six to two to close the UJA. One of the "no" votes was cast by Prime Minister David Ben-Gurion, the former head of the Jewish Agency: "A government cannot give an immigrant a new cup of tea. We should keep the UJA." Ben-Gurion's argument led them to reconsider and carried the day.[7] It should be noted that during this early period in Israel, the UJA provided more than 20 percent of the Israel welfare budget. Support was directly linked to *aliyah* and *k'litah*, the ingathering of new immigrants and their integration into Israeli life.

The period from 1948 to 1967 is the story of ever-increasing UJA campaigns. Despite the fact that most American Jews did not identify strongly as Zionists, they were starting to identify with Israel.

The UJA campaign succeeded because of voluntary leadership. Fundraising is more of an art than a science. Solicitors were trained in how to ask for a gift and how to tell the story of the needs of Israel. Direct solicitation, face-to-face, became the preferred method for the campaign. One of the major methods used was "card calling" at public meetings. The chair would announce his or her gift and then proceed to call out people's names, asking for them to rise and announce their gift.

The UJA ran donor trips called "missions" to Europe and Israel as part of their campaign strategy. Harriet Sloane was an early leader of the UJA Women's Division and eventually its chair. She often told the story of a UJA mission to Europe and Israel in the late 1940s visiting a displaced persons (DP) camp. A child was crying so Harriet offered her a piece of chocolate. The child continued to cry so Harriet offered the entire candy bar, but the crying continued. Finally the mother turned to Harriet and said, "My child has no idea what chocolate is." Such experiences became the emotional narratives that informed fundraising and infused fealty to the cause.

The stories about lay leaders' efforts for the UJA campaign are legendary. "Harry the House" in Reno, Nevada, was known for making the circuit of the houses of ill repute, emerging with large sums of cash. In Iowa, Dave was known as the "arm twister." If he came to your office and the gift wasn't big enough, he would literally twist your arm. Irving from Chicago was known as the "chair breaker." There were volunteer solicitors in every community who were afforded these affectionate names.[8]

UJA often framed its campaigns by utilizing Jewish texts, such as "It is not your responsibility to finish the work, but neither are you free to desist from it" (*Pirkei Avot* 2:16) and "All Jews are responsible for one another" (*Sifra Vayikra, B'chukotai* 7:5). The most famous UJA slogan was "We Are One." The message was that there is one Jewish people, seemingly without division in their support for the State of Israel.

"It matters who is on the bus." This is how Mort Mandel of Cleveland, Ohio, a major Jewish philanthropist, discussed Jewish leadership. In 1960, at the Waldorf Astoria Hotel in New York City, UJA convened the first national Young Leadership Conference. Those attending represented ninety-one cities in twenty-five states. These men—men's and women's fundraising organizations were still separated by gender—were primarily the sons of successful Jewish businessmen who were already major donors. The conference led to the establishment of the UJA Young Leadership Cabinet.

The cabinet's first meeting, held in New York City, had twenty-three select men in attendance. One of the highlights of the gathering was a private meeting with former New York governor Herbert Lehman, who by then was in failing health. At the following year's cabinet meeting, the members attended his funeral. The aura of being the best and the brightest, an elite group who had special responsibility to their people, was created by Rabbi Herbert Friedman, a graduate of the Hebrew Union College who served as CEO of UJA.

The UJA Young Leadership Cabinet, eventually joined by the Women's Cabinet, became the premiere training ground for the next generation of Jewish philanthropic leadership. By 1980, it was hard to find a Federation, JCC, or American friends group that did not have among its leaders an alumnus of these cabinets.

The Six-Day War impacted American Jewish fundraising tremendously. Jews from all walks of life took great pride in Israel's military accomplishments, and for the first time there was mass identification with Israel. In fact, there is a story, perhaps apocryphal, that tells of a Jewish corporal in the U.S. Army who was having a hard time with his drill sergeant, who did not seem to like Jews. The day after the Six-Day

War, the sergeant walked up to him, put his arm around his shoulder, and said, "Damn, you guys can really fight." A new acceptance of Jews began to emerge in America because of Israel.

Israel had suffered economic setbacks due to the war and was in desperate need of cash. Between 1968 and 1970, the UJA Israel Emergency campaign set a goal of $500 million in addition to the annual campaign. The UJA wanted to help the government of Israel but could not provide those funds directly, as per U.S. law. In 1970, the United Israel Appeal, using the funds from the UJA campaign, acquired half of the Israeli government's public housing stock. With its partner, the Jewish Agency, it created a not-for-profit enterprise called Amigor, which continues to operate today. The acquisition of some forty thousand apartments is a unique example of donors collectively deciding on the use of their own funds.

Israel-based organizations began establishing "American friends" groups during the early 1970s. In addition to traditional efforts like Hadassah and the American Friends of Hebrew University, new groups included American Friends of Tel Aviv University, American Committee for the Weizmann Institute of Science, American Friends of the Israel Philharmonic Orchestra, American Society for Yad Vashem, supporters of numerous Israeli hospitals—and the list continues. Interestingly enough, the UJA campaign continued to increase even with the addition of so many other Israel-focused philanthropies.

Donors wanted a direct influence on the use of their gifts, and they had a desire for capital projects as well. The Israel Education Fund was founded in 1964, led by Joseph Meyerhoff of Baltimore and Charles Bensley of New York. The IEF was established to address the nascent state's critical shortage of high school buildings, resulting from the major *aliyot* of the 1950s and subsequent increased birth rate.[9]

In the early 1970s, the major donor community, represented by the United Israel Appeal, also wanted a larger say in the operation of its agent, the Jewish Agency for Israel. An effort to have seats on the board of the Jewish Agency was led by Max Fisher from Detroit. Max Fisher was a singular figure in American Jewish life, having been president of the Council of Jewish Welfare Federations, chairman of the United Jewish Appeal, chairman of the United Israel Appeal, and a close confidant of presidents of the United States starting with Eisenhower. His efforts led to donors, through their collective organizations, now controlling 50 percent of the Jewish Agency board and thus having an equal say in the distribution of funds and programs.

Throughout the 1970s and 1980s, American Jewish philanthropy continued to be highly focused on Israel through the UJA and the American friends organizations. This benefited the growing presence of "American friends" as well as other efforts such as the American Israel Public Affairs Committee (AIPAC). At the same time, communal efforts to save Soviet Jewry became public. This movement would become a new pillar in the public advocacy work in the American Jewish community.

There were two schools of thought: one said Soviet Jews should be able to go anywhere in the world, and the other said they must go to Israel. Despite these differences, American Jews staged the largest (to date) demonstration in Washington, DC, with over 250,000 Jews. While Gorbachev met with Reagan, Jews demanded freedom for their brothers and sisters.

In an earlier effort to free Soviet Jewry, many were allowed to emigrate between 1970 and 1972. In 1974, Congress mandated that the U.S. government begin to provide a grant for the resettlement of Jewish refugees in Israel. The United Israel Appeal was the recipient of the grant. As of 2017, this grant has provided more than $1.7 billion as a gift from the people of the United States to the Jewish people in order to facilitate their homecoming.

Project Renewal was another effort of the UJA–UIA–Jewish Agency to involve donors and Federations. Encouraged by Menachem Begin, Federations twinned with Israeli communities, focused on urban renewal. This trend of donor designation of gifts continued to expand. Project Renewal became Partnership Together, creating a direct relationship between Israelis and Americans.

In 1978, the Reform and Conservative Movements also formally came to the Israel activist/fundraising community through their own organizations. The Conservative Movement formed Mercaz USA, and the Reform Movement formed ARZA, the Association of Reform Zionists of America. Each joined the World Zionist Organization and received seats on the Board of Governors of the Jewish Agency for Israel. The ARZA and Mercaz voices became energized in the 1980s over the question "Who is a Jew?" Their efforts, combined with those of the United Israel Appeal, led by Shoshana S. Cardin of Baltimore, ensured Jewish Agency funding of the Reform, Conservative (Masorti), and modern Orthodox streams in Israel. This fundraising stream eventually reached $6 million annually at its height. The allocations were agreed to be 20 percent modern Orthodox and 40 percent each for the liberal movements, since they received no government funding. This was a unique shift, where individual groups' needs were funded through the collective.

These allocations provided for such activities as the building of congregations, American rabbinical students in Israel, and the Israel Religious Action Center. Hebrew Union College–Jewish Institute of Religion (HUC-JIR), in coordination with the World Union for Progressive Judaism and the Union of American Hebrew Congregations (in 2003 renamed the Union for Reform Judaism, or URJ), established an Israel presence through the HUC-JIR Jerusalem campus. The United Synagogue for Conservative Judaism founded the Schechter Institute of Jerusalem and the Tali School system, which added a larger non-Orthodox Jewish component to Israeli secular schools. The Conservative Movement (Masorti) established Kibbutz Hanaton in the Galilee, and the Reform Movement (Israel Movement for Progressive Judaism) founded Kibbutz Yahel and Kibbutz Lotan in the Arava.

Annual UJA-Federation campaigns in the 1980s, while continuing to increase, allocated more and more funds for U.S. needs. In 1980, the majority of federations designated 70 percent overseas and 30 percent locally. There were approximately eight hundred thousand donors. In the same period, the percentage of JDC programs in Israel increased dramatically. By the late 1980s, with the UJA annual national campaign running at $800 million, the split on average was 60 percent overseas and 40 percent local. The split today has been, more or less, inverted.[10]

Women, as donors, wanted recognition for their own contributions. The model of a "sisterhood," or a women's auxiliary, was not satisfying. In 1972, the Greater Miami Jewish Federation UJA campaign established a giving group for women called the "Lion of Judah." For a specific minimum gift, one received a gold pendant of the Lion of Judah. This grew to be a national enterprise. Women's Divisions, now called Women's Philanthropy, focused heavily on Israel, specifically on the needs of Israeli women.

American Jewish philanthropic culture is both Jewish and uniquely American. In 1980, playing off football frenzy, the Jewish Federation of Greater Washington (DC) established the "Super Sunday" phonathon. Held on the day of the Super Bowl, Super Sunday volunteers gathered in a central place to call fellow Jews to ask for their gifts to the annual UJA campaign. For the next twenty-five to thirty years, Super Sunday became a staple of many Federation campaigns, although it is now almost never held on Super Bowl Sunday.

In October 1989, the Jewish Agency decided to begin closing its absorption centers due to lack of both funds and new immigrants. However, in December 1989, thanks to glasnost, 25,000 Soviet Jews came to Israel. In 1990, the figure was 189,000, and in 1991 it was 170,000. To meet these needs, as well as the Ethiopian *aliyah*, the UJA-Federation campaigns ran special efforts. Campaigns such as Passage to Freedom, Operation Exodus, Operation Moses, and Operation Joshua brought more than one million immigrants in the 1990s from the former Soviet Union and Ethiopia to Israel.

Israel's model of social welfare developed as an outsourced enterprise. Rather than providing direct service, the government supported many NGOs. In the mid-1980s, many of these NGOs began direct outreach to American donors, although the lion's share of Israel-oriented giving remained with UJA-Federation and the American friends campaigns. Each year brought more Israel-based NGOs to the American Jewish fundraising market. In 1980, Israel had approximately one thousand registered NGOs. By the year 2000, the number was thirty-five thousand. While not all focused on American fundraising, the market was increasingly crowded, and donors were voting with their dollars.

In 1952, the UJA campaign of approximately $100 million provided nearly 25 percent of Israel's social welfare budget. By the year 2000, American Jewish philanthropy for Israel, now over $2 billion annually, was more focused on social issues and Jewish identity than on the hard work of building a state. These changes reflect the evolving relationship between Israel and the American Jewish community.

What we learned in American philanthropic trends in the second half of the twentieth century was as follows: (1) Israel held great importance; (2) crisis fundraising was generally successful, such as responses to a war in Israel or to a cause like saving Soviet Jewry; (3) issues such as religious pluralism in Israel or increasing Jewish education in America captured donor imagination; (4) major philanthropists and foundations increasingly played a role in shaping Jewish life as the number of donors diminished (e.g., Birthright Israel, Wexner Fellows, Clal); and (5) American Jewish philanthropic entrepreneurship began to emerge with the likes of Mazon, American Jewish World Service, Jewish Funders Network, and the New Israel Fund.

Our hopes for American Jewish philanthropy in the twenty-first century are the following: (1) philanthropic support for Israel will continue without and despite political differences; (2) there will be a reconfiguration of legacy within Jewish organizations in order to serve a more disparate American Jewish population; (3) mega-donors and foundations will include the general Jewish community in their decision-making process; and (4) the emergence of a strong Jewish philanthropic collective will be based on Israel and American Jewish needs, not partisan or parochial perspectives.

Israel-focused philanthropy is clearly a unique example of the combined mitzvot of *tzedakah* and *aliyah*. American Jews have been, and hopefully will continue to be, integral to the unique national project of our people, the State of Israel. An additional benefit of fulfilling these two mitzvot was the expansion of general Jewish philanthropy. This story of people, passion, and perseverance, and the building of the state, including American Jewish philanthropic contributions, is unique in the annals of history.

NOTES

1. Today, KKL-JNF remains the title holder of vast stretches of the Land of Israel, and the government of Israel contributes about 90 percent of KKL-JNF's budget: http://land.gov.il/en/Pages/AboutUs.aspx (93 percent of land belongs to the Israel Land Authority, and an undefined portion of that belongs to the JNF).
2. Hadassah remains the largest women's Zionist organization in America. Its current membership is approximately three hundred thousand, down from a high of eight hundred thousand: http://www.hadassah.org/about/history.html; http://www.hadassah-med.com/about/hwzoa/hwzoa-members.aspx.
3. The Israel Endowment Fund is a donor-designated enterprise providing in excess of $70 million a year for Israeli NGOs.
4. Ernst Stock, *Partners & Pursestrings* (Landham, MD: University Press of America, 1987).
5. Leonard Slater, *The Pledge* (New York: Pocket Books, 1970).
6. Menahem Kaufman, *An Ambiguous Partnership* (Detroit: Wayne State University Press, 1991), 238.
7. Based on private conversations with Rabbi Herbert Friedman, who knew the participants of the meeting personally and frequently spoke of the account.
8. Though these affectionate names were long kept from the public, we record them here from Rabbi Daniel Allen's firsthand knowledge and personal connection to these men.
9. The United Israel Appeal, because of the Israel Education Fund campaigns, holds title to more than eleven hundred educational properties in Israel and seventy-five operating companies.
10. Contemporaneous internal UJA campaign reports as given at UJA board meetings.

14

FINANCING ZION

Looking Back to Shape Today

Rabbi Joshua Weinberg

> Wealth and riches are in his house, and his righteousness
> endures forever.
>
> *Psalm 112:3*

As the old joke goes, a Zionist is one who raises money from another
to send a third person to Israel. Funding and philanthropy have been
at the core of Diaspora Zionism since its inception. Where most
Zionist movements throughout the world centered on the ideology of
hachsharah (training for life in Israel) and *aliyah* (immigration), American Zionism was always centered on providing financial support and
later political support for the Zionist enterprise and the Jewish state.
Raising essential funds for the fledgling state was historically the core
value for so many North American Jews. Today this is undergoing
considerable change, given shifts in the realities of both contemporary
Jewish life and Israel.

Historical Background

Since biblical times, we have known a model of Diaspora-based philanthropy to Israel. As the short-lived exile to Babylonia during the sixth
century BCE was coming to an end, the Persian king Cyrus issued a

proclamation offering all Jews the opportunity to return to Jerusalem and reestablish their commonwealth:

> Anyone of you of all God's people—may God be with them, and let them go up to Jerusalem that is in Judah and build the House of the Eternal God of Israel, the God that is in Jerusalem; and all who stay behind, wherever they may be living, let the people of their place assist them with silver, gold, goods, and livestock, besides the free-will offering to the House of God that is in Jerusalem. (Ezra 1:3–4)

There were many who chose to stay behind, offering instead to send gifts of material wealth to support the "people of their place." Why did they do that? Perhaps uprooting oneself for the rugged and potentially insecure conditions of an unsown land proved a price so high to pay that many preferred to remain outside the Land of Israel. Instead, they willingly offered to offset their physical presence with gifts and donations.

As in ancient times, so it is today. While a minority of Jews did leave to pursue life in Israel, most Jews remained outside the Land, with a commitment to support the Zionist enterprise. As the movement for a sovereign Jewish political entity began to take shape, with it came new funding initiatives from abroad.

One such initiative was the "Zionist shekel," a program instituted in 1897 by Theodor Herzl, which ensured the right of participation in the elections of the Zionist Congress. The Zionist shekel, named after the half-shekel tax collected in biblical times to support the Temple, was the dues of membership. Every shekel-paying member, aged eighteen and over, was entitled to a vote in the election of delegates, while those aged twenty-four or over were also able to be elected as delegates to the Zionist Congress, the supreme legislative institution of the World Zionist Organization. The final decisions concerning the activities of the Zionist Organization were in the hands of the delegates to the Zionist Congress. Thus, the shekel payers directly influenced the development of the Zionist movement and were responsible for the affairs of the Zionist Organization, similar to the sovereign peoples of the democratic countries. The shekel solidified the notion that a donation or even a quasi-tax system enabled input and influence within the organization, providing a way for direct participation in the formation of policy and implementation of ideological values. The more shekels a certain group provided, the more sway it would have.[1]

Part and parcel of the strategy to achieving a political mandate in Palestine was to raise the necessary funds to purchase land. On December 29, 1901 (9 Tevet 5562), the delegates to the Fifth Zionist Congress in Basel, Switzerland, voted to establish a Jewish National Fund (Keren Kayemet LeIsrael [KKL]). Haim Kleinman, a bank clerk from Nadvorna, Galicia, soon placed a collection box in his office and sent off a letter to *Die Welt*, the Zionist newspaper in Vienna, notifying it accordingly:

> In keeping with the saying, "bit and bitty fill the kitty" and following the Congress resolution on KKL's founding, I put together an "Eretz Israel box," stuck the words "National Fund" on it and placed it in a prominent spot in my office. The results, given the extent of the experiment so far, have been astonishing. I suggest that like-minded people, and particularly all Zionist officials, collect contributions to KKL in this way.[2]

The Blue Box, or *pushke* as it was commonly referred to in Yiddish, was more than just a fundraising device. From the beginning, it was an important educational vehicle, spreading the Zionist word and forging the bond between the Jewish people and their ancient homeland by providing a tangible symbol of the connection between Diaspora Jews and Israel.

After the establishment of the State of Israel, the leadership of the young country called on all Jews to fulfill the Zionist mission and make *aliyah*. However, the sense of negation or rejection of Diaspora Judaism became a source of tension for the largest and most established Jewish community outside of Israel, the United States.

A historic correspondence between Israel's prime minister David Ben-Gurion and AJC chairman Jacob Blaustein established an agreement as to the expectations and responsibilities of each community. Both men then agreed that American Jews would lobby, donate to, and raise money for the new nation without meddling in Israeli policies and politics. Israel, for its part, recognized the allegiance of American Jews to the United States. It, too, would not meddle in the internal affairs of Diaspora Jewry. Individuals who chose to make *aliyah* were needed and would be warmly welcomed, but those remaining in America would not be disparaged as exiles. Neither American nor Israeli Jews would speak on behalf of the other.[3]

Throughout the first decades of the state's existence the need for philanthropy was obvious as a result of the shortage of material wealth in Israel. This was the case before the Israeli economy took off in the early 1990s. There wasn't just a measurable difference in income and quality of life. Until about thirty years ago, the basic creature comforts of average middle-class life in the United States were unimaginable to the great majority of Israelis.[4]

American Jews have consistently proved to be a major source of philanthropic support for the Israeli state and Israeli society. A network of Jewish fundraising and advocacy groups have long organized collective donations and lobbying efforts. These groups make major donations to large Israeli nonprofits, like the Jewish Agency for Israel and the Joint Distribution Committee, which then distribute them to smaller, local nonprofits.[5]

Israeli scholar Menahem Kaufman argued that Israel became so central to American Jewish philanthropic efforts as a result of the Six-Day War to the point where leaders of the United Jewish Appeal were and continue to be supportive of almost every decision of almost every Israeli government, at times becoming actual lobbyists for Israeli government policy. The UJA leadership acts in this manner partly out of its own convictions and partly with the tacit support of a broad cross section of the American Jewish population. For example, in 1990 more than 70 percent of American Jewish baby boomers agreed with the statement "The need for funds for services and program in Israel is greater now than five years ago." Although some have argued, such as former deputy foreign minister Yossi Beilin, that Israel is a modern, growing society and no longer needs American Jewish charity, there is every reason to assume that Israel is still a major recipient of American Jewish philanthropy.[6] Though knowledge about the actual scope of Jewish philanthropic contributions to Israel is limited, data collected by researchers at Brandeis University indicate a steady increase from $1.05 billion annually in 1975 to $2.05 billion in 2007 in real dollars.[7]

The Present

Times have in fact changed. While there is still a considerable Israeli population living below the poverty line, many Israelis experience a relatively high standard of living, travel abroad with great frequency, and have access to the material life similar to that of many North American and European Jews. This is leading to a gradual change in approach for philanthropy, transitioning from a general need for funding the State of Israel to a cause-based philanthropic system. Israel today boasts the highest number of per capita NGOs, many of which seek funds from abroad. Funding comes from foreign governments, private foundations, and a host of "American Friends of" organizations supporting universities, hospitals, museums, cultural institutions, kibbutzim, settlements, the Israel Defense Forces, and even non-Orthodox congregations that receive no state funding. Through these organizations, individual Diaspora Jews can contribute to the cause of their choice, essentially replacing the Zionist shekel of yesteryear, favoring instead the de-institutionalized smaller nonprofit organizations, which reflects a trend of more direct giving and tangible impact.

Financiers and Their Causes

Despite the growing trends that might suggest that Jewish philanthropy to Israel is on a decline, we still see major donors contributing to Israeli causes. Larry Ellison, the world's wealthiest Jew, made his fortune by founding the database-software giant Oracle Corporation. He and his wife have donated millions to various causes in Israel. Most notably, they donated $9 million in a lump sum to the soldiers of the Israel Defense Forces through the American-based Friends of the IDF (FIDF). On a visit in 2007, upon touring a community center in the southern city of Sderot, which often comes under rocket attacks from Gaza, he immediately pledged $500,000 toward reinforcing the center against rockets.[8]

Another such financier, Sheldon Adelson, who made his fortune owning and operating Las Vegas casinos, is one of the largest Israel donors in the world. He has given nearly $100 million to Birthright Israel. In 2006, Adelson gave $25 million to Jerusalem's Holocaust memorial, Yad Vashem. He has also given $5.2 million to FIDF and established a $4.5 million Jewish studies center in Israel. A summit hosted by Adelson raised $20 million toward organizing against anti-Israel boycotts and activities on U.S. campuses. A close ally of Israeli prime minister Benjamin Netanyahu, Adelson has advocated strongly for Israel's conservative Likud party and personally finances Israel's leading free daily newspaper, *Yisrael Hayom*.[9]

The Reverse Trend: Boycott and Divest

While for much of its existence Israel has seen significant support, the BDS (Boycott, Divestment, Sanctions) movement is a global campaign promoting various forms of boycott against Israel. It hopes to hold Israel accountable for what the campaign describes as "Israel's obligations under international law," defined as withdrawal from the occupied territories captured in the 1967 Six-Day War, removal of the separation barrier in the West Bank, full equality for Arab-Palestinian citizens of Israel, and promotion of the right of return of Palestinian refugees.[10]

The campaign, organized and coordinated by the Palestinian BDS National Committee, was started on July 9, 2005, by over 170

Palestinian nongovernmental organizations in support of the Palestinian call for boycott of Israel, divestment from Israel, and international sanctions against Israel, citing a body of UN resolutions and specifically echoing the anti-apartheid campaigns against white minority rule in apartheid-era South Africa.[11] Protests and conferences in support of the campaign have been held in a number of countries around the world.

Advocates of BDS target multinational companies, college communities, and well-known institutions, with the express goal of building "international support for Israel's oppression of Palestinians and pressure Israel to comply with international law."[12] College and university campuses, especially, have become battlegrounds.

A 2015 Knesset report concluded that the global movement to boycott the Israeli economy is having no discernible impact even though Israel's export-dependent economy is vulnerable, according to the Knesset Research and Information Center. "Foreign trade figures, mainly exports to Europe, show that the impact of efforts over the last decade to impose a boycott have not hurt the Israeli economy on the macroeconomic level," concluded the study written by Eyal Kaufman.[13]

The BDS movement has not made a significant impact on the Israeli economy and has only succeeded in riling up many Jewish organizations and Israeli government agencies to stand together against its opposition outside of Israel, as a significant PR challenge to Israel and to many young Jews particularly on college campuses.

While I personally may easily dismiss the BDS movement as being largely unsuccessful in its efforts to force Israel to be held accountable, Nathan Thrall, an American journalist and analyst covering the Middle East, claims that it has actually transformed the entire debate:

> For many diaspora Jews, BDS has become a symbol of evil and repository of dread, a nefarious force transforming the Israel-Palestine debate from a negotiation over the end of the occupation and the division of territory into an argument about the conflict's older and deeper roots: the original displacement of most of the Palestinians, and, on the ruins of their conquered villages, the establishment of a Jewish state. The emergence of the BDS

movement has revived old questions about the legitimacy of Zionism, how to justify the privileging of Jewish over non-Jewish rights,
and why refugees can return to their homes in other conflicts but
not in this one. Above all, it has underscored an awkward issue that
cannot be indefinitely neglected: whether Israel, even if it were to
cease its occupation of the West Bank and Gaza, can be both a
democracy and a Jewish state.[14]

While BDS may not be successful in impacting Israel's economy or
causing financial reason to be held accountable for behavior that some
determine to be egregious, it is an example of how some choose to use
money as a weapon or as a tool in achieving political goals. There are many
who use tactics of BDS to undermine the Jewish state and those who use
it to influence policy. Some proponents of these tactics are clearly antisemitic, and some see themselves as using their financial resources to reflect
values and use this sacred exchange as a means to an end.

Money = Values

In ancient times Jews were required to tithe—to give 10 percent of
their income or net worth to the Temple. Since the destruction of the
Temple, some have interpreted this to now mean that we as Jews are
required to tithe and give to charitable causes. For modern Reform
Zionists, who harbor no aspiration for the rebuilding of the actual
Temple in Jerusalem, the State of Israel can be the embodiment of
the Third Temple or an incarnation of the Third Commonwealth of
Jewish sovereignty in our ancestral homeland. Therefore, our tithed
money should, at least in part, be reserved for the continued building
of Israel, and specifically to support the institutions that reflect our
values, namely our Reform Movement.

Although American Jews still donate more to Israel amid wartime
emergencies, there has not been giving as large as during the Six-Day
War, for example, when compared to donations following the major
military operation in Gaza in 2012 or in 2014 when the conflict in Gaza

flared again. And overall, the proportion of Jewish giving going to Israeli causes is decreasing. "Meanwhile, donations to Jewish causes outside Israel are rising," as explained by Dr. Hannah Bar Shaul, a postdoctoral fellow at Brandeis University.[15]

While Israel's increasingly conservative social and religious policies may be gradually eroding Jewish philanthropic support for Israeli causes, this could also be a motivating factor for U.S. Jews to increase their investment and support for those organizations that are working toward a more pluralistic and tolerant Israeli society. Many in the Diaspora today see Israel as rejecting their Jewish practice and discounting their political opinion, yet still expecting their financial support, which will doubtlessly erode in the coming years.

The Reform Movement has spoken out on many occasions strongly condemning BDS. However, our response to the BDS movement has, by and large, been to invest in what we believe in and support the organizations on the ground doing the work that advances our values. There have been both public and behind-the-scenes efforts to combat BDS, as in Rabbi Rick Jacobs's appearance at the convention of the Presbyterian Church to dissuade them of a BDS resolution and in the leadership of the Reform Pension Board's working to ensure that other religiously oriented pension boards and investors do not succumb to BDS pressure.

In addition to openly campaigning against those who choose to boycott or divest from Israel, we vociferously advocate for all those who are disturbed, bothered, concerned, and highly critical of Israel to invest and reinvest in Israel. We advocate for financial support of our values and our movement in Israel as a way to engage and to work together for the betterment of Israeli society.

In his address to the URJ Biennial of 2017, Rabbi Rick Jacobs clearly stated our commitment to financially support our Movement and our values:

> My friends, leaders of this great Movement, this is not a moment for us to watch from the sidelines. Between now and our next Biennial, our North American Movement will double its financial

investment in growing Reform Judaism in Israel. In the past seven years—our Israeli Reform Movement—the IMPJ—has doubled the number of Israelis who self-identify as Reform Jews, so now when we double our investment, we can continue to grow more rapidly our Israeli movement and its influence.[16]

While this rallying cry for financial support did not come as a direct response to the international communities' call for boycott, divestment, and sanctions, it can be said that our Movement's response is to significantly increase our support for Israel, using our financial wherewithal to champion the organizations and movements who are working for change.

We in the Reform Movement often make the claim that we are the largest movement in Jewish life worldwide, yet our financial impact in Israel is relatively low compared to some North American–based organizations dedicated to funding various aspects of Israeli institutional life and civil society. As a movement we have the opportunity to impact Israel if we were to mobilize and give uniformly. In the same way that political action committees (PACs) work to finance candidates that uphold their values and support their political successes, we can also use our wealth in North America to support our values in Israel. That means putting serious capital into growing the Reform Movement in Israel. With significant financial backing we could quickly expand exponentially the number of congregations and communities throughout Israel and increase the reach of our legal advocacy wing, the Israel Religious Action Center (IRAC). Funding would also increase our ability to reach the next circle of potential members and engaged Israeli Jews. It would allow us to promote both our programs and our values of equality, tolerance, pluralism, and justice throughout Israeli society, beyond our individual members and congregations.

Conclusion

Since before the founding of the State of Israel, the American Jewish community has centered on providing financial support, and later political support, for the Zionist enterprise and Jewish state. Today we can soundly say that Israel has grown to be a powerful and successful country, a high-tech center, and an advanced industrial democracy. While some advocate that the wealth of Diaspora Jewry should remain local in order to invest in solving the ails of American Jewy, we still need strong support for Israel and specifically for the Israeli Reform Movement and its efforts to ensure that Israel be a Jewish and democratic state. Soon to become the largest Jewish community in the world, Israel provides a great deal for us. Israel is the cultural and spiritual center of the Jewish world. We, as Diaspora Jews, gain from Israel the perspective of a complete Jewish society, steeped in a nationalist and religious Jewish life with Jewish public culture and the revival of the Hebrew language. The creation of an ethno-nationalist state leaves a tremendous impact on Jews around the world; they visit and return inspired and motivated to engage positively in their local Jewish communities, to deepen their Jewish studies, and to live fuller Jewish lives. With that, it is upon us to invest in Israel and to support the causes that reflect our values and that have significant impact on the ground.

For the multitudes of Diaspora Jews who choose to live outside of the State of Israel, financial support and involvement in key organizations is an essential way to maintain a relationship with the Jewish state and to bring our two communities closer together. If we don't stand up and support our Reform cause, no one else will. The current increasingly conservative social and religious trends in Israel will only increase, and the forces looking to silence the progressive and liberal movements will only strengthen.

Diaspora Jewry's financial support of Israel is a critical element in the relationship between Jews around the world and those within Israel. The Reform Movement, especially, must continue its work in defining what it means to be Jewish in the Jewish state.

NOTES

1. "Zionist Sheckel," Encyclopedia and Dictionary of Zionism and Israel, accessed October 16, 2018, http://www.zionism-israel.com/dic/Zionist_ Shekel.htm.

2. "The Blue Box," Keren Kayemeth LeIsrael–Jewish National Fund, accessed October 16, 2018, http://www.kkl-jnf.org/about-kkl-jnf/ the-blue-box/.

3. "David Ben-Gurion and Jacob Blaustein Agree That American Jewry's Prime Loyalty Is to the United States, August 23, 1950," in *The Jew in the American World: A Sourcebook*, ed. Jacob R. Marcus (Detroit: Wayne State University Press, 1996), 489–94. The agreement was reported in the *New York Times*, August 24, 1950. For a full account of this and subsequent agreements, negotiations, difficulties, and the critical role of Blaustein as lobbyist/diplomat, see Zvi Ganin, *An Uneasy Relationship: American Jewish Leadership and Israel, 1948–1957* (Syracuse: Syracuse University Press, 2005).

4. Anshel Pfeffer, "Help Israel: Stop Giving It Money," *Haaretz*, February 15, 2018, https://www.haaretz.com/opinion/premium-help-israel-stop-giving-it-money-1.5824188.

5. Hanna Shaul Bar Nissim, "Why Jewish Giving to Israel Is Losing Ground," The Conversation, August 15, 2018, https://theconversation. com/why-jewish-giving-to-israel-is-losing-ground-100946.

6. Chaim I. Waxman, "Center and Periphery: Israel in American Jewish Life," in *Jews in America: A Contemporary Reader*, ed. Roberta Rosenberg Farber and Chaim I. Waxman (Hanover, NH: University Press of New England for Brandeis University Press, 1999), 212–25.

7. Eric Fleich and Theodor Sasson, *The New Philanthropy: American Jewish Giving to Israeli Organizations* (Waltham, MA: Brandeis University, Cohen Center for Modern Jewish Studies, 2012), http://www.brandeis.edu/ cmjs/pdfs/TheNewPhilanthropy.pdf.

8. Abra Forman, "Meet America's Top 20 'Zionaires': Billionaires Who Support Israel," Breaking Israel News, October 28, 2015, https://www.breakingisraelnews.com/52318/exclusive-americas-top-20-richest-pro-israel-zionaires-technology-and-business/.

9. Forman, "Meet America's Top 20 "Zionaires.""

10. Charles Tripp, *The Power and the People: Paths of Resistance in the Middle East* (New York: Cambridge University Press, 2013), 125–26.

11. "Palestinian BDS National Committee," BDS, July 9, 2005, https:// bdsmovement.net/bnc.

12. BDS, https://bdsmovement.net/.

13. Ora Cohen and Zvi Zerahya, "Knesset Report: BDS Movement Has No Impact on Economy," *Haaretz*, January 9, 2015, https://www.haaretz.com/.

premium-knesset-report-bds-movement-has-no-impact-on-economy-1.5358260.

14. Nathan Thrall, " BDS: How a Controversial Non-violent Movement Has Transformed the Israeli-Palestinian Debate", *Guardian*, August 14, 2018, https://www.theguardian.com/news/2018/aug/14/bds-boycott-divestment-sanctions-movement-transformed-israeli-palestinian-debate.

15. Nissim, "Why Jewish Giving to Israel Is Losing Ground."

16. Rabbi Rick Jacobs, "D'var Torah to the URJ Biennial 2017," Union for Reform Judaism, December 9, 2017, https://urj.org/blog/2017/12/09/read-rabbi-rick-jacobs-dvar-torah-urj-biennial-2017.

15

IRAC BUILDS DEMOCRACY
THROUGH THE POWER OF MONEY

Rabbi Noa Sattath

The gang of priests is like the ambuscade of bandits who
murder on the road to Shechem, for they have encouraged
depravity.

Hosea 6:9

For the lips of a priest guard knowledge, and men seek
rulings from his mouth; for he is a messenger of the God
of hosts. But you have turned away from that course: You
have made the many stumble through your rulings; you have
corrupted the covenant of the Levites—said the God of hosts.

Malachi 2:7–8

The work of the Israel Religious Action Center (IRAC) is deeply
entangled with the issue of money, resources, funding, and their
relation to equality in Israel. Our work on these issues is inspired by
the prophetic commitment to fight corruption. The prophets were
adamant in calling out and rejecting all forms of corruption in ancient
Israelite society, no matter who was the perpetrator, from cow herders
to the kings. However, the prophets had a specific emphasis on the
damages of corruption among the *kohanim*, the priests. As read above,
Hosea railed against the corrupt priests, calling them murderers. In
the second passage, Malachi, the last of the prophets, elaborates on

the ideal priest and the effect of corruption by priests on the people. The words of both prophets are, unfortunately, equally needed today to critique the misuse of power and money by modern Israel's official religious leaders, the state-funded rabbis.

At IRAC we find inspiration in *Pirkei Avot* 3:17, "If there is no flour, there is no Torah." Every day, we strive to equalize funding sources for the Reform and Conservative Movements and institutions, as well as to challenge and stop funding of institutions that pervert democracy and work against our values. We know the forces that undermine a pluralistic Judaism in Israel often find their fuel in state funding.

In this chapter I will describe three different cases in which IRAC chose to pursue legal action and discuss the role of money in Israeli political and religious life. The work of IRAC is focused on two axes, corruption in state-funded religious services and discrimination against the Reform Movement.

The Israeli government spends over three billion shekels (close to $900 million) every year on maintaining and strengthening the Orthodox monopoly,[1] while giving the Reform and Conservative Movements in Israel a fraction of a percent of that sum. The success and growth of the Reform Movement in Israel is astounding, as our congregations face competition from institutions receiving not only funding but also the challenge of lack of recognition from the Israeli government.

The Orthodox monopoly is known to be corrupt. The Israeli media often covers stories (some from clients of IRAC) about this corruption—for example, sexual harassment of women in conversion processes, harassment and gender segregation of relatives trying to mourn their loved ones by state rabbis officiating at funerals, and kashrut inspectors demanding money for official kosher certificates while not even looking in the kitchen, to name just a few. A former chief rabbi (the most senior rabbi in the state rabbinate structure) is currently serving a prison sentence for accepting bribes. In addition, nepotism is ubiquitous in the rabbinic system; the two men currently serving as chief rabbis are sons of previous chief rabbis.

The impact of all this corruption is monumental. Annual comparative surveys by the Organisation for Economic Co-operation and Development (OECD) of perceived corruption in governmental and societal institutions find again and again that Israelis perceive the rabbinic institutions to be the most corrupt institutions in Israel—more corrupt than the banking system or the political establishment. Israel and Japan are the only countries in the OECD where the religious establishment is perceived as the most corrupt institution.

In our effort to revolutionize the power structure around religion, as well as the perceptions of the Israeli public about the Reform Movement and about Judaism in general, we are not seeking to build an alternative Reform monopoly on religion. We know that it is not Orthodox tradition or values that create the corruption. Rather, it is the marriage of power, money, and religion that generates corruption.

In some of our cases funding and recognition are tied together. One of the struggles we take profound pride in is our victory in the Supreme Court representing Rabbi Miri Gold. The Israeli government employs community rabbis for neighborhoods, cities, and small towns. Over a thousand rabbis are employed by the Ministry of Religious Affairs in a community rabbi position. In 2007 we went to the Supreme Court demanding a salary for Rabbi Miri Gold of Kibbutz Gezer. We chose to represent her because we thought she would be the best test case for a precedent-setting petition to the Israeli Supreme Court. We had 100 percent of the residents of Kibbutz Gezer sign affidavits that Rabbi Gold was their rabbi and that they didn't want the services of an Orthodox rabbi. It took seven years in court to get the groundbreaking decision of the court mandating the state to equally fund our rabbis in small towns.

In our first hearing, during the first year, the court indicated to the government that the type of discrimination they were advocating (funding only Orthodox rabbis) would not be accepted by the court and urged the representatives of the government to offer us a compromise.

Following two years of negotiations, the government came back with the following offer: Rabbi Miri Gold could receive 90 percent of the salary of an Orthodox rabbi, but she would be referred to as "head of community," not "rabbi." It was significant to the state to retain a symbolic discrimination in funding, to demonstrate the lesser monetary value of our rabbi, in addition to denying her recognition of the authority of her title.

The Reform Movement rejected that offer, and we were back in the courtroom. The judges immediately rejected the idea of unequal pay for our rabbis. It was easy for them to see the blatant discrimination in funding. It took four more years for them to understand that we were not only seeking funding, but demanding equal recognition. In 2014 Rabbi Miri Gold became the first Reform rabbi to be recognized by the State of Israel as a non-Orthodox rabbi and to receive an equal salary. This victory granting both recognition and funding is a first step toward a larger revolution. The Reform and Conservative Movements in Israel spend large portions of their budgets on salaries for our Israeli congregational rabbis. When we are able to receive full funding for all of our rabbis (this is still being discussed in the Supreme Court as of summer 2018), it will free up the budgets of the liberal movements to build on their current success, by investing more in outreach, education, publicity, and building additional new congregations.

Some of our struggles focus exclusively on money and corruption; the Orthodox monopoly in Israel is strong and enjoys high-level political power. Our strategy to topple it is a step-by-step approach in dismantling the power structure. The rabbinate controls huge sums of money that sustain it. Cutting lines of funding is essential to toppling the monopoly. One such struggle is to open the kashrut market. When in 1983 the Knesset passed a law against fraud in kosher certificates, it also created a monopoly for the chief rabbinate to issue these certificates. The kashrut industry generates 2.8 billion NIS (approximately $770 million) annually and raises costs of food in Israel by 4 percent.[2] The monopoly means that a business owner wanting to sell kosher food is held captive by the chief rabbi's local kosher inspector. The inspector can make insane demands, demanding more money or not visiting the kitchen at all. The business owner must comply, as the kosher certificate can only be given by that inspector, and having a kosher certificate is crucial to the survival of many businesses in Israel. IRAC partnered with two restaurant owners who cared deeply about kashrut. They wanted to meticulously observe kosher laws in their kitchens, and they wanted to present to their customers a certificate they could stand behind. They were overseen by corrupt inspectors, who wouldn't go into their kitchen, who demanded they only buy produce from certain suppliers (who were paying them off), and who kept coming up with more and more demands for money. They were faced with the choice of complying with the reprobate demands or relinquishing the kosher certificates. The latter would lead to another awful choice: lose clients or present themselves as kosher without the tainted certificate and face heavy fines (because of the fraud laws). They wanted an alternative way to be kosher. In a long hearing with an extended panel of Supreme Court justices, we exposed the corruption of the kosher certificate industry. IRAC lawyer Riki Shapira Rosenberg argued that the monopoly hurts business owners and customers. In a landmark decision in August 2017, the Supreme Court ruled that there must be another path to selling kosher food in Israel other than the chief rabbinate. Less than a year later, Tzohar, a major Orthodox rabbinic union, has announced that it will launch an alternative kashrut certificate service. More kosher certificate providers are expected to emerge in the coming years. This will eventually pose a real threat to the main source of funding for the rabbinate. In this case we both fought corruption and cut the funding to control the lives of all Israelis, excluding all other forms of Judaism except for Orthodoxy. This is a crucial step in the dismantling of the power structure.

Money can be an incredibly effective motivator for change. IRAC took on the case of gender segregation on Israeli buses in 2002. After a long effort of creating networks and alliances, collecting data, and building our case, in 2010 the Israeli Supreme Court gave a decision outlawing gender segregation on Israeli buses, stating that segregation is discrimination. We felt (and still feel) immense pride at setting such a significant pillar of democracy. However, our allies and clients in the ultra-Orthodox community reported to us that there was no change on the ground. The bus drivers, who had instructed women to go to the back of the bus in 2009, were still doing it in 2011, even after the Supreme Court ruling. Bus drivers, who served the same segregated routes for years, were pressured by members of the ultra-Orthodox communities on their routes to continue to enforce segregation.

The victory in the Supreme Court opened the door to sue drivers for discrimination if they tried to segregate buses. And that is what we began to do. One of IRAC's youngest clients, Ariella, a thirteen-year-old Orthodox girl from Beit-Shemesh, was told by the bus driver that she had to move to the back of the bus on her way home from school. She represented herself in a small-claims suit against the driver. She won 13,000 NIS (about $3,700). It's a tiny sum of money in comparison to the huge sums invested in the struggle for and against segregation. But it's more than a month's salary for a bus driver. Ariella's suit and the small-claims suits of six other clients managed to produce the fastest, most decisive process of social change in IRAC's history. Immediately after the victorious suits, within the space of days, we saw drivers shift attitudes completely. From being enforcers of segregation, they became protectors of women.

Money and power are clearly connected. At its best, money can be used as a forceful incentive for change and equality. At IRAC we use all of our legal tools to make sure that money and funding in Israel promote the prophetic values of Judaism, creating a society of justice.

NOTES

1. According to a data provided by the Knesset Information Center, 2014.
2. According to a data provided by the Knesset Information Center, 2017.

16

FULL FAITH AND CREDIT

Jewish Views on Debt and Bankruptcy

RABBI EDWARD ELKIN

The wicked one borrows and does not repay.

Psalm 37:21

Every seventh year you shall practice remission of debts.

Deuteronomy 15:1

From the biblical period until today, the Jewish textual tradition has reflected contradictory impulses regarding debt.[1] Some texts understand the offering of loans as an act of *tzedakah* for the needy borrower, and that conception informs the way in which a loan may be extended, its terms and conditions, and how we deal with loan default. Other texts see the incurring of debt as being in the business interests of both lender and borrower, as well as serving the interests of the wider economy. This conception yields a very different regulatory regime governing the transaction.

The purpose of this chapter is to explore the Jewish values at play as we consider our response to debt in our time, both in terms of how we conduct our own individual financial affairs and how we consider public policy as citizens of a democratic society. While many naturally associate the phrase "Jewish values" with such obviously ritual aspects of our lives as Shabbat, holidays, prayer, and so on, the way we conduct our day-to-day lives is as important, if not more so, in revealing what our Jewish values are. Decisions in financial matters have long been particularly susceptible to the human propensity to greed, to self-interested willful blindness, and to ethical laziness. But even if we are determined to conduct our lives according to the highest Jewish values in this area, we quickly find out that contradictory impulses reflected in the textual tradition, resulting from different conditions in different historical settings, as well as different approaches to the tension between the ideal and the real, mean that simple decisions about our conduct in this area may elude us.

This chapter will survey Jewish sources from the biblical, Talmudic, medieval, and modern periods. In particular, it will focus on the phenomenon of bankruptcy: What does Jewish tradition have to say about the situation in which borrowers cannot meet their obligations? Whose interests does the tradition defend most urgently in this scenario—the creditor or the borrower? And finally, what can a liberal Jewish perspective add to this discussion?

The Biblical Period

The situation in which a borrower does not have the resources to repay a loan is well-known in the Bible. When an Israelite man could not repay, the assumption in biblical days is that he would go into debt slavery, becoming what is known as an *eved ivri*, "Hebrew slave." Often his wife and children would be bonded into servitude as well. In one example, a widow comes to the prophet Elisha and tells him that creditors are about to seize her two children as slaves. He miraculously makes enough oil for her to sell to pay off her debt and support her family (II Kings 4:1–7). The prophet Amos denounces those who "sell the needy for a pair of sandals" and "recline by the altar on garments taken in pledge" (Amos 2:6–8, 8:6). Nehemiah, a leader trying to rebuild the community in the Land of Israel after the return from Babylonian exile in the fifth century BCE, hears the people cry out that they are being forced to sell their sons and daughters into slavery, because they have borrowed money against their fields and vineyards in order to pay their taxes and cannot repay these loans (Neh. 5:1–5). He reprimands the nobles and the prefects for calling in the loans they had extended to the poor: "Are you pressing claims on loans made to your brothers? . . . We have done our best to buy back our Jewish brothers who were sold to the nations; will you now sell your brothers so that they must be sold [back] to us?" (5:7–8). Ultimately, following Nehemiah's own example, the nobles agree to abandon their claims against the poor.

All these texts confirm the fact that debt slavery was a feature of Israelite life. If a man could not pay his debts, a legal—if regrettable—recourse was for that person to become an *eved ivri*. However, biblical law sought various ways to mitigate the worst features of this kind of servitude. The association of this kind of slavery with the Israelite experience in Egypt was simply too powerful to ignore. In the Decalogue itself, the *eved ivri* is granted the right of Sabbath rest along with every other Israelite (Exod. 20:10). A master's right to beat debt slaves is severely limited (Exod. 21:26–27), and fugitive slaves may not be extradited (Deut. 23:16–17). A procedure for a kinsman to redeem debt slaves is established, and if debt slaves gain the means, they may even redeem themselves (Lev. 25:47–55). Most importantly, a limit is placed on their years of service: six years in Exodus (21:2) and Deuteronomy (15:12); until the next Jubilee year in Leviticus (25:54).

The corresponding term for a female Hebrew debt slave is *amah ivriyah*. A woman may become indentured because of her own insolvency or that of her husband or father. Like the *eved ivri*, the *amah ivriyah* also serves a maximum of six years (Deut. 15:12). A father may sell his minor daughter into slavery (Exod. 21:7–11), and the assumption appears to have been that in this case either the master or his son would marry her. Certain additional rights are hers if so; if she does not receive these rights, she must be freed. Because the status of women in regard to owning or inheriting property was so different in the biblical era from that of men, their legal status in regard to debt was very different. However, women could of course still be afflicted by poverty, and one of the ways available to deal with that situation was for her to become an *amah ivriyah*.

According to Deuteronomy, debts are annulled altogether at the end of the six-year cycle:

> Every seventh year you shall practice remission of debts [*sh'mitah*]. . . . All creditors shall remit the due that they claim from their fellow; they shall not dun their fellow [Israelites] or kin, for the remission proclaimed is of the Eternal. You may dun the foreigner; but you must remit whatever is due you from your kin. (Deut. 15:1–3)

And even during the period when the debt is owed, the creditor is required to "stand outside" and not enter the debtor's home to collect a pledge (Deut. 24:10–11). Exacting interest on loans is prohibited (Exod. 22:24; Lev. 25:35–37; Deut. 23:20).

Biblical legislation regarding the provisions of the Sabbatical year that apply to debt and debt slavery are complex and sometimes contradictory. But overall, we see in the Bible a recognition that insolvency, and the servitude that could result, is a societal phenomenon that cannot be eliminated but whose worst effects must be alleviated. The extension of credit is assumed to be a critical part of that societal response. People of means who might be prone to withholding loans from the poor as the Sabbatical year remission approaches are exhorted to overcome that impulse (Deut. 15:7–11).

We do see glimpses in the biblical period that there might be a problem with debtors of means refusing to pay their debts. "The wicked one borrows and does not repay his debts" (Ps. 37:21) stands out in this regard. But the bulk of the biblical material on this subject reflects the imperative to help the needy, not creditors who are owed money.

The Talmudic Period

A full examination of the issue of credit and debt in Rabbinic literature is beyond the scope of this chapter. However, two important points must be made. First, the Rabbis establish that the repayment of loans is a positive commandment. This becomes clear in a discussion between Rav Kahana and Rav Papa in the Babylonian Talmud, *K'tubot* 86a. Both agree that repayment is a mitzvah, a religious obligation. Rav Papa also maintains that repayment is also an obligation whose violation could lead to flogging *ad sheteitzei nafsho*, "until his soul departs." Regardless of the punishment, their discussion reflects the fact that the Rabbis begin to view debt not just in the framework of *tzedakah* but also as a commercial transaction in which, at times, people of means refuse to meet their obligations—necessitating a societal consequence.

Historically, there is strong evidence that the Sabbatical year provisions regarding farming and remission of debts were still widely observed throughout the Second Temple period. Following the destruction of the Temple in the year 70 CE, the situation of the Jews in the Land of Israel deteriorated. As a result, observing the Sabbatical year became increasingly difficult for farmers, so the Rabbis relaxed some of the agricultural provisions.

Regarding debt, the key factor from the Talmudic period is the development of Hillel's *prosbul*. The *prosbul* is often cited in liberal Jewish circles as a precedent for rabbis responding to the changing circumstances of the times. But the actual content of the *prosbul* technique is important for our discussion. Hillel noticed that leading up to the Sabbatical year, the biblically mandated seventh year in which debts were canceled, people were not issuing loans in the years leading up to the Sabbatical year. As we've seen, the Bible had already anticipated this problem when it warned against people withholding loans to the needy as the seventh year approached (Deut. 15:9). However, the problem clearly existed into the Rabbinic period, and exhortations to lend were not enough to keep credit flowing. Hillel devised a legal formula that enabled a creditor to still claim his debts following the Sabbatical year by giving the bonds to the court before the advent of the Sabbatical year (BT *Gittin* 36a). The biblical prohibition against collecting that debt was applied to individuals but not to the court, so the creditor would get his money back after all.

The *prosbul* was controversial in its time. Several authorities claimed that they would abolish it if they could, on the basis that it constituted an abrogation of a Torah law. But it is noteworthy that Rav Chisda explains the term *prosbul* as being derived from the phrase *p'ruz buli u-buti* (BT *Gittin* 37a), meaning that it is an advantage for both rich and poor—that is, the rich creditors got repayment on their loans and the poor had access to much needed credit, which they had been hitherto been deprived of in the years leading up to the Sabbatical year. This comment reflects the more balanced approach characteristic of Rabbinic texts on debt. By the Middle Ages, the *prosbul* was no longer being used, in keeping with the increasingly tenuous connection of the Jewish people to the Sabbatical laws now that they were away from the Land of Israel for so long. But the Rabbinic principle of balancing the needs of debtors and creditors had, by then, been firmly established.

The Rabbis in the Talmudic period also faced the challenge of dealing with the biblical prohibition on charging interest, given the practical societal need to achieve a flow of credit. As they did with the *prosbul*, they devised a legal means of working around this biblical prohibition. Their technique is called a *heter iska*, "permission to do business," transforming prohibited interest into added value for the partnership between the lender and the borrower, something that is permitted in the business context (BT *Bava M'tzia* 104b). The institution of *heter iska*, which is still used in loan agreements among strictly observant Jews, is another example of the development of the conception of borrowing beyond the *tzedakah* context.

The Rabbis did of course stand by the protections for debtors that they had inherited from the Bible. Some were even extended. For example, while the Torah prohibits a creditor from entering the house of a debtor to collect what is owed, the Rabbis say that prohibition also applies to a *shaliach* (officer of the court) who has been appointed to collect the assets of the debtor (BT *Bava M'tzia* 113a). The Gemara also explicates what arrangement must be made for debtors (*sidur l'baal chov*), that is, what assets they must be left with, even if the creditor or the *shaliach* does collect their assets to pay off the debt. For example, two couches and a mattress must be left for a wealthy man, and two couches and matting for a poor man (BT *Bava M'tzia* 113b).

For all these safeguards for the debtor, however, the establishment of repayment as a mitzvah and the institution of the *prosbul* and *heteir iska* reflect the fact that a new perspective on lending and borrowing had taken root in the Rabbinic period. Whereas the focus in the Bible was on protecting debtors as much as possible, the Rabbinic period displays an additional sensitivity to the rights of creditors and a recognition of the importance of the flow of credit for everyone. Not all debtors were in fact poor. Some were people of means who did not want to repay their loans.

A new system that balanced the needs of creditors and debtors had to be devised.

Maimonides

Maimonides builds on the Rabbinic inheritance in the twenty-seven chapters of his *Hilchot Malveh V'Loveh* in the *Mishneh Torah*. The extent of this material reflects the sophistication of legislation regarding financial matters, *dinei mamonot*, in the medieval period, and also the complexity of the subject.

Maimonides reiterates that it is a positive commandment to lend to the poor and considers this commandment to be even greater than the commandment to give charity. The person asking for alms has crossed the psychological barrier already and so doesn't suffer as much humiliation, whereas the person asking for a loan has not yet faced that particular shame (*Mishneh Torah, Hilchot Malveh V'Loveh* 1:1). Maimonides also says that it is a transgression to press a poor Israelite for repayment if the creditor knows he doesn't have the means (1:2). It is also forbidden for a creditor to frighten or embarrass a debtor (1:3). Debtors may not be imprisoned, nor may they be required to bring proof that they are indeed poor (2:1). In all these examples, Maimonides is in keeping with the biblical emphasis on protecting the rights of poor debtors.

However, in seeming contradiction to this approach, Maimonides also states:

> When a lender demands payment of a loan—even if he is wealthy and the borrower is in a pressing situation and struggles to support [his family]—we are not merciful in judgment [*ein m'rachamin badin*]. Instead we expropriate all the movable property that the person owns to pay the last penny of the debt. If the movable property he owns is not sufficient, we expropriate his landed property after issuing a ban of ostracism against any person who possesses movable property or knows of movable property he possesses and does not bring it to court. (1:4)

Moreover, even if a debtor will be imprisoned by gentiles if his property is expropriated by the *beit din*, the court still has the right to expropriate it (1:6)—at that point, the mitzvah of *pidyon sh'vuyim*, "redemption of the captive," becomes operative, but that fact shouldn't stop the court from implementing the expropriation. If a debtor claims not to have the means to repay, he should be required to take a solemn oath to that effect called an *ein li*, "I have no means." The only exception to the requirement that this oath be sworn is when a debtor has an established reputation for being poor and virtuous (2:3–4).[2]

Maimonides details a few exemptions to the principle of expropriation. The debtor must bring everything he owns to the *beit din*, but he is allowed food for thirty days, appropriate clothing for a year, a mattress, his sandals, and his *t'fillin*. A craftsman may keep two tools. He keeps only what he needs for himself, not for his family (it appears that this would be too much consideration to ask of a creditor).

In all these provisions, Maimonides stresses the rights of creditors. By raising the possibility of *cheirem* (excommunication) for those debtors who have property that they don't report to the court (2:2), he demonstrates an awareness that sometimes debtors hide their assets. A system that is too "kind" to debtors would result in a system in which people of means would not want to lend. *Ninalah delet lifnei lovin*, "the door would be bolted against those who sought loans" (2:2). As we have seen, that would be detrimental to both rich and poor.

For Maimonides, the goal is to make as clear and specific as possible how the court should achieve the balance between the competing goals of compassion for the poor on the one hand and maintaining a viable commercial system on the other—a system in which people are deterred from reneging on their debts and lenders are prepared to take appropriate risks and keep credit flowing to those who need and want it.

The Modern Period: Bankruptcy

Bankruptcy in modern Western societies is a legal means whereby debtors can discharge all or part of their debt. The debt is eliminated, even if the debtor later becomes wealthy, so bankruptcy represents a major concession to the rights of debtors over their creditors. The purpose of bankruptcy laws is to allow for an orderly and equitable distribution of assets that remain when a debtor cannot meet obligations.

As outlined by Rabbi Steven Resnicoff, professor at DePaul University College of Law, bankruptcy protection serves several important additional social functions: it allows debtors to have a fresh start; it minimizes the likelihood that debtors will engage in immoral conduct such as stealing in order to survive; it reduces the likelihood that the debtor will go on welfare; it encourages creditors to extend their credit wisely, because they know about bankruptcy protection going into the loan; and it encourages entrepreneurs to take out loans necessary to develop their business and thereby grow the economy.[3]

The question for us is whether this remedy may be considered Jewishly valid. As we have seen, Jewish law requires debts to be repaid. There is no provision for discharging debts; in fact, some authorities consider such a discharge to be the equivalent of theft by the debtor. If a debtor can't pay at the time the debt is due, he must repay it when he can. Bankruptcy as we know it therefore simply does not exist in the Jewish legal tradition. Can it be justified?

Resnicoff cites various halachic strategies employed to justify bankruptcy. One such strategy is called *minhag hasocharim*, "common business practice," in which local custom is assumed to govern any commercial agreement, even when that custom is different from Torah law on the matter. Since bankruptcy is part of the law of our wider society, it can be halachically justified on this basis.

However, even when bankruptcy can be legally justified, that doesn't mean that the *poskim*, rabbinic judges, approve of it. Rabbi Ezra Basri is an example of a modern *posek* who agrees creditors must accept bankruptcy discharges set by secular courts. However, he uses strong rhetoric to denounce those who take advantage of this procedure if they have means:

> Those who go bankrupt while their homes are full of valuables and do not pay their creditors, even if they do so through secular courts, have stolen merchandise in their hands. They will ultimately have to give an accounting. There is not enough space to expound upon the enormity of their guilt, especially if they do so with respect to non-Jewish creditors, because they profane God's name and cause non-Jews to say, "This is what Jews do." One cannot describe the extent of their punishment.[4]

We can see by the extreme nature of this rhetoric that Rabbi Basri is concerned that allowing bankruptcy on the basis that it is the custom of the society might lead nefarious people to take advantage, a development that must be deterred however possible, because it brings Jews into ill-repute among their gentile neighbors.

The general halachic approach to bankruptcy at this point would best be characterized by the term "necessary evil." It is not a solution that emanates from Jewish sources and so should be discouraged. But it is an established procedure in the wider society and has its uses, so therefore it must be borne.

Reform Movement Approaches

There has not been extensive discussion of commercial matters by the Responsa Committee of the Reform Central Conference of American

Rabbis. However, in 1961, the committee discussed whether a congregation may use the secular courts to collect delinquent building pledges.[5] It ruled then that such matters should *not* be brought to gentile courts, in part because to do so would represent a *chilul HaShem*, "desecration of God's name."

A 2004 CCAR responsum disagrees with the stance taken in the 1961 ruling.[6] While acknowledging that there is a long tradition going back to the Talmud of not relying on gentile courts, the more recent ruling maintains that our circumstances vis-á-vis the wider society have changed so radically that this notion no longer applies:

> These are not "gentile" courts, but *our* courts, belonging to "us," just as much as to "them." To suggest that Jews should not avail themselves of our nation's courts on the grounds that they are "secular" or "gentile" tribunals is to imply that our legal position in this society is not that of equal citizenship.

Similarly, the 2004 responsum addresses the *chilul HaShem* argument, claiming that we no longer need to be excessively fearful of presenting a negative image to the general public, because we are now more confident of our position in society.[7]

As a result of this more recent responsum, we can say that the Reform legal tradition would provide no barrier for debtors seeking protection from their creditors in secular bankruptcy court. But the committee has not specifically addressed the legitimacy of bankruptcy in general.

In the year 2000, the U.S. Congress passed a law intended to tighten bankruptcy laws by subjecting bankruptcy applicants to a means test that would steer most applicants to a much stricter payment plan. At the time, the Religious Action Center urged President Clinton to veto this bill. Rabbi David Saperstein explained the RAC's position as follows:

> Crushing the poorest Americans beneath unrealistic payment plans would force them to make impossible choices—between repaying credit card debt and feeding their families, between repaying

a loan and meeting child support. And since these provisions will particularly hurt divorced families living in poverty, this legislation can only deepen child poverty.

In biblical times, debt-relief was structured into the Sabbatical, or seventh year, remission of debt. It is specifically referred to as "God's remission of debt." *A fair and equitable bankruptcy system plays the same role in our society.*[8]

The language used by Rabbi Saperstein in his criticism of legislative efforts to make filing for bankruptcy protection more difficult makes it clear that he sees lending in the social justice context. Similarly, the resolution on predatory lending adopted by the Union for Reform Judaism's Commission on Social Action in 2007 reveals a *tzedakah* perspective. The background paper for this resolution stresses that unfair lending practices affect the most vulnerable in society and mentions specifically impoverished individuals, rural borrowers, people on fixed incomes, women, minorities, seniors, and military personnel. The resolution does use language acknowledging that interest rates should "appropriately recognize the risk that lenders incur" but otherwise focuses on protecting debtors rather than creditors. This emphasis is much more consistent with the biblical approach to lending as an act of compassion than with the more balanced rabbinic trend that considers the commercial imperative to keep credit flowing by minimizing fraud and protecting the rights of creditors, as well as the plight of poor debtors.

As we have seen, there is no single view of bankruptcy among contemporary Jewish legal scholars. The issue is complex, because it involves a mechanism of redress that does not stem from within the halachic system itself but rather comes from the outside. Any discussion of the topic necessarily leads to the difficult question of the relationship of Jews to the norms of the wider society in which we live. In the ever-present tension between the rights of creditors and the rights of debtors, secular bankruptcy represents a major shift to the rights of debtors in that it allows for some debts to be discharged altogether—a measure not contemplated in the halachah, at least not since the biblical remission of debts in the seventh year fell out of use.

Conclusions

We have seen that the Jewish textual tradition does not have one clear message on the issue of debt and credit. It is a complex topic that yields complex responses. What is it possible to say about Jewish values in this area? I derive five insights from Jewish sources that are applicable to us as we grapple with these questions:

1. Credit is important. Going back to biblical times, potential lenders were warned not to freeze credit out of fear that they wouldn't be repaid. Moving forward into the Rabbinic period, as the economy grew more sophisticated, the importance of having a system in which creditors could have confidence that they would be repaid even during the Sabbatical year was affirmed by means of the *prosbul*, and the right of creditors not to be defrauded and to charge interest by means of the *heter iska* was legally recognized. In this regard Judaism reflects a very pragmatic approach. Human nature is respected. There is a limit to how much people will give as *tzedakah*. Without the protection of creditors' rights, credit wouldn't flow—and that would be bad for both those who needed/wanted loans and those who had the means to provide them. Today, our economy is even more complex. But still the imperative to remove impediments to lending remains. Maimonides's injunction *Ein m'rachamin badin*, "Show no mercy in judgment" (in regard to borrowers who can't or won't repay), sounds harsh, but there do need to be rules that systematically protect those who are in a position to extend loans.

2. However important credit is in society, we must be restrained in our use of it. Living within our means and being circumspect in our risk-taking are worthy goals both individuals and businesses should strive for. The biblical model of loans is that they were an act of *tzedakah* for the desperately poor. But even when in later generations people began taking out loans for other reasons, the

financing of a flashy lifestyle through easily available credit was not in keeping with Jewish values around modesty and humility. Debtors should consider whether their purpose in taking out the loan meets the highest Jewish and ethical standards and whether they indeed can realistically expect to repay it. Creditors should curtail the aggressive marketing of credit at exorbitant interest rates to people who clearly cannot afford these terms.

3. There are many good and honest people on both sides of the credit equation. However, there are also creditors preying on the most vulnerable, as there are borrowers defrauding those who have extended loans in good faith. Our *yetzer hara* (evil inclination) is particularly active in regard to financial matters. The temptation to greed is powerful, in both rich and poor. We need a justice system that recognizes this essential truth of human nature. If greed leads us down the path to becoming either an exploiter or a swindler, there must be legal consequences for our actions.

4. The bankruptcy system, which has evolved in most Western countries, seems to work reasonably well, balancing the rights of creditors and debtors. Depending on who is in power, the system can be tinkered with to the advantage of one side or another, and we must be vigilant about providing correctives if it goes out of whack. Bankruptcy is certainly a more humane way to address unpaid debt than indentured servitude or debtors' prison. It does not emanate from Jewish sources, but nevertheless it is one of those areas where our sages have found ways to accommodate a useful outside innovation.

5. Maintaining a strong social support system is essential. There is no precedent in our tradition for a social Darwinian position in which the poor and vulnerable are left to their own devices. The question is: Who should be responsible for their support—creditors (by a societal insistence that they forgo repayment on loans), society at large (through taxpayer-supported social programs or bailouts), or private charity? If we

feel that all have a role to play, how do we sort out the various responsibilities of each? These are challenging questions, but the complexity should not deter us from seeking answers. The sector that we have most direct involvement in and influence over is our own Jewish community, and although we no longer have powers of taxation among our community, at times of economic distress we must redouble our effort to remind our members of their covenantal obligation to help support those in need. Nehemiah used the power of his rhetoric to move his peers to do right by those who were in debt to them; we need similar rhetorical skill today to move ourselves and our community to do right by the most vulnerable members of our society—both in terms of our own *tzedakah* and in terms of our activism on behalf of social programs designed to help the needy. And our rhetoric needs to be matched by our deeds. The biblical provision for remission of debt is not legally applicable any more, nor has it been for many centuries. But it should inspire us to support a generous approach when it has been determined that debtors are in fact impoverished.

Although the economic and societal context in which we live today is vastly different from that of our ancestors, they did explore many of the same issues that we face in our time. Our tradition never took the route of saying that these matters were secular, and therefore outside the pale of Jewish concern; rather, Jewish texts and traditions understand that all of life is properly the subject of covenantal obligation. Jewish texts and traditions also demonstrate an understanding that a proper balance between covenantal ideals and human reality needs to be reached. Some texts veer more toward ideals to which we should aspire; others more toward pragmatic reality. As a totality, they display an inevitably imperfect balance between the two. The experience and insights reflected in our long and varied tradition on debt can help us work our way through the challenges we face in this area today in a Jewishly authentic way.

NOTES

1. This chapter is an updated version of Edward Elkin, "Full Faith and Credit: Jewish Views on Debt and Bankruptcy," *CCAR Journal: The Reform Jewish Quarterly* 57, no. 2 (Spring 2010): 7–22.
2. See Menahem Elon, "Execution," *Encyclopaedia Judaica* (Jerusalem: Keter, 2007), 6:597.
3. Steven Resnicoff, "Bankruptcy—A Viable Halachic Option?," *Journal of Halacha and Contemporary Society* 5 (Fall 1992): 26–28.
4. Rabbi Ezra Basri, *Dinei Mamonot*, vol. 1 (Jerusalem: Ktav Institute, 1985), 68n4.
5. "Collecting Synagogue Pledges through Civil Courts," no. 17 in *American Reform Responsa: Collected Responsa of the Central Conference of American Rabbis*, ed. Walter Jacob (New York: CCAR, 1983), 58–60; *CCAR Yearbook* 72 (1961): 127–29; CCAR Responsa, https://www.ccarnet.org/ccar-responsa/arr-58-61/.
6. CCAR Responsa Committee, "Collection of Debts to the Congregation," no. 5764.1, in *Reform Responsa for the Twenty-First Century: Sh'eilot Ut'shuvot*, ed. Mark Washofsky (New York: CCAR Press, 2010), 2:291–98; CCAR Responsa, https://www.ccarnet.org/ccar-responsa/nyp-no-5764-1/.
7. Having ruled that bringing this case to a secular court is permissible, the committee goes on to discuss whether it is advisable in this particular case, but that discussion is beyond the scope of this chapter.
8. RAC press release, May 2, 2000; my italics. Another version of this bankruptcy reform law was passed by Congress and signed by President Bush in 2005. The intent of this law, which was supported especially by the credit card companies, was to cut down on fraud and abuse by making it harder for people to file for bankruptcy and have their debts discharged.

ETHICS IN FOCUS

When You Hire a Rabbi in Israel

RABBI AYALA RONEN SAMUELS, PHD

"We truly like you and the egalitarian wedding you suggested. But we cannot have you as our officiating rabbi, because my grandmother would not feel comfortable with a woman rabbi."

"We loved studying with you for the past year [in preparation for a Reform conversion]. However, while we admire you, my brothers are traditionalists, and they will not attend a wedding officiated by a woman rabbi."

"I really want my son to have an egalitarian bar mitzvah ceremony, but he and my husband will not cooperate with a woman rabbi."

"Can you recommend a male Reform rabbi?"

These are typical responses Israeli female rabbis (IFRs) repeatedly hear. When Israelis, or even Diaspora Jews, choose a rabbi for life-cycle events (*b'rit milah*, *b'rit bat*, bar/bat mitzvah, weddings, funerals, and other ceremonies), they have several alternatives to the state-funded, Orthodox *rabanut rashit* (principal rabbinic establishment). Officiants representing Conservative, Reform, and civilian options are available, but they present challenges from legal and cultural perspectives. While these challenges are often discussed, the sexism that impacts IFRs is seldom recognized openly.

With rare exceptions, IFRs officiate at one to four weddings per year on average, compared to ten to twenty per year by many of their male colleagues.[1] The same gap is true for bar mitzvah ceremonies. Because of the disappointment and insult of frequently being rejected solely for being a woman, some senior IFRs have stopped offering life-cycle ceremonies beyond their congregation.

The Israel Movement for Progressive Judaism (IMPJ) offers a special phone number for Israelis to call and inquire about egalitarian weddings. The clerk who answers these calls makes it a point to ask candidates if they want a female rabbi to officiate. Nine out of ten callers indicate they want only a male rabbi. Many people explain, "It is such a big step for us to have a Reform wedding, a woman rabbi is just too much." On the positive side, calls to this IMPJ number have doubled in 2017, but the percentage of callers requesting a female rabbi has remained constant.[2] This is by no means a Reform issue. In an Israeli secular organization offering life-cycle ceremonies the situation is only somewhat better, with 80 percent of couples demanding a male to lead the event.[3]

Why is this happening? Israel, even in its more progressive communities, is still a largely conservative and patriarchal society. The state-supported and ever-present Orthodox establishment influences perceptions and expectations of non-Orthodox Jews, especially in the realm of religion. While women are equal to men by law, Israelis still feel more comfortable with men in authoritative and leadership roles. Therefore, even when people embrace a more egalitarian wedding ceremony where both the groom and the bride speak the words of *kiddushin* (words spoken during the ring exchange), they find it too extreme for a woman to officiate at the ceremony. Accepting a woman in the role of a rabbi is simply too progressive for most people.

There are serious economic and social implications for the inequality between male and female Israeli Reform rabbis. It is common that wedding fees either supplement the congregation's budget for the rabbi's expenses or provide additional income directly to the rabbi (a much-needed addition, since the salaries of Reform rabbis in Israel are usually very low). Also, weddings and bar/bat mitzvah ceremonies are the most visible venue for Reform rabbis. This is where they have contact with Israeli Jews beyond their small congregations and gain exposure to the general public. Naturally, the more ceremonies one performs, the more one gets invited to lead other ceremonies. This means that most IFRs are simply out of sight!

The challenge for liberal Jews at large is to recognize this glass ceiling. The moral task is to promote gender equality among officiating rabbis, just as we demand justice in the greater world. Diaspora Jews can impact Israeli society by promoting IFRs, choosing them to officiate at ceremonies celebrated in Israel. It is not uncommon for IFRs to officiate at more weddings of Diaspora Jews performed in Israel than at weddings for Israelis. Likewise, IFRs typically lead more bat mitzvah ceremonies for North American girls (in Israel) than for Israeli girls. Each of these celebrations provides extra income, additional experience, and much-needed exposure to the broader Israeli society.

When you have your life-cycle ceremony in Israel, you support Reform Judaism in Israel. By choosing a female rabbi for your personal ceremony, you also fulfill the mitzvah of *tikkun olam* (fixing the world). *Pirkei Avot* 1:6 suggests that you make a conscious decision to *aseih l'cha rav* (literally, "make for yourself a rabbi," meaning choose a rabbi). When you select an Israeli rabbi for life-cycle events, you should include these considerations when making your decision. Your choice supports the fight for pluralism and egalitarianism in Israel!

NOTES

1. This number is based on an informal survey among IFRs in 2016.
2. Here are the numbers: A recent study of Jewish weddings performed in Israel in 2017 outside of the chief rabbinate shows an 8 percent increase from 2016, continuing stable growth over the last decade. This brings the

total of such weddings in 2017 to 2,434. Fifty-five percent of those opting for non-official ceremonies are secular Jews, doing so for ideological reasons. Another 33 percent are former Soviet Union immigrants who have problems proving their Jewish identity, and the rest are LGBQ couples. At the same time, there is a documented 10 percent decrease in the total number of weddings officiated by Orthodox rabbis (also a steady trend). Unfortunately, the study does not include the issue of male versus female officiation in non-Orthodox weddings.

3. Havaya (http://www.havaya.info/havaya-english/). This information was presented by the Havaya representative to a conference of Maram—Reform Israeli Rabbis in the summer of 2016.

TALKING ABOUT MONEY

Etrog Envy

RABBI MARY L. ZAMORE

My *etrog* envy hit a new height last year when a colleague proudly posted a picture of himself accepting a huge, gorgeous yellow fruit grown expressly for his congregation by the local arboretum. After I saw this impressive *etrog*, I dreamed of having one just like it. Of course, *etrog* envy is not unique to me. Many Jews obsess over their yearly purchase for the holiday of Sukkot. As commanded in Leviticus 23:40, "On the first day you shall take the product of *hadar* trees, branches of palm trees, boughs of leafy trees, and willows of the brook, and you shall rejoice before the Eternal your God seven days," we gather together the four species—*etrog*, willow, myrtle, and palm—during this festival, with its agrarian themes. Many Jews will pore over the selection of *etrogim* for sale, examining their shape and texture, dismissing any candidate for the slightest blemish. This is not my type of *etrog* envy. I don't care about cosmetic perfection; I am more than pleased with an *etrog* that reflects its owner, fragrant and comely, but discernibly imperfect. I, instead, desire an *etrog* grown free of distasteful political strings. Most plainly, I don't want to give my money to people who oppose me, a Reform woman rabbi, and the causes liberal Judaism supports.

Every year when I buy my *etrog* set, I feel like I must choose which bad cause I want to fund, albeit indirectly. Do I buy my *etrog* from the missionizing Jews who undermine my local Jewish community and whose Judaica store is a patriarchal world in which I am ignored by salesmen who schmooze up the male customers? Or do I go with my other, less local choice? I used to make the pilgrimage to New York's Lower East Side, bringing groups of congregants to see the pop-up *etrog* market and experience a touch of the Old World, as we haggled over the prices. It reminded me of my childhood visits with my grandparents, when they would happily kibitz in Yiddish with the storeowners. But standing in the street caught in my nostalgic bliss, negotiating with young ultra-Orthodox men or middle-aged Sephardic sellers, I would spy the pictures of their rebbe or rabbi adorning their stalls and be forced to wake up to the stark reality that my dollars were going to people who spent a lot of money opposing Jewish pluralism and me. No matter where I purchase it, the ultimate truth emerges when I read the copious text on the *etrog* box. These fruits are grown in Israel in communities that surely do not reflect my values, with the rabbinic oversight I neither welcome nor want to pay for.

Here in the New York City metropolitan area, I can forage for the needed willow, myrtle, and palm branches, but *etrog* does not belong to my gardening zone 6 climate. With no hope of growing my own, I am left to envy the rabbi who has an amazing community partner with a professional greenhouse, as well as my other colleagues living in warm climates who plant *etrogim* among their citrus trees. In the meantime, I need to tuck away my jealousy and decide which bad cause I support with my *etrog* money.

· Part Four ·

We Are All Employers

As employees, we readily recognize the injustices committed against us. However, when we are the employer, it is harder to see those inequalities and have the motivation to amend them, especially when remedies impact the profit margin. Yet, in a manner, we are all employers, as, either directly or indirectly, we shape the laws, policies, and customs, as well as their implementation, that govern our workplaces, as well as the marketplace. Jewish ethics call upon us to understand that whether we are in direct relationship or part of the global economy, our actions impact others and shape the communities in which we live.

In her chapter "Partnership and Mutual Respect," Rabbi Jill Jacobs writes of the inherent dignity of the worker and their work, highlighting the legal opinion of by Rabbi Ben-Zion Meir Chai Uzziel, the Sephardic chief rabbi of Mandate Palestine/Israel from 1939 to 1953:

> Employers are obligated to behave toward workers with love and honor, and with goodwill and generosity. And the workers, for their part, act faithfully and give themselves fully to the work that they were hired to do. . . . The relationship between the employer and the worker needs to be a relationship of fellowship, as with

an equal, and not a relationship in which one person is of inferior status, as such a relationship can lead to acts that are insulting or that induce shame. (*Mishp'tei Uzziel* 4, *Choshen Mishpat* 42)

Rabbi Jacobs also shares Jewish teachings on fair and mutual pay, living wage, and the right of workers to organize and unionize. Building on Rabbi Jacobs's chapter, Rabbi Mary L. Zamore's "The Family as Employer" focuses Jewish employment ethics on domestic workers, emphasizing that family employers must realize their obligations as employers. Rabbi Zamore shares Jewish laws and their practical application to the employment of domestic workers.

The foundational values of Reform Judaism include egalitarianism and social justice. However, this does not make us immune to the sexism that causes a gender-based wage gap among the female Jewish professionals employed by our synagogues and institutions. Rabbi Esther L. Lederman and Amy Asin's "What Is Possible: Striving for Gender Pay Equity for Congregational Employees" outlines the challenges and the interventions to reach pay equity in the Reform Movement.

In "Bread and Roses: Jewish Women Transform the American Labor Movement," Judith Rosenbaum, PhD, shares the extensive Jewish involvement in the founding of the American labor movement, sharing the fascinating narratives and contributions some of its seminal female Jewish leaders. Rabbi Arthur Gross-Schaefer, JD, CPA, in "Jewish Values in the Marketplace," expands this part's discussion to include the ethics of the marketplace. He underscores key Rabbinic ethics and applies them to current scenarios. In his "Dreaming a New American Economy," Rabbi Andy Kahn surveys the current economy and its impact on workers and proposes a new way, guided by Jewish ethics and values.

Related to Rabbi Lederman and Amy Asin's chapter, "Ethics in Focus: Responsum on Equal Pay," by Rabbi Jonathan Cohen, PhD, on behalf of the CCAR Responsa Committee, offers the official Reform Jewish opinion on the legal imperative to pay women appropriately.

In "Talking about Money: Mutual Benefits," Rabbi Amy Schwartzman and Kevin Moss share their efforts to be fair, respectful employers to the women who have worked for their family, illustrating in their narrative many of the values discussed in the prior chapters, especially Rabbi Zamore's chapter.

17

EMPLOYMENT

Partnership and Mutual Respect

RABBI JILL JACOBS

Six days you shall labor and do all your work, but the seventh day is a Sabbath of the Eternal your God.

Exodus 20:9–10

The commandment to observe Shabbat simultaneously asserts the sanctity and value of work. Just as God worked for six days of Creation and rested on the seventh, human beings spend six days contributing to the world and one day enjoying the fruits of our labor. *Pirkei Avot* even demands that we "love work" (1:10). An early commentary on this text explains, "A person should love work and not hate work. Just as the Torah was given through the covenant, so too work was given through the covenant, as it says, "For six days you shall labor" (*Avot D'Rabbi Natan* 1, chapter 11).

While the Rabbis of the Talmud idealized a life immersed in Torah study, without the need to work, they also recognized both the necessity of work and its inherent dignity: "Skin carcasses in the marketplace and collect your wages, and do not say, 'I am a *kohein* and a great man, and this is below my dignity'" (BT *P'sachim* 113a). Even the most important leader should not consider skinning animals—considered one of the most unpleasant types of work—to be below one's dignity, if economic need demands.

From the Rabbinic fantasy of a life devoted only to Torah study, and from Adam's punishment, "by the sweat of your brow shall you eat bread" (Gen. 3:19), we might conclude that Judaism views work as a necessary evil. But this is not the only or even the majority view. God purposely leaves the world unfinished and tasks human beings with completing this world. That's why we are commanded to work for six days, yet only to rest for one. As Rabbi Chaim David HaLevy, the Sephardic chief rabbi of Tel Aviv from 1973 to 1998, puts it, "In the Jewish worldview, work is sacred—it is building and creating and is a partnership with God in the work of Creation."[1]

If work is sacred, then the workplace must be treated as a holy place, in which everyone strives to make divinity manifest. According to one midrash, "Everyone who does business honestly, such that people feel good about them, is considered as though they have fulfilled the entire Torah" (*M'chilta D'Rabbi Yishmael* 15:26). Whereas we might be inclined to think of synagogues and other sacred spaces as being the sites of religious practice, our tradition asserts that workplaces, too, belong in this category. Therefore, employers must take measures to ensure that workers are paid fairly, are respected, and are ensured a workplace worthy of being called sacred.

This approach to the relationship between workers and employers emerges in a *t'shuvah* (legal opinion) of Rabbi Ben-Zion Meir Chai Uzziel, the Sephardic chief rabbi of Mandate Palestine/Israel from 1939 to 1953, and HaLevy's primary teacher. Uzziel writes:

> Employers are obligated to behave toward workers with love and honor, and with goodwill and generosity. And the workers, for their part, act faithfully and give themselves fully to the work that they were hired to do. . . . The relationship between the employer and the worker needs to be a relationship of fellowship, as with an equal, and not a relationship in which one person is of inferior status, as such a relationship can lead to acts that are insulting or that induce shame.[2]

These ideals sound beautiful, but how do we put them into practice? As always, the Jewish legal corpus translates these ideals into specific laws regarding workplace practices.

Two Categories of Workers: *Po-eil* and *Kablan*

The Talmud distinguishes generally between two general classes of workers: the *po-eil*, a day laborer who is paid at the end of each day and is generally understood to be poor and dependent on that day's salary; and the *kablan*, an artisan who is paid a price for a completed product, regardless of the amount of time spent working. Laws regarding the *kablan* tend to view this worker as less likely to be living hand-to-mouth than the *po-eil*, but still in need of the protection of organized labor, as we will see later.

Laws regarding the *po-eil* focus on the obligations of the employer to treat this person fairly and to understand the extent to which the *po-eil* depends on the day-to-day wages. This concern begins with the Torah, which commands:

> You shall not abuse a needy and destitute laborer, whether a fellow Israelite or a stranger in one of the communities of your land. You must pay out the wages due on the same day, before the sun sets, for the worker is needy and urgently depends on it; else a cry to the Eternal will be issued against you and you will incur guilt. (Deut. 24:14–15; cf. Lev. 19:13)

Interpreters of this passage understand the desperate situation in which day laborers likely find themselves. The Talmud comments, "Why does [the worker] climb a ladder or hang from a tree or risk death? Is it not for his wages? Another interpretation: 'His life depends on them' means that it is as if anyone who denies a hired laborer his wages takes his life from him" (BT *Bava M'tzia* 112a). The medieval commentator Nachmanides (Rabbi Moshe ben Nachman; Catalonia, 1194–1270) explains:

> The verse commands payment on that day . . . so that the worker may use his wages to buy something to eat that night for himself, his wife, and his children. . . . If he does not collect the wages right away, as he is leaving work, he will go home, and his wages will remain with you until the morning, and he will die of hunger that night.

This warning hammers home the consequences of not paying the low-income working promptly: God will hold the employer responsible for the death of the worker. While it is unlikely that a worker will die as a result of missing dinner one night, the cumulative effect of stolen wages certainly may be death.

Nachmanides's formulation also sets the foundation for a Jewish approach to a living wage. He assumes that workers who are paid on time *will* be able to purchase food—and presumably a home—for themselves and their families. Contrast this assumption with the reality in the United States, in which more than 50 percent of the people who apply for the Supplemental Nutrition Assistance Program (SNAP) have jobs.[3]

How Do We Determine Workers' Wages?

The foundational Talmudic text on workplace conditions establishes the principle that "the custom of the land" determines practices incumbent upon all employers:

> One who hires workers and instructs them to begin work early and to stay late—in a place in which it is not the custom to begin work early and to stay late, the employer may not force them to do so. In a place in which it is the custom to feed the workers, he must do so. In a place in which it is the custom to distribute sweets, he must do so. Everything goes according to the custom of the land. (BT *Bava M'tzia* 83a)

Though it doesn't mention wages, let alone contemporary concerns such as health care, pensions, or disability insurance, this text sets a precedent for all employers to hold to the labor practices that have become customary within a given area.

But where do these customary practices come from? Some writers have tried to suggest that the Talmud supports laissez-faire economics, in which the market determines wages and other labor conditions.[4] By this measure, the "custom of the land" magically arises from the free market and only then becomes incumbent on employers. However, the text of the Talmud itself belies this assertion. The Rabbis declare, "The people of the city are permitted to stipulate weights and measures and to set workers' wages and to establish penalties for breaking the rules" (BT *Bava Batra* 8b). These "people of the city"—which may refer to all members of a community or to their elected representatives—actively determine appropriate wages and impose these on all local employers.

In a comment that becomes one basis for Jewish support of unions, the thirteenth- to fourteenth-century scholar Rabbi Asher ben Yechiel (known as "the Rosh") wrote, "From here, we learn that all members of a trade are able to make stipulations among themselves, and they are considered 'the people of the city' in regard to labor."[5] That is, the workers themselves determine appropriate wages and other working conditions for their sector, and these agreements become the "custom of the land" that all employers must follow.[6]

A few medieval and modern texts are even more explicit about the necessity of paying adequate wages. Maimonides (Spain/Egypt, 1135–1204) establishes a base salary for certain communal workers:

> The official proofreaders of biblical manuscripts in Jerusalem, and the judges who tried robbers in Jerusalem, received their salaries out of the Temple fund. How much did they receive? Ninety *maneh* (9,000 *zuz*) annually. If this was insufficient for their maintenance, they were given, whether they wanted it or not, enough additional pay to provide for their own needs and the needs of their wives and children and other members of their households.[7]

HaLevy explains that this base salary was necessary "in order for these workers to devote their full energies to their important tasks, and in order that they will be able to focus on fulfilling their duties, without concerns about the needs of their families weighing on them."[8]

What is important here is not the precise worth of ninety *maneh*, but rather the assertion that workers must earn enough to take care of themselves and their families and to focus entirely on their tasks without being overwhelmed with financial concerns. Paying workers appropriately thus benefits not only the workers themselves, but also the employer and, in the case of communal workers, the entire community. We see this principle reflected also in restrictions against workers moonlighting in second jobs, lest they not have the energy to devote themselves fully to their first job (see, for example, *Tosefta Bava M'tzia* 8:2). Such restrictions, of course, assume that a single job pays enough for workers to support their families without taking on additional work.

Uzziel goes even further and obligates employers to pay a living wage:

> This mitzvah obligates every employer to pay his workers an amount that enables the worker to sustain himself in a way that is consistent with the standard of living in the place where he is working. This is not said explicitly, but is said in general terms, as it says regarding an Israelite indentured servant [*eved ivri*]: It should be good for him with you. And the Rabbis explained that this means "like you in regard to food; like you in regard to drink," in order to obligate the master to bring the servant to his own standard of living (BT *Kiddushin* 20a). From this, we learn regarding the law of workers that even though the employer is not obligated to bring the worker to his same level, since the worker does not eat at his table, in paying wages, the employer is obligated to pay enough that the worker can live according to the standard of living in the place of his work.[9]

Organizing and Unions

We have seen that halachah establishes an ideal in which workplaces reflect the divine presence, in which employers and workers treat one another with dignity, and in which all workers—even those at the bottom of the hierarchy—earn enough to support their families at the median standard of living. But how should this ideal be achieved?

From the Talmud through the present day, Jewish law asserts that organized labor offers the best means of achieving this standard. Within the Talmud, we learn that the family that baked the showbread for the Temple once refused to bake until their wages were doubled. In the midst of this labor strike, another set of bakers is recruited as scabs, but their bread becomes moldy and therefore unusable. The strike succeeds, and the family agrees to return for double their previous wages (BT *Yoma* 38a).

One early Rabbinic text lays the groundwork for guilds by declaring:

> The wool workers and the dyers are permitted to say, "We will all be partners in any business that comes to the city." The bakers are permitted to establish work shifts among themselves. Donkey drivers are permitted to say, "We will provide another donkey for anyone whose donkey dies." . . . Merchants are permitted to say, "We will provide another ship for anyone whose ship is destroyed." (*Tosefta Bava M'tzia* 11:24–26)

In this case, the workers are kablanim—members of skilled trades, who organize among themselves to prevent competition that negatively affects all members of the trade.

Modern legal thinkers give broad permission for workers to organize unions and to declare strikes, especially if other means of achieving acceptable conditions have been exhausted. For example, Rabbi Moshe Feinstein, one of the preeminent American Orthodox authorities of the twentieth century, writes, "In the case in which workers decide that they will not work until they receive a raise in salary or a similar thing, this is considered a stipulation, and the majority may force the minority to observe it."[10]

Uzziel offers an even clearer rallying cry for organized labor:

> Logic dictates [permission for unions] in order that the individual worker not be left on his own, to the point that he hires himself out

for a low wage in order to satisfy his hunger and that of his family with a bit of bread and water and with a dark and dingy home; in order that the worker may protect himself, the law gives him the legal right to organize, and to establish stipulations that benefit the members of his profession regarding the fair distribution of work among the workers, and to achieve fair treatment and a wage appropriate for the work and sufficient to sustain his household at the standard of living as the other residents of his city . . . all of these things can only be fulfilled through a workers' union. Therefore, the Torah gave the Jewish people the full and legal right to organize these, even though it is possible that [such unions] will result in a financial loss for the employers.[11]

Finally, Rav Abraham Isaac Kook, the first Ashkenazic chief rabbi of Israel, sees a larger purpose in workers' organizing:

Within the workers' organization, which is formed for the purpose of guarding and protecting the work conditions, there is an aspect of righteousness and uprightness and *tikkun olam* [literally—repair of the world]. The workers' organization may sue both the employer and the worker who causes this problem, for unorganized labor brings damage and loss of money to workers. For the unorganized worker works under worse conditions—both in regard to wages and in regard to working hours, etc. And this is likely to make working conditions worse in general.[12]

Kook most likely does not understand *tikkun olam* in the way that many of our communities use it today—as an overall vision of repairing the world. Rather, he probably has in mind the Mishnaic understanding of this term, as a means of changing a law or eliminating a loophole or technicality in order to make the system more just in general, and particularly for those with little positional power in society.[13] Here, he asserts that organized labor—whether expressly required by halachah or not—represents the best way to ensure a just working situation for those most likely to be exploited.

We have seen Jewish law and narrative text offer a series of specifics regarding the relationship between employers and workers, including requirements regarding fair and timely pay, expectations of mutual respect, and encouragement for workers to form unions and even initiate strikes when necessary. Ultimately, all of these details aim to create a workplace that lives up to the ideal, articulated by HaLevy, that our labor should feel like a "partnership with God in the work of Creation."

NOTES

1. Chaim David HaLevy, *Aseih L'cha Rav* 2:64.
2. Ben-Zion Meir Chai Uzziel, *Mishp'tei Uzziel* 4, *Choshen Mishpat* 42.
3. Brynne Keith-Jennings and Raheem Chaudhry, "Issue Brief: Most Working-Age SNAP Participants Work, but Often in Unstable Jobs," Center on Budget and Policy Priorities, March 23, 2018, https://www.cbpp.org/research/food-assistance/issue-brief-most-working-age-snap-participants-work-but-often-in-unstable.
4. For example, Aaron Levine, "The Living Wage and Jewish Law," *Tradition* 41, no. 4 (2008): 8–32.
5. Commentary of the Rosh on *Bava Batra* 9a.
6. For a more extensive discussion of the above Talmudic passage and its continuation and of the living wage in Judaism, see Jill Jacobs, *There Shall Be No Needy* (Woodstock, VT: Jewish Lights, 2009).
7. Maimonides, *Mishneh Torah, Hilchot Sh'kalim* 4:7, in Philip Birnbaum, *Maimonides' Mishneh Torah (Yad Hazakah)* (New York: Hebrew Publishing Co., 1989), 96–97.
8. HaLevy, *Aseih L'cha Rav* 5:23.
9. Uzziel, *Mishp'tei Uzziel* 4:44.
10. Moshe Feinstein, *Iggerot Moshe, Choshen Mishpat* 59.
11. Uzziel, *Choshen Mishpat* 52:6.
12. Abraham Isaac Kook, quoted in Tzvi Yaron, *Mishnato shel HaRav Kook* (Jerusalem: ha-Machlakhah lechinuch ule-tarbut Toraniyim ba-golah, 1974), 164.
13. For a more extensive exploration of the history of *tikkun olam*, see Jacobs, *There Shall be No Needy*, chap. 2; and Jane Kanarek, "What Does *Tikkun Olam* Actually Mean?," in *Righteous Indignation*, ed. Or Rose, Jo Ellen Kaiser, and Margie Klein (Woodstock, VT: Jewish Lights, 2008).

18

THE FAMILY AS EMPLOYER

Rabbi Mary L. Zamore

When we work outside of the home, the roles of employer and employee are clearly delineated, with oversight by state and federal laws and agencies, often with HR departments to oversee their enforcement. When we employ others in our own households, however, even though state and federal laws also apply, it can be harder to view our home as someone else's workplace. But of course, we must. Fortunately, we have Jewish ethical teachings to guide us in this employee-employer relationship.

Teaching children and teens not only opens a window to the attitudes and values upheld in their individual homes, but also holds up a mirror to our greater society. I have learned much concerning our views of employment from the young citizens in my classes. When I teach employment ethics to teens, I start the lesson by asking them whom their family employs. Usually, my question is greeted with complete silence, the students believing their families hires no one. Sometimes a teen will offer that their parents own a business and it has employees. Then, finally, a student will catch on and share that their family pays another adult to drive them to activities after school. From there, the list will accumulate to include housekeepers, babysitters, nannies, elder-care providers, tutors, dog walkers, landscapers, and pool cleaners. Many are reluctant to acknowledge that their families are employers. Yet, when the conversation switches and I ask the teens about their experiences as employees, everyone is excited to tell their employment stories.

The employee question yields an interesting conversation, because the jobs young teenagers do are frequently informal arrangements, not usually governed by working papers, 1099 forms, or HR departments. This type of work frequently takes place in neighbors' homes. The teens babysit, do yardwork, tutor, and more rarely, help adults, usually relatives, with their paid work. When I ask them about the clarity of these arrangements concerning hours, pay, and work conditions, the narratives vary greatly. Most share happy tales of their first employment experiences, but others complain of poor communication of hours, pay, and expectations. There are stories of neighbors not coming home at a reasonable hour to let the babysitter leave on a school night; there are scary narratives of using heavy-duty landscaping equipment without training or safety precautions; there was the teen who was driven home after babysitting by a drunk adult. Using their personal experiences, we can quickly create a list of ethical guidelines for all employment. It seems, as reflected by our youngest citizens, it is easy to identify yourself as an employee, deserving of rights, but it is difficult to recognize that our families are also employers and the workplace is our home.

When speaking of the workers employed by our families, many say these working folks are "like family." This creates a dangerous fiction that shields the family, you and me, from facing the reality of the responsibilities we have as employers. Family members live together and do the work that sustains daily function, from child care to elder care to cooking and cleaning. While all of this is real work, no one is paid, hours are not limited, working conditions are not considered, and retirement rarely funded. Family members, in fact, are encouraged to sacrifice for each other, for the collective good. And studies show that the women in our families, even when they also work outside of the home, shoulder the greater burden of caregiving, cooking, and cleaning for others.[1] So too our employed domestic workers are most likely to be female.[2] These are the people who enable men and women to work outside of the home, have respite from family responsibilities, and accomplish tasks for which we are not suited. We must not take their employment for granted, as sometimes we take the labors of our own family members for granted. Yet, when we refer to these workers as family, we avoid the uncomfortable reality that we must think legally and ethically about the employment relationship. As much as we want the employees of our household to be warm, loving, and responsible substitutes for our own care and work, they are not family.[3]

As described above, when the teens were asked to create a list of rules to protect themselves as employees, they quickly produced ethical guidelines for all employment, beautifully illustrating the power of Hillel's ethic of reciprocity, "That which is hateful to you, do not do to your fellow. That is the whole Torah; the rest is commentary; go and learn it." (BT *Shabbat* 31a). While it would be tempting to leave this text as the sole guide for home employment, the commentary is needed. Rabbi Jill Jacobs discusses the Jewish ethics of employment in her chapter earlier in this book. Here we will explore these and other ethical values, applying them to home-based employment.

Rabbi Jacobs shares the Jewish textual argument supporting the worker's right to organize in labor unions. When we discuss domestic workers, it is important to understand that this class of workers had been (until 2015) purposefully excluded from our nation's labor laws from the beginning of the New Deal. As activist and MacArthur fellow Ai-Jen Poo explains:

> This special treatment is rooted in the legacy of slavery. Farm work and domestic work had been the work of slaves, so when labor laws were passed in the 1930s, southern members of Congress refused to sign on to the labor package of the New Deal if farmworkers and domestic workers—who at the time were largely African Americans—were included. In the deal that Congress struck, those two workforces were excluded.[4]

This exclusion left domestic workers in isolation. In recent years, there have been notable improvements in labor laws, as well as efforts to organize domestic workers. In 2007 Ai-Jen Poo was among the group who founded the National Domestic Workers Alliance (NDWA) to support and organize what she calls "the nearly invisible workforce employed inside homes across America."[5] Despite these positive steps forward, and others described below, domestic workers continue to be isolated, vulnerable, underpaid, and underappreciated.

In addition to traditional labor unions, two other models are emerging to give much needed empowerment to privately hired independent cleaners and caregivers. The cooperative movement and the digital age enable these individuals the ability to organize and to have greater control over their employment. As described in journalist Alissa Quart's *Squeezed: Why Our Families Can't Afford America*, the cooperative movement is a counterbalance to the "Uber-ization" of employment in which workers are forced to shift from an employment model to a gig economy. The latter does not include protections like minimum salaries or benefits such as health care. Pointing out that since 2000 over 150 new worker-owned co-ops have been created, Quart highlights the Brooklyn, New York–based Beyond Care Childcare Cooperative, which is run by the nannies with support from Cooperative Development Program at the Center for Family Life.[6] Representing the positive impact of the digital age on employment, the well-known platform Care.com, which connects caregivers to employers, is not a cooperative. However, this for-profit web-based platform partners with the nonprofit Who Cares Coalition to advocate for caregiver rights, as well as transparency between employers and employees.[7] When you hire a caregiver or any other type of household help, it is important to consider the mode by which you connect to your future employee and how it impacts them.

Home employment, by its very nature, is extremely intimate. We are inviting another person into our private space, often to do the most trusted of tasks: help raise our children or care for our parents in our absence. Since ancient times, those employed by families have completed very personal responsibilities, from Abraham's servant securing Isaac's future wife (Genesis 24) to Rebekah's former wet nurse who accompanies her into her new life with Isaac (Gen. 24:59) to the later example of Rabbi Yehudah HaNasi's maid who recognizes it was time for him to die (BT *K'tubot* 104a). As much as we need to be able to trust those we invite to work in our homes, we must recognize the great confidence the employee places in us to treat them with respect and to ensure their safety as they enter our homes, isolated behind closed doors.

Protecting our employees' physical safety by upholding the Jewish value of *pikuach nefesh*, literally "saving a life," broadly applied to mean avoiding endangerment of a person's health or safety, is primary. For example, this value directs us to ensure our employees' health by outfitting them with the appropriate safety precautions, like good-quality gloves and masks when they are caring for the sick or infirm and safe cleaning products and proper ventilation when they are cleaning our homes. Creating a reasonable list of responsibilities for an employee is also part of protecting their health. In describing how the Egyptian's embittered the Israelite slaves' lives, one midrash describes the young adult Moses coming to an awareness of his people's servitude, for the Egyptian slave masters "had put a heavy burden on a small person and a light burden on a large person; a man's burden on a woman and women's burden on a man" (*Sh'mot Rabbah* 1:27). We can learn from this extreme example the importance of gauging our employees' workload appropriately. For example, we should not expect a single caregiver to lift a large person without the appropriate apparatus to do it safely. The moral imperative of *pikuach nefesh* should also extend beyond the borders of our homes. For example, if the employment involves working at odd hours, we must consider if the employee will have a safe method to get home. If the answer is no, then you, the employer, should provide cab money as part of the compensation.

Not only must the family employer be reasonable in the expectations of an employee's responsibilities and the task performed, but we must also be judicious in the hours of employment. As described by the

Talmud, commenting on Deuteronomy 24:15, workers may be willing to take jobs with dangerous tasks because they need the money desperately (BT *Bava M'tzia* 112a). We should also be aware that such need disempowers the employee from objecting when the family employer lengthens or switches work hours. Sometimes we unwittingly replicate the worst of corporate practices when we are family employers. Recently, major corporations have been using "just-in-time" scheduling, an erratic method that gives the minimum-wage employee little notice of, pattern for, or control over work hours. While both worker objection and government employment laws have been fighting this inhumane method of scheduling, it leaves a societal expectation that workers will be available as needed, with little notice and little choice.[8] In some ways, this is a modern problem, facilitated by computer algorithms creating workers' schedules to ensure the employer the largest profit margin possible. However, deviating from the set expectation for a worker's hours is also an ancient issue discussed in the Talmud, which warns against hiring workers and then instructing them to work earlier or later than the local custom. The Talmud also warns against giving employees a raise and then demanding they work beyond their regular work hours. Instead, the Talmud teaches that the extra money is for the quality of work, unless it is clearly stated when the extra money is given that the expectation is that the worker will stay outside of the regular workday (BT *Bava M'tzia* 83a). The family employer must be clear about work hours and responsibilities. Changes must be done in a timely manner, only with the worker's fullest consent and with the appropriate compensation.

Pikuach nefesh should also lead the family employer to help full-time (and perhaps, in part, for limited-service employees) employees obtain health insurance and to include paid sick days. While concern for your employee's health should be the motivating force behind these benefits, they also protect the employer by helping the employee to be healthy and to stay at home when sick. Full-time caregivers employed by agencies are more likely have employer-provided health insurance, with one in four receiving this benefit. Only one in five caregivers receive health insurance when privately employed.[9] Pension also falls under the category of *pikuach nefesh*, as this financial safety net can make a huge difference in the quality of life one has in retirement. Unfortunately, among privately employed caregivers, only one in ten participates in an employer pension plan.[10]

As explored elsewhere in this book, consideration for one's household employees is native to Judaism, starting with the Ten Commandments, "Six days you shall labor and do all your work, but the seventh day is a Sabbath of the Eternal your God: you shall not do any work—you, your son or daughter, your male or female slave, or your cattle, or the stranger who is within your settlements" (Exod. 20:9–10). Here resting from work is a privilege extended to all within the household. In the modern setting, this should be applied to Jewish employees by not expecting them to work on Shabbat or Jewish holidays, and in addition, the family employer should facilitate time off for any employee's religious observance, being aware of others' holy day calendars.

Paying a worker on time is highlighted in the Holiness Code, in Leviticus 19:13, "The wages of a laborer shall not remain with you until morning," and in the related text of Deuteronomy 24:15, "You must pay out the wages due on the same day, before the sun sets, for the worker is needy and urgently depends on it; else he will cry to the Eternal will be issued against you and you will incur guilt." The law to pay the worker on the same day is explored and expanded in the Babylonian Talmud (*Bava M'tzia* 111a–113a).[11] The family employer should not only pay the employee promptly at the proper time, but should also consider the best method of payment so that the employee does not incur high fees to access the money. As the Torah emphasizes, the employee depends on this money. Unfortunately, many domestic workers are the working poor. With, for example, 40 percent of caregivers working less than full time,[12] the family employee may live gig to gig, without even the security of a regular paycheck. Your employee may not have a regular bank account,[13] a privilege many of us take for granted. If you provide payment in the form of a check, your employee may have to use a check-cashing service, which can charge exploitive fees as high as eight dollars per check.[14]

Because of the intimate relationship between employer and employee in the household, the family employer may become aware of financial struggles plaguing the employee. Therefore, the employer may want to support the worker with offerings of *tzedakah*, either in the form of material items or money. As Rabbi Ruth Adar discusses (see p. 90 in this book), Maimonides teaches that the poor of one's own household are a priority for *tzedakah* giving.[15] However, it is vital not to confuse *tzedakah* for paying a living wage. Giving an employee *tzedakah*, either directly or indirectly in the form of a gift or interest-free loan (as Maimonides instructs for cases in which giving *tzedakah* directly may cause embarrassment),[16] must stay in the realm of *tzedakah* and not be mistaken for appropriate compensation or a raise.

The people we employ in our households do vital work, allowing many of us to go to our own places of employment without worry or have tasks performed without concern. We entrust these employees with our most precious beloveds, our children and our parents; we give them our keys and access to our material possessions. Working in our homes, these employees deserve safe work conditions, a living wage, the assurance of health insurance and retirement benefits, and control over their work hours. We, the family employer, must see our homes as their place of employment, ensuring these basic rights.

NOTES

1. Kim Parker, "Despite Progress, Women Still Bear Heavier Load Than Men in Balancing Work and Family," Pew Research Center, March 10, 2015, http://www.pewresearch.org/fact-tank/2015/03/10/women-still-bear-heavier-load-than-men-balancing-work-family/.

2. Ai-Jen Poo, *The Age of Dignity: Preparing for the Elder Boom in a Changing America* (New York: New Press, 2015), 82.

3. Sociologist Mary Romero writes extensively about the fiction created when referring to domestic workers as family. See especially Mary Romero, *Maid in the U.S.A.* (New York: Routledge, 2002), 7–8.

4. Poo, *The Age of Dignity*, 88–89.

5. Poo, *The Age of Dignity*, 5.

6. Alissa Quart, *Squeezed: Why Our Families Can't Afford America* (New York: Ecco, 2018), 158–59.

7. Quart, *Squeezed*, 254; Who Cares Coalition, http://whocares.org/.

8. Quart, *Squeezed*, 70–71.

9. Poo, *The Age of Dignity*, 86.

10. Poo, *The Age of Dignity*, 86.

11. Rabbi Jill Jacobs discusses these laws in greater depth in her chapter (p. 223) and connects them to the concept of a living wage.

12. Poo, *The Age of Dignity*, 87.

13. According to the FDIC, 7 percent of Americans are considered to be "unbanked," meaning they do not have access to banking services, but 19.9 percent of Americans are "underbanked," meaning they have a bank account but still elect to use services like check cashing, money transfers, payday loans, and pawnshops. All of these services are very expensive to use. Madeline Farber, "The Percentage of Americans without Bank Accounts Is Declining," *Fortune*, September 8, 2016, http://fortune.com/2016/09/08/unbanked-americans-fdic/.

14. David Lazarus, "Banks Greed on Full Display with Check-Cashing Fee for Non-customers," *Los Angeles Times*, July 21, 2017, http://www.latimes.com/business/lazarus/la-fi-lazarus-bank-check-cashing-fees-20170721-story.html.

15. Maimonides, *Mishneh Torah, Hilchot Mat'not Aniyim* 7:13.

16. Maimonides, *Mishneh Torah, Mat'not Aniyim* 7:9.

19

WHAT IS POSSIBLE

Striving for Gender Pay Equity
for Congregational Employees

RABBI ESTHER L. LEDERMAN AND AMY ASIN

Our tradition differentiates between *olam hazeh* and *olam haba*, "this world" and "the world-to-come." *This* world seems obvious—the living, breathing, messy lives we inhabit. The world-*to-come*—generations upon generations of Jewish scholars and thinkers have postulated what that world-to-come will be: resurrection, a return to the Land of Israel, the messianic era.

Parker Palmer, scholar, thinker, teacher, and activist, developed a similar binary to describe the world—the binary of the hard realities and what we know is possible. More important is his conception that we must live in the "tragic gap" between reality and the possibility to make changes.[1]

It is in this gap that we exist today concerning pay equity in our Reform Movement. We know achieving fair and equitable pay for our male and female professional employees is possible. Although the overall numbers from the 2016–17 CCAR salary study show that there is indeed a pay gap between male and female rabbis, there are pockets of equity. For example, female senior rabbis of the URJ's largest congregations (with more than eight hundred households) are paid just over 95 percent of what their male colleagues make.[2]

And yet, the reality for the vast majority of our male and female Jewish professionals and clergy is different. Female rabbis in senior or solo positions in congregations with fewer than six hundred households make about 90 percent of what their male colleagues are paid.[3] Starting salaries for newly ordained rabbis in assistant positions are more equitable between men and women. By the time a woman is an associate rabbi, the salary difference can range between 82 and 103 percent.

Similar data exists for women in other synagogue positions—cantors, executive directors, and educators. Salary survey data from NATA, the National Association for Temple Administrators, shows that, overall, female executive directors and temple administrators earn 82 percent of the average salary of males. And yet, the survey also shows progress, part of what Palmer referred to as the "what we know is possible." The data shows less of a gap for newer hires compared to tenured executive directors. Female directors with fewer than three years at their current congregation earned 102 percent of what their male counterparts earned. In addition, females with an MBA or other master's degree showed the smallest gender gap in pay.[4]

Let us return for a moment to Palmer's tragic gap—to living in the space between what we know is possible and where things are. Palmer encourages all of us to live in that gap and not to choose a side—either the cold hard facts of reality that lead us down the road to corrosive cynicism or the world of "wouldn't it be nice if," which he refers to as irrelevant idealism.[5] Many of our congregations are financially strained. When we speak to our congregational leaders and we ask about challenges, budget constraints are often at the top of the list. We cannot ignore that real challenge. Yet, congregations are built with the mission of fixing our broken world, including the broken parts in our own system, and modeling just practices. Therefore, we need to wrestle with the challenge that running a congregation is costly, while at the same time recognizing we should not declare "we can't afford it" when the wage gap is unfair and unjust. We need the courage and patience to really wrestle with this challenge. Part of the world that needs to be repaired is our own internal congregational world.

Before we address the best practices to help achieve pay equity in congregational life, let us first address a necessary ingredient to the successful foundation of all congregations: sacred partnership.

Sacred Partnerships

At the Union for Reform Judaism, we spend an incredible amount of time speaking about the sacred partnership between professional staff and lay leaders. It is the very foundation by which our congregations achieve their mission and purpose. There is almost nothing our congregations can achieve without recognizing how valuable this partnership and connection is. Some of our congregations do this extremely well, and some are still challenged by this concept.

In a congregation with a healthy degree of sacred partnership, contract negotiations are more likely to be defined by trust, open dialogue, and a desire to make each partner feel good about the end result. These are the congregations that have a deep understanding of the *b'rit*, the covenant, between the congregation and its clergy and professional staff. They understand that this is much more than an employee contract. In the clergy and staff, they see the individual who buried their parent, who held them when their child was sick, who prepared their child for a bat mitzvah, or who introduced Jewish summer camp to their kids. And for the clergy and professional staff, they don't necessarily see the board as an employer but as partners in a sacred relationship, as a group of people who strive to build the kind of institution that brings compassion, justice, and wholeness to the world.

Unfortunately, there are some congregations that see the position of rabbi or cantor, or any other staff, as just a job that needs filling. There is no sense of covenant or trust. The worst practices from the business world, particularly as it relates to employment, are borrowed. Comments such as "If the rabbi doesn't do what we want him or her to do, then we can always get another rabbi" are heard. Thankfully, the vast majority of our congregations are unlike this. However, it is important to recognize that we will not be able to close the gap on pay equity in our congregations if we don't recognize the sacred partnerships that make our congregations unique places of employment.

What can we do in congregations to get closer to pay equity? There are a number of best principles and concrete steps that can be taken. Let us begin with the principle of transparency.

Transparency

Transparency is important for everyone who has a stake in reaching pay equity in the Reform Movement, both for congregational leaders who make hiring decisions and clergy and other professionals who work in our institutions. Something is transparent when it is easy to perceive or detect. Key to success is transparency around salary and accompanying benefits.

When a congregation advertises a position for a cantor, rabbi, educator, or other professional staff, it is important that from the moment the job is posted, a specific salary amount and benefits are included. Words like "competitive" or "commensurate with experience" are not helpful. If we want to try to end the pay inequity in our movement, it is important that candidates know the starting salary for the position. One central reason this is important is that it prevents the candidate from having to ask early on in the interview process, which for women is harder and comes across as more aggressive than when a man asks. In addition, leaders in the field of pay equity, such as the National Women's Law Center, have argued that if negotiating for salary and benefits is acceptable, employers should make that explicit in the job description and/or at the point of a job offer. This will both increase the likelihood that a woman will negotiate and will also reduce the stigma often placed on women for engaging in such behavior.[6]

It is also important that synagogue professionals get to a place of trust and transparency with one another where they can share with each other what they make, in confidence. When a female candidate is trying to figure out what the standard salary should be for a particular position in a particular size congregation, it is critically important that she learn what her male colleagues are making, not just her female colleagues. If she learns only what her female colleagues are making, she may have a depressed baseline, as we know that women, on average, make less than their male counterparts.

As part of the effort at transparency, it is important that each of the respective professional associations continue to provide timely salary studies or surveys and that these be shared equally with congregational leaders and professionals. Crucial to these studies and surveys is being able to see the difference in pay scales for men and women in different size congregations.

Implicit Bias Awareness

All of us have implicit bias. How do we define it? The following definition is taken from the Perception Institute:

> Thoughts and feelings are "implicit" if we are unaware of them or mistaken about their nature. We have a bias when, rather than being neutral, we have a preference for (or aversion to) a person or group of people. Thus, we use the term "implicit bias" to describe when we have attitudes towards people or associate stereotypes with them without our conscious knowledge.[7]

Many of us, irrespective of our gender, have implicit gender bias. Having a female chair of the search committee or having women on the committee does not end implicit gender bias against women. It is crucial that the individuals who are involved in hiring professionals in our congregations and movement institutions receive implicit bias training.

The challenge with implicit bias is that it is *not* explicit. Bias is not the same as misogyny or racism. Implicit bias training helps us to become more of aware of the stereotypes and prejudices we all have, even though we may not be aware of them.

Project Implicit, out of Harvard University, offers implicit bias tests around many categories, including gender-career.[8] We invite everyone, search committees and candidates themselves, to take the ten-minute test and engage in some self-reflection on the results. It is important to note that the results do not label individuals as bad people; rather they help identify how our actions may be affected by societally held biases.

One of the suggested strategies to erase implicit gender bias in the workplace is to remove the name and identifying gender markers from resumes.[9] This has not yet been attempted through our respective professional associations such as the Central Conference of American Rabbis (CCAR), the National Association for Temple Administration (NATA), the Early Childhood Educators of Reform Judaism (ECE-RJ), or the Association of Reform Judaism Educators (ARJE), although it has been suggested.[10] This would allow search committees to judge resumes based on experience and ensure that callbacks are not influenced by a gender lens. Another option might be to have search committees commit to looking at a certain number of candidates from each gender. Although congregations cannot control who applies for the job, they can control how many women they choose to interview, both during first rounds and callbacks, based on who submits resumes.

Negotiations

According to the National Women's Law Center:

> Using negotiation to set compensation can lead to gender wage gaps. Women are less likely to negotiate their salaries than men, and in many instances, that may be for good reason. Indeed, studies show that employers react more favorably to men who negotiate salaries, while women who negotiate may be perceived negatively and penalized for violating gender stereotypes.[11]

In an excerpt from her book *Lean In: Women, Work and the Will to Lead*, Sheryl Sandberg writes on the different ways men and women are perceived when they negotiate:

There is little downside when men negotiate for themselves. People expect men to advocate on their own behalf, point out their contributions, and be recognized and rewarded for them. For men, there is truly no harm in asking. But since women are expected to be concerned with others, when they advocate for themselves or point to their own value, both men and women react unfavorably. Interestingly, women can negotiate as well as or even more successfully than men when negotiating for others . . . because in these cases, their advocacy does not make them appear self-serving. However, when a woman negotiates on her own behalf, she violates the perceived gender norm.[12]

This plays out constantly in our congregational environment. A number of female clergy have shared that when they tried negotiating for salary or benefits, they were viewed as "aggressive and greedy" or "unladylike."[13] Women have been told they don't need to be paid as much nor do they need health insurance, since their husbands work. Some have been told "it's unbecoming of you to ask." If women in general violate the gender norm by negotiating, women clergy do so in particular, as clergy are viewed as serving, selfless beings.

Research has shown that when women do choose to negotiate, they need to negotiate differently than men.[14] It is critical that we provide negotiation training for our female clergy and professionals, either through Hebrew Union College–Jewish Institute of Religion or through our respective professional organizations. At the 2017 URJ Biennial in Boston, the Reform Pay Equity Initiative (RPEI), led by Women of Reform Judaism and the Women's Rabbinic Network, sponsored a workshop on negotiation skills for women that was very well attended. There is a critical need for this type of continuing education. One workshop will not be enough.

As stated earlier, it could have an impact on how women are perceived in congregations if negotiating was explicitly encouraged. If the terms of employment, both salaries and benefits, were viewed by the search committee as an opening offer, then perhaps women won't be viewed so negatively when they do ask for more.

Paid Family Leave

We could have called this section "maternity leave," but that language creates a false narrative about the reality of life. *Family* leave acknowledges that at some point in our working years, each of us will likely need to take some protected time off to care for a child, a dying parent, or an ill spouse, irrespective of our gender. Paid family leave is built on the notion that none of us should have to risk our jobs or lose money to do that.

We must stop seeing paid family leave as a luxury or benefit that only women need. As a movement, we must push our society to a place where this is a non-negotiable—dare we say a right—that every working member of society should have.

In the Ten Commandments, the fifth commandment is "honor your father and your mother" (Exod. 20:12). What kind of honor is it we give to parents when we require them to negotiate for time off to take care of the most vulnerable—babies, the sick, and the dying? It is a Jewish value to care for our parents and children.

We realize that expecting every congregation and institution in our movement to change its policy immediately will be a little like waiting for *olam haba*, the world-to-come. In the meantime, we would like to suggest the following strategies that will help.

If it becomes standard for every male professional in our congregations to ask for paid family leave, even if they don't anticipate using it, then it will be more likely that this will become a norm across the Reform Movement. Remember that when men negotiate, they are not penalized the way women often are, and they are often granted their request. In addition, when a male professional has successfully asked for paid family leave and then leaves the position, he has paved the way for a female professional who succeeds him to gain the same benefit without having to ask for it. Clearly, each individual has to assess the situation for himself, and each situation is unique. We encourage our male professionals to ask themselves if this is something they can do in their next contract or annual review.

Some senior rabbis, particularly senior male clergy, are well positioned to advocate for paid family leave for the employees they supervise. In those situations where the senior rabbi has the relationships, the trust, and the clout with the board, he or she can be quite successful in advocating for fair compensation packages for female employees, with a particular focus on equity in the field.

It must be stated that it is impossible to discuss the issue of paid family leave without acknowledging the gap between what we provide for our senior professional staff and what we offer our administrative and support staff. We will not have achieved full pay equity until such a time as our congregations and movement institutions live up to the standard that we have argued for in the greater society. In 2015, the URJ passed a resolution in support of paid family leave, stating that "the Union for Reform Judaism . . . urges our congregations and all arms of the Reform Movement to provide, to the extent feasible, paid family and medical leave for their employees, and set an example for their communities."[15] Indeed the URJ's own policy is to offer up to eight weeks of paid family leave for its full-time employees in the United States, plus an additional 4.6 weeks of paid sick leave, thus satisfying family advocacy groups and the CCAR's recommendation of a minimum of 12 weeks paid leave. It is time that the gap between what we believe and what we practice is closed.

Motherhood Penalty

One of the key challenges that affects the wage gap in society in general is what is known as the "motherhood penalty." This term has become such a known entity that it has its own Wikipedia entry.[16] The term was coined by sociologists to name the phenomenon that working mothers are paid less than working fathers, as well as less than working non-mothers. The American Association of University Women (AAUW) states that it typically takes working mothers five extra months to be paid what working fathers are paid in just one year.[17]

This impacts mothers not only in the private and public sector, but in our congregations as well. When female staff raise the subject of family leave, especially when negotiating a first contract, eyebrows get raised and comments such as "Is there something you aren't telling us?" or "Are you planning on getting pregnant?" are often heard across the table.[18] Congregations are concerned when hiring female clergy or professionals that they will take time off to have kids—a question that rarely is raised when men are being considered.

According to a recent *New York Times* article, entitled "Children Hurt Women's Earnings, but Not Men's (Even in Scandinavia)," changes in the behavior of fathers is key to having an impact:

> There is evidence that the gap would shrink if fathers acted more the way mothers do after having children, by spending more time on parenting and the related responsibilities. "At the very least, men have to take a larger role," said Francine Blau, an economist at Cornell who has studied the gender pay gap and family-friendly policies in the United States and Europe. "It does become a distinction in the eyes of employers between potential male and female workers, and it may reinforce traditional gender roles." . . .
>
> "If you know that both men and women will go off and take care of children, not just women, what that does is remove the motherhood penalty," said Heejung Chang, a sociologist at the University of Kent. [19]

Some Remaining Dos and Don'ts

Lastly, we want to provide some final helpful tips, particularly for congregations beginning to think about their next hire.

There are a number of questions to avoid when interviewing candidates, particularly as they contradict recommended hiring procedures of the Reform Movement. Types of questions to avoid including asking about the candidate's age, family make-up and family plans, whether the candidate is pregnant, what the spouse does for a living, as well as salary history.

Why is asking about salary history particularly challenging? Given that most women applying for new jobs are already at a salary disadvantage as compared to male candidates, learning their salary history generally only perpetuates the pay inequity between men and women. Congregations should not set the salary for jobs based on what the person earned previously.

In addition, asking a job candidate about previous earnings has recently become illegal in a number of states and cities across the United States. In April 2018, the United States Court of Appeals for the Ninth Circuit declared it illegal to pay a woman less than a man based on her prior salary.[20] It is important that we note, however, that most religious institutions, including URJ congregations, are exempt from such labor laws. Yet, our stance as a movement compels us to engage in the best practices that will further reduce the gender gap in pay in our Reform institutions.

Don't offer a higher salary at the expense of offering paid family leave. Neither should family leave be used as an excuse to lower a woman's pay compared to anyone else's salary.

Don't begin by deciding if you want to hire a man or a woman. Decide upon the qualities you want. In addition, don't assume that a woman will be good with families because she is assumed to be more maternal or that a man will be a better visionary or scholar. Stereotypes, as implicit bias tests show, are hard to shake.

Final Thoughts

It is not all bad news. The data from the 2016–17 CCAR salary study shows that for some categories the pay gap between men and women has improved slightly since the last salary study in 2012. Similar results are evident in the NATA salary survey. We as a movement have made strides in this arena. It is now time to commit ourselves even more to addressing this challenge.

And let us remember what the Mishnah comes to teach: *Lo alecha ham'lachah ligmor v'lo atah ben chorin l'hibateil mimenah*, "It is not incumbent upon us to complete the work, but neither are we free to desist from it" (*Pirkei Avot* 2:21). Let us continue to live in the tragic gap between the hard reality of the world and what we know is possible. We likely will not reach *olam haba* anytime soon, but that doesn't mean we can't try to create a more equitable, fair, and just situation for the clergy and professionals of our congregations.

NOTES

1. Alicia von Stamwitz, "If Only We Would Listen: Parker J. Palmer on What We Could Learn about Politics, Faith, and Each Other," *The Sun*, November 2012, https://www.thesunmagazine.org/issues/443/ if-only-we-would-listen.
2. "2016–2017 Study of Rabbinic Compensation," Central Conference of American Rabbis and Union for Reform Judaism, June 2017, http://www. ccarnet.org/wp-content/uploads/2017/09/2016-2017_salary_study_.pdf.
3. "2016–2017 Study of Rabbinic Compensation."
4. "2016–2017 Study of Rabbinic Compensation."
5. Stamwitz, "If Only We Would Listen."
6. "Advancing Equal Pay: Innovative Employer Approaches," National Women's Law Center, June 2016, https://nwlc-ciw49tixgw5lbab.stack-pathdns.com/wp-content/uploads/2016/06/Advancing-Equal-Pay-Innovative-Employer-Approaches-1.pdf.
7. "Implicit Bias," Perception Institute, accessed September 21, 2018, https://perception.org/research/implicit-bias/.
8. Project Implicit, accessed September 21, 2018, https://implicit.harvard. edu/implicit/takeatest.html.
9. Rebecca Knight, "7 Practical Ways to Reduce Bias in Your Hiring Process," *Harvard Business Review*, June 12, 2017, https://hbr. org/2017/06/7-practical-ways-to-reduce-bias-in-your-hiring-process.
10. "Best Practices," Women of Reform Judaism, accessed September 21, 2018, https://wrj.org/best-practices.
11. "Advancing Equal Pay: Innovative Employer Approaches," National Women's Law Center, June 10, 2016, https://nwlc.org/resources/ advancing-equal-pay-innovative-employer-approaches/.

12. Sheryl Sandberg, *Lean In: Women, Work, and the Will to Lead* (New York: Knopf, 2013), 45–56.

13. Taken from individual correspondence with female clergy via e-mail and private conversations.

14. For more information on the unique challenges women face when negotiating, please see Linda Babcock and Sara Laschever, *Women Don't Ask: The High Cost of Avoiding Negotiation and Positive Strategies for Change* (New York: Bantam Dell, 2007).

15. "Resolution in Support of Paid Family Leave," Union for Reform Judaism, adopted 2015, https://urj.org/what-we-believe/resolutions/resolution-support-paid-family-leave.

16. "Motherhood Penalty," Wikipedia, last edited July 21, 2018, https://en.wikipedia.org/wiki/Motherhood_penalty.

17. Amy Becker, "At Work, Dads Get a Bonus, but Moms Get a Penalty. What Gives?," AAUW, May 6, 2016, https://www.aauw.org/2016/05/06/dads-get-a-bonus-but-moms-get-a-penalty/.

18. These comments come from one of the authors' personal experiences as well as comments made by female clergy in private conversations.

19. Claire Cain Miller, "Children Hurt Women's Earnings, but Not Men's (Even in Scandinavia)," The Upshot, *New York Times*, February 5, 2018, https://www.nytimes.com/2018/02/05/upshot/even-in-family-friendly-scandinavia-mothers-are-paid-less.html?rref=collection%2Fsectioncollection%2Fbusiness&action=click&contentCollection=business&region=stream&module=stream_unit&version=latest&contentPlacement=18&pgtype=sectionfront.

20. Maura Dolan, "Prior Salary Can't Justify Wage Gap between Men and Women, U.S. Appeals Court Rules," *Los Angeles Times*, April 9, 2018, http://www.latimes.com/local/lanow/la-me-ln-equal-pay-9th-circuit-20180409-story.html.

20

BREAD AND ROSES

Jewish Women Transform
the American Labor Movement

Judith Rosenbaum, PhD

The American labor movement was shaped by the activism of immigrant workers, and few played as prominent a role as the young Jewish women who worked in the garment industry of the early twentieth century. We recall few of their names despite that—as scholar Alice Kessler-Harris has written—"in early twentieth-century New York, Philadelphia, Boston, and other large cities, only the exceptional unmarried woman did not operate a sewing machine in a garment factory for part of her young adult life."[1]

At the turn of the twentieth century, a perfect storm of Jewish mass immigration and the growth of the garment industry resulted in unprecedented opportunities for work—and for unionization. This was particularly true for young Jewish women, who in American immigrant families were an essential part of the family economy. With many jobs available for young women who could sew, they worked to help pay the rent, to buy groceries, to keep their brothers in school, to support relatives back in Europe, or to bring relatives to America. Though most women stopped working in garment factories when they married, they often remained part of the garment industry by bringing home piecework.[2]

Working conditions in sweatshops and garment factories at the turn of the twentieth century were dangerous and demeaning at best. Garment industry laborers regularly worked fourteen-hour days, six days a week, and hours could be added on Sundays during peak work seasons. There was neither a minimum wage nor overtime pay, and girls and women were regularly paid less than boys and men for doing the same jobs. Wages were deducted for late arrival, broken machinery, going to the bathroom without permission, not completing enough work in the time allotted even when workers were forced to keep a break-neck pace, and for other reasons beyond the control of the worker. Despite their meager wages, workers often had to provide their own machinery and supplies (such as thread). With few child labor laws and minimal enforcement of those that did exist, children as young as six years old could be found snipping loose threads and sewing labels into finished garments. Lighting and sanitation were poor. The heat was unbearable in the summer, and the shops and factories were freezing in the winter. Exits were locked. The noise was deafening. Sexual abuse was common but rarely reported and even more rarely punished.[3]

To Jewish immigrants who had come to America seeking greater freedom and opportunity, the oppression they experienced in the workplace felt reminiscent of the political oppression that had inspired their families to leave Europe. For some, it also echoed their collective memory of the history of Jewish oppression. Still, they believed in the promise of America and the possibility of holding America to that promise. Labor activism—already familiar to many from the radical political movements they had encountered and in some cases led in Europe—was a natural and obvious channel for their commitment to social change.

Though Jewish men readily found a place for themselves within trade unionism, the labor movement did not immediately recognize the potential of working women and their commitment to the garment industry—and therefore to improving its conditions—and dismissed them as capable union members. It took the tireless work and brave activism of leaders like Pauline Newman, Clara Lemlich Shavelson,

Rose Schneiderman, Bessie Abramowitz Hillman, and Rose Pesotta—and tens of thousands of their fellow workers—to prove otherwise.[4]

Pauline Newman began working in a hairbrush factory at age nine and by eleven was at the notorious Triangle Shirtwaist factory. In 1907, at age sixteen, she helped organize a major rent strike by applying principles of union organizing to women's neighborhood networks. In recognition of her prominent role in organizing the garment industry strikes of 1909–10, she was appointed the first female general organizer of the International Ladies Garment Workers Union (ILGWU), and she continued to work for the ILGWU for more than seventy years. In 1913, after the Triangle fire, Newman worked to improve factory safety standards by serving on the Joint Board of Sanitary Control. A vice president of the National Women's Trade Union League as well as a board member for various U.S. and UN committees on labor, Pauline, along with her partner Frieda Miller, was also part of Eleanor Roosevelt's inner circle.[5]

Clara Lemlich Shavelson began organizing women for the ILGWU in 1905, insisting that the union could not succeed without women workers. Her fiery oratory, building on her years of organizing, helped spark the "Uprising of the 20,000," the largest strike by women workers to that date. After the strike, she was blacklisted from factory work, but she continued to organize, first for the suffrage movement and then organizing housewives around cost-of-living issues, such as the 1917 kosher meat boycott and the 1919 rent strike movement. In 1929, she helped create what became the Progressive Women's Councils, running anti-eviction demonstrations, marches on Washington, and a meat boycott that shut down forty-five hundred butcher shops in New York. Shavelson remained a devoted activist into her final years, even organizing the orderlies at her nursing home.[6]

Rose Schneiderman went to work at thirteen and began her career as a labor organizer at twenty-one. The first paid organizer of the Women's Trade Union League (WTUL), she helped organize the Uprising of the 20,000 for the ILGWU in 1909. She went on to become NYWTUL president in 1917 and president of the national

WTUL in 1926. She also fought for women's suffrage and ran for the United States Senate as a Labor Party candidate in 1920. Her friendship with Eleanor Roosevelt and their conversations on labor issues led to Schneiderman's appointment to the National Labor Advisory Board in 1933, where—as the only woman on the board—she fought to include domestic workers in social security and argued for equal pay for women workers.[7]

From age fifteen on, Bessie Abramowitz's life centered around the fight for workers' rights. She even announced her engagement on a picket line! After immigrating to Chicago alone as a teen, Abramowitz found work sewing buttons in a garment factory while attending night school at the famous Hull House settlement house. She led walkouts over pay cuts and poor conditions, inspiring her future husband Sidney Hillman to become a striker and labor leader himself. Abramowitz organized workers for the WTUL before becoming education director of the Laundry Workers Joint Board in 1937. Through Laundry Workers, which had many non-white workers, Abramowitz became involved in civil rights issues. She also served on the Child Welfare Committee of New York, the Defense Advisory Commission on Women in the Services, and President Kennedy's Commission on the Status of Women.[8]

Rose Pesotta was known for her ability to organize workers across gender and ethnic lines. Pesotta, an anarchist, immigrated to America in 1913 rather than marry. She began factory work and joined the ILGWU, creating their first education department in 1915 and, in 1920, joining the ILGWU Local 25's executive board. She received further training at the Bryn Mawr Summer School for Workers and Brookwood Labor College. In 1933, she spearheaded the Dressmakers General Strike in Los Angeles, mobilizing the Mexican workforce through Spanish-language radio and newspaper ads. She served as vice president of the ILGWU from 1934 to 1942, ultimately resigning to call attention to the absence of female leadership in an organization whose membership was 85 percent female. In her eight years of ILGWU leadership, she mobilized workers in places as diverse as

Puerto Rico, Detroit, Boston, Montreal, and Salt Lake City, among others.[9]

All these women (except Pesotta, who had not yet arrived in the United States) helped lay the groundwork for the turning point that transformed the labor movement and the place of women within it. The Uprising of the 20,000—as the major strike of shirtwaist makers in the winter of 1909–10 is popularly called—was not a spontaneous uprising. Rather, it grew out of years of organizing women in the garment industry.[10] Shirtwaist makers held a series of small strikes throughout the summer and fall of 1909, but by early November, it was unclear if and how the strikes would go forward. ILGWU Local 25—then a small local of only one hundred members—called for a general strike to shut down the entire shirtwaist industry, and on November 22, thousands of garment workers attended a meeting at Cooper Union to discuss this recommendation. After many labor leaders gave speeches lacking in any meaningful suggestions for action, twenty-three-year-old Clara Lemlich, one of the strike leaders, took the stage and delivered a rousing call for a general strike. Her bold words energized the women in the crowd, and they pledged to strike.[11]

The next day, between twenty thousand and forty thousand girls and women working in the six hundred shirtwaist factories in New York City got up from their machines, walked out onto the city's streets, and went on strike. Demanding their rights to better working conditions, better pay, and union membership, they risked their jobs, arrest, and possible deportation, rough physical treatment on the picket line at the hands of thugs hired by their bosses, and in some cases, the disapproval and rejection of their families.

The strike lasted eleven weeks, and while it was not a complete victory, it did win some significant demands. Most of the garment shops agreed to a fifty-two-hour workweek, at least four holidays with pay per year, no charge for tools and materials, no discrimination against union members, and the right for unions to negotiate wages with employers. By the end of the strike, 85 percent of all shirtwaist makers in New York had joined the ILGWU, and Local 25 had grown from one hundred members to more than ten thousand. Perhaps most importantly, the Uprising of the 20,000 demonstrated that women workers could be organized into a powerful force, sparking five years of strikes that turned the garment industry into one of the best-organized trades in the United States. For the young women involved in the strike, it was a powerful experience that proved their worth; many of them considered it one of the defining moments of their lives.[12]

These young strikers—many of them teenagers—not only proved their mettle on the cold and harsh picket lines, but also introduced new ideas into the labor movement. The women expanded their demands beyond the usual calls for higher wages and shorter hours, articulating their right to dignity and respect. This took the form of calling for improvements ranging from sanitation to a recognition of sexual harassment on the job to a hook on which to hang one's cherished hat, bought with pennies saved by skipping lunch for weeks. Their vision of a broader unionism was captured in the concept of "Bread and Roses." Though the origin of the slogan is unclear, it appeared in a 1911 poem by James Oppenheim and was popularized by Jewish labor activist Rose Schneiderman in the context of a women's suffrage campaign in 1912; in later years, it was also applied to a 1912 strike of primarily women workers in Lawrence, Massachusetts.[13]

Schneiderman—who began organizing women workers in 1903, setting much of the groundwork for the women's strikes to come—had learned pragmatism early on and sought support for working women's rights from middle-class women as well as from male unionists. Her conviction that the vote would help working women by giving them the power to improve their conditions through legislative change brought her to the suffrage movement. In speaking to her middle-class suffrage sisters, she articulated a vision of working women's human rights:

> What the woman who labors wants is the right to live, not simply exist—the right to life as the rich woman has the right to life, and the sun and music and art. You have nothing that the humblest

worker has not a right to have also. The worker must have bread, but she must have roses, too.[14]

Though captured in this exchange with middle-class women, the vision represented by "Bread and Roses" also pushed working-class men to expand their goals for the labor movement. In large part due to the contributions and insights of women workers, unions came to understand that they needed to address not only workers' basic needs of higher wages, shorter hours, and safer working conditions, but also the greater human needs for education, community, beauty, and dignity. Women's entry into the unions as members and organizers, and the vision they brought with them, was crucial for the growth and success of the labor movement. The unions not only addressed worker grievances; they tried to support workers in every aspect of their lives, offering educational programs in subjects such as English language, literature, and politics; social and cultural programs such as dances, shows, and concerts; and even opportunities to get out of the city and enjoy vacations in the country at union-run camps.[15]

As the labor movement expanded the range of services it offered workers to encompass education and social life—a trend known as "social unionism"—its role as the primary vehicle of Americanization for immigrant workers became even stronger. Unions helped shape their new American identities, providing a context in which they could connect with fellow workers, learn about the labor movement and other topics, and socialize. With the help of union activities, immigrants learned English, American social customs, fashion, and politics. The labor movement also worked in tandem with and helped strengthen mutual aid societies, such as the Arbeter Ring (the Workmen's Circle). These fraternal clubs offered social and educational programs geared at American Jewish workers, designed to cultivate new ways of being Jewish in America based on leftist politics, commitment to social justice, Yiddish culture, and working-class identity.[16]

Jewish women labor activists also helped the labor movement to recognize the value of legislation and government regulation in improving workers' lives. The Triangle Shirtwaist factory fire in 1911, which resulted in the deaths of 146 workers (mostly Jewish immigrant women between the ages of sixteen and twenty-three), served as a devastating wake-up call to the need for better safety regulations. Galvanized by the tragedy, labor activists and other progressive reformers campaigned for protective legislation to establish industrial safety standards and regulate working conditions. They created state investigative commissions, testified before state legislatures, and helped draft new factory legislation, limiting the number of occupants on each factory floor relative to the dimensions of staircases, prescribing automatic sprinkler systems, and offering new protections for women and children at work. This work also created a springboard for some of the leaders and programs that would take on national significance during Roosevelt's New Deal.[17]

The Depression bolstered union activism in the 1930s and the New Deal—with the help of Jewish labor leaders like Bessie Abramowitz and her husband Sidney Hillman, Rose Schneiderman, Pauline Newman, and Frieda Miller—institutionalized many aspects of social unionism, such as unemployment insurance, health insurance, pensions, and fair labor standards. Jewish women also began to organize in other industries into which Jews were entering during this period, such as teaching, social work, office work, and retail sales.[18]

The decades that followed, however, brought a decline in Jewish labor activism, as the Red Scare and McCarthyism purged unions of those Jews who had been communists or communist sympathizers decades earlier. For women workers, debates over the value of protective legislation, which could function to limit women's access into certain fields or roles, led many women to organize outside of the union, applying their activism instead to the Equal Rights Amendment and other causes.[19]

When Jews shaped the labor movement, they did so primarily as workers themselves, though of course Jews were also represented among the owner and management class. Yet in the mid-twentieth century a significant economic and cultural shift took place in the

American Jewish community. Whereas the majority of Jewish workers until the 1930s and '40s had been skilled and unskilled "blue-collar" laborers, after the 1930s and '40s the majority of Jews became "white-collar," professional workers. While Jews weren't the only immigrant group to experience this shift, it marked a profound change for the American Jewish community. Often within just one generation, the level of education achieved among many Jews, the professional status accessible to them, and the standard of living it afforded Jews as a group increased substantially. Parents who worked in the factories and shops of the Lower East Side saw their children go to college and move into the professional class.[20]

In some fields, becoming white-collar workers meant moving away from the labor movement, with the exceptions of teachers and writers, where Jews remain well-represented among union members and leadership. However, many of the children of union members retained the values about fair treatment of workers that they had learned from their parents.

In twenty-first-century America, Jews fall on all sides of debates about labor and the role of unions. Many still feel a sense of Jewish identification with the labor movement, even if they are not personally involved with it; some advocate specifically as Jews on behalf of oppressed workers today. Others, however, do not feel that the historical relationship between American Jews and the labor movement has any relevance to contemporary labor conditions and to their own position within labor relations. The contraction of the labor movement in the late twentieth and early twenty-first centuries and Jews' distance from their own history as workers and labor activists mean that the Jewish community is increasingly alienated from the significant role Jews played in the shaping of the American labor movement.

This alienation and amnesia represent a missed opportunity for American Jews to comprehend, take pride in, and learn from our impact on America's social movements and policies, to connect and build solidarity with other American immigrant communities who are currently experiencing labor challenges, and to access rich and varied points of connection to American Jewish identity. Without an understanding of our history—in all its complexity, not merely the laudable aspects—we draw on an impoverished picture of what is possible and how change is made. In twenty-first-century America, we can not afford to neglect or discard the riches of our history.

NOTES

1. Alice Kessler-Harris, "Labor Movement in the United States," in *Jewish Women: A Comprehensive Historical Encyclopedia*, Jewish Women's Archive, March 1, 2009, https://jwa.org/encyclopedia/article/labor-movement-in-united-states.
2. Susan A. Glenn, *Daughters of the Shtetl: Life and Labor in the Immigrant Generation* (Ithaca, NY: Cornell University Press, 1990), 63–72.
3. Annelise Orleck, *Common Sense and a Little Fire: Women and Working-Class Politics in the United States, 1900–1965* (Chapel Hill: University of North Carolina Press, 1995), 31–35.
4. Kessler-Harris, "Labor Movement in the United States."
5. Annelise Orleck, "Pauline Newman," in *Jewish Women: A Comprehensive Historical Encyclopedia*, Jewish Women's Archive, March 20, 2009, https://jwa.org/encyclopedia/article/newman-pauline.
6. Annelise Orleck, "Clara Lemlich Shavelson," in *Jewish Women: A Comprehensive Historical Encyclopedia*, Jewish Women's Archive, March 20, 2009 https://jwa.org/encyclopedia/article/shavelson-clara-lemlich.
7. Annelise Orleck, "Rose Schneiderman," in *Jewish Women: A Comprehensive Historical Encyclopedia*, Jewish Women's Archive, March 20, 2009, https://jwa.org/encyclopedia/article/schneiderman-rose.
8. Antonio Ramirez, "Bessie Abramowitz Hillman," in *Jewish Women: A Comprehensive Historical Encyclopedia*, Jewish Women's Archive, March 20, 2009, https://jwa.org/encyclopedia/article/Hillman-Bessie-Abramowitz.
9. Ann Schofield, "Rose Pesotta," in *Jewish Women: A Comprehensive Historical Encyclopedia*, Jewish Women's Archive, March 20, 2009, https://jwa.org/encyclopedia/article/pesotta-rose.
10. Orleck, *Common Sense and a Little Fire*, 60.
11. Tony Michels, "Uprising of 20,000 (1909)," in *Jewish Women: A Comprehensive Historical Encyclopedia*, Jewish Women's Archive, March 20, 2009, https://jwa.org/encyclopedia/article/uprising-of-20000-1909.
12. Michels, "Uprising of 20,000 (1909)."

13. Sarah Eisenstein, *Give Us Bread but Give Us Roses: Working Women's Consciousness in the United States, 1890 to the First World War* (London: Routledge & Kegan Paul, 1983).

14. Eisenstein, *Give Us Bread but Give Us Roses*, 32.

15. Kessler-Harris, "Labor Movement in the United States."

16. Tony Michels, *A Fire in Their Hearts: Yiddish Socialists in New York* (Cambridge, MA: Harvard University Press, 2005), 179.

17. Hadassa Kosak, "Triangle Shirtwaist Fire," in *Jewish Women: A Comprehensive Historical Encyclopedia*, Jewish Women's Archive, March 20, 2009, https://jwa.org/encyclopedia/article/triangle-shirtwaist-fire%20.

18. Kessler-Harris, "Labor Movement in the United States."

19. Kessler-Harris, "Labor Movement in the United States."

20. Henry L. Feingold, *A Time for Searching: Entering the Mainstream, 1920–1945* (Baltimore: Johns Hopkins University Press, 1992), 145, 152.

21

JEWISH VALUES IN THE MARKETPLACE[1]

RABBI ARTHUR GROSS-SCHAEFER, JD, CPA

When we think of the marketplace, whether it be the mall, a local store, or the internet, ethical issues quickly arise in terms of fair pricing, honest representations of merchandise, responsible marketing, fair competition, and reasonable actions by both buyers and sellers. The way one chooses to deal with these complex issues will often depend on the lens used. Many turn to Adam Smith's *The Wealth of Nations* (1776), which established him as the father of free market economics. Simply put, Smith taught that the "invisible hand" of the marketplace will dictate a fair price, allowing buyers and sellers to equally and honestly benefit without government interference. Others may support the need for government regulation, as indicated in Ralph Nader's 1965 book *Unsafe at Any Speed*, a significant work in the development of consumer protection laws. Yet, Jewish tradition has a lot to say about economic theory, as well as the role of buyers and sellers in the marketplace. Many of these detailed ideas come from our first Jewish code, the Mishnah, codified around 200 CE, far in advance of Ralph Nader, or even Adam Smith.

Below is a sampling of several of the Jewish economic and consumer-related concepts that will not only reveal the Rabbis' awareness of these complex business ethics issues, but also illustrate the realistic insights and solutions they provided. Each ancient concept is then applied to modern business scenarios to show the durability of Jewish law.

Profit Limitations on Necessary Items

"One-sixth of the of the purchase price counts as defrauding" (*Mishnah Bava M'tzia* 4:3).[2] Many of us grew up understanding that the free and open marketplace was the best vehicle to determine a fair profit. Adam Smith's idea of the "invisible hand" proposes that the marketplace itself would fairly allow a willing buyer and a willing seller to be able to determine a fair price for a given item. We may therefore be surprised that back in 200 CE there was a concept advanced in the Jewish tradition of a limitation on profits of around 17 percent for primarily consumer goods. The concept of limits on profits in specific situations is a rebuke to the overriding notation of a free market theory of price setting.

We may never know the Rabbis' specific reasons for introducing price limits, but they may have had the same concerns that we still have today about fairness in a free market system. First, there is often an imbalanced amount of power between merchants and consumers. We need only look at secular legal acts such as antitrust laws, initially aimed at stopping monopolistic power with the Sherman Act of 1890 and subsequent legislation. These regulations tried to stop activities that significantly lessened competition or limited profits. For example, after an earthquake, there may be a shortage of wood to cover broken windows. Both Rabbinic law and our secular laws often prevent price gouging in situations in which the consumer is without power because of a crisis.

Second, for markets to be fair, both consumers and merchants must have equal access to information such as price comparisons, product availability, or product options. Individuals with better information may be able to corner the market faster, switch to alternative products, or find the cheapest prices more quickly. Today this is clearly a concern addressed by many of the securities regulations that prevent those who are "insiders" from using their access to information to give them significant advantages in the stock market.

Third, there is a fear that private companies will buy up necessities such as access to water, gas, and electricity. For example, Coca-Cola has acquired significant water rights around the world. Companies who own water rights, such as Coca-Cola, are in very powerful positions to control prices for water and can even set unreasonably high prices, despite water being a necessity. Consumers therefore would have very few options but to pay whatever price is demanded.

The Mishnah uses the word *onaah* to communicate that unfair profits are fraudulent. The word is often translated as "fraud," meaning "unfairness." Jewish law believes it is simply unfair for sellers in certain circumstances to profit more than one-sixth over their costs.

Based on the above discussion of profit limitations, a strong argument for an application of reasonable price limits for today could be used for basic items such as food, clothing, and shelter. For example, reasonable price limits may be needed, as the cost for renting or buying a home is often beyond the financial ability of many consumers. Price limitations may be appropriate to help reduce gouging, deal with unfair marketing tactics, and ensure that basic life needs are readily available to all people. In this approach, one could also suggest that price restrictions would be appropriate for medical care and prescription drugs. Price limitations are not always easy or workable solutions in our complex economies; however, it is significant to note that our ancestors were worried about many of the same issues in terms of pricing that we are facing today.

Not Hiding Old Produce

"Produce may not be mixed together with other produce . . . fresh with old" (*Mishnah Bava M'tzia* 4:11). How many of us have bought a basket of strawberries where the top ones look perfectly bright red, only to find that those at the bottom are squashed, overripe, or sometimes moldy? Certainly not appetizing and very frustrating for the consumer who chose to buy the fruit based on the appearance of the top, visible layer. Jewish law from 200 CE questions such practices in which the intent is to deceive the consumer. In effect, the notion of *caveat emptor*, "buyer beware," is precluded. Sometimes buyers are simply unable to fully protect themselves. When you add an app to your computer and click on the box to agree to all the terms, do you fully understand what you may have given up, especially regarding how your personal information will be used? This robust concept, *caveat emptor*, for so much of our secular legal history, required the buyer to check the quality and suitability of goods being purchased. Are we really able to check what rights we are giving up when we download apps or buy a complex product like a car? Recently Volkswagen was caught conduct-ing false testing regarding their diesel engines to fool the regulators and ultimately the consumers. And there have been numerous examples of companies selling dangerous products, such as cigarettes, DDT, and asbestos. In short, the ethical guidelines included in this ancient tradition are quite modern in their outlook and should be taken very seriously. Not only are merchants forbidden to hide bad produce under the guise of good produce, but also the merchant has a duty to disclose the negative effects and dangers of products. This and subsequent *mishnayot* reject the old notion of *caveat emptor* and effectively uphold the concept that sellers must be fair in disclosing information about a product in a manner that consumers understand.

Not Covering Up Old or Damaged Items

"One should not dress up that which one sells" (*Mishnah Bava M'tzia* 4:12). The demise of *caveat emptor* continues with this mishnah passage that instructs one not to paint over used items to make them look new or have cattle drink beer before a potential sale, increasing their weight. Today's consumers may have had the experience of buying a home where cracks in the foundation or in the walls from earthquake damage were covered up and not disclosed. Using deceptive techniques to hide defects was not uncommon in ancient times and is certainly not uncommon today. Clearly, today there are secular laws to help reduce these practices. However, the real objective of our tradition is to reject actions that deceive buyers. Our Jewish tradition provides us with an imperative to let the buyer know what they are getting, so that they have the right and the agency to make fair and informed decisions. Given the growing trend of direct consumer-to-consumer selling through online platforms, it is necessary to apply these Jewish laws to our own practices. When we ourselves are the seller via online platforms, or even the informal yard sale, we must be forthright, telling the potential buyer what we know about our item, especially if the damage is not apparent.

Misrepresenting What You Are Selling

"One [the seller] should not sift them [crushed beans] at the entry of the store" (*Mishnah Bava M'tzia* 4:12). Once again, our ancient tradition takes aim at *caveat emptor* through the deceptive practice of showing one thing and then attempting to sell something very different. Simply put, this mishnah supports the notion, novel for its time and a necessary concept for modernity, that the seller has an ethical duty to be fair and transparent. The example criticized in this mishnah is similar to the tactic customarily known as "bait and switch." This unethical method is generally understood as showing or advertising one's goods with the intent to sell the consumer something else, either an item of less quality or one that is more expensive. To understand the context of this original prohibition, one needs to appreciate that beans were generally grown in sandy soil. So, one could sell beans weighed down with a lot of residual soil or beans that have been cleaned, with minimal sand. No consumer wants to pay for the weight of sand or for beans that have not been cleaned. If the consumer saw sifted beans at the store entrance, the false presumption would be that the beans sold within the store had been cleaned in the same manner.

Many modern consumers have been subject to bait and switch situations. We arrive at a store to get an item on sale only to find that the merchant has "run out" of the sale item and attempts to sell us another, more expensive item in its place. Certainly, a seller may unintentionally run out of a sale item or may try to sell another product better matching the consumer's needs, but this ancient rule was created to stop intentional actions of deception.

Not Nice to Entice Children with Gifts

"A storekeeper may not distribute parched grain or nuts to children" (BT *Bava M'tzia* 4:11). Another approach to getting customers into one's store or making them feel obligated to buy something is to offer their children gifts. This can include having candy or balloons readily available or having some special computer game they can play. In this ancient legal section, the term "parched grain or nuts" is used. Akin to modern popcorn, "parched grain" is believed to have been grain that had been cooked by dry roasting.[3] It was clearly a favorite treat for children, used to draw the youngsters into a store and therefore attract their parents as well. The Rabbis were concerned about using children as bait for selling products to their parents. Today the prohibition can be broadened to address any noncommercial technique, such as free giveaways or prizes to interest customers. From the view of this law, the only attraction should be the quality of one's product at a fair price.

Do Not Destroy Competition through Unfair Practices

"One [a seller] may not lower the price" (BT *Bava M'tzia* 4:12). It was not that the Rabbis were against a good deal, but they were concerned if there was a more nefarious goal for selling goods for less than the fair market price. The Rabbis of the third century CE did not know complex terms such as "predatory pricing," the practice of selling goods for less than market value in an attempt to eliminate the competition, which can be held to be illegal under modern antitrust laws. Nevertheless, they did understand that if one were to sell goods at a cheaper price than a competitor, the rival might be forced out of business.

It is interesting to note that not only was there a limit on profits, as previously discussed, but there was also a limit on selling goods at a rate below that which was necessary to make a fair profit by other merchants. In effect, the writers of this mishnah were supporting the need for merchants to make a profit in order to stay in business. Of course, the Rabbis were not aware of the eventual vicious clash between brick-and-mortar stores with internet sellers, who can often charge cheaper prices. Some claim that this is simply the new reality of online shopping, but the Rabbis would say otherwise. While this reality may be true, perhaps we should attempt to shop at our local stores, so that they may continue to provide more than just products, like the intangible benefits of living in a community with people shopping and talking with one another.

Take Responsibility for How Your Product May Be Presented to Future Consumers

"A person whose wine is mixed with water . . . may not sell it to a merchant . . . since it would be bought only to deceive others" (*Mishnah Bava M'tzia* 4:11). This is one of the most fascinating pronouncements from our tradition and still very novel in today's secular legal landscape. To understand this mishnah, one must understand that watering down wine was not permitted unless the buyer was aware of such practices. The fear governing this rule was that if one sold such watered-down wine to a seller, it could be eventually resold without proper description, thus making the initial seller a party to the deception of the final consumer.

To this day, many manufacturers, middlemen, and merchants do not take responsibility for the ultimate, and perhaps even harmful, use of their products. Examples abound, including the production of dangerous pesticides, such as DDT or building materials that may include asbestos products, that may be unlawful to sell locally but are sent to foreign countries whose laws or enforcement are less stringent. This Rabbinic restriction places the onus clearly on the seller, enforcing the notion that the seller's responsibility does not stop at the point of sale, but continues to the eventual user of their product. This far-reaching tenet of responsibility and accountability may seem excessive. However, current business practices such as sending products abroad that are known to have health risks, or simply turning a blind eye to the known dangerous uses of products, present numerous modern applications of the law. This mishnah suggests that we should not ignore the ethical demand of taking responsibility for products that one reasonably knows may be used to deceive or harm another.

Be Careful of Using Words in the Marketplace That May Create Unfair Expectations or Even Cause Pain

"One [a buyer] may not say, 'How much is this thing?' if one [the buyer] does not wish to buy it" (*Mishnah Bava M'tzia* 4:10). The Jewish tradition understands that words can create, as exemplified when "God says, 'Let there be light' and there was light" (Gen. 1:3). Our tradition is also aware that words can hurt and even destroy (BT *Arachin* 15b). This Rabbinic ordinance, inserted in the midst of a discussion of business ethics, prompts us to be careful with our words even when we are in the marketplace. If, as this selection instructs, we have no intent to buy an object, it is not fair to falsely raise the expectation of the seller that there is a chance for a possible sale. Immediately after this law, in this mishnah we also read that it is unfair for us to remind someone that they are a convert or have done harmful past actions if that person had made proper amends through the process of *t'shuvah*, or repentance. This implies that the consumer also causes pain to the seller, in addition to wasting her time, by inquiring about an item he does not intend to buy. Today, many use brick-and-mortar stores as a live showroom, asking the salesclerks for extensive advice. Yet these customers actually have no intent to buy the product in that particular store. Rather, they plan to go home and order the item online. "What is hateful to you do not do to another" (Hillel, BT *Shabbat* 31a) is a golden rule that we should follow. The Rabbis are warning us that we can cause harm with our words, and we need to be careful, even when engaged in business, whether we are the buyer or the seller.

What does it mean to act in the marketplace guided by Jewish ethics? Both consumers and merchants have an obligation to create and maintain a commerce system that allows for fair profits and respects the autonomy of the buyer by not attempting to manipulate them or mislead them. We work together to create an honest, transparent, and fair marketplace steeped in the dignity of both buyers and sellers, even to the extent of being careful of the words we use and the expectations we create. Our commerce must always be concerned with not only selling products of value, but also being people of values.

NOTE

1. Several concepts used as background for this article were derived from Rabbi Meir Tamari, *With all Your Possessions: Jewish Ethics and Economic Life* (New York: The Free Press, 1987).
2. Principle translations of the Mishnah are derived from Herbert Danby, *The Mishnah*, (Oxford, UK: Oxford University Press, 1977).
3. Noam Zion and David Dishon, *A Different Night: The Family Participation Haggadah* (Jerusalem: Shalom Hartman Institute, 1997), 25.

22

DREAMING A NEW AMERICAN ECONOMY

Rabbi Andy Kahn

The American economy has undergone a quiet revolution over the past few decades, drastically changing the relationship between work, quality of life, and wealth. Where we once assumed job stability to equate with familial economic and social stability, we now find a world in which most jobs no longer provide adequate income for an individual, let alone a family. In 2016 there was no state or county in the nation where a minimum wage job (based on the federal mandate of $7.25 an hour) afforded a two-bedroom apartment at market rate. Nineteen percent of all households, after excluding the value of the family car, have zero wealth. These are manifestations of compensation and productivity having become decoupled, with more hours and harder work not leading to an equivalent increase in pay.[1]

The United Way's ALICE (Asset Limited, Income Constrained, Employed) study takes a close look at this downturn for the lower economic layer of society. The number of households with income below the ALICE threshold increased in all states from 2007 to 2014, ranging from a 4 percent increase in Washington to a 40 percent increase in Maryland.[2] These families experience consistent food insecurity, insufficient housing conditions, inconsistent child care, unreliable transportation, and lack of access to health care.[3]

The lack of opportunities for these families to provide adequately for their basic needs has led to systemic problems of desperation, illness, and overall unlivable hardship. This trend is predicted to be exacerbated by the rise of automation and artificial intelligence.

A study undertaken by the Executive Office of the President in 2016, found that

> 83 percent of jobs making less than $20 per hour would come under pressure from automation, as compared to 31 percent of jobs making between $20 and $40 per hour and 4 percent of jobs making above $40 per hour. Furthermore . . . 44 percent of American workers with less than a high school degree hold jobs made up of highly-automatable tasks while 1 percent of people with a bachelor's degree or higher hold such a job.[4]

For most, work hours are longer, jobs provide less compensation, and economic and social stability are decreasing. These difficulties are only one piece of a much bigger shift in the American economy that not only impacts individual lives but undermines many of the basic assumptions that Americans have about the relationship between work, achievement, and socioeconomic advancement. Over the past twenty-five years, college tuition has continually increased, while both overall postgraduate employment and pay have decreased.[5] On the other end of the career timeline, retirement is becoming a distant dream for younger generations. A recent study has shown that millennials can not look forward to retiring until they are seventy.[6]

On the surface it may appear from the continual growth of the American GDP and stock markets, along with falling unemployment, that the U.S. economy is doing well. Yet, these gains are not spread out equitably among the population. For the past decade the strongest wage increases have gone to the top 10 percent of earners. For instance, from 2016 to 2017, strong wage growth continued at the top (1.5 percent at the 95th percentile), but the 10th percentile saw the strongest growth at 3.7 percent, while median wages grew only 0.2 percent.[7] Similarly, the richest 10 percent of Americans own 84 percent of all stocks, stock market gains then only representing a continuation of wealth accrual among a small, already wealthy subset of the population.[8] In short, America's recent economic growth has overwhelmingly enriched the most wealthy without benefiting the rest of the country.

The central notion of the American Dream, that every person is equally capable of working toward a life of prosperity and happiness, may remain, but only as a dream. That ideal based itself upon the belief in an equal playing field for all Americans.[9] Through tax legislation, corporatization, dismantling of social safety net programs, and wealth channeling directly to the upper echelons of the economic elite, the nature of the system upon which the American Dream rested has been altered in such a way that this dream no longer corresponds to reality.[10] In the face of this situation, Judaism can provide us with excellent examples of responses to similar dramatic change. We can, with the power of our visionary tradition, construct a new dream for the American future based on Jewish values.

Old Dreams: Scriptural Sources for a New Jewish Prophetic Dream

Rabbi Lawrence Kushner once suggested that we "suppose Scripture were like a dream, and we were its vessels. Like ones in a dream."[11] Kushner's mystical understanding of our relationship to Scripture, or Torah, places us in the role of the ones who embody the dreams of our people. Torah, rather than a record of history or ideas, becomes a system of symbols containing deep truths about our lives. Interpreting it as a guide to eternal aspects of our world, we become active vessels of the messages contained within. As vessels of Torah, we can return to our dreams from the past as guides to help us forge a new way forward in America. Like the prophecies of Isaiah,[12] this new dream must aid all people in our country in finding their way to a better, more sustainable life. I suggest three sources of guidance: Cain and his descendants' reaction to their world changing, the Israelites' response to a new mode of collectivity in the desert, and the dreams of the future yet to come—that of the messianic era.

When we consider Cain and Abel, we tend to focus on the tragedy of the story: the first murder in our Scripture and the next step in removal from the Edenic paradise. Cain, when cast out of Eden and cursed to have his work on the land never yield fruit, was placed in a brand-new world. He, unlike Adam, was given no directive as to how he would survive—only that he wouldn't be murdered himself. His response to this new reality? To construct the first city.

Enoch, the first city of the *Tanach*, is named after Cain's son (Gen. 4:17), a character who spawned his own extra-biblical books about his ascension into the heavenly realms (Gen. 5:21–24). This city, then, is a place of consecration and learning,[13] which is abundantly clear in its yield, the invention of the next steps in humanity's technological ascent: animal husbandry, music, and metalworking (Gen. 4:19–22).

Cain, having been notified that agriculture was no longer an option for him, went to work cultivating a collective that birthed new modes of production into the world. Rather than languishing in irrelevance or merely becoming a beggar, Cain and his offspring found new ways to contribute to society. By providing others with previously unseen metal tools to use, with music for entertainment and spiritual fulfillment, with reliable sources of meat and dairy to supplement their diet, the Cainites were able to contribute to agricultural society *and* advance and beautify the human world. By channeling their creative impulses into innovation, the offspring of Cain supported and enriched not only themselves, but also the rest of humanity.

From Cain and his children we learn that we can view our own new, scary economic reality as an open canvas. We can choose the palette with which we paint. It is almost impossible to imagine our current society without the fundamental technologies attributed to Cain and his offspring. Now, how innovative can we become to create equally new and groundbreaking ways of being and expressing humanity?

Such innovations are already afoot if we look in the right place. But instead of venturing into the fringe of today's innovators, let us look at the second source from Torah of new community the *Tanach* holds for us: the *Mishkan*, the Tabernacle.

The Israelites in the desert were emerging from generations of slavery in Egypt and were in need of a new way of organizing themselves. Just like Cain, Moses brought forth a new, this time God-ordained, technology—the *Mishkan*, an innovation meant to maintain connection between the people of Israel and God (Exod. 25:8). When divinely directed to collect the resources for the *Mishkan*, the Israelites were specifically asked to do so with *n'divut lev*, the free will of their hearts (Exod. 35:5–29). In practice, this meant that people with particular skills or resources volunteered what was needed for the project. Skilled weavers, women who were "wise of heart," wove all the fabrics that were part of the *Mishkan*, as well as the tent (*ohel*); the chieftains, the richest among the people, brought precious stones, fine oils, and incense. Every person and group contributed based on their own personal proclivities, rather than being commanded top-down. In the instance of the *Mishkan*, this method worked *too* well. The people had to be told to stop bringing their freewill gifts (Exod. 36:5–6). An overflow of resources, an abundance of desire to contribute, even from these slaves-turned-refugees wandering the desert, was the outcome of simply broadcasting the proposed project with its specific needs and asking the people to give.

This new social formulation gives us insight into our Scripture's view of human and communal nature. The Israelites' willingness to give was not framed as a God-derived miracle. Instead, they went above and beyond of their own accord. In our day and age, this is a revolutionary outlook. It is often assumed that people are unlikely to contribute resources or energy to projects without extrinsic rewards or punishments, which leads to the common prejudice in America that the unemployed or impoverished are simply lacking initiative. Further, full-time jobs in American society are often unrelated to individuals' *n'divut lev*, or the mode in which they most deeply wish to give. These jobs are still viewed as a, if not *the*, centerpiece of a person's identity and social worth. We also frequently refer to jobs, whether or not we like them, as "how we make our living" or "our livelihood." In short, jobs have become synonymous with both the ability to survive and individual worth, regardless of the individual's personal connection to the job itself. Due to this, the jobless or impoverished are often devalued to the point of being dehumanized (referred to as "drains on the system," for instance), and individuals seek jobs, and in particular socially valued jobs, at any cost, whether or not they have a desire to perform the actual role.

God's mode of directing the construction of God's own place of dwelling tells us much more about the basic nature of humanity. Humans, according to this piece of Torah, when in meaningful community and given a clear, direct need, will jump at the chance to contribute. Giving people the opportunity to contribute on their own terms leads to abundance—a greater amount of resources than even needed. This view is continued in the grand Torah of the future—the messianic age.

According to Maimonides (Spain/Egypt, 1135–1204), in the messianic age

> there will be no famines and no wars, no envy and no competition. For the Good will be pervasive. All the delicacies will be as readily available as is dust. The world will only be engaged in knowing God. Then, there will be very wise people who will understand the deep, sealed matters. They will then achieve knowledge of the Creator to as high a degree as humanly possible, as it says, "For the earth shall be filled of knowledge of the Eternal, as the waters cover the sea" (Isaiah 11:9).[14]

For Maimonides, then, the ultimate state of redemption is one in which people no longer have to compete for resources. In essence, this means that all needs will be provided for, and the individual will be able to pursue one's own knowledge of God. Perhaps we can tie this vision to the *Mishkan*, and the individual knowledge of God may be construed as the individual's *n'divut lev*, one's own free will to enact one's own God-given abilities in pursuance of collective Good. This vision is an extension of our own collective dream as rendered by the prophet Micah:

> Thus God will judge among the many peoples,
> And arbitrate for the multitude of nations,
> However distant;
> And they shall beat their swords into plowshares
> And their spears into pruning hooks.
> Nation shall not take up
> Sword against nation;
> They shall never again know war;
> But every person shall sit under their grapevine or fig tree
> With no one to disturb them.
>
> (Micah 4:3–4)

A New Dream: Economics of the Messianic Era

If our Scriptures are our dreams, and we their vessels, it is up to us to enact those dreams in this world. As we have seen, the American economy and dream are both in a state of deep transition. The destination of this transition is anything but decided. Our Scriptures teach us that according to the story of Cain and his offspring, in times of extreme change we ought to seek inventive, new ways to engage in the world; according to the story of the *Mishkan*, each person should ideally be able to give of their own free will based on their capacity and skill; and according to the ideal of the messianic age, all people should have their basic needs met so that they can pursue peace, self-knowledge, and their God-given gifts. How do we translate this dream into reality today?

One of the contenders in the debate for a new economic structure that most closely fits our new dream has been universal basic income (UBI). In short, UBI is the policy that every resident of a community or country is guaranteed enough income to live on.[15] At the moment, those proposing UBI in America wish to provide all adult citizens with

$1,000 per month.[16] According to Annie Lowry, author of a recent book on the subject and renowned journalist on economics and politics, UBI is more than an economic policy. It is an expression of values of "universality, unconditionality, inclusion and simplicity, and it insists that every person is deserving of participation in the economy, freedom of choice, and a life without deprivation."[17]

These values echo our new Jewish dream very clearly. Even the cursed Cain and his offspring were able to participate in the economy. The Israelites in the desert were able to follow their freedom of choice in order to be a part of their grand project. And the basis for the dream of the messianic era has always been focused upon life without deprivation.

The somewhat utopian idea of UBI isn't without its problems. The tax burden it would create would be unlike anything America has undertaken before.[18] There are many creative thinkers, such as Bill Gates,[19] working on innovative ways of raising money for such a policy, but all of them focus on this being a governmentally driven undertaking. In a country whose past few decades of legislation has continued to funnel wealth upward into the hands of corporations and the wealthy, it is unlikely such a radical new piece of policy will be adopted in the near term. If we accept UBI as unlikely to be actualized through our current government but agree with the values it expresses in its methods and outcomes, what can we do in our own communities to help bring about a shift that embodies our Jewish dream without relying upon the government?

Douglas Rushkoff, a prominent academic, media theorist, and social activist, writes that the shift from an economy focused on individuals being honored and valued only when they are in well-paid full-time jobs can be undertaken in a bottom-up fashion. We are in a stage of economics Rushkoff refers to as digital industrialism. This is a mixture of the growth- and productivity-centric industrial ethos, which focused on consolidating "the power of those at the top by minimizing the value and price of human laborers,"[20] and the digital revolution, in which human work is replaced with mechanical labor.[21] Rushkoff sees the combination of digital technology and the industrial economic ethic having led to corporations extracting value from society, usually in the form of money, and then holding onto that value and passively investing it in other corporations rather than using it to enrich those who created the value in the first place. Unfortunately for the corporations, this has now led to a situation in which the extracted and held value no longer has a way to grow.[22] He charts the tapering off of the goal of unlimited growth in the corporations of the postwar economy as a sign that the economy itself is turning a corner and that as more and more corporations recognize that unlimited growth is no longer a viable model, some are opting for new visions for their future.[23] Rushkoff suggests a new approach for the future: digital distributism.

Digital distributism empowers individuals to create, breaks up centralized means of production, and creates cheap means of exchange between peers.[24] Its goal, rather than pushing for exponential growth and the continual upstream movement of value toward the already wealthy, is that of communal empowerment and sustainable prosperity.[25] At its most realized state, upon attaining sustainable prosperity, Rushkoff claims that a digitally distributist society would "seek some sort of collective or spiritual awareness."[26]

In an economy focused on digital distributism, rather than extracting wealth from local communities, corporations would either cease to exist or begin to function as conduits for those within local communities to exchange their creations. Much like the project of the *Mishkan*, individuals within communities would be able to contribute of their own free will, and by keeping the value of the labor circulating among the people contributing, rather than centralizing the value within a corporation, more value would be distributed more evenly.

This dream has been enacted, on a small scale, in multiple ways already. For example, the Massachusetts BerkShare is a local currency implemented in the Berkshires region, facilitating the communal circulation of both local wealth and wealth brought into the region from tourists and strengthening the local economy.[27] The Japanese invented "Caring Relationship Tickets," in which people throughout the country (and sometimes beyond) cared for each other's elderly in a time exchange that allowed those who had moved far from home to bank hours of care that they provided for the loved ones of others to be cashed in directly for use for their own loved ones.[28] These examples only scratch the surface of what might be possible when switching from the industrial ethos to the distributionist ethos.

The dreams found within our Scriptures point us toward a Jewish value system strongly akin to Rushkoff's digital distributism. By looking to empower individuals to both contribute and benefit from shared systems (Cain and his offspring's innovative ways of remaining part of society while enriching it) and striving to create a society based on collective or spiritual awareness (the collective project of creating the *Mishkan*) and pursuit of a steady state of prosperity for all, rather than continual growth (the messianic vision of freedom from deprivation), digital distributism fits squarely into the Jewish dream. After it is implemented on the small scale, digital distributism could lead to a much wider version, akin to that imagined by proponents of UBI.

As the 1999 CCAR Pittsburgh Platform states, "Partners with God in *tikkun olam*, we are called to help bring nearer the messianic age. . . . We are obligated to pursue *tzedek*, justice and righteousness, and to narrow the gap between the affluent and the poor . . . to protect the earth's biodiversity and natural resources, and to redeem those in physical, economic, and spiritual bondage."[29]

These values central to the Reform Movement commit us to pursuing a new Jewish dream for America's future. We, the vessels of such a boldly hopeful Torah, can take the lead in realizing a new vision for the future of our beloved home in America. As we stride bravely into the uncharted territory of our country's future, the guiding values of our Torah will provide us the dreams we need in order to build a new, better future, free of bondage for all people.

NOTES

1. "The Souls of Poor Folk: Poverty," Institute for Policy Studies, 2017, https://ips-dc.org/souls-of-poor-folks/.
2. United Way, *ALICE Executive Summary—A Multi-State Comparison: A Study of Financial Hardship*, Winter 2016, http://alice.ctunitedway.org/files/2014/11/2016-ALICE-Multi-State-Comparison.pdf, 5.
3. United Way, *ALICE: The Consequences of Insufficient Household Income*, 2017, http://alice.ctunitedway.org/wp-content/uploads/2018/03/2017-ALICE-Consequences-Report.pdf, 82.
4. Executive Office of the President, *Artificial Intelligence, Automation, and the Economy*, December 20, 2016, 14, https://obamawhitehouse.archives.gov/sites/whitehouse.gov/files/documents/Artificial-Intelligence-Automation-Economy.PDF.
5. Beth Akers, "Assessing the Plight of Recent College Grads," Brookings Institute, October 30, 2013, https://www.brookings.edu/research/assessing-the-plight-of-recent-college-grads/.
6. Alicia H. Munnell, "Millennials and Retirement: How Bad Is It?," *Politico*, June 7, 2018, https://www.politico.com/agenda/story/2018/06/07/millennials-preparing-for-retirement-000670.
7. Elise Gould, "The State of American Wages 2017," Economic Policy Institute, March 1, 2018, https://www.epi.org/publication/the-state-of-american-wages-2017-wages-have-finally-recovered-from-the-blow-of-the-great-recession-but-are-still-growing-too-slowly-and-unequally/.
8. Rob Wile, "The Richest 10% of Americans Now Own 84% of All Stocks," *Time*, December 29, 2017, http://time.com/money/5054009/stock-ownership-10-percent-richest/.
9. We must also recognize that this equal playing field never truly existed for all people and has always been particularly difficult to reach for people of color and for women.
10. Donald L. Bartlett and James B. Steele, *The Betrayal of the American Dream*, (New York: PublicAffairs, 2012), xvii–xx.
11. Rabbi Lawrence Kushner, *The River of Light: Jewish Mystical Awareness* (Woodstock: Jewish Lights, 2013), loc. 337–38, Kindle.
12. In particular, Isaiah 2:3: "And many peoples shall go and say: 'Come, let us go up to the mountain of the Eternal, to the House of the God of Jacob; that God may instruct us in God's ways, and that we may walk in God's paths.' For instruction shall come forth from Zion, the word of the Eternal from Jerusalem."
13. Two different, but related, definitions of the Hebrew word translated as Enoch, *chanoch*.
14. Rambam, *Mishneh Torah, Hilchot M'lachim Umilchamot* 12, trans. adapted from Reuven Brauner, *Laws of Kings and Wars* (2012), Sefaria,

accessed September 23, 2018, Sefaria.org, https://www.sefaria.org/Mishneh_Torah%2C_Kings_and_Wars.12.1?lang=bi&with=About&lang2=en.

15. Annie Lowrey, *Give People Money* (New York: Crown, 2018), 4–5.

16. Lowrey, *Give People Money*, 6.

17. Lowrey, *Give People Money*, 11.

18. Lowrey, *Give People Money*, 187.

19. Lowrey, *Give People Money*, 189.

20. Douglas Rushkoff, *Throwing Rocks at the Google Bus: How Growth Became the Enemy of Prosperity* (New York: Penguin, 2016), 39.

21. Rushkoff, *Throwing Stones at the Google Bus*, 33.

22. Rushkoff, *Throwing Stones at the Google Bus*, 151–52.

23. Rushkoff, *Throwing Stones at the Google Bus*, 188.

24. Rushkoff, *Throwing Stones at the Google Bus*, 428–29.

25. Rushkoff, *Throwing Stones at the Google Bus*, 408–9.

26. Rushkoff, *Throwing Stones at the Google Bus*, 429.

27. Rushkoff, *Throwing Stones at the Google Bus*, 280–82.

28. Rushkoff, *Throwing Stones at the Google Bus*, 293–94.

29. Central Conference of American Rabbis, "A Statement of Principles for Reform Judaism, Pittsburgh, 1999," CCAR, accessed June 26, 2018, https://www.ccarnet.org/rabbinic-voice/platforms/article-statement-principles-reform-judaism/.

ETHICS IN FOCUS

Responsum on Equal Pay

RABBI JONATHAN COHEN, PHD,
ON BEHALF OF THE CCAR RESPONSA COMMITTEE

Responsa (the plural of "responsum") are the body of Jewish literature in which rabbis act in a legal capacity and answer contemporary questions not directly addressed by the sacred Jewish canon. The process of responsa starts with someone asking a question, sh'eilah, and a single Jewish legal expert or a group of experts offering a t'shuvah, an answer. The response to the question starts with a process of examining related issues discussed in other sacred texts in order to show how the expert is extrapolating the answer.

This question-and-answer system has its roots in the geonic period, the early medieval period, in Babylonia and continues to today. The Reform Movement has its own responsa body, the CCAR Responsa Committee, which steeps its answers in not only the entire body of Jewish law, but also an understanding of the development of that law and its interaction with Reform values specifically.

*Here in this "Responsum on Equal Pay," Rabbi Jonathan Cohen, PhD, on behalf of the CCAR Responsa Committee, navigates the halachah, recognizing that Jewish legal texts often support the disparate treatment of men and women. He then applies a framework to his t'shuvah to uphold the foundational assumptions that "(1) that women **are** paid for their work, and (2) that women and men do **comparable** work." Then, he explores the* *interaction of Jewish and secular law, as he examines the concept of reward and renumeration in both, leading to the final conclusion to the t'shuvah.*[1]

Responsum on Equal Pay

Sh'eilah: Is there an obligation under Jewish law to pay men and women the same for comparable labor?

Submitted by Rabbi Marla Feldman, Women of Reform Judaism, and Rabbi Mary L. Zamore, Women's Rabbinic Network, on behalf of the Reform Pay Equity Initiative

T'shuvah:[2] In responding to your question we must recognize that the formulators and proponents of halachah throughout the centuries have recorded, defended, and in many instances also promoted distinctions and inequalities between men and women, including ones that have occurred in the realm of work and its remuneration. To cite one example, it was accepted that under many circumstances women would not be entitled to compensation for their work; rather, the revenue generated through their efforts would be directed to their fathers or husbands.[3] In addition, even when women were offered payment for their work, there is evidence to suggest that much of their work was defined by then accepted gender and family roles.[4] However, our response to your question is shaped by two assumptions: (1) that women *are* paid for their work, and (2) that women and men do *comparable* work. On this basis, we turn to the question of pay regulation and equity.

Starting during the Talmudic period questions of payment or remuneration for work (in Hebrew *sachar*) were resolved on the basis of local customs and jurisdictions.[5] We note a tendency to level, or render equal, payment and protect workers among Talmudic Sages. For example, in a discussion on the obligation of the employer in cases where the stipulation of pay to laborers does not include a specific wage and the employer's commitment is based on local custom, R. Joshua requires a minimum payment of the lowest wage paid for comparable work in the locality, while the Sages rule that an average wage must be paid.[6] In addition, the Talmud indicates that members of a Jewish jurisdiction or polity may regulate rates, weights, and measures as well as wages.[7] In other words, wage-fixing and regulation are explicitly permitted in these sources. Further, this rule is cited by leading respondents. For example, the Rashba explains that such regulations may be approved by members of a professional or trade association without the approval of others in their city and that these enactments carry the weight of Torah law,[8] and the Rosh addresses the possibility that in certain monetary matters courts of law may depart from Torah law on the basis of this rule.[9] Also, this Talmudic rule includes the stipulation that members of a jurisdiction may establish monetary sanctions to enforce their regulations.[10] In addition, citing Rambam, the Beit Yosef teaches us that the two-pronged purpose informing such sweeping administrative authority is to regulate the affairs within a jurisdiction and to enable the success or thriving of its subjects, citizens, or inhabitants.[11]

In addition, generations of *poskim* identified certain matters as subject to the rule *dina d'malchuta dina*—in other words, matters that fall under the recognized jurisdiction of non-Jewish law. In brief, the application of this principle has been restricted in three principal ways. It applies to:

i. matters that are specifically in the interest of the ruler or of government (taxes and other sources of revenue for the state, for example); or

ii. government regulation for the well-being of inhabitants in the jurisdiction; and

iii. legislation or regulation that does not directly contravene or uproot *din Torah*.[12]

We note that there are a number of potential difficulties that arise with respect to the application of this rule to the regulation of employment and wages. Beyond the need to consider the position of certain *poskim* who ruled that *dina d'malchuta dina* depends upon the legitimacy of the ruler, administrator, or legislator,[13] a number of halachic authorities restrict its scope to matters touching on real property.[14] The Hatam Sofer famously rejects the application of this rule to an employment issue in part because in his view the ruler (or king) enjoys the power to act arbitrarily (and unfairly) in hiring decisions.[15] However, R. Elijah b. David Tayeb is understood to have opined that the rule does apply to relations of employment.[16] Needless to elaborate, arguments such as the concern with the arbitrary use of power do not apply to our current condition with respect to the regulation of employment. Indeed, upon consideration, we hold that the question with which we are presented raises a matter that is central to the public good, that we cannot assail the legitimacy of our legislation and regulation, and that pay equity does not in any way contravene *din Torah*. Recognizing the complexity of this issue, we suggest that *dina d'malchuta dina* would apply to most aspects of employment legislation and regulation in general and the principle of equal pay for comparable work in particular.

It bears noting that the Hebrew word *sachar* touches upon notions of reward and merit that the words "payment" or "remuneration" do not necessarily denote. Thus, to cite a famous example, R. Elazar and R. Tarfon's dictum—"[Recognize that] the master of your work is trustworthy to pay the *sachar* of your actions"—refers to the divine reward for the engagement in mitzvot.[17] Yet the Sages clearly frame their analysis of this aspect of the relationship between humanity and its maker in the context of the employment relationship. Our tradition also teaches that the *sachar* for the performance of mitzvot is determined on the basis of the depth of one's commitment and faith or the quality of one's performance of the commandments.[18] Indeed, we learn that the *sachar* for Rachel's modesty was the reward of ancestry to Israel's first king, Saul, and that in turn, the *sachar* for Saul's modesty would be the merit of being a forefather to Queen Esther.[19] These demonstrate that the quality of one's character and actions is the divine criterion for the setting of *sachar*, as opposed to gender identity. With considerations of equity in mind, we may emphasize the explicit equivalences in both comportment and reward and recompense to both men and women in this text. Similarly, in yet another midrash, Miriam's ability to nourish Moses is identified as an example of divine *sachar* for the righteous in general.[20] In addition, we learn that in reward, *sachar*, for the righteousness of women entire generations of Israel were saved and redeemed, reminding us that the very survival of our tradition has depended on divine recognition and reward offered on account of women's actions.[21]

The Reform Movement has had a long record of advocacy on the issue of equal pay, and its repeated statements have fallen within the purview of the halachic mandate to promote regulation of wages for the sake of social repair and justice for employees regardless of gender identity and orientation.[22] Recognizing that equal pay is an issue that touches on individuals and families and therefore affects every man, woman, and child in our society, we address it in the context of our application of the rule *dina d'malchuta dina*. Informed and inspired by the teaching of our Sages, who lived within conditions wherein women were all too often treated unequally and unjustly, and who nevertheless conceived of an equitable, gender-neutral system of divine *sachar*, we continue to pray for and act toward the implementation of a vision of justice, repair, and full recognition for all who labor in our society and world. May the words of the midrash describing the righteous as *"mitkasher b'm'lachto"*—one becoming worthy and meritorious through the qualities of his or her labors—be realized,[23] may we merit the Psalmist's blessing that we consume the fruit of our labors, rejoice, and be blessed with goodness,[24] and may our efforts lead all to the recognition in the inherent value of labor, as Rabbi Simon taught, "Great is labor, for it brings dignity to the person who engages in it."[25]

NOTES

1. This responsum was previously published in *CCAR Journal*, Fall 2019.
2. Thank you to Rabbi Dr. Joan Friedman for her assistance in reviewing the texts used throughout this responsum.

3. *Mishnah K'tubot* 4:4; *Mishneh Torah, Hilchot Ishut* 3:1; *Shulchan Aruch, Even Haezer* 37:1; 80:1.

4. For example, in *Exodus Rabbah* 1:11 and BT *Sotah* 11b we note a distinction between the labors of men as opposed to those of women. Indeed, the assignment of men's work to women and vice versa was identified as an oppressive Egyptian practice during the period of slavery, one that required men and women to function in ways that did not correspond to their "natures." For listing of married women's labors and tasks, see *Mishnah K'tubot* 5:5; *Mishneh Torah, Hilchot Ishut* 21:7.

5. BT *Bava M'tzia* 87a.

6. Ibid.

7. BT *Bava Batra* 8b; *Tosefta Bava M'tzia* 11:23.

9. Rashba 4:185.

9. Rosh 55:10.

10. See Rashi, s.v. להסיע על קיצתם, BT *Bava Batra* 9a.

11. *Beit Yosef, Choshen Mishpat* 231:20.

12. See the *Siftei Kohen* on *Shulchan Aruch, Choshen Mishpat* 369:11.

13. For example: *Mishneh Torah, Hilchot G'zelah* 5:18.

14. Beit Yosef, *Choshen Mishpat* 369:14, citing R. Eliezer of Metz "we do not pronounce."

15. Responsa Hatam Sofer, *Choshen Mishpat* 19.

16. Responsa *Sha'al Haish, Choshen Mishpat* 1; also see Responsa *Tarshish Shoham, Choshen Mishpat* 100.

17. *Mishnah Avot* 2:14, 16.

18. For example, see Albo's *Sefer Haiqarim* 1:10 or *Exodus Rabbah* 2:2.

19. BT *M'gillah* 13b.

20. *Exodus Rabbah* 1:25.

21. BT *Sotah* 11b and see Rashi, s.v. "הנס באותו היו הן שאף" and the Tosafot citing Rashbam, s.v. "הנס באותו היו," BT *Pesachim* 108b.

22. A 1928 resolution of the CCAR with respect to women in industry calls for safe and sanitary conditions, a maximum of eight hours of work per day, and pay equality with men for equal work; an additional resolution on pay equity followed in 1984, and it was re-affirmed in 2017.

23. *Exodus Rabbah* 2:2 and *Ecclesiastes Rabbah* 5:11.

24. Psalm 128:2.

25. BT *N'darim* 49b.

TALKING ABOUT MONEY

Mutual Benefits

RABBI AMY SCHWARTZMAN AND KEVIN MOSS

Nanny, housekeeper, babysitter, child-minder, caregiver, home administrator—all of these titles describe our only employee, but none fully capture the extent of work she takes on each day and week. Early on, beginning nearly twenty years ago, the daily duties related mostly to our infants and their care: feeding, cleaning, playing, strolls outside, reading and singing and games inside. As our children grew, the responsibilities shifted to homework-encourager and music lesson driver and Hebrew school picker-upper. While the two women who cared for our kids, Raquel for their first five years, and Maria from then until today, provided attention, care, and tremendous love for our girls, we also were the fortunate beneficiaries of their great gifts and skills and of their love as well. As our partners in parenting and the overseers of our household, Raquel and Maria enabled us to fulfill our professional goals, to work full-time in jobs we love.

When we hired Raquel, we paid her a salary that reflected the economic demands of our area (Washington, DC), as we knew that minimum wage would not provide a sustainable income. The job of caring for and protecting our children certainly deserved a respectable salary, and she deserved to live securely, as we did. How could we expect her to come to work energized and enthusiastic if in her own life she didn't have all that she needed?

Years later, when we hired Maria, who did not have health insurance, we added a contribution into her benefits package to enable her to join the ranks of the insured. Not only was this the right thing to do ethically, but we also wanted her to remain healthy, as the best thing for the health of our family. In the years that followed, our understanding of Maria's financial situation grew, as did our personal connection. As we aged and looked toward our own retirements with the support of our own benefits packages, we realized that we had an obligation and desire to provide this for Maria too. We discussed an approach with her and started saving to help her in the time when we would no longer need her and she would no longer want to work full-time. We hope we have and will continue to contribute to her financial security, as she has made it possible for us to have financial security too.

Our values, Jewish and humanitarian, guided our actions. Support for our nannies over and above minimum thresholds also addressed our desire to help others move up the economic ladder beyond philanthropy. As most caregivers are women, minorities, and immigrants, we hoped our approach contributed to transferring wealth to those who often have a less secure foundation for growth. Indeed, after her time with us, Raquel opened a child-care business in her own home.

The two women who served as our nanny–housekeeper–babysitter–child minder–caregiver–home administrator have done much more than taken great care of our children; they have enabled us to be good parents as well as fulfilled professionals. Both Raquel and Maria allowed our family to grow and meet our own aspirations. As loving individuals with many needed skills, they made our family complete. While we have been committed to providing more than a living wage, their worth to us is immeasurable, and we hope they know how valued they are in our lives.

Part Five

Religious Life and Money

While *The Sacred Exchange* is dedicated to a multivocal conversation about the intersection of money and Judaism, this part focuses a bit more sharply on Jewish practice and its institutions. Rabbi Leah Lewis, in "The Value of Membership," passionately defends synagogue membership, using the argument of value proposition to show the priceless benefits of community. In "The Cost of Dying Jewishly," Stephanie Garry and Rabbi Eric J. Greenberg share the history of Jewish funerals and mourning practices through the economic lens. They then challenge the Jewish community to take an honest look at the high costs of modern Jewish funerals and recognize the negative impact on engagement and ritual observance. They offer suggestions to cap costs, making funerals more accessible to all. Addressing happy life-cycle celebrations, Rabbi Douglas B. Sagal, in his *"Mazal Tov* to Life-Cycle Parties," makes the surprising, yet cogent argument for being more tolerant of conspicuous consumption in parties. His chapter creates an important dialogue with Rabbi Neal Gold's chapter in part 1, as Rabbi Gold forcefully argues for a more tempered use of wealth.

In "Money and Transaction in Jewish Liturgy and Ritual," Rabbi Robert Scheinberg reveals what has always been in plain sight, as he guides us through the prayer book and Jewish rituals, drawing our attention to the numerous references to money and transaction. By doing this, Rabbi Scheinberg demonstrates that Judaism addresses daily living, including our concerns about money. In the next chapter, "Dividends of Meaning: Jewish Rituals for the Financial Life Cycle," Rabbi Jennifer Gubitz makes the compelling argument for the creation of new rituals to engage modern Jews. As she examines several existing examples of new rituals for the financial life cycle, Rabbi Gubitz explains the need for new rituals and calls upon the Jewish community to create them. In *"Gelt,"* Rabbi Deborah Prinz provides a concise history of coined money in the Chanukah story and celebration, reminding us that this chocolate holiday treat has deep and important roots.

"Ethics in Focus: Copyright Infringement and the Synagogue," by Rabbi Hara E. Person and Rabbi Sonja K. Pilz, PhD, reminds us of the ethical imperative to be scrupulous in our use of copyrighted material, especially for religious uses. This chapter illustrates not only the connection of Jewish money ethics and rituals, but also the truism that our financial decisions, such as whether to pay the appropriate licensing fees, affect other people's livelihoods. Once again, we are reminded that we are all employers.

Rabbi Idit Solomon shares her personal infertility narrative in "Talking about Money: Be Fruitful and Multiply, and Go into Debt." Describing her and her husband's struggle to become parents, with its huge financial impact, Rabbi Solomon also writes about her nonprofit organization Hasida, dedicated to helping fund and support Jews struggling with infertility.

23

THE VALUE OF MEMBERSHIP

Rabbi Leah Lewis

There was not a shred of anger or hostility in her voice when a young woman—an attorney, an active preschool parent, a wife, and mother of three young children—told me that she was not renewing her membership in the synagogue where I serve as her rabbi. The decision was a rational one: "It makes more sense to pay the non-member premium for preschool tuition than it does to pay for membership."

For many in the first, second, and third generations of American Jews, maintaining memberships with local synagogues and other communal institutions, regardless of how often they did or did not utilize their services, was "just what we did."[1] In the 1950s and early 1960s, a time in which suburbs were booming and American Jews were settling en masse into the American lifestyle, various demographic studies showed that rates of affiliation with the organized Jewish community hovered anywhere between one-half and three-quarters of the population.[2]

Like in every generation, in the 1950s and 1960s there were as many reasons for people choosing whether to affiliate as there were people. Among the majority of American Jews who affiliated, some did so because there was a perceived "need" to have a place where they belonged during a time when there remained significant corners of American life where they were not welcomed. Others affiliated out of a sense of obligation or desire to support the communal effort to build Jewish institutions.

The landscape of life for American Jews has changed. Challenges with integration into mainstream American life are a thing of the past. So too is the presumption on the part of synagogues and other Jewish institutions that communal support will manifest in a significant way from any sort of perceived obligation. The statistics are on the side of the woman in my synagogue. According to the 2013 Pew Research report, less than a third of American Jews claim to affiliate with a synagogue.[3] It is clear to me that those numbers are not likely to increase anytime soon. It behooves those of us who work in the synagogue world to understand why.

While finances are an essential reason why people choose whether to affiliate, financially based decisions are never simply a matter of dollars and cents. As they impact choices about synagogue affiliation or engagement with Jewish organizational life, finances are often a matter of perceived worth. In the case of this woman, it was clear that belonging to a synagogue at this point in the life of her family was first and foremost an expense—one that simply did not make any rational sense. "We only participate in preschool-related activities: school of course, and an occasional Tot Shabbat or High Holy Day family experience. Paying synagogue dues feels to me like a multi-thousand-dollar donation to the synagogue, which, at this point in our lives, is not in the cards." She and her family would rejoin, she said, when her children were older and ready to benefit from more of the services that the synagogue provides.

For this woman and an increasing number of individuals and families like her, participation in the organized Jewish community is a value proposition. Our world is filled with an overwhelming number of choices about how to allocate precious resources of time and money, and an affiliated Jewish life is an investment of both. If a person wants to worship in a synagogue during the High Holy Days, for a few hundred dollars most synagogues will be happy to sell that person a ticket to attend. This is a moderate expense compared to synagogue membership, which can cost thousands. If a person wants to participate in a lecture series, many synagogues or JCCs will happily welcome that person for a non-member rate, sometimes a few dollars more than the rate being charged to members. If a person wants to have a rabbi or cantor officiate at a baby naming or a bar mitzvah or a wedding or a funeral, they can certainly do so, for a set fee. There are clergy available to hire for any life-cycle event, and connecting with them is as easy as a single internet search. Most often, this pay-as-you-go approach to Jewish life is significantly less expensive than formal affiliation. When resources are limited, constructing a Jewish life this way stands to reason. But by definition, religious life has never been a rational endeavor. During the great communal enterprise of building the Tabernacle as a ritual home for God and the Israelites during their wanderings in the wilderness, the Torah describes the census, with its mandatory contribution of the half-shekel:

> Everyone who is entered in the records, from the age of twenty years up, shall give the Eternal's offering. The rich shall not pay more and the poor shall not pay less than half a shekel when giving the Eternal's offering as expiation for your persons. You shall take the expiation money from the Israelites and assign it to the service of the Tent of Meeting; it shall serve the Israelites as a reminder before the Eternal, as expiation for your persons. (Exodus 30:14–16)

In ancient Israel, when it was time to step up, be counted, and participate in the ritual life of the community, there was a clear sense of shared responsibility. Though the modest half-shekel alone could not have sustained Jewish life even in the days of the Tabernacle, requiring it as part of the census sent a clear message that like anything, building a spiritual life requires resources and commitment from the entire community, regardless of how direct any individual's benefit from it would be.

Even after the Tabernacle ceased to exist, the Rabbis of the second century CE affirmed this sense of obligation toward communal giving when they wrote about the half-shekel. After giving people ample time to make their contribution, they would use those funds to "repair the paths and the roads and the pools of water" (*Mishnah Sh'kalim* 1:1). The timing was such that they would ensure the work was complete in preparation for the Passover pilgrimage to Jerusalem. Clear paths, safe roads, and clean water sources are hardly the stuff that attracts most major gifts of the heart or excites supporters to contribute toward innovation and change. But clear paths, safe roads, and clean water sources represent the infrastructure that was essential to guarantee that the spiritual journey could take place. It was incumbent upon everyone to support the communal endeavor.

Well into the twenty-first century now, the American Jewish community faces the mixed blessing of assimilation and cultural integration. We are succeeding in education, in business, in social, cultural, and political life in every corner of our society. And because we are no longer the first generation of American Jews to inherit this opportunity, we are also heirs to an American mind-set about participation and spending that flies in the face of the Exodus-era obligation of the half-shekel. To be American is to ask logical questions about the return on investment for the dollars spent to live a Jewish life and to make choices about where and when to invest, based on the answers. To live with a traditional Jewish mind-set is to support the communal endeavor, regardless of personal gain. It follows, then, that the goal of the leadership of the American Jewish community today ought to be ensuring that the communal endeavor provides meaningful and worthwhile return for those who invest in it.

In today's communal landscape there exist unprecedented opportunities for engagement in Jewish life: synagogues, day schools, summer camps, community centers, youth groups, retreats, social service agencies, *tzedakah* opportunities, Israel travel opportunities, environmental movements, food choices, online learning centers, Jewish start-up opportunities, and more. The people who create and innovate and lead the community are providing more Jewish opportunities than ever before. At the same time, the very people we are trying to engage face more choices about where to invest their time and money, and why. Before committing, Jews ask: What will be the return on my investment? Will the educational and programmatic needs of my family be met in a time and space and budget that fit in my life? For increasing numbers of American Jews, the days of supporting the community simply because doing so is expected are gone.

This cost-benefit approach certainly makes the work of those of us who spend our days trying to build a vibrant Jewish community more challenging. But the greater loss lies with the individual who may never be around to gain from Jewish life and all that it has to offer. Judaism and Jewish life provide essential tools to help people thrive, to live a life of meaning and belonging and purpose—all things that become even more valuable with each passing day.

In the summer of 2017, there was an opinion piece printed in the *Los Angeles Times* claiming, "It's too expensive to be Jewish."[4] Leslee Komaiko, the author, is a mother who, like many, is busy trying to make the puzzle pieces of her family's life fit together. She wrote the article when it was time for her twelve-year-old son to begin studying for his bar mitzvah. She was unable to find a tutor who was, to her, affordable. When one reads the hourly costs for bar mitzvah tutoring, it is easy to see her logic. Families who grapple with the mounting costs of modern life must make difficult choices about where engagement with Jewish life fits in their budgets.

The dilemma lies in this: most often, it is precisely those individuals and families who have not already made Jewish affiliation a part of their lives, and who are not already reaping the benefits, for whom the perceived high cost does not compute. Jewish life, understood as a fee-for-service enterprise, is understandably "too expensive." Case in point—hiring a private bar mitzvah tutor. When bar mitzvah preparation or any other Jewish activity is introduced into a life in which resources of time and money are already strained, it can feel like an obligation that needs to be squeezed between ballet lessons, baseball practice, and braces . . . simply more charges on the credit card and more places to be.

When Jewish life in general, and synagogue life in particular, is conceptualized as yet more things to be squeezed out of already tight calendars and bank accounts, Jewish life will lose out nearly every time. Everyone, regardless of age or family makeup, has other demands pulling on limited resources. Judaism simply cannot be another thing to *do*. Instead, we would benefit from a reminder of what Jewish life was like when, with the census, universal participation was expected in order to maintain the infrastructure of sacred life. The half-shekel, contributed by everyone, served as evidence that to be Jewish was to be counted and to be part of something greater than ourselves.

I am glad that we have advanced beyond the Tabernacle in the wilderness and the Temple in Jerusalem. Today, Jewish life exists wherever we build it. The vibrant Jewish choices about where and what to build provide remarkable potential to impact people in a manner that speaks to them today. At the same time, it is no longer reasonable to think we can expect participation simply because it is articulated by our sacred texts or even by our parents and grandparents. What we can do is to make Jewish life accessible and engaging so that when people do affiliate, the experience of living a Jewish life rises above a litany of programs and services to *do*, becoming once again an essential part of who the individuals and families that affiliate ultimately *are*. In our ever-isolating world, being part of something greater than ourselves is priceless.

While it is always possible to arrange for a bat mitzvah or funeral or any other life event without identifying with or supporting the broader Jewish community, it is within community that these moments are more than isolated occasions. These sacred moments, celebrated and mourned within the community by a person or family calling that community home, have a lasting impact not only on the individual or family, but on the community as a whole as well.

For Jews, living a ritual and a spiritual life has never been an individual endeavor. We gather in a minyan, the language of our prayer is in the plural (*our* God, *we* have gone astray, *we* bow down, *we* give thanks), and the community exists to support those within it. There is no denying that financial hardship is a reality and affiliation with synagogues and other Jewish organizations, with their professional staff and overhead, cost money. For those who want to participate and be counted in the Jewish community, though, money should not be a barrier. The Jewish community must continue to make affiliation affordable. But that required subvention can only happen when everyone contributes.

I do not know whether Leslee Komaiko and her son managed to find the time and the money to arrange for a tutor or if he ever had a bar mitzvah service. I certainly hope he did. I do know that the woman in my synagogue ended up rejoining the synagogue so that she could be part of strengthening the connection between the preschool and the broader synagogue community. But for these women and the staggering numbers of people like them who are constantly juggling the very real challenges of building a Jewish life that is part of who they are and how they live every day, the story is not done being told. It may never be. But the potential remains . . . to move beyond *having* a bar mitzvah (or any other celebration of Jewish life) to be able to celebrate a young person *being* a bar mitzvah—a young person who will carry the Torah and his *and our* heritage, with a sense of belonging, into the next generation.

NOTES

1. Spoken often by my grandmother, *z"l*, and many grandmothers I know.
2. The Los Angeles Communal Survey of 1953; The Baltimore Survey of Jewish Attitudes of 1963; *Social and Economic Characteristics of the Detroit Jewish Community, 1963.*
3. Pew Research Center's Religion and Public Life Project, *A Portrait of Jewish Americans* (Washington, DC: Pew Research Center, October 1, 2013), chap. 3; 31 percent of American Jews report belonging to a synagogue.
4. Leslee Komaiko, "It's Too Expensive to Be Jewish," *Los Angeles Times*, July 30, 2017 http://www.latimes.com/opinion/op-ed/la-oe-komaiko-cost-of-hebrew-lessons-20170730-story.html.

24

THE COST OF DYING JEWISHLY

STEPHANIE GARRY WITH RABBI ERIC J. GREENBERG

Concern over the cost of a proper funeral is nothing new for the Jewish people. About two thousand years ago, the ancient Rabbis took it upon themselves to implement new rules to prevent poor Jews from feeling ashamed because they could not afford the same opulent funerals as their wealthy neighbors. The situation was so bad, the Babylonian Talmud (*Mo-eid Katan* 27a) reports, "the expense of burying the dead was harder on the family than the death itself, so the family abandoned the corpse and fled." In response to the plight of the poor, Rabban Gamliel, president of the Sanhedrin in the first half of the first century CE, took matters into his own hands. At his death, instead of being dressed in expensive garments that only the wealthy could afford, Gamliel left instructions that his own body be carried out in a simple flaxen shroud. The Talmud says that seeing his example, all the people followed his lead and had themselves also carried out in flaxen shrouds. Two hundred years later, Rav Papa, referring to the simple shroud, reported that "nowadays, all follow the practice of being carried out even in a canvas shroud that costs but a *zuz*."[1] The Rabbis didn't stop there to bring cost equity to dying. They instituted a series of changes to make the funeral service affordable for all Jews.

During the time of the Talmud, the faces of corpses from wealthy families would remain uncovered, while the faces of poor people were covered—because their faces quickly became blackened from famine. Out of concern for the dignity of the poor, the Rabbis declared that all faces should be covered (BT *Mo-eid Katan* 27a). The deceased from rich families had been carried out in ornate stately beds, while the poor were placed on a common bier—a plain, flat board. The Rabbis instructed that everyone was to be carried out on a simple bier. Even the shivah, the first seven days of mourning, with its custom of bringing food to the house of mourners, did not escape the critique of the Rabbis. For wealthy mourners, guests would bring food in baskets of gold and silver and provide drinks in expensive white glass. In contrast, to the home of poor mourners, food was brought in simple wicker baskets made of peeled willows, and drinks were brought in cheap colored glass. Therefore, the Talmud reports, the poor people were embarrassed. But the Rabbis changed this too: they declared that out of deference to the poor, all food should be brought in wicker baskets made of peeled willow, and drinks in the inexpensive colored glass.

The importance of a proper burial with its financial dimension goes all the way back to the beginning, literally. The Book of Genesis records Abraham's purchase of a field and cave of Machpelah, located near Hebron, so he can bury his wife Sarah (Gen. 23:9). The Torah states that Abraham purchased the land from Ephron the Hittite for the full market price of 400 silver shekels. The cave served as the family burial plot for Abraham, Isaac, Rebekah, Jacob, and Leah (Gen. 49:29–33, 50:25–26). Further demonstrating the importance of a proper burial, when Jacob's beloved wife Rachel dies in childbirth along the road to Bethlehem, the patriarch stops to bury her, setting up a pillar to mark the site (Gen. 35:19–20), known as Rachel's Tomb.

About eight hundred years later, during the period of the Jewish Kingdoms of Israel and Judah, through the Second Temple period and even up the Middle Ages, Jews buried their dead in caves outside the town or city. It was a two-step process: After death, the body was brought to an outer room of the cave and placed on the floor. About a year later, after the flesh decomposed, the family collected the remaining bones and moved them into an inner room to join the bones of their ancestors, in a process called *likut atzamot* (bone gathering). During the Second Temple period, a new innovation was introduced: Jews began putting the bones in small stone boxes called ossuaries. As Roman influence increased in the region after the Second Temple was destroyed in 70 CE, Jews increasingly used caskets for burial. Famously, the great leader Rabbi Y'hudah HaNasi (Judah the Prince), the redactor of the Mishnah, was buried in a casket, dressed in a plain white linen shroud, when he died in 217 CE. It is also during the third century CE that the cost of Jewish burials increased, as some Jews, under the influence of Roman culture, began to spend extravagantly to dress up the deceased and create ornate burial sites like their pagan neighbors. In response, the Rabbis rejected these practices taken from foreign cultures, labeling them as excessive.[2]

During the Talmudic era, family obligation to bury the deceased slowly evolved into a community responsibility, and thus emerged the concept of mutual burial societies. There is a reference to this in the Talmud (BT *Mo-eid Katan* 26b) in the story of Rabbi Hamnuna, who while visiting a town, is surprised to learn that the locals continued to work at their jobs after a death was announced instead of helping bury the deceased. He was informed that a group, or *chevrah*, took care of the burial.

Later in the Middle Ages, family caves were replaced by community cemeteries that were cared for by a voluntary Jewish burial group. In the beginning, the mutual burial societies were just that: groups of Jews made agreements they would bury each other's dead when the time came. This process evolved into the establishment of nonprofit groups dedicated to giving all the Jews in the town a proper, halachic Jewish burial. The *chevrah kadisha* incorporated in Prague in 1564 is the earliest of these communal institutions on record. Membership in these new burial groups was generally reserved for the wealthy and prominent in the town, and this privilege was passed down to children for a substantial donation. Members were taught the art of a proper Jewish burial: how to wash bodies, dig graves, and teach grieving families about the laws and customs of mourning. Today, *chevrei kadisha* are not strictly voluntary societies, but some are organized nonprofits, the majority Orthodox. Volunteer *chevrei kadisha* exist in Conservative and Reform communities as well. They provide a valuable sacred service for both affiliated and unaffiliated Jews. In modern Israel, *chevrei kadisha* can be an arm of local government supported by taxes or a private association affiliated with a particular religious organization.

In the twenty-first century, Jews are still being buried in cemeteries, but a growing percentage are choosing to be cremated. As in the ancient world, customs and expenses continue to shift today, as the price of dying Jewishly remains a topic of community concern. The funeral bill has changed significantly in recent years. In 1970, according to National Funeral Directors Association, the average cost of a Jewish funeral in the Northeast was $708, or $4,207.53 adjusted to 2015 dollars.[3] In 2015, the average cost of a Jewish funeral was $8,000. "People go into debt for funerals. They take out loans. They do some crazy things," said David Zinner, vice president of the Jewish Funeral Practices Committee of Greater Washington.[4] As a result, Jews in the last decade have increasingly taken costs into consideration when planning a funeral, including reexamining the need for some luxury expenses, as well as some traditional religious rituals. Changes in both technology and the American Jewish family are key to this new dynamic.

Two generations ago, members of a nuclear family generally stayed in close proximity to each other. But with families now spread out around the country, if not the world, some question the need to spend thousands of dollars on a grave they are never going to visit. Both parents and children evaluate the economic sense of paying thousands to open, close, and maintain a grave that is no longer connected to the children geographically. Therefore, concern over costs leads some families to choose to bury the deceased where they died, not in the family burial plot purchased decades ago, now thousands of miles away from descendants. Similarly, elders now retire far from their family roots, and children must choose what to do, especially if it is less expensive to bury in the retirement locale, rather than taking on the cost of burial in the distant family plot or near adult children.

Another factor is the profound change in the traditional role of the synagogue in American Jewish life. Historically, the vast majority of synagogues had cemetery plots, purchased even before the sanctuary was built. But the synagogue, which was the pillar of the community and therefore would dictate where Jews were buried—likely in the cemetery plots that belonged to the synagogue—is not serving that function as it was twenty years ago. Changes are also more apparent in suburban synagogues, which are struggling economically more than the urban congregations. With the rising cost of real estate, suburban congregations are increasingly not buying more land for burial plots when their synagogue plots fill up. Cutting the obligation or choice to use the cemetery associated with the family synagogue creates more options for Jews.

Today, the Jewish consumer planning a funeral must consider several key factors that contribute to the overall price tag for a Jewish funeral and burial: the funeral chapel, the price of a casket, cemetery charges, and other costs related to traditional religious customs.

Caskets: A Return to Tradition

It should first be noted that Jewish burial costs and customs vary around the world. In the Middle East and Eastern Europe for example, caskets are rarely used. In Israel, too, there is no casket. Instead, a body is buried wrapped in a shroud and buried directly in the ground. (An exception is made for Israeli soldiers, who are buried in a shroud and a plain wooden casket in deference to the mortal damage done to their bodies.)

However, in the West, Jews are routinely buried in caskets. For many years, the price of caskets has been one of the key factors in driving up the cost of Jewish funerals. The average cost of a funeral can more than double, depending on the casket chosen.

For example, costs for a Jewish funeral are typically $8,000, which include the basic charges for transferring the body to the funeral chapel and then the cemetery, preparing the body, usually with a traditional white linen shroud, arrangements for a graveside service, and a hearse. But that $8,000 cost can jump to $15,000 with the choice of a luxury casket made of mahogany, oak, or walnut and lined with velvet.[5] In recent years, Jews from all streams have been returning to tradition and choosing plain pine caskets, as the ancient Rabbis directed. One explanation has to do with end-of-life issues and religious observance. People tend to cling to ritual regarding death, even when they are not observant other times in their lives. Yet, in the last generation, there was a sense that buying a more extravagant casket was a way to honor one's dead, to show care for the deceased. But the notion that the more expensive the casket, the more love shown is no longer the conventional wisdom. As Jews attend funerals and witness the increased use of plain pine caskets, they feel the permission to do the same. Even the wealthiest members of the Jewish community are following the trend. Rabbi Y'hudah HaNasi and the Talmudic Sages clearly understood human nature.

A handful of nonprofit community-owned and community-operated funeral chapels have been established in the United States to return to the basic service of the community caring for one another at this most sacred moment. Purposefully, the profit motive has been taken out of the equation. For example, in 2001, a group of New York City Jewish community leaders (along with UJA-Federation of New York and the Jewish Communal Fund) acquired Plaza Memorial Funeral Chapel from a national for-profit funeral home chain to create for the first time in New York a nonprofit community-owned and community-operated funeral chapel, now known as Plaza Jewish Community Chapel. In San Francisco, Sinai Chapel has operated as a nonprofit for the Jewish community for more than a century.

Of course, there are other expenses associated with a Jewish funeral. Jewish tradition calls for a *shomeir*, or watcher to guard the body until burial, and for *tahorah*, the ritual washing of the body before it is dressed in a simple white shroud. These rituals are often performed by the local Jewish burial society, or *chevrah kadisha*, whose services are engaged by funeral chapels and cost about $400.[6] Then there is the decision whether to have clergy officiate at the funeral. Depending on the synagogue, a rabbi or cantor officiating at a funeral can be part of the benefits of congregational membership. But in cases where it is not and for unaffiliated Jews, having a rabbi or cantor officiate runs between $500 and $600.[7] While it can be comforting to have clergy conducting the funeral, there is no religious requirement to have a professional perform the funeral service. And families are increasingly choosing to forgo using a rabbi or cantor at the service for a number of reasons. According to one New York City survey from 2017, about 15 to 20 percent of funerals did not have clergy involved. This compares to about 1 to 2 percent a decade before.[8] This reflects cost, but also the rise of unaffiliated and interfaith families who have no connection to a family rabbi or cantor. They do not feel the need to pay for that ritual, instead reciting the traditional prayers and giving eulogies without professional guidance.

Cemetery Costs

One of the biggest charges, one that often leads to confusion and misunderstanding, is from the cemetery. In fact, cemetery costs can represent as much as half the total cost of a Jewish funeral/burial bill. The price includes the cemetery's charge to open and close the burial plot, which can run as high as $4,000. Yet the bill presented by the funeral chapel often includes the cemetery charges. This can be confusing for the grieving family, who can mistakenly think the cemetery charges come from the funeral chapel. It helps if all charges are on one bill, so the family must write only one check. However, a licensed funeral director should carefully review the bill with the family, making sure they understand that the cost of opening and closing the grave is not going to the funeral chapel, but to the cemetery, which may or may not be regulated by a government agency, depending on location.

Cremation

As a result of funeral and cemetery costs and major changes in the lifestyle of American Jews, cremation has become a growing alternative, despite its historical prohibition by Orthodox and traditional legal authorities. Indeed, halachah, or Jewish law, mandates that corpses be buried. In the Book of Genesis (3:19), after the sin of the Tree of Knowledge, God says to Adam, "For dust you are, and to dust you shall return." In Deuteronomy 21:23, the Torah commands that the body of an executed criminal must be buried on the same day. Historically, cremation was also associated with pagan practices, which the Torah commands the Jewish people to abhor. The mandate to bury the dead was later codified in Rabbinic literature, including the Talmud, Maimonides's *Sefer HaMitzvot*, and the *Shulchan Aruch*.[9] After the Shoah, cremation took on another layer of negativity, with the horrific vision of millions of Jews being burned in Nazi crematoria. Proponents of cremation note there is no explicit prohibition against cremation in Jewish legal sources. They also note biblical sources that suggest ancient Jews may have burned dead bodies in rituals. The Book of Samuel reports that the men of Jabesh-Gilead took the bodies of King Saul and his three sons mutilated by the Philistines and burned them as an act of faithfulness (I Sam. 31:9–13; II Sam. 2:5). There are also references to "making a fire" at the funeral of certain biblical kings, although it is not clear what exactly is being burned (Jer. 34:5; II Chron. 16:14; 21:19).

Given the preponderance of arguments against it, rabbinic leaders in the Orthodox and Conservative streams hold that cremation is prohibited. The Reform Movement holds differing viewpoints; however, in recent years leaders have stated that while cremation is not a violation of Jewish law, it should not be encouraged.[10] Nevertheless, centuries of tradition and continued rabbinic opposition to cremation can cause tension for families.

In recent years, a confluence of factors has eased the traditional restrictions against cremation. For one, cremation has become more common among non-Jews. The challenging costs of a traditional funeral have led Jews to seek alternatives, and the price of cremation can be half that of a no-frills traditional funeral with a plain casket. The percentage of Jews choosing cremation depends on location, but today hovers between 10 and 14 percent of total Jewish funerals, compared to about 3 to 5 percent a decade ago. "I think it's become a more accepted, preferred form of disposition," said Mindy Botbol, president of the Jewish Funeral Directors of America and a funeral director at Shalom Memorial Park and Funeral Home in Arlington Heights, Illinois.[11]

Cremains are legally disposed of in several ways. Some relatives choose to keep them in an urn. Other families divide the cremains among themselves. Another option is to scatter them at sea, but they must be taken out at least three nautical miles from land, according to U.S. Environmental Protection Agency regulations. The cost of ocean disposal varies. In addition, some families choose to bury them in a family mausoleum, which results in added cemetery opening costs as much as several thousand dollars.

The board of directors at Plaza, which includes Orthodox, Conservative, Reform, Reconstructionist, and Renewal rabbis, approved Plaza to assist families when requesting cremation. This decision is the result of Plaza's mission, which is to "ensure that every member of the Jewish community receive a dignified Jewish burial." It is up to each individual to decide what is appropriate for their family.

Gravestones

The cost of dying Jewishly doesn't end after the burial. Several months after burial, the process of ordering a gravestone usually begins. Erecting a gravestone has great significance, religiously, historically, and culturally, as it comes straight from the Bible in Genesis 35:20, where it is reported that Jacob established a marker for Rachel when she died on the road in Bethlehem. And much Jewish history has been gleaned from information contained on gravestones. But the price of an upright gravestone can start at about $2,000, which is out of reach for many families, especially after the other funeral costs.

One of the reasons for the higher cost of gravestones is that Jewish cemeteries and synagogues are using them to offset the cost of other funeral-related charges, including providing discounted funerals to those who die on Medicaid. "It's the only way we can police the loss of revenue to the Jewish Cemetery Association," said Stan Kaplan, executive director of the Jewish Cemetery Association of Massachusetts.[12] Other after-funeral costs can include a foundation pouring fee required to stabilize headstones and the cost of perpetual care, which together can cost many additional thousands of dollars.

The cost of dying Jewishly fluctuates, often in response to the changing lifestyles of the American Jewish communities. It could be seen as a series of contradictions. On the one hand, a return to simple pine caskets, do-it-yourself funeral services, a move to using synagogues rather than funeral chapels, and more people choosing the less expensive option of cremation should mean lower costs for Jewish funerals. Yet at the same time, with steep cemetery costs and the increase in basic vendor services like limousines, funeral costs continue to be a concern for many.

To meet the challenge of rising costs, it is in the interest of Jewish leaders of all denominations and communities to reexamine the teachings of our ancient Sages and to strategize about how best to make Jewish funerals more financially accessible, rather than leaving it to individual families to look for ways to cut costs at a very stressful and emotional time. Following the model of Rabban Gamliel and the other rabbis of the Talmud, the Jewish community should seek ways to help Jews save money and make the process more transparent, through the creation and promotion of more nonprofit Jewish funeral chapels, working with the Jewish community to find ways to lower and stabilize funeral costs, pre-planning to lock in costs, and making no-interest loans available to the needy. And, of course, who knows what other innovations could be thought of if the Jewish community works together to help make Jewish rituals accessible for the dead and their mourners.

NOTES

1. Elon Gilad, "The History of Jewish Burial," *Haaretz*, April 21, 2015.
2. Gilad, "The History of Jewish Burial."
3. "CPI Inflation Calculator," Bureau of Labor Statistics, United States Department of Labor, calculated on June 10, 2018, https://www.bls.gov/data/inflation_calculator.htm.
4. Melissa Gerr and Marc Shapiro, "The Cost of a Dignified Burial," *Baltimore Jewish Times*, June 4, 2015.
5. "How Much Does a Jewish Funeral Cost?," CostHelper, accessed on July 29, 2018, http://personalfinance.costhelper.com/jewish-funerals.html.
6. Based on pricing in the New York metropolitan area in the spring of 2018.
7. Based on pricing in the New York metropolitan area in the spring of 2018.
8. As tracked by Plaza Jewish Community Chapel, Inc.
9. BT *Sanhedrin* 46b; Maimonides, *Sefer HaMitzvot*, aseih 231; *Shulchan Aruch, Yoreh Dei-ah* 362:1, 348:2–3.
10. Victor Appell, "What Is Reform Judaism's Position on Cremation?," ReformJudaism.org, accessed September 24, 2018, https://reformjudaism.org/practice/ask-rabbi/what-reform-judaisms-position-cremation.
11. Josh Nathan-Kazis, "More Jews Opt for Cremation," *Forward*, June 27, 2012.
12. Julie Masis, "Luxuries for Poor as Jewish Burial Groups Cut Back," *Forward*, December 1, 2016.

25

MAZAL TOV TO LIFE-CYCLE PARTIES

RABBI DOUGLAS B. SAGAL, DD

God showed Moses a shekel made of fire.

Midrash Tanchuma on Exodus 30:13

To teach us that like fire, money can warm and nourish, or destroy and degrade.

Rabbi Elimelech of Lizhensk (d. 1787)

Many years ago, an older mentor, an esteemed rabbi, gave a High Holy Day sermon that got him into some trouble. In the era before digital video, it had become the custom in affluent Jewish communities to create a bar or bat mitzvah invitation in a VHS format. The bar mitzvah boy or bat mitzvah girl would be featured in a short film, mailed as a package, at great expense, to all the invited guests. One Rosh HaShanah, noting this trend, my mentor stated, "When the bar mitzvah invitation is larger than the mailbox, you know you have a problem."

Needless to say, some in the congregation, particularly those who either had sent this type of invitation or were planning to, were offended and infuriated. "How dare the rabbi tell us how to spend our money—and on a Jewish event too!" In other words, the offended congregants felt that they had the right to spend their resources as they saw fit, and after all, it was for a religious purpose. Who was the rabbi to admonish them?

As it turns out, my mentor was not the first to question extravagant expenditures on Jewish events. In the sixteenth century, Polish rabbi Solomon Luria derided bar mitzvah celebrations as "occasions for wild levity, for the purpose of stuffing the gullet."[1] Four hundred years later, Benjamin Efron and Rabbi Alvan D. Rubin echoed Luria, in "The Reality of Bar Mitzvah," published in the *CCAR Journal*, bemoaning, "The extravagant consumption, the waste and the crudity of these affairs are becoming a Jewish scandal."[2]

In recent years, the media has been filled with stories about extravagant, multimillion-dollar *b'nei mitzvah* celebrations, complete with hired celebrities to entertain. In fact, a well-received 2006 movie, *Keeping Up with the Steins*, dealt with this issue as its main theme. Before we get too deeply into piously lamenting that Jews have become too "over the top" in our contemporary celebrations, let's remember that the first party celebrating a religious event was organized by none other than the founder of the faith, Abraham. Three thousand years ago the patriarch threw a party for his son Isaac, on the occasion of his weaning (Gen. 21:8). While there is no discussion of whether there was a DJ or motivational dancers or balloons spelling out "ISAAC," it was probably a very nice party.

The tradition of a *s'udat mitzvah*, literally "a meal in honor of a mitzvah," is ancient and well established in the Jewish tradition. Although it began with our ancestor Abraham, the idea of having a celebratory meal connected with the performance of a mitzvah is reflected in the literature of the Talmud, the Middle Ages, and up to our present day. It is the common practice to have a meal, and even a party, associated not only with a bar or bat mitzvah, but also with a *b'rit milah* or a *b'rit bat*, baby namings, and of course, a wedding. Even the most expansive and expensive celebrations almost always include a nod to the fact that the event is connected to a religious rite of passage. Without being too cynical, how often does the most hedonistic bar mitzvah party begin with an elderly relative (often a grandparent) reciting *Motzi* or *Kiddush*? The question I pose is: Has all this become too much from an economic point of view? In other words, we can argue over the tastefulness (or tastelessness) of having Kanye West or Aerosmith perform at your son's bar mitzvah or a wedding where the hosts fly all four hundred guests to an exotic locale, but should we even be spending our money on such events? Or is it mandated by tradition that we be more restrained in our spending on the *s'udot mitzvah* and their accompanying celebrations? Certainly, our tradition values the idea of moderation and restraint. Most famously Moses Maimonides (Spain/Egypt, 1135–1204) advocated the "middle path"—that is adopting a practice of moderation in all things.[3] Some argue that exorbitant spending on life-cycle celebrations could better be directed toward worthy causes. However, according to Maimonides, a person should live neither in extreme abstinence nor in extreme gluttony. The early Rabbis disapproved of the biblical institution of the Nazirite, the Jew who voluntarily abstains from wine and other pleasures of life, which the Rabbis believed should be enjoyed. The preponderance of evidence suggests that the Jewish tradition encourages us to enjoy and celebrate the significant moments of life but to do so while clinging to a "middle path."[4] It is also undeniable that our tradition requires us to contribute *tzedakah* to support the poor, to ameliorate suffering, to sustain our religious institutions. The Torah itself is replete with examples of laws that demand a mandatory contribution to assist the poor, as well as to maintain the Tabernacle and the priesthood.

It is not clear that those who spend large sums on life-cycle events are not also generous and philanthropic. Although the media relishes stories of selfish people who make large parties while ignoring social ills, in my congregational experience there are many who spend a great deal on life-cycle events and are equally generous and philanthropic. Not long ago some pundits in the Jewish community condemned an "over the top" bar mitzvah in Texas until it was discovered that the parents who spent millions on their son's event were among the most generous and philanthropic in their Jewish community. Is the current practice of some in the Jewish community spending exorbitant sums on life-cycle celebrations permitted, or should we be working to curb the expense connected to these celebrations? To seek an answer, I turned to the work of Carmel Chiswick, professor of economics at George Washington University, who wrote *Judaism in Transition: How Economic Choices Shape Religious Tradition*. In this short book, Chiswick examines the economic history of the American Jewish community and explores how wealth influences religious choices that Jews make.[5] First, Chiswick establishes that American Jews are, in fact, wealthy. Although there are many American Jews who are poor and lower middle class, a majority fall into the category of wealthier Americans. As Chiswick states, "It is clear that in the year 2000 [the year of the study she cites] the well-educated American Jewish community had a high proportion of families with earnings in six figures."[6] Furthermore, the fact that many Jewish families could now count on several generations of family wealth means that even a Jewish family earning a middle-class income can most likely afford an upper-class lifestyle. After several generations of economic success in America, many Jewish households might find themselves with firmly middle-class wages, but fully upper-middle-class lifestyles, thanks to these other sources of income.[7] This is quite apparent in many synagogues, as families spend a great deal of money on life-cycle events assisted by wealthy parents and grandparents. Even the family in *Keeping Up with the Steins*, who forgoes a bar mitzvah at Dodger Stadium in favor of a more modest backyard barbecue, live in an enormous mansion, and that "backyard" is the size of a football field. Chiswick comes to the novel conclusion that American Jews see "purchasing" Jewish experiences in the same manner that they purchase any commodity. In the enviable position of having high incomes at their disposal, Jews tend to see "purchasing Jewish" as a good, like a boat, car, or expensive vacation. Steven Weiss, who interviewed Chiswick for an article in the *Atlantic*, writes:

> "Religion is a good," Chiswick told me in an interview. While it's unconventional to think of religion that way, the transaction of exchanging time and money for a particular experience retains

certain core qualities whether that experience is religious or secular. For example, though it might seem more wholesome than buying a boat, paying for religious schooling is still a purchase of a luxury good. Heading to church or synagogue might make one feel more righteous and community-oriented than going golfing on a weekend morning, and that's pretty much the point: The feelings and knock-on effects gathered from spending time in a certain way are part of the overall purchase.[8]

In other words, according to Chiswick, the Jewish consumer will choose to "buy Jewish" if he or she receives the kind of pleasure and satisfaction that comes from purchasing any good on the market. Similarly, Judith Lichtenberg, professor of philosophy at Georgetown University, has argued that critiques of consumption often unfairly indict human character. She writes, "An appreciation of the complexities of consumption shows why it is often reasonable and respectable for a person to consume when others do; more generally it illuminates certain puzzles about human desires and wellbeing."[9] According to Lichtenberg, it is simplistic to condemn those who spend large sums on items or events that give them pleasure.

The ancient Sages themselves argued that there are certain circumstances that demand the display of even ostentatious wealth. The Babylonian Talmud (*Yoma* 34b–35b) describes approvingly the ornate garments of the High Priest, worn on Yom Kippur, and even delineates the value of each item. The Sages add that if the High Priest was wealthy, he could augment the fine garments with even finer, more expensive clothes and accessories. They tell the story about Rabbi Elazar ben Harsum (believed to be a High Priest) whose mother made him a garment worth twenty thousand *dinar*, approximately 2.12 million grams of silver.[10] The other Sages would not let him wear it, not because it was too expensive, but because the linen was so fine he appeared naked underneath![11] Almost one thousand years later Moses Maimonides comments that golden vessels were used in the Temple service simply to display wealth, and therefore that in a place of wealth, there is no need to display poverty, meaning that in a place in which

328 · THE SACRED EXCHANGE

conspicuous consumption is the norm, there is no need to display false modesty.[12]

When my rabbinic mentor criticized the VHS bar mitzvah invitations, people were outraged not because he was perceived as mocking their choices, but because he called into doubt the intense satisfaction they received from making the videos, sending them to friends, and enjoying the responses. Not dissimilar from a person who proudly buys a new car only to have people tell her that the model is fraught with problems, is ugly, etc., this leads me, as a congregational rabbi, to the following conclusion. I serve a congregation in which a significant percentage of members can afford to spend a great deal of money on life-cycle events—and often do. (There are many members of my congregation of modest means as well.) Following Jewish tradition, I urge moderation and walking a middle path in planning and funding these events. I find the occasional competition between families and the extreme "one-upmanship" to be distasteful, but that is rarer than one might think. We are living in an age in which choice, rather than obligation, is the driving force behind much of the American Jewish community. The decision to live Jewishly, to observe Jewish ritual, to belong to a synagogue, and to support Jewish institutions is very much a matter of individual choice. If spending considerable wealth on a *b'rit bat*, *b'rit milah*, bar/bat mitzvah, or wedding is the choice of a Jewish family, it is not for us to judge. That family derives satisfaction from "purchasing Jewish," and we must realize that this purchase provides the family with genuine satisfaction and a sense of well-being. There are too many opportunities for Jewish families and individuals to simply drop out of Jewish life; therefore, a family spending their wealth on a Jewish life-cycle experience is something we should applaud, rather than condemn for its excess. Yes, there are the occasional scoundrels who embarrass the community by ostentatious displays of wealth, but for every one of those, there are hundreds more who spend large sums in sincerity and, yes, even in piety, derive great joy from the *s'udat mitzvah*, turning their celebration into a sacred meal. We should applaud them and wish them a *mazal tov*!

NOTES

1. Jeffrey K. Salkin, *Putting God on the Guest List: How to Reclaim the Spiritual Meaning of Your Child's Bar or Bat Mitzvah* (Woodstock, VT: Jewish Lights, 2010), 83.
2. Benjamin Efron and Alvan D. Rubin, "The Reality of Bar Mitzvah," *CCAR Journal: The Reform Jewish Quarterly* 8, no. 3, no. 31 (October 1960): 32.
3. Maimonides, *Mishneh Torah, Hilchot Dei-ot* 1:4.
4. For example, see BT *Taanit* 11a; BT *N'darim* 10a.
5. Carmel U. Chiswick, *Judaism in Transition: How Economic Choices Shape Religious Tradition* (Stanford, CA: Stanford University Press, 2014), 21.
6. Chiswick, *Judaism in Transition*, 45.
7. Steven I. Weiss, "A Cost-Benefit Analysis of Being Jewish," *Atlantic*, October 3, 2014, www.theatlantic.com/business/archive/2014/10/a-cost-benefit-analysis-of-being-jewish/381009/.
8. Weiss, "A Cost-Benefit Analysis of Being Jewish."
9. Judith Lichtenberg, "Consuming Because Others Consume," *Philosophy and Public Policy Quarterly* 15, no. 4 (1995): 156–57.
10. The Talmud does not specify the type of currency; *dinar*, according the Steinsaltz commentary. Approximation to silver, as calculated from Yitzhak Frank, *The Practical Talmud Dictionary* (Jerusalem: Ariel Institute, 1991), appendix 4, "Coins and Weights."
11. BT *Yoma* 35b. Thank you to my teacher Dr. Elana Stein Hain for bringing this text to my attention.
12. Maimonides, *Commentary on the Mishnah, Tamid* 3:4. The exact quote is, "There is not poverty in a place of wealth."

26

MONEY AND TRANSACTION
IN JEWISH LITURGY AND RITUAL

Rabbi Robert Scheinberg

For many, the word "spiritual" is best understood in contrast with the word "material." According to this interpretation, objects in the physical world are necessarily less "spiritual" than the soul, emotions, values, experiences, and other intangibles. A spiritual person may focus less on the body and in fact may engage in techniques to escape it and journey outside of it.

The perspective of Jewish tradition is different. Jewish texts have never implied that God is unconcerned with the world of the material; in fact, our material existence is one route into relationship with God. An example of this comes from the Chasidic tradition, which draws a contrast between *gashmiyut* (the material dimension of the world) and *ruchaniyut* (the spiritual dimension of the world), but there is never an assumption that God is concerned only with *ruchaniyut*. In fact, one ideal of a Chasidic life is *avodah sheb'gashmiyut*, service of God through our connection with the mundane material world.[1]

Money may be the paradigmatic example of *gashmiyut*, the material, in our lives. Money is exchangeable for nearly every other kind of material in the world. In fact, we use the word "materialistic" to refer to someone who is overly concerned with money. The mere mention of money has the power to transform an emotional and heartfelt interaction into a transaction that feels crass or even ugly and exploitative. Furthermore, many religions have been criticized for the "un-spiritual" role that money has played in the religion—from the Catholic Church's sale of indulgences that helped to prompt the Protestant Reformation, to the lavish lifestyles of various diverse religious leaders, to accusations of corruption among religious leaders in many centuries and many places around the world.

Despite these negative associations with money, Judaism understands the potential for wealth to be an instrument of *avodah sheb'gashmiyut*, of the possibility of deepening one's spiritual life and serving even using this paradigmatic example of "the material." This chapter collects examples of references to and uses of money in Jewish prayer and ritual. Not all of these examples resonate with every Jewish community, but they highlight that Jewish tradition has rejected a strict dichotomy between the material and the spiritual.

Lending and Borrowing in Jewish Prayer Texts

Casual observers of Jewish liturgy and ritual may be surprised just how frequently Jewish prayers and rituals include or discuss money and transaction. One category of such references centers around lending and borrowing. This motif is found most prominently in the *Birkat HaMazon*, Blessing after Meals:

וְנָא אַל תַּצְרִיכֵנוּ יְיָ אֱלֹהֵינוּ, לֹא לִידֵי מַתְּנַת בָּשָׂר וָדָם וְלֹא לִידֵי הַלְוָאָתָם, כִּי אִם לְיָדְךָ הַמְּלֵאָה הַפְּתוּחָה הַקְּדוֹשָׁה וְהָרְחָבָה, שֶׁלֹּא נֵבוֹשׁ וְלֹא נִכָּלֵם לְעוֹלָם וָעֶד.

> Make us not dependent on the gifts of other human beings or on their loans, but rather on Your full and ample, generous,[2] and wide-open hand, that we may never be shamed or humiliated.[3]

This petition implies that for all that Jewish tradition encourages people to be generous to others, there is an element of shame and humiliation that is felt by one who receives charity, and while praying for ample food, one prays for self-sufficiency. This petition is located within the blessing about the rebuilding of Jerusalem, which represents Jewish self-sufficiency on a national scale. The specific reference to loans reminds us that in the Hebrew Bible, loans are mentioned only as a way to assist the poor, rather than as a necessary component of a capitalist economy.[4] This passage in *Birkat HaMazon* echoes the passage in Deuteronomy 28:43–44, within the list of curses that would befall the people of Israel if they neglect God's laws:

> The strangers in your midst shall rise above you higher and higher, while you sink lower and lower: they shall be your creditors, but you shall not be theirs; they shall be the head and you the tail.[5]

The implication of the conclusion of the *Birkat HaMazon* text, however, is that it is only shameful to receive gifts and loans from "flesh and blood," but not directly from God. There are various texts that suggest that all we have and benefit from in the material world is a gift or a loan from God; the Talmud even indicates that one of the functions of blessings before food is to prompt God to release God's property for human consumption. In other words, all property, including all food, belongs to God, and one who eats without having said a blessing has actually misappropriated sacred property (Babylonian Talmud, *B'rachot* 35a). Even the human body is described as being divine property that is on long-term loan to the individual.[6]

Prayers for Economic Well-Being

In the statutory portions of Jewish liturgy (i.e., the portions of Jewish liturgy that have their basis in the Talmud, as opposed to later medieval and modern additions), the most prominent petition for economic stability is within the weekday *Amidah*, in the *Birkat HaShanim*, Blessing of the Years. In its traditional Ashkenazic formulation, this blessing is as follows:

ברך עלינו יי אלהינו את השנה הזאת ואת כל מיני תבואתה לטובה, ותן ברכה על
פני האדמה, ושבענו מטובך, וברך שנתנו כשנים הטובות. ברוך אתה יי, מברך השנים.

Adonai our God, make this a blessed year for us; may its varied
harvest yield prosperity. May the land be blessed [*in winter add:* with
dew and rain] and satisfy us with its goodness. Bless this year, that it
be like the best of years. Blessed are You, Adonai, who is the source
of blessing of each year.[7]

This blessing addresses material well-being in general terms, but
there are other prayer texts that are more overt in requesting material sustenance. The Talmud indicates that one who wants to pray
for individual needs is encouraged to do so within the daily *Amidah*'s
blessing *Shomei-a T'filah*, "Who Hears Prayer." Thus, many prayer
books include such an optional prayer for sustenance in that section;
the following example is found in the prayer book of Rabbi Isaiah
Horowitz (first printed in Amsterdam in 1717):

אתה הוא יי האלקים, הזן ומפרנס ומכלכל מקרני ראמים עד ביצי כנים, הטריפני לחם
חקי, והמצא לי ולכל בני ביתי מזונותי קודם שאצטרך להם, בנחת ולא בצער, בהתר ולא
באסור, בכבוד ולא בבזיון, לחיים ולשלום, משפע ברכה והצלחה משפע ברכה עליונה, כדי
שאוכל לעשות רצונך, ולעסוק בתורתך, ולקיים מצוותיך, ואל תצריכני לידי מתנת בשר
ודם, ויקויים בי מקרא שכתוב, פותח את ידך ומשביע לכל חי רצון.

You are Adonai, God, the one who sustains and grants food, from
the horns of the wild oxen to the eggs of lice,[8] grant me my portion
of bread,[9] and provide food for me and all the members of my household before I need it, with pleasure and not with sorrow, permissibly
and not through prohibition, with honor and not with degradation,
for life and peace, from the bounty of blessing and success from the
"upper pool,"[10] so that I will be able to fulfill Your will and occupy
myself with Your Torah and fulfill Your commandments. Do not
make me dependent upon the gifts of flesh and blood. Fulfill for me
the verse: "You open Your hand and sustain every living thing with
favor."[11]

There is also a tradition of reciting the passage from the Book of Exodus about the manna (Exodus 16) at the conclusion of the daily morning service, usually cited to a passage from the Talmud of the Land of Israel,[12] accompanied by petitions for material sustenance, like the following:

יְהִי רָצוֹן מִלְּפָנֶיךָ, יְיָ אֱלֹהֵינוּ וֵאלֹהֵי אֲבוֹתֵינוּ, שֶׁתַּזְמִין פַּרְנָסָה לְכָל עַמְּךָ בֵּית יִשְׂרָאֵל, וּפַרְנָסָתִי וּפַרְנָסַת אַנְשֵׁי בֵיתִי בִּכְלָלָם, בְּנַחַת וְלֹא בְצַעַר, בְּכָבוֹד וְלֹא בְּבִזּוּי, בְּהֶתֵּר וְלֹא בְאִסּוּר, כְּדֵי שֶׁנּוּכַל לַעֲבֹד עֲבוֹדָתֶךָ וְלִלְמוֹד תּוֹרָתֶךָ, כְּמוֹ שֶׁזַּנְתָּ לַאֲבוֹתֵינוּ מָן בַּמִּדְבָּר, בְּאֶרֶץ צִיָּה וַעֲרָבָה.

> May it be Your will, Adonai our God and God of our ancestors, to provide sustenance for all Your people, the House of Israel, and sustenance for me and all the members of my household, with pleasantness and not with suffering, with honor and not with degradation, through permissible activities and not forbidden activities, so that we will be able to serve You and to learn Your Torah, just as You sustained our ancestors in the wilderness with manna in a dry and desert land.[13]

Following the manna passage in some prayer books would be the following statement, which echoes the concern about borrowing that is found in some other texts we have examined:

אַתָּה הוּא יְיָ לְבַדֶּךָ אַתָּה עָשִׂיתָ אֶת הַשָּׁמַיִם וּשְׁמֵי הַשָּׁמַיִם הָאָרֶץ וְכָל אֲשֶׁר עָלֶיהָ הַיַּמִּים וְכָל אֲשֶׁר בָּהֶם וְאַתָּה מְחַיֶּה אֶת כֻּלָּם וְאַתָּה הוּא שֶׁעָשִׂיתָ נִסִּים וְנִפְלָאוֹת גְּדוֹלוֹת תָּמִיד עִם אֲבוֹתֵינוּ גַם בַּמִּדְבָּר הִמְטַרְתָּ לָהֶם לֶחֶם מִן הַשָּׁמַיִם וּמִצּוּר הַחַלָּמִישׁ הוֹצֵאתָ לָהֶם מַיִם וְגַם נָתַתָּ לָהֶם כָּל צָרְכֵיהֶם שִׂמְלוֹתָם לֹא בָלְתָה מֵעֲלֵיהֶם כֵּן בְּרַחֲמֶיךָ הָרַבִּים וּבַחֲסָדֶיךָ הָעֲצוּמִים תְּזוּנֵנוּ וּתְפַרְנְסֵנוּ וּתְכַלְכְּלֵנוּ וְתַסְפִּיק לָנוּ כָּל צָרְכֵנוּ וְצָרְכֵי עַמְּךָ בֵּית יִשְׂרָאֵל הַמְרוּבִּים בְּמִלּוּי וּבְרֶוַח בְּלִי טֹרַח וְעָמָל גָּדוֹל מִתַּחַת יָדְךָ הַנְּקִיָּה וְלֹא מִתַּחַת יְדֵי בָשָׂר וָדָם:

יְהִי רָצוֹן מִלְּפָנֶיךָ יְהֹוָה אֱלֹהַי וֵאלֹהֵי אֲבוֹתַי שֶׁתָּכִין לִי וּלְאַנְשֵׁי בֵיתִי כָּל מַחֲסוֹרֵנוּ וְתַזְמִין לָנוּ כָּל צָרְכֵנוּ לְכָל יוֹם וָיוֹם מֵחַיֵּינוּ דֵּי מַחֲסוֹרֵנוּ וּלְכָל שָׁעָה וְשָׁעָה מִשְּׁעוֹתֵינוּ דֵּי סִפּוּקֵנוּ וּלְכָל עֶצֶם מֵעֲצָמֵינוּ דֵּי מִחְיָתֵנוּ מִיָּדְךָ הַטּוֹבָה וְהָרְחָבָה וְלֹא כִמְעוּט מִפְעָלֵינוּ וְקוֹצֶר חֲסָדֵינוּ וּמִזְעֵיר גְּמוּלוֹתֵינוּ וְיִהְיוּ מְזוֹנוֹתַי וּמְזוֹנוֹת אַנְשֵׁי בֵיתִי וְזַרְעִי וְזֶרַע זַרְעִי מְסוּרִים בְּיָדְךָ וְלֹא בְּיַד בָּשָׂר וָדָם:

You are Adonai alone; You made the heavens and the higher heavens, the land and all that is in it, the seas and all that is in them, and You keep everything alive. You are the one who always made the great miracles for our ancestors. In the wilderness, too, You rained down bread for them from the heavens, and You brought them water from the flinty rock, and You provided for all their needs, and their clothing did not wear out.[14] So, in Your great mercy and abundant kindness, sustain us and support us, and provide for our needs and the great needs of Your people Israel, with fullness and abundance, without burdensome labor, from Your pure hand, and not from the hand of flesh and blood.

May it be Your will, Adonai my God and God of my ancestors, to provide for me and the members of my household all that we lack, and to provide for all our needs, giving us each day what we lack and giving us each hour enough for our needs, and to provide each of our limbs enough to thrive. May it come from Your good and generous hand, and not in accordance with the paucity of our deeds and our limited kindnesses. May my food and the food of the members of my household, my children and my children's children, be given to us from Your hand, and not from the hand of flesh and blood.[15]

Like the passage from *Birkat HaMazon*, the repeated motif in this passage is that there may be no such thing as true self-sufficiency, as everything comes from God, but the deepest hope is that one will not have to rely on charitable giving. Rather, one's sustenance will be provided directly from God, which is the equivalent to earning it oneself.

In yet another example, the *Kaddish D'Rabanan*, the special form of the *Kaddish* that is recited following study, includes a prayer for the welfare of scholars, teachers, and students. Along with prayers for long life, peace, grace, and mercy, we pray that they may have *m'zonei r'vichei*, "ample food," which may be a sad reference to the material sacrifices that often characterized a life of scholarship.

Communal Fundraising
during Jewish Prayer and Ritual

Prior generations in the Jewish community seem to have had a greater comfort with discussion of the need for material sustenance during synagogue services, which later generations often regarded as inappropriate. For example, it had been a common practice to auction off synagogue honors during synagogue services. This auctioning of honors and the accompanying purchasing of prayers in honor or in memory of individuals were referred to in Ashkenazic communities as *shnuddering*, based on the Hebrew word *shenadar*, meaning "who has donated," which would often be included in such prayers.[16] Over time, the auctioning of honors and the overt discussion of finances during synagogue services were increasingly regarded as unseemly and uncouth. In fact, in 1825, opposition to such fundraising during synagogue services was one of the core principles of Charleston's Reformed Society of Israelites, the first organization in the United States to promote religious reform.[17] Nearly a century later, fundraising during synagogue services was considered such an objectionable practice to some early twentieth-century Orthodox Jews that they founded the Young Israel movement in part to create synagogues that would avoid this practice. One of the most prominent Orthodox synagogues in New York City, Kehillath Jeshurun, abolished *shnuddering* in 1943, defending this decision by saying that this practice "imparted an unsavory commercial character to one of the most sacred parts of the service."[18] It is possible that such commercial activity was considered more acceptable in earlier years when the community was in a more precarious financial condition; once the community was wealthier, there was an assumption that it would make a separation between fundraising and religious ritual.

One of the most beloved Jewish rituals, the *Yizkor* memorial service, is also associated with charitable donations from its very origins. As early as fourteenth- to fifteenth-century Germany, rabbinic sources demonstrate a direct connection between the *Yizkor* memorial prayer, recited on Pesach, Shavuot, Sh'mini Atzeret, and Yom Kippur, and the concept of *mat'nat yad*, or "the gift of one's hands." This phrase refers to the passage in Deuteronomy 16:17 (traditionally read on the festival days when *Yizkor* is recited) that describes how each person coming to Jerusalem for the Pilgrimage Festivals would bring a gift appropriate for that person's means. This phrase came to refer to donations that individuals would make to their communities at the time of the Pilgrimage Festivals.[19] In Ashkenazic communities, it has been customary for the *Yizkor* prayers to include a phrase like "I pledge to give charity in his/her memory." Sometimes, the phrase "without taking a formal oath" is inserted into this pledge so that it is considered appropriate to declare on the holiday and so that the consequences of not carrying out this pledge are less dire.[20]

The original Reform prayer book from the Hamburg Temple, in 1819, included such a charitable pledge in its *Yizkor* memorial service.[21] Since that time, some non-Orthodox prayer books have included such a pledge during the *Yizkor* prayer to give charity, and others have not. The overall trend, however, appears to be toward the reintroduction of this financial pledge language in the *Yizkor* prayer, perhaps demonstrating a growing level of comfort with financial references in the context of Jewish prayer.[22]

Jewish Rituals That Include or Refer to Currency

There are a few Jewish rituals that either revolve around money or make special reference to money. For example, coins are central in the ritual of *pidyon haben*, "redemption of the firstborn." While the *kohanim*, the priests descended from Aaron, became the ritual leaders of the community, the Torah describes this as a revision of the original plan. Rather, according to Exodus 13:2, the firstborn of every family was to be "holy to God" and was to serve as a priest. However, this plan is revised when Aaron and his descendants are appointed as the *kohanim*. The ritual of *pidyon haben* is described in Numbers 3:47, in which a father is required to redeem his month-old son from a *kohein* in exchange for five shekels of silver. This ritual continues to be practiced in traditional communities and infrequently in liberal circles (often with an egalitarian twist): when a firstborn baby boy is born into a family in which neither the father nor the mother is a *kohein* or a Levite, the parents engage in this ceremony, which involves a brief dialogue with a *kohein* and the presentation of five silver coins to the *kohein* to redeem the baby boy. The ritual traditionally takes place in the context of a festive meal. The value of the silver coins has varied from community to community; the nineteenth-century prayer book *Seder Avodat Yisrael* specifies that the mitzvah of *pidyon haben* can be fulfilled with "five brabanter thalers" (currency of Frankfurt region), "five Prussian thalers" (currency of Prussia), or "five Russian rubles" (in Russia).[23] Today, American silver dollars are often used, as are special *pidyon haben* silver coins minted in Israel. By and large, Reform Judaism does not observe or encourage the ritual of *pidyon haben*, because the ceremony perpetuates tribal and gender distinctions, though some communities have adapted elements of the *pidyon haben* ritual to create *tzedakah*-oriented ceremonies to honor a firstborn child (of any gender).[24]

Another ritual that refers to actual currency is the *ketubah* at a wedding ceremony. The traditional text of the *ketubah* includes specific reference to currency, stipulating that in the event of the dissolution of the marriage, whether because of divorce or because the husband predeceases the wife, the wife would receive a payment of 100 to 200 *zuz*, depending on the wife's previous marital status. (That the *zuz* has not been transferrable currency for many hundreds of years is one among many reasons why these numbers in the *ketubah* are not actually put into practice.) Reform weddings typically use modern versions of the *ketubah* without financial references.

A related issue that has prompted significant controversy is that classical Jewish sources in the Torah and Rabbinic literature indicate that marriage itself is an act of transaction and acquisition, in which the husband "acquires" the marital rights of the wife through the act of *kiddushin*, "betrothal." For some in Reform Judaism and elsewhere in the Jewish spectrum, the discomfort with this fact is so great that they suggest that the entire institution of *kiddushin* should be eliminated and substituted with a different ritual. Dr. Rachel Adler, for example, has suggested the creation of a new marriage ceremony based on a different aspect of Rabbinic property law: *shutafut*, or "joint partnership."[25] For Adler, it is not problematic that Jewish marriage uses terminology and a form borrowed from the business world; rather, what is problematic is that the particular business analogy traditionally used for marriage (*kinyan*, or "acquisition") is so manifestly inequitable, leading her to substitute that business analogy with the more equitable business analogy of *shutafut*.

Tzedakah and Charitable Giving in Jewish Liturgy and Ritual

Is giving *tzedakah*, charitable donations, an example of an ethical act or a ritual act? The answer seems simple: giving *tzedakah* is an affirmation of Jewish ethics, and there is nothing ritual about it. But the giving of *tzedakah* is also ritualized, at various points in a Jewish day or year.

Many siddurim indicate that a particular point in the daily morning service, during the recitation of a passage from I Chronicles 29:12 shortly before the Song at the Sea, is the appropriate time for charitable giving; in some traditional synagogues, this is the point when a *tzedakah* box gets passed around during weekday prayer services. In some synagogues it is passed around during the public recitation of the *Amidah*.[26]

Traditional sources also refer to a practice on the evening of Purim during which one would donate three half-shekels in commemoration of the half-shekel tax that was collected around the time of Purim for the upkeep of the Temple. This practice, adapted from Exodus 30:11–16, is first associated with the holiday of Purim in medieval

Ashkenazic sources.[27] Traditional synagogues will often acquire three Israeli half-shekels (or three American half-dollars or other coins that are one-half the value of the predominant local currency) so that those who come to the synagogue can "purchase" these coins with whatever money they wish to donate for *tzedakah* and then donate these coins back to the community. Donating to *tzedakah* using coins that belong to the community may be a way to express ritually that *tzedakah* is both an individual and communal obligation.

In Conclusion: The Spirituality of Money

Whatever the source of our modern discomfort with the intertwining of money and religion, it does not appear that such discomfort is native to Judaism. We have seen numerous references to money in Jewish prayer texts and religious rituals. Concerns about money and the use of money appear not to be taboo in Jewish religious settings. Inspired by these examples, perhaps we could stand to benefit from greater overt discussion of money in Jewish religious spaces, as individuals and as communities. Money may be part of the material world, but it provides a doorway into the world of the spirit.

NOTES

1. See, for example, the discussion in Michael Strassfeld, *The Book of Life: Embracing Judaism as a Spiritual Practice* (Woodstock, VT: Jewish Lights, 2002), xiii.
2. In most versions, this word is rendered *hak'doshah*, "holy," rather than *hag'dushah*, "ample" or "generous," but Rabbinical Assembly publications have preferred the versions that include the word *hag'dushah*, which is more similar in meaning to the other synonyms in this list.
3. Translation from *Siddur Lev Shalem* (New York: Rabbinical Assembly, 2016), 89, except that I have amended the translation to render *hal'vaatam* more literally as "loans," rather than as "generosity" as it is found in the original *Siddur Lev Shalem* translation.

4. See Elkin, p. 195 in this volume.

5. See also Deut. 28:12, in which the converse of this is specified as a blessing: "You will be creditor to many nations, but debtor to none."

6. This is considered an implication of biblical sources including Ps. 24:1, "The earth and all that fills it belongs to the Eternal, the earth and those who dwell on it."

7. *Siddur Lev Shalem*, 274.

8. See Babylonian Talmud, *Avodah Zarah* 3a.

9. See Prov. 30:8.

10. A kabbalistic reference to the *s'firah* (divine emanation) called *Binah*; see George Robinson, "What Are the *Sefirot*?," My Jewish Learning, accessed September 25, 2018, https://www.myjewishlearning.com/article/sefirot/. Translation of the Horowitz prayer is my own.

11. Ps. 145:16.

12. Rabbinic sources cite this tradition to Tractate *B'rachot* (see *P'risha, Orach Chayim* 1:5), but such a citation is not found in printed or manuscript versions of the Talmud of the Land of Israel to which we have access. Thus, it is not possible to confirm whether this tradition dates back to the Talmudic era.

13. Translation is my own.

14. Deut. 8:4.

15. Translation is my own.

16. For the early history of this practice in medieval Europe, see Rabbi Daniel Judson, *Pennies for Heaven: The History of American Synagogues and Money* (Waltham, MA: Brandeis University Press, 2018), loc. 1020ff., Kindle. For a discussion of this practice in twentieth-century Orthodox communities in the United States, see Jenna Weisman Joselit, *New York's Jewish Jews: The Orthodox Community in the Interwar Years* (Bloomington: Indiana University Press, 1990), 37.

17. Judson, *Pennies for Heaven.*

18. Joselit, *New York's Jewish Jews*, 40.

19. See Solomon Freehof, "Hazkarath Neshamoth," *Hebrew Union College Annual*, HUCA 36 (1965), 181–83; also in Lawrence A. Hoffman, *May God Remember: Memory and Memorializing in Judaism—Yizkor* (Woodstock, VT: Jewish Lights, 2013), 77–89.

20. Jonathan Sacks, *The Koren Sacks Siddur* (Jerusalem: Koren, 2009), 799.

21. Jakob Petuchowski, "*Kaddish* and Memorial Services," in Hoffman, *May God Remember*, 90ff.; Eric L. Friedland, "*Yizkor*: A Microcosm of Liturgical Interconnectivity," in Hoffman, *May God Remember*, 104ff.

22. See Annette M. Boeckler, "'Service for the Souls': The Origin of Modern Memorial Services, 1819 to 1938," in Hoffman, *May God Remember*, 113ff.

The following is a survey of contemporary American prayer books on this question. Among Conservative prayer books, *The Sabbath and Festival Prayer Book* (New York: Rabbinical Assembly, 1946) does not include such a financial pledge in the *Yizkor* prayer, but later Conservative liturgical publications do, including *Mahzor for Rosh Hashanah and Yom Kippur* (New York: Rabbinical Assembly, 1972), 686–88; *Siddur Sim Shalom* (New York: Rabbinical Assembly, 1985), 518–20; *Siddur Lev Shalem* (New York: Rabbinical Assembly, 2016), 335. Reconstructionist prayer books do not include the financial pledge; see *Kol Haneshamah: Mahzor Leyamim Nora'im* (Elkins Park, PA: Reconstructionist Press, 1999), 1027. Among American Reform prayer books, most do not include the financial pledge, including *The Union Prayer Book* (New York: CCAR, 1940), I:268–73; *Gates of Repentance: The New Union Reform Prayerbook for the Days of Awe* (New York: CCAR, 1978), 491; and *Mishkan T'filah: A Reform Siddur* (New York: CCAR Press, 2007), 580. However, *Mishkan HaNefesh: Machzor for the Days of Awe*, vol. 2, *Yom Kippur* (New York: CCAR Press, 2015), 570–71, does include the financial pledge in the *Yizkor* prayer, inspired in part by the article by Rabbi Margaret Moers Wenig, "For I Pledge *Tz'dakah* on Her Behalf," in Hoffman, *May God Remember*, 219–22.

23. Seligmann Baer, *Seder Avodat Yisrael* (Rödelheim, 1868), 584.

24. See Daniel Syme, "What Is *Pidyon HaBen?*," ReformJudaism.org, accessed October 19, 2018, https://reformjudaism.org/what-pidyon-haben; Anita Diamant, *The New Jewish Baby Book*, 2nd ed. (Woodstock, VT: Jewish Lights, 2005), 207–8.

25. See Rachel Adler, *Engendering Judaism: An Inclusive Theology and Ethics* (Philadelphia: Jewish Publication Society, 1999), 192ff.

26. See http://www.daat.ac.il/daat/toshba/minhagim/ash-tfi.htm.

27. See *Shulchan Aruch, Orah Chayim* 694:1 (gloss of Isserles).

27

DIVIDENDS OF MEANING

Jewish Rituals for the Financial Life Cycle

RABBI JENNIFER GUBITZ

When Hyman retired from his job, he gathered with his community and rabbi to ritualize this major transition in his life. This Jewish ritual began as many do—his wife Ann placed a *kippah* on Hyman's head, they lit candles, and they blessed wine. Then Hyman put his briefcase down on the ground and asked aloud, "As I enter the years of retirement and aging: Will I be bored or stimulated? Will I feel useless or valuable? Will I be lonely or involved with others? Will I feel despair or hope?"

"Only the years to come can answer those questions," the rabbi responded, "but tonight we can do several things to help Hy through his transition. First, we have brought seven gifts. Second, we can follow the traditional Jewish custom of offering *tzedakah* in Hy's honor. The money will be given to the Philadelphia Unemployment Project. Third, we can scare away the demons as our ancestors did with the blast of the shofar."

Upon the conclusion of a final shofar blast, Hyman was declared a *bar Yoveil*, a "son of the Jubilee," released from professional employment with the opportunity to move on to a new stage in life.[1] To mark his new status, Hyman also took on an additional Hebrew name.

A donation dedicated to the Philadelphia Unemployment Project, a briefcase, candles, and the shofar—from the mundane to the holy, these are the ritual items used to mark a financial and life transition. This category of ritual does not celebrate the eight-day-old baby, a child entering Jewish adulthood, or the beloveds under their wedding canopy, but the retiree, enhancing a significant moment of the secular financial life cycle. In addition to celebrating retirement, Jewish ritual and wisdom have the means to frame and celebrate seemingly amorphous and mundane financial moments, from opening a bank account to getting a first credit card; from purchasing and owning a car to the first or the last mortgage payment on the place called home; from receiving a scholarship to remitting that final student loan payment to submitting a final tuition payment for a child's education; from cutting up credit cards to tackling debt to earning money through labor and investments and accruing money through saving; from retiring from a primary career to transitioning to a second or third.

However, a personal survey of literature and clergy's stories among various faith traditions revealed surprisingly few rituals, prayers, or poems to mark these significant moments in life. The distinct transitional moments of the financial life cycle clearly lie beyond the arc of the traditional framework of Jewish ritual and its marking of loving relationships, childbearing, welcoming, learning, illness, and loss. Judaism brims with ritual and recognition of the formal family life cycle, yet these days many of us live longer, causing the gap in time between classic Jewish life-cycle events to increase dramatically. Moreover, the only experiences in life we all have in common today are birth and death. Many of us do not even aspire or are able to reach or mark the traditionally ritualized moments of the Jewish life cycle that happen in between, causing a dearth of ritual in progressive Jewish life.

There is tremendous opportunity to broaden the scope of private and communal Jewish ritual to encompass moments of the life cycle in connection to money and finances. With sensitivity to the many in our midst who work endless hours and years without reaching the financial milestones that would relieve them of their crippling debt or acknowledge their life's investment, this type of ritual innovation can have a transformative impact on the Jewish community, particularly on the demographics of people least attracted or immediately connected to Jewish living, such as millennials and baby boomers. Money and its impact on our lives are part of the reality of living in the world. We are not, yet, allowing Judaism to permeate this part of our lives, bridging the realities of secular living and Jewish practice. That said, over the last twenty years Jewish ritual has been the subject of many innovations, and some of our new rituals do attempt to make our financial life cycle part of our spiritual lives.

Rituals mark transformative moments in our lives: when we change our status, experience a transition, enter a new life stage, or move beyond current hopes and dreams to pursue new ones. Anthropologist Barbara Myerhoff teaches:

> Ritual makes things sacred. It sets them apart. It sanctifies them by announcing and calling attention to their specialness. . . . Ritual is an occasion when one takes the chaos within the world and within oneself and pours it into a vessel that gives it shape and gives it order and power and form.[2]

Do financial changes signify identity change in a way that needs to be marked ritually? Some more than others, but many financial changes yield a transition in focus and reallocation of energy, signifying an accomplishment or a new investment. At the core of any new rituals for the transitional moments of our financial lives have to be an expression of reflection (and, if apt, gratitude), the teaching of our financial values and decision-making processes, and (if apt) space for feelings of regret over wrong decisions. Ritualizing these moments and the feelings accompanying them can imbue financial changes with dividends of meaning.

Ritual Resources and Inspiration

Buying a Home

When first-time home buyers Rachel and Will bought their three-bedroom fixer-upper in Metrowest Boston, after years of living in (read: squeezing into) one-bedroom rental apartments sans washer/dryer, their very first act of celebration was to do loads of laundry. This ritual was followed by popping a bottle of champagne and endless trips to Home Depot. Upon further reflection, Rachel noted, "This is the first time we feel like we can use nails to hang our mezuzah. Until now, we've always used double stick tape." For millennials like Rachel and Will, this is what it means to be your own landlord, to own the doorposts upon which you ritually affix the blessings for *your* house. A member of a generation blessed with student loan debt and financial struggle unlike any other, Rachel acknowledged that although she and Will were broke after putting a down payment on their house, they were lucky to be able to purchase it in the first place.[3]

The catch is, of course, that Rachel and Will don't yet own their house in full. They have a significant debt due to the bank that they will pay off over a long mortgage period while living in the house. Aside from the traditional ritual of affixing a mezuzah to every doorpost in their home (yes, even the laundry room), how else could they ritually claim this space as they continued to pay back their debt? Canadian spiritual leader Kohenet Annie Matan considered this question: After each mortgage payment, she suggested, "imagine for yourself as if drawing a line and reciting aloud, 'The front steps are now mine . . . the entryway is now mine . . . the kitchen sink now belongs to me.'" Acknowledging the shared investment with the bank and the capacity to save money for a down payment transforms the mundane task of paying a monthly mortgage installment into something sacred.

Kohenet Matan also shared the ritual she and her husband perform to claim a new space: they placed salt in pockets and corners of each room,[4] ritualizing the medieval belief that salt-despising demons resided in corners of new houses. Though most of us will think of such beliefs as superstition, salt also shows up in another old, much more universal ritual for moving into a new home: the gifting of bread and salt by the first guests to a new house. Amy W. Helfman writes that "by bringing bread and salt to a new home, one is making it possible for the people who have just moved to sustain themselves."[5] The Jewish practice of this ritual, most often associated with hospitality, helps sustain someone right after they've moved into a new house and is also an intentional acknowledgment of a meaningful and difficult personal financial transition.

Innovating Rituals of Release, Exemption, and Dismissal: Paying Off Loans, Getting Out of Debt, Completing a Mortgage, Cutting Up Credit Cards

Beyond the ceremonial mezuzah hanging in a new home and the somewhat superstitious salting of a new living space, how else might we create or adapt other rituals in Jewish life to acknowledge the financial life cycle? Consider the following two ritual moments as opportunities for innovation.

Early Rabbinic literature (*B'reishit Rabbah* 63:10) records a special blessing recited by fathers upon their sons' coming of age: *Baruch atah, Adonai Eloheinu, Melech haolam, shep'tarani mei-onsho shelazeh*. In reciting this prayer, the father publicly declares, "Blessed is God who has now freed me from the responsibility for this one." The word in focus is *patar*, "exemption" or "dismissal," which can also mean "to distance" or "to remove." This blessing is traditionally said during the bar mitzvah celebration. The ritual symbolizes parents exempting themselves from certain responsibilities as they release their child into a world of new Jewish responsibility. Reform rabbi Joel Mosbacher reframes the traditional blessing. He invites parents to stand at a distance from their child as they recite the Torah blessing aside a daughter or a son to show the child's growing self-reliance.

We can imagine, then, the innovative use of this prayer as one makes a final payment on a loan, credit card debt, mortgage, car payment, or tuition. Finally *patur*, exempt from the responsibility of these payments and the burden of financial commitment, they can remove the payee from their bank account autopay list, mail in their final check, receive the deed or final account balance, and recite an adapted *Baruch Shep'tarani* blessing to symbolically distance themselves from the weight of this financial obligation.

In addition, the ancient ritual of *tashlich*, symbolically throwing away one's sins at Rosh HaShanah by casting breadcrumbs in the water, could be adapted for a ritual of cutting up credit cards, to begin the process of tackling debt, creating a path to solvency. To mark the beginning of the process of unchaining oneself from creditors and the weight of living beyond one's means, we can imagine a small gathering of friends or family surrounding their loved one, who is holding a special pair of scissors. The individual, who is dedicating him- or herself to ending debt, cuts up the credit cards, throws them into the garbage, and recites the *Shehecheyanu*, expressing gratitude for starting this journey to being debt-free. The power of ritualizing the beginning of the journey, surrounded by family and friends, can support the individual, reinforcing the resolve to be debt-free.

Retirement

Perhaps the best-documented rituals related to the financial life cycle focus on retirement. In addition to Hyman's *bar Yoveil* (son of the Jubilee) retirement ritual shared at the beginning of this chapter, there are a number of other retirement rituals.

When Rabbi Laura Geller was in rabbinical school at Hebrew Union College–Jewish Institute of Religion, she had an epiphany when one of her teachers claimed, "There are no important moments in a Jew's life for which there is not a blessing." After hearing that, Laura started cataloguing all the moments in her life that had gone unmarked,[6] including many women's life-cycle events. After a distinguished congregational career, Rabbi Geller honed her focus to organizing community and developing a religious framework for the baby boom generation's ritual moments, including downsizing homes, cleaning out a loved one's belongings, retirement, and more.[7] In a personal interview with her colleague Rabbi Beth Lieberman, Rabbi Geller said:

> One of the things that start to happen as we grow older is that these family traditions get passed down to the next generation. For

instance, when the Passover seder takes place at the house of our children, we begin to sit in the seats that our parents and grandparents once sat in, as younger generations now lead the seder. The same thing is true with the money. If we are in a position to leave money to our children, we might have our own hopes regarding its future investment. One way to ensure that might be to add a condition to the heritage. We can ask our children to create a new kind of "*ketubah*"—a document that reflects our expectations regarding the future use of assets. The problem with what I'm saying is that it assumes partnership and trust.[8]

Irwin Kula and Vanessa Ochs describe a retirement ritual in *The Book of Jewish Sacred Practices*,[9] and the CCAR's *L'chol Z'man v'Eit: For Sacred Moments—New Rabbi's Manual*[10] includes a ritual for rabbinic retirement written by Rabbi Danny Burkeman. Cantor David Mintz and Rabbi Michael R. Boino, from Manhattan's B'nai Jeshurun Center for Prayer and Spirituality, developed a retirement ritual utilizing *Hadran Alach* (We Will Return to You), a prayer traditionally recited upon the completion of learning a tractate of Talmud. This last ritual gives words and gestures to feelings of completion, abundance, and gratitude through text study, poetry, and blessings.

While "abundance" may be a code word for "money," few of these rituals for retirement actually speak of the financial import of the transition. They do not acknowledge the financial changes that retirement brings: receiving a final paycheck or ending a salary, beginning to collect the return on investments, or struggling to make ends meet.

Despite the general dearth of retirement rituals that explicitly mention money, here is one example worth highlighting. Rabbi Ellen Weinberg Dreyfus created a mikveh ritual for her retirement from congregational life.[11] She wrote her own blessing, using Mayyim Hayyim's suggested ritual framework of three immersions representing past, present, and future. The text of this ritual, like most, speaks of money in metaphor, acknowledging her life's work and financial earnings through natural harvest imagery of seeds planted and bounty reaped. Here are the texts of the first two immersions:

First Immersion: Past

I have had decades of busyness,
of work with meaning,
of excitement and challenge.
I have had wonderful opportunities
and also feelings of limitation.
I have done what I could do,
which never seemed to be enough.
I have grown where I was planted.
I have given of my time and energy,
and I have accomplished a great deal.
I have loved my work, and it is hard to let go.
I have amazing memories, much experience,
and many stories to tell.
Now it is time to put that behind me, and move on.

Second Immersion: Future

As today I celebrate my life's continued unfolding, I am
awestruck by the wonder of my being. And so I pray that
kindness and compassion may be on my lips, that strength and
courage may be with me in my comings and my goings, and
that I may continue to learn from and to teach those dear to
me. O God, my Creator, as You are the first and the last, may
my life ever be a song of praise to You.

(Excerpted from Richard F. Address,
To Honor and Respect)[12]

The possibilities are endless. The future is open. That is
somewhat scary, but I will need to create my own structure,
and make my time meaningful.

To take the first step
To sing a new song—
Is to close one's eyes
and dive

into unknown waters.

For a moment knowing nothing risking all

But then to discover
The waters are friendly
The ground is firm.
And the song—
The song rises again.
(Ruth Sohn)

Rabbi Dreyfus's ritual is a wonderful opportunity not only to mark the moment of retirement, but also to engage in a conversation regarding the next steps in one's financial life. Well before retiring, one may want to consider these questions: How will I choose to invest my money moving forward? Which values will guide me when I will give *tzedakah* (charity)? What is the financial legacy I want to leave for future generations of my family or communities I cherish?

Of the rituals that do acknowledge the financial life cycle, most speak of money through metaphor, speaking of trees and harvests. We take comfort in metaphor, as if hiding behind beautiful and relatable images. However, perhaps we can expand beyond the comfort of metaphor and encourage more honest, direct money talk. How could ritual help us express more honestly the vulnerability we experience around money? What blessings might we develop to articulate the uncertainty of wealth or express optimism in the face of scarcity?

Moving toward a Ritual Language
of Money and Finances

As we embrace and develop more rituals to acknowledge the financial life cycle, we must also maintain deep sensitivity and awareness for those whose financial struggles are a barrier to their engagement in Jewish

354 · THE SACRED EXCHANGE

life. We can imagine the single adult whose financial circumstances prevent retirement, or the once financially comfortable couple whose investments are depleted due to prohibitive health-care costs, or the millennial burdened with so much student debt that home ownership will never be possible. If not considering the variety of financial stability in our communities, ritualizing the financial life cycle might further alienate some of us from organized Jewish life. We must take their needs into account as we forge this new ritual frontier. Vanessa Ochs writes that "an invented Jewish ritual is a practice, liturgy or object that comes about at a particular time and setting because something has changed, something is missing or something needs marking or remembering."[13] Times have changed, and generations of Jews, especially millennials and baby boomers, are more and more disconnected from the traditional family life cycle. Amid financial uncertainty and success, the dearth of markers and remembrances that acknowledge financial transition opens tremendous creative possibility to develop rituals acknowledging the broadest span of being human. These rituals can root life's financial peaks and valleys in gratitude, reflection, community, and transformation. Dividends of meaning abound.

NOTES

1. "Passages" class at the Reconstructionist Rabbinical College in 1983. The ritual is published online as "Bar Yovel: A Retirement Ritual," Ritualwell, https://www.ritualwell.org/ritual/bar-yovel-retirement-ritual.
2. Barbara Myerhoff, as quoted in Barbara Binder Kadden and Bruce Kadden, *Teaching Jewish Life Cycle: Traditions and Activities* (Denver: ARE, 1997), 138.
3. Richard Fry, "5 Facts about Millennial Households," Fact Tank, Pew Research Center, September 6, 2017, http://www.pewresearch.org/fact-tank/2017/09/06/5-facts-about-millennial-households..
4. For the historical background of the ritual, see Ron Eisenberg, *The JPS Guide to Jewish Traditions* (Philadelphia: Jewish Publication Society, 2004), 588.
5. See Amy W. Helfman, "What Is the Meaning behind the Tradition of Bringing Bread and Salt to Someone When S/he Moves into a New

Home?," ReformJudaism.org, accessed October 19, 2018, https://reform-judaism.org/what-meaning-behind-tradition-bringing-bread-and-salt-someone-when-she-moves-new-home.

6. Patricia Karlin-Neumann, "Creating Jewish Ritual," in Kadden and Kadden, *Teaching Jewish Life Cycle*, 135–38.

7. Rabbi Laura Geller is a founder of ChaiVillageLA (https://www.chaivillagela.org/content.aspx?sl=973432017), TEBH Next Stage (https://tebh.org/community/boomers-beyond/), and, with Richard Siegel, *z"l*, author of *Getting Good at Getting Older: A New Jewish Catalog* (Millburn, NJ: Behrman House, 2019).

8. Rabbi Laura Geller in conversation with Rabbi Beth Lieberman, Los Angeles, August 14, 2018.

9. Irwin Kula and Vanessa Ochs, eds., *The Book of Sacred Jewish Practices: CLAL's Guide to Everyday & Holiday Jewish Practices & Blessings* (Woodstock, VT: Jewish Lights, 2001).

10. Don Goor, ed., *L'chol Z'man v'Eit: For Sacred Moments—New Rabbi's Manual* (New York: CCAR Press, 2015).

11. Additional resources are the innovative rituals of the mikveh, led by Anita Diamant and Aliza Kline at Mayyim Hayyim: Living Waters Community Mikveh, in Newton, Massachusetts (https://www.mayyim-hayyim.org/). Mayyim Hayyim has developed numerous immersion rituals for transformative and transitional times.

12. Richard F. Address, with Andrew L. Rosenkranz, *To Honor and Respect: A Program and Resource Guide for Congregations on Sacred Aging* (New York: URJ Press, 2005), 61.

13. Vanessa Ochs, "The Courage to Reinvent Jewish Ritual," in *Contact*, Winter 2010, http://www.steinhardtfoundation.org/publication/winter-2010/.

28

GELT

Rabbi Deborah Prinz

I have vivid memories of my mother decorating the Chanukah party table with glittering chocolate gelt and stuffing it into plastic dreidels. Gelt marked the season, and I gobbled more than my share. (Those were the days before I attended to the quality of the chocolate I ingest.) I now realize that neither my mother nor anyone else in our family had any idea why or how chocolate gelt was part of the Chanukah celebration. Sure, I vaguely knew about the tradition of giving Chanukah money in lieu of other gifts, but that seemed like a distraction. The sparkly satisfaction of a sweet tooth was all that mattered to me. Although later as a rabbinical student and then as a rabbi I learned much about the customs and traditions of our people, the stories of Chanukah gelt never surfaced. We distributed it each year to our religious school students without thinking beyond the golden exterior. I tossed multiple coins amid my own Chanukah bling at home. No one asked me and I did not think to question: Why gelt, meaning actual money, for Chanukah? How did coins come to be part of Chanukah festivities in the home? And, how did chocolate enter the mix?

Only as I researched the many stories of chocolate and Jews for my book *On the Chocolate Trail* did I begin to understand the value of gelt.

It turns out that money and Chanukah go way back and that gelt, the real money, evinces power and exalts Jewish values of education and *tzedakah*. The Hasmoneans, the descendants of the Maccabees, issued shekels to symbolize their hard-fought autonomy. As the Book of I Maccabees records, Syria's King Antiochus VII said to Simon Maccabeus, "I turn over to you the right to make your own stamp for coinage for your country" (15:6). Some of those early Israelite coins produced during the rule of Antigonus Matityahu (40–37 BCE), the last in this line of Hasmonean kings, portray a seven-branched menorah on one side and the shewbread offering on the other. Each symbol recalls the centrality of the ancient Jerusalem Temple to the Jewish people and of course the Maccabean victory. Unfortunately, the Roman destruction of the Second Jerusalem Temple in 70 CE ended this freedom. With the establishment of the modern State of Israel, the Israeli Coins and Medals Corporation reforged this connection between sovereignty and the holiday by minting Chanukah medals. These political and national expressions of Chanukah currency have been integral to the festival.

The gelt of Chanukah also reflects Rabbinic values. At its earliest roots, the coins recall the booty that the Maccabean victors distributed to the Jewish widows, soldiers, and orphans at the rededication of the Jerusalem Temple (II Maccabees 8:28). This gift giving entered later Jewish custom to ensure access to the festivities of the eight days. Italian and Sephardic Jewish communities encouraged donations of clothing to teachers and students. At Chanukah, poor people were allowed to beg from door to door.

The basic three-letter Hebrew root for the holiday, usually defined as "dedication," also came to be associated with the Hebrew word for education, *chinuch*. In the days of the Baal Shem Tov (1698–1760), rabbis often traveled to distant Eastern European villages to instruct illiterate Jews in Torah, generally refusing payment. However, at Chanukah the instructors accepted coins and food as tokens of gratitude.[1] The *Kitzur Shulchan Aruch* (139:1) notes that Chanukah especially called for *tzedakah* for students of Torah.[2] Chanukah gelt signified appreciative compensation for Jewish education.

The chocolate expression of gelt may come from the miracle stories of Saint Nicholas, the Catholic patron saint of sweets. The feast day of Saint Nicholas and its use of chocolate coins recalls that Nicholas, from Asia Minor, tossed bags of gold coins to an impoverished father to keep his daughters from lives of prostitution. Saint Nick's *geld* surprisingly and sweetly flows right into Chanukah's gelt—or, perhaps, the other way around. These Christian and Jewish golden coin stories, each originating from the Mediterranean area, each of them centuries old, each with inspiring accounts of courage and liberation, also indulge and nurture a love of chocolate.

Over time the money of Chanukah shifted from its military sources to Jewish compassion for the poor and tangible support for Torah learning, just as the holiday itself had been spiritualized in rabbinic retellings. Chanukah gelt can return us to those priorities of Jewish identity and meaning. Whether the gelt ends up on the table or in a dreidel or in our mouths, whether it is dark or milk, when I unwrap my next fair-trade chocolate gelt I will be uncovering the gratifying and sustaining stories of the festival and of our people.[3]

NOTES

1. Eliezer Segal, *Holidays, History and Halakhah* (Northvale, NJ: Jason Aronson, 2001), 88.

2. David Golinkin, "Why Do We Give Hanukkah Gelt and Hanukkah Presents?," *Responsa in a Moment* 9, no. 2 (December 2014), http://www.schechter.edu/why-do-we-give-hanukkah-gelt-and-hanukkah-presents/.

3. Based on the research for Deborah Prinz, *On the Chocolate Trail: A Delicious Adventure Connecting Jews, Religions, History, Travel, Rituals and Recipes to the Magic of Cacao*, 2nd ed. (Nashville, TN: Jewish Lights, 2017).

ETHICS IN FOCUS

Copyright as a Jewish Ethical Issue

RABBI HARA E. PERSON AND
RABBI SONJA K. PILZ, PhD

From our very beginnings, our most sacred text describes the original act of creation, while crediting the creator. *B'reishit bara Elohim eit hashamayim v'eit haaretz*, "In the beginning, God created the heavens and the earth" (Gen. 1:1). In the postbiblical era the idea was introduced of appropriately attributing an idea through the Rabbinic principle from *Pirkei Avot* of *b'shem omro*, or "in the name of."

However, since the advent of the printing press, those publishing Jewish books have had to confront a difficult ethical dilemma: Which is more important, our obligation to increase Torah learning in the world, or our obligation to enable those who provide this content the ability to earn a living? Even though it may be obvious that the study of Torah can only be worthwhile when undertaken in a moral way, the two values sometimes clash with each other, especially in the modern world.

In today's world of easy duplication, where just about anything can be scanned and downloaded, copied and pasted, pirated and reposted, the questions of who owns content and how to properly credit and use it have become vastly more complicated. Think about how often we happily use free content found online, without making sure that we actually have the right to use or reproduce it. The argument that if content is being used for educational or religious purpose it can therefore be freely copied and distributed is simply inaccurate. Doing so may increase Torah learning in the world, but it may also be illegal and is certainly unethical, because those who created the content aren't being compensated for their work and investment.

The invention of the printing press made Jewish books more readily available, yet the questions surrounding reproduction of content had to be addressed. A body of Jewish law known as *haskamah* developed to deal with these new challenges and protect the rights of those who invest in the publication of Jewish content. *Haskamah* served two purposes: the granting of this rabbinic approval (1) allowed an author to print a book and have it recognized as worthwhile by the community, and (2) like copyright, protected the investment of the printer by prohibiting republication by another printer for a defined number of years.

The modern, secular legal concept of copyright applies to the right to produce, publish, and distribute content. The holder of copyrighted material controls how the content can be used and by whom; those who use the work without permission or payment are violating the copyright of the rights holder. Payment is not always required, but permission must always be sought.

In 1974, the CCAR Responsa Committee was asked: "Is it right, according to Jewish legal tradition, to photostat or Xerox and sell books that have been published by other publishers?" The responsum states that "the ethics of the Jewish copyright *Haskama* means to protect the author and the publisher, and thus encourage them to continue their work," meaning that without this protection, no one would enter into publishing. The responsum cites a decision from the early nineteenth century, *Chosen Mishpot* 41 by Moses Sofer, addressing the question of whether one may copy and sell books that have been previously published by other publishers. It argues for the protection of the publisher, stating "that if he were not protected, he would never invest his money and labor, and thus the study of the Torah would be more difficult for lack of availability of books." The responsum ends with the following statement: "There is no question that large-scale copying for the use of a school, for example, is definitely against Jewish religious ethics."

As we look at the boundary between the Jewish value of learning and the Jewish value of ethical use of content, we need to differentiate between three different categories of Jewish content:

1. **The Hebrew or Aramaic versions of sacred text:** This includes the books of the *Tanach*, the corpus of Rabbinic literature, and the historical texts of Jewish prayers. This content belongs to the Jewish people; no one owns it. In fact, great efforts have been made to make these texts available to as many Jews as possible and to enhance Torah in our world.

2. **Commentary on sacred text:** Ownership of the content in books like prayer books and rabbinic commentaries to the Torah or the Talmud have been historically difficult to regulate. These sacred texts are generally accessed in the form of publications that include translations, commentaries, explanations, and poetic additions—and this material belongs to the author, editor, or publisher. For that matter, it may be that the fonts themselves, carefully chosen to enhance the educational and prayer experience, are proprietary and owned by the publisher, as is the case with the Shlomo font used in *Mishkan HaNefesh* and other CCAR Press publications. While the original sacred text belongs to all of us, it is the publisher who has invested in the editorial process, the design, the printing, and when relevant, the e-book or app. This also applies to musical settings of sacred text; the text may belong to the Jewish people, but the translation and music belong to the composer. Therefore, anyone wishing to reproduce this content, distribute it, put it online, or project it must request permission from the rights holder.

3. **Contemporary content:** This third category, which would apply, for example, to a collection of essays on a Jewish theme, or a textbook, or a contemporary Jewish song, is more straightforward. This body of content belongs to the realm of civil law and as such is part of the legal category of *dina d'malchuta dina* (adhere to the [civil] law

of your country). It is also protected by Jewish law, which maintains that if an author, publisher, or composer put in all the money and work it requires to publish, they must receive the profit they deserve for their work and have the right to choose how it may be used.

Haskamah ensures that quality Jewish content can be produced for the good of the community. Secular copyright deals with the issues surrounding the legal use of content. As Jews, we have to uphold both these standards. Synagogues, Jewish schools, camps, and the whole Jewish community must adhere to legal and ethical standards, paying for and properly crediting content being used. If the community does not support the production of content, it is only a matter of time until such content is no longer produced.

NOTES

1. CCAR Responsa Committee, "Copyrighting Books," Central Conference of American Rabbis, 1974, https://www.ccarnet.org/ccar-responsa/corr-245-252/.
2. To use content from CCAR Press, contact CCAR Press directly. There are various other ways of being copyright compliant today, not all of which require multiple license negotiations. Within the Reform Movement, this includes JLicense for music, which is administered by Transcontinental Music (jlicense.com) through the American Conference of Cantors. Depending on the content and intended usage, there are also various open content and open-source licensing sources, such as en.wikipedia.org.wiki/Open_ Source_Judaism and the Copyright Clearance Center (www.copyright.com).
3. CCAR Responsa Committee, "Copyrighting Books."
4. CCAR Responsa Committee, "Copyrighting Books."
5. CCAR Responsa Committee, "Copyrighting Books."
6. See BT *N'darim* 28a; BT *Gittin* 10b; BT *Bava Kama* 113a; and BT *Bava Batra* 54b–55a.
7. Jewish law speaks about this halachic concept as *Zeh neheneh vezeh chaser* ("One has all the profit and the other is lacking!"; BT *Bava Kama* 20a).

TALKING ABOUT MONEY

Be Fruitful and Multiply, and Go into Debt?

Rabbi Idit Solomon

We spent close to $100,000 on fertility treatments. At some point, the details of the numerous bills became a blur. I focused on ordering and administering complicated medication protocols, appointments, and keeping emotions under control through invasive tests, painful procedures, shots, and many losses. In contrast, my husband shouldered more of the worries about the finances. This was the easiest division of labor. My privilege of financial ignorance was quickly supplanted by stress about my body, withering hope, and trying to stay sane.

In three years we created a bit of financial carnage. We began with an economic cushion, fertility insurance, which was really helpful. That coverage included our first few months on fertility drugs, some of the labs and test procedures, most of our three intrauterine inseminations, and our first couple of IVFs. We paid thousands, but most people paying out of pocket would have already spent $50,000.

The losses, however, continued. They included failed treatments and multiple miscarriages. They were devastating. So we headed to another clinic. Our expenses at this new place were just beginning.

The two-day, eight-appointment clinic adventure involved a training seminar, an ultrasound, blood tests, genetic counseling, and a financial consultation. My husband kept stepping outside to talk to the guy providing him with consulting work, so we could pay for this entirely out-of-pocket attempt to build our family. At my second blood test, I knew they were going to ask for my credit card again, so I had it in hand. As I sat alone in the lab, one arm had a needle drawing blood and the other held out the credit card. Our commitment to *p'ru ur'vu*, "be fruitful and multiply" (Gen. 1:28), was draining my blood and my bank account at the same time.

That trip didn't end with a baby, nor did the IVF after that. The next one, costing almost $40,000 paid up front, did finally result in parenthood. I felt indebted for the gift of parenthood. To express this gratitude, I founded a nonprofit organization to support people experiencing infertility or fertility challenges, filling in where the Jewish community was previously lacking.

The stories of financial barriers to parenthood, however, never cease to amaze me. Most people imagine it all starting with a romantic dinner or frisky smile. People facing fertility challenges have different stories: "The doctor visits and stress are affecting my work, but we need the income to pay for this." "Maybe I should crowdfund and ask my friends." "We moved in with his parents for a year to save money."

The average out-of-pocket cost of a single IVF treatment is $24,000. The average spent on treatment exceeds $65,000.

The Jewish community sinks tens of thousands of dollars into incentives and programs for raising Jewish children. Yet for so many couples, *having* a child creates a financial crisis. When Jews discuss the importance of *tzedakah*, the role of mitzvot, and the need to help others, we ought to include issues related to *p'ru ur'vu*. Every life has infinite value. In the face of fertility challenges, however, the cost of having a child can be painful and prohibitive.

· Part Six ·

Uncomfortable Conversations

While this final part of *The Sacred Exchange* is entitled "Uncomfortable Conversations," talking about the topics described, of course, does not need to be awkward or pained. However, each subject raised in this part seems to raise discomfort for many. Here the authors provide a road map, educating us how to talk about these topics. And in doing so, they show us that shame, embarrassment, and reticence do not need to be part of any money conversation. Rather Jewish theology, history, law, and ethics can lead us to money talk that is open, honest, astute, and therefore productive.

Joshua Holo, PhD, tackles the shame of the Jewish history of money lending in "Moneylending and Jews: Falsehoods, Stereotypes, and Shame." For some Jews, any discussion about Jews and money conjures antisemitic stereotypes, creating an aversion to any related topic. Yet, Dr. Holo argues for a different view of the history of Jews and money. In "Monetizing *T'shuvah*: Reparations and Returning Valuables," Patty Gerstenblith and Rabbi Samuel N. Gordon work together to present a primer on the legal history of returning and paying reparations for stolen and misappropriated art and other cultural treasures, including those stolen from Jews by the Nazis. This legal history is framed in a discussion of the Jewish view of repentance.

In "Embracing Dave Ramsey: A Financial Literacy Model for the Jewish Community," Rabbi Amy B. Cohen and Rabbi Alan Freedman describe their congregation's efforts to teach the Evangelical Christian Financial Peace University developed by talk radio star Dave Ramsey of Ramsey Solutions. In doing so, Rabbis Cohen and Freedman create a compelling example of why synagogues and other Jewish institutions should be teaching financial literacy skills as part of their regular educational offerings. Deborah Niederman, RJE, reminds us that the first and most influential teachers are parents. In "Using Jewish Values to Teach Your Children about Money," Niederman explores her and her husband's own discomfort with money talk and provides guidance on how to teach children about wealth through Jewish values. Rabbi Barry H. Block addresses the role of examining partner attitudes and financial health during premarital counseling. In "Marriage, Money, and Musar," Rabbi Block demonstrates how the values learned from the study of Musar can shape these conversations.

In "Saying Goodbye: Honoring Your Congregation's Legacy," Rabbi David Burstein Fine and Beth Burstein Fine describe the process of dissolving a congregation, emphasizing the decisions to be made concerning assets and memory-laden objects. In writing about this rarely discussed scenario, the Burstein Fines offer much wisdom not only for closing a synagogue, but also for anyone considering the meaning of their wealth and material possessions. Rabbi Richard F. Address, DMin, offers advice in "Ethics in Focus: Ethical Estate Planning." Starting with the halachah of estate distributions, Rabbi Address opens other possibilities from a Reform perspective. He is sensitive to Jewish values and the importance of legacy and always striving for *sh'lom bayit*, peace among family members.

Written by Marcie Zelikow, "Talking about Money: A Time to Give, a Time to Refrain from Giving" is the closing chapter of both this part and *The Sacred Exchange*. A poignant adaptation of a letter she and her husband, Howard, wrote during a time of financial challenge, this chapter models a caring, open discussion about personal finances. These words recognize the dependency of nonprofits on their donors, the heart of a philanthropist, and the importance of forthright money talk.

29

MONEYLENDING AND JEWS

Falsehoods, Stereotypes, and Shame

Joshua Holo, PhD

The Root of the Stereotype
and Jewish Embarrassment

It seems obvious that we should cringe at stereotypes regarding Jews and money. Any caricature stings, and worse, it puts its subject on the defensive against a phantom accusation, a loaded proposition that cannot be refuted without reinforcing the charge itself. In the specific case of Jews and money, the stereotype casts Jews as stingy and sometimes predatory. It further implicates Jews in class conflict, by presuming that Jews are wealthy enough to leverage the poor. Most of all, we know that this and other stereotypes have armed antisemites with a language of hate, which they have deployed as an excuse for the commission of crimes, great and small, against Jewish people.

We also cringe at this stereotype for another, more problematic reason: we are embarrassed by its historical association with European medieval moneylending. Consequently, we often distance ourselves from that history. We tend to explain Jewish moneylending away, dismissing it as a consequence of medieval restrictions imposed by Christian European rulers: the Jews could not own land, so they had to lend money; the potentates preferred to corner the Jews into an exploitable financial situation; etc.

The shame that Jews express (often tacitly) about the history of moneylending merits a critical look, for two reasons. First, the connection between moneylending and the stereotype belies and masks a much more complicated, nuanced, and surprising set of attitudes. Second, the received history of Jewish moneylending itself tends to misrepresent the facts. Underneath the simplistic story of Jews being cornered into moneylending lies an intricate network of relationships, both between Jews and Christians and within each religious community. If, in the end, we accept the fact that charging interest inevitably disgruntled some, we also must appreciate that it underpinned the credit system that helped bring Western Europe into the modern age.

Evolving Attitudes toward Moneylending and Charging Interest

If the stereotype began with the Jews' lending at interest to Christians in medieval Europe, the original suspicion of moneylending goes far deeper and much closer to home. Torah demands, "If your kin, being in straits, come under your authority . . . do not exact advance or accrued interest, but fear your God" (Lev. 25:35–36; see also Exod. 22:24). Effectively, Scripture characterizes the charging of interest as a tool of oppression and alienation. In so doing, it enshrines an attitude that has haunted all three Abrahamic religions for millennia.

This distaste for interest does not grow out of Israel's antiquity or Middle Eastern origins; other contemporary cultures embraced the practical benefits of moneylending at interest without qualms. Remarkably stable interest rates took hold as early as Bronze Age Mesopotamia, for example, based on the local six-based numerical system, resulting in an annual interest rate of 20 percent.[1] By contrast, ancient Israel's aversion to charging interest derives from its very specific socioeconomic perspective: that of the borrower "in straits."

Torah does not take up the cause of the commercial borrower, who would leverage the loan, or that of the creditor, who would lend more readily at interest.[2] Adopting the point of view of the *vulnerable borrower*, Torah responds, first and foremost, with an ethical imperative to float an interest-free loan—a lifesaver. Viewed thus, charging any form of interest undermines Torah's very precise ethical purpose. In fact, there is no need to distinguish between *usury* (understood as *excessive* interest) and moderate interest, because Torah prohibits both equally.

This highly adversarial understanding of interest functions in two opposite moral directions: not only does Torah protect "kin" from it, but Torah also deploys interest as a tool against the "other" to distance Israel from alien nations.[3] While you may not charge interest within your circle of solidarity, "you may deduct interest from loans to foreigners" (Deut. 23:21). In all, Torah takes one step further than a mere moral injunction against interest; it freights the practice of charging interest with the baggage of belonging versus otherness. This, in a religious context where the question of covenantal and national belonging undergirded the entire project.

In the age of the Talmud (first to fifth centuries CE), the Rabbis still bound themselves to the restrictions of Torah, even if those did not entirely suit the types of borrowing that an increasingly mercantile economy required. As a matter of religious commitment, the Rabbis accepted the biblical prohibition and the values that shaped its contours, including the permission to charge interest to non-Jews. As opposed to the prohibitive element in Jewish law, this permission promoted vital business with non-Jews in the Land of Israel and Mesopotamia; it also validated the still-dominant worldview whereby different religious and ethnic communities respected both the cultural and legal boundaries that separated them.

At the same time, the Rabbis also sought to grease the wheels of trade and promote the flow of money among Jews, which cut against the grain of the biblical prohibition on charging interest to "kin." The increasingly commercial, urban Jewish community needed credit, or something very much like credit, to promote business.[4] To meet these needs, the Rabbis elaborated on the Torah's prohibition extensively and with great technical precision. At the same time, their rulings addressed all kinds of potential loopholes, evasions, and efforts to distribute risk and to put capital to work. The Rabbis also distinguished between interest and usury (excessive interest) to a degree alien in Scripture. This propensity to find Torah-legal modes of leveraging capital expanded during the Middle Ages (sixth to fifteenth centuries CE), as those urban and mercantile forces continued to engage an increasing portion of the Jewish population and society at large.

All the while, the biblically rooted rejection of interest followed Judaism, Islam, and Christianity throughout their respective histories, generating economic and social tensions—in particular for the Jews of Christian medieval Europe, where the story of Jewish moneylending truly takes place. Functioning as a litmus test for inclusion versus exclusion— "kin" versus "foreigner"—in the Bible, moneylending at interest took on a very charged meaning among Christians in relation to Jews. First, they queried: Who falls into the category of Torah's "foreigner"? In the early Middle Ages, this question, triggered by Deuteronomy's double standard for the charging of interest, roiled Christian sensibilities in at least two ways. First, Christians understood their own religion as entirely universal, effectively dispensing with the notion of the "other" altogether. In theory, all were brethren. Second, Christians, numerically and politically dominant in the setting of medieval Western Europe, could hardly imagine Torah's designation of "foreigners" as applying to themselves and, even less so, that they should be disenfranchised by a text that enfranchises the Jews as the "kin" of the biblical perspective. For both of these reasons, some (not all) leading Christian thinkers declared *all* interest forbidden, without regard to the affiliation of the parties in question.

Somewhat at odds with this religious perspective, political powers varied in their degree of respect or disregard for this position. Meanwhile, as demand for credit increased in urbanizing Christian Europe, the Jews offered sorely needed capital—at interest. Gathering steam in the thirteenth century, Western Europe was emerging as an urban and mercantile center, with keen demand for credit; church, state, and individuals alike turned to the Jews, as well as other Christians for loans at interest. Though the church's Fourth Lateran Council banned "heavy or immoderate usuries" in the year 1215, it implicitly kept the door open for moderate interest.[5] The attribution of ugly stereotypes to the Jews responded to many deeper, interreligious tensions, but anxieties about moneylending clearly sparked and exacerbated them, especially when borrowers defaulted, as took place in an anti-Jewish riot in fourteenth-century Spain.[6]

Nevertheless, regardless of the Jews, moneylending at interest gained ground, and in Italy, *monti di pietà*, or poverty banks, took root as early as the fifteenth century. These *monti di pietà* afforded cheap loans, guaranteed with a pawn at annual interest rates as low as 4 percent, to the needy (though sometimes the well-heeled took advantage of them as well). These poverty banks alternatively rendered Jews redundant and cooperated with them, but in all cases, they were losing propositions that required charitable subvention. In Venice, Jews, rather than Christian charities, funded the equivalent of *monti di pietà* out of their own pocket, as a precondition for permission to engage in larger-scale moneylending for profit.[7]

All the while reflecting Torah's adverse sensibilities, some Jews then, as today, felt squeamish about their own moneylending, for fear it might imply enmity toward their creditors. At the very least, it reflected interreligious resentments. In seventeenth-century Venice, Simone Luzzatto conceded that Jewish charging of interest from Christians was a necessary evil—with a defensive emphasis on "necessary." Luzzatto presented Jewish moneylending as a justification for their residence in Venice:

> Moved by . . . the exemplary piety directed toward the needy, it was additionally imposed upon the Jews that they should tend to the needs of the poor by opening [poverty] banks, at the annual rate of a mere 5% . . . so low that the expenses of rent, agents and bankers and other expenses exceed such low interest.[8]

Sometimes in competition, other times complicitly, Jews and Christians alike walked the tightrope between their inherited antipathy to interest, on the one hand, and their modernizing appreciation of its usefulness, on the other. Burgeoning urban economies promoted trade in coin—as opposed to barter—which needed the fuel of ready cash, in ways that foreshadow our own use of credit today.

The distaste for charging interest makes sense from the very particular perspective out of which it was born: Torah's defense of the vulnerable borrower. Unfortunately, however, the narrowness of that perspective established a blanket attitude toward interest, which does not apply well to other situations in the spectrum of human interaction. In fact, insofar as charging interest can promote even charitable lending, Torah's prohibition may have sometimes undermined its own purpose. More obviously, however, it ignored all the other ways in which moneylending at interest promoted a better life. And finally, the prohibition set the tone for viewing interest as predatory, which seeded one of the most harmful stereotypes about Jews, with which we still contend today. European society worked through this ambivalence, but in such a way as to layer it onto the minority experience of a competing religion. As such, negative attitudes of predation and otherness competed with social and financial pressures, complicating attitudes over time and in various contexts.

Medieval Jewish Moneylending and the Particular Stereotypes about Money

When we think of the anti-Jewish stereotypes around money, and when we connect them to the experience of medieval moneylending in Christian Europe, we face two distinct historical problems. First, the moneylending in question pertained only to particular situations. Second, moneylending and its proxy forms of extending credit leavened the emerging urban economies of Europe and the Mediterranean, which foreshadowed our own, modern economy. Far from defensively explaining Jewish moneylending away, this accurate historical perspective illustrates the utility, and even necessity, of moneylending as a source for economic growth, and it therefore forces us to reevaluate the negative stereotype.

As for the particularity of the phenomenon of Jewish moneylending, there are a few myths that bear debunking. First, the Jews did not function as monopolists, although in some cases, they counted among very few who could afford to extend sufficient credit to satisfy the needs of kings, as in Angevin England (twelfth to thirteenth centuries). Christians also lent money at interest to one another. For example, the Lombard Christians from Northern Italy (and Cahorsins from Southern France) played a prominent role in the marketplace, with the Jews sometimes making headway by undercutting their rates. In Byzantium, the government regulated interest rates in a thriving credit market among both Orthodox and Catholic Christians.[9] Second, in late medieval and Renaissance Italy, Jews negotiated rights for large-scale moneylending, as indicated above, in the context of highly developed Christian moneylending, both charitable and otherwise. Third, the Jews, though sometimes limited in their scope of occupation, were not relegated solely to moneylending, nor were they prohibited from owning land.

Ultimately, the fact that Jews numbered among other parties who also lent at interest should not motivate us to distance ourselves from our historical role, as if to share the blame, but rather the opposite, to point out the utility of moneylending at interest. Jews lent money because it was useful and profitable, as it was for many others.

Inevitably, the business of moneylending created tensions, even internally among Jews, but all these concerns merely reflected the utter necessity of credit. Two of medieval Judaism's greatest thinkers illustrate this paradox. On the one hand, we know of an entire realm of economic pursuits dedicated to working around the prohibition against charging interest from fellow Jews. Thus, Maimonides points out, "There are practices that resemble interest, but which are permitted," though they are heavily regulated.[10] He recognized the relentless need for credit in bustling Cairo, where Muslims also worked within their own set of rules and where both communities traded copiously among themselves and with each other. By the same token, Rashi, a century prior, also understood how money requires investment for growth. However, he felt compelled to admonish his readers not to rationalize charging interest as though "a permissible matter, on account of the fact that his money will otherwise remain idle."[11] Rashi, Maimonides, and countless others lived in an increasingly urban and mercantile economy, struggling with the limits imposed by Torah's inapposite prohibition.

In relation to Christians, Jews increased moneylending in Western Europe, beginning in the thirteenth century. Christian restrictions on fellow Christians tightened (but never fully abolished the practice) and promoted Jewish lending to fill the void. Sometimes extremely lucrative, other times almost a subsistence business, moneylending generally made sense for the Jews of Christian Europe. It conformed, in part, to the ideological biases that distanced Christians from Jews—the mutual "othering" associated with the charging of interest—and they could make a living. A historian of Jews of the Middle Ages, Norman Roth, argues simply that "the ever-increasing tax burdens, on the one hand, and the relatively large profits to be made with virtually no risk, on the other, encouraged Jews to engage in moneylending on ever larger scales."[12] Roth perhaps understates the risks, not only of default but also of animosity. Still, the rewards proved worth pursuing in a growing marketplace hungry for reliable credit.

Conclusion: Unreasonable Embarrassment

The shame (even though relatively mild and often implicit) that Jews today sometimes exhibit about the history of moneylending poses a very special problem: It displaces our appreciation of a productive, jostling, and multifaceted history in favor of a specious stereotype. In this regard, as a historical viewpoint, the story of the Jews in Western Europe (where Jewish moneylending materially mattered) deserves a reboot.

Though cogs in a social machine that needed capital and acquired it from many parties, the Jews contributed to medieval Europe's emerging financial sophistication. At the same time, they bore the brunt of society's deep suspicion toward moneylending—a suspicion embedded into Judaism's own constitution and, regrettably, bequeathed to the cultures that would ultimately project that suspicion back onto the Jews themselves. A cogent appreciation of this complex history defangs the shame and casts the Jews as part of a more interesting and rich chapter in Western European history.

But what of the stereotype and the harm that grows out of its capacity to flatten and oversimplify this complicated history? An interlocutor of bad faith can readily distort even accurate history, and that, even when presented with proper nuance. Some simply vilify all of capitalism's precedents, including Jewish moneylending, as intrinsically detrimental in nature. Others may attribute disproportionate power and influence to the Jews and imperfectly cite this history as proof. In fact, regarding Jewish prominence, philosemitic tropes and antisemitic tropes converge in ways that force us to contend with all stereotypes, even the positive ones.

These stereotypes will not disappear, but a truer historical perspective does ultimately put the lie to them. For that reason alone, Jews should shed the implied embarrassment of deflection. But there is another reason for us to espouse the fuller story: it can serve to bolster the half-century-long, gradual disabusal of the antisemitic myth. According to the 1964 Anti-Defamation League Global 100, the international survey of antisemitic attitudes, 29 percent and 30 percent of Americans felt, respectively, that "Jews have too much power in the business world" and (as a separate question in the poll) that "Jews have too much power on Wall Street." By contrast, the 2015 update to the poll indicates that only 16 percent of Americans affirm those same attitudes. In other words, we have reason to believe that the stereotype of Jews and money can give way to reasoned discussion, and our own attitude to our history can help shape that change.

NOTES

1. Michael Hudson, "How Interest Rates Were Set, 2500 BC–1000 AD: *Máš, tokos* and *fœnus* as Metaphors for Interest Accruals," *Journal of the Economic and Social History of the Orient* 43 (Spring 2000): 134–35.

2. See Elkin in this volume (p. 198): "The bulk of the biblical material on this subject reflects the imperative to help the needy, not creditors who are owed money." Deut. 23:20 does not refer to a borrower in straits, but Nachmanides, in his commentary on this verse, refers to Lev. 25:25–28, which does, again, refer to a fellow Israelite in dire straits, this time in relation to buying back (redeeming) land the person was forced to sell off, due to financial pressures. It echoes some of the same principles at the root of the biblical prohibition against charging interest:

> If one of your kin is in straits and has to sell part of a holding, the nearest redeemer shall come and redeem what that relative has sold. If a person has no one to be redeemer but prospers and acquires enough to redeem with, since its sale shall be computed and the difference shall be refunded to the person to whom it was sold, so that the person returns to that holding. If that person lacks sufficient means to recover it, what was sold shall remain with the purchaser until the Jubilee; in the Jubilee year it shall be released, so that the person returns to that holding. (Lev. 25:25–28)

3. Benjamin Nelson, *The Idea of Usury*, 2nd ed. (Chicago: University of Chicago Press, 1969).

4. John Pryor, "The Origins of the Commenda Contract," *Speculum* 52, no. 1 (January 1977): 5–37; Elkin, p. 195 in this volume.

5. Solomon Grayzel, *The Church and the Jews in the XIIIth Century*, rev. 2nd ed. (New York: Hermon Press, 1966), 306–9.

6. Grayzel, *The Church and the Jews in the XIIIth Century*, 283; Maya Soifer Irish, "The Problem of Old Debts: Jewish Moneylenders in Northern Castile," *Sefarad* 74, no. 2 (2014): 300. In 1360, in Miranda, Spain, residents took advantage of political turmoil and a vacuum of power to attack the Jewish residents.

7. Brian Pullan, "Jewish Banks and the Monti di Pietà," in *The Jews of Early Modern Venice*, ed. Robert C. Davis and Benjamin Ravid (Baltimore: John Hopkins University Press, 2001), 65.

8. Simone Luzzatto, *Discorso circa il stato de gl'Hebrei* (Venice, 1638), 33a–b; Benjamin Ravid, "Moneylending in Seventeenth-Century Jewish Vernacular Apologetica," in *Jewish Thought in the Seventeenth Century*, ed. Isadore Twersky and Bernard Septimus (Cambridge, MA: Harvard University Press, 1987), 280–82.

9. Gilbert Dacron, "The Urban Economy, Seventh–Twelfth Centuries," in *The Economic History of Byzantium*, ed. A. E. Laiou (Washington, DC: Dumbarton Oaks, 2002), 437–38; Angeliki Laiou, "Exchange and Trade, Seventh-Twelfth Centuries," in Laiou, *Economic History of Byzantium*, 710–11.

10. Maimonides, *Mishneh Torah, Hilchot Malveh V'Loveh* 5:14.

11. Rashi on Lev. 24:36.

12. Roth, Norman, "Jewish Moneylending," https://www.myjewishlearning.com/article/jewish-moneylending/.

30

MONETIZING *T'SHUVAH*

Reparations and Returning Valuables

PATTY GERSTENBLITH, PhD, JD AND
RABBI SAMUEL N. GORDON

In the *Mishneh Torah*, *Hilchot T'shuvah* 2:9, Moses Maimonides (Spain/ Egypt, 1135–1204) writes:

> Neither Rosh Hashanah nor Yom Kippur atones for anything but sins between a human being and God (for example, eating forbidden foods or engaging in [consensual] illicit relations). Sins between one human being and another (for example, harming, cursing or stealing from another person) are never forgiven until one repays the debt and placates the injured party.
>
> Even though the monetary debt is paid, one still needs to placate the injured party and ask for forgiveness. Even if the wrong was only a matter of an argument, one must appease an injured party, requesting repeatedly until forgiveness is granted.

While Maimonides's understanding of *t'shuvah*, "repentance," would be valid in most situations, there are certain cases where monetary compensation and requests for forgiveness are inadequate means to undo the harm. This is particularly true when cultural heritage has been vandalized or destroyed, as exemplified by attempts in recent history by the Nazis to destroy Jewish memory and cultural tradition. While financial compensation and the return of objects cannot fully undo the harm to a precious heritage, these types of restitution are still needed. In this chapter, we will discuss the interaction between the American secular court system and those families and countries seeking justice after their personal artwork and cultural objects were stolen. Some of the cases begin in the horror of the Holocaust; others reflect dishonest dealings in antiquities. For both, the reader is encouraged to keep in mind the Jewish definition of repentance, as articulated by Maimonides, and ask if true restitution, in the sense of making the injured party whole, came in the cases presented. In the process of exploring this area of restitution, the reader should also reflect on how material objects may transcend their monetary worth.

In many legal disputes, the successful plaintiff directly seeks or is willing to accept damages (monetary compensation) as the result of either a court decision or settlement. However, disputes concerning artworks and cultural objects are different. Artworks and cultural objects (often referred to as cultural property or tangible cultural heritage objects) are objects that carry particular artistic, religious, historical, or archaeological significance. A body of distinct law has developed around the question of the proper disposition of cultural objects, which reflects, in part, the circumstances under which an object was taken from an individual, a family, or some other entity, which is now attempting to recover the object. The goal of this body of law is to recognize the unique values of cultural objects and to vindicate the interests of those who have been deprived of those rights. Here we will discuss two types of legal disputes involving cultural objects in which monetization, the acceptance of a monetary payment in place of recovery of the object itself, is not considered, by itself, to constitute adequate compensation. The following two types of disputes are considered: disputes where a known object was stolen from its rightful owner and disputes involving looted archaeological artifacts. A common characteristic of these disputes is that because of the unique values associated with a cultural object, the parties to the dispute are typically not willing to accept monetary compensation, but rather are willing to undergo the rigors of a full and often very contentious legal proceeding in order to recover the object itself or to achieve some other, less tangible resolution. By the same token, payment of monetary compensation and often restitution of the cultural object typically do not adequately compensate for the harm that was done.

Cultural objects and monuments are particularly vulnerable during time of war. The paradigmatic example of stolen art works occurred during the Holocaust. Not content with murdering six million Jews and six million other Europeans, the Nazis also were determined to eradicate the memory of the presence of Jews from the European continent. Hitler and the other leaders of the Third Reich caused the largest movement and destruction of cultural objects ever to have occurred in world history. While many forms of property were stolen from victims of the Holocaust during World War II, artworks raise unique problems because they are valued for far more than their economic worth. Many Jews were themselves artists, but even more so they were renowned dealers and collectors of many types of art, particularly art of the late nineteenth and early twentieth centuries. Many prominent collections were formed by the Rosenberg family, the Rothschilds, Julius Cassirer, the Mauthners, the Gutmann (now Goodman) family, and others.

As the Nazis conquered Western Europe, their pattern was to gather the most prominent art collections, both public and private. Commissioned by the Third Reich, the Kümmel Report had earmarked specific artworks, either because Germany felt it had some particular claim on the work or because the work was viewed as a replacement for something taken from a German city by Napoleon or at the end of World War I. Those works not desired by the Germans (especially Impressionist and modern art) were resold, often through Switzerland, onto the international art market. The Germans were meticulous in dealing with records. As major collections were brought into the central depository established at the Jeu de Paume Museum in Paris, the individual works were often marked with the collection from which they derived before they were redistributed to Germany, to individual Nazi leaders or for resale abroad.

In the earlier years of the war, these works were sometimes "purchased" from their owners. Jews and others desperate to escape from the Nazis were sometimes given exit visas on condition that they sign over their collections, often for a fraction of their true worth or for no payment at all or for payment into a "blocked" account, meaning the owner could not access the funds. Other times owners sold their works privately to raise the cash needed either to buy exit visas or to pay the costs of travel to a safe haven. Sometimes the Nazis simply expropriated all property, particularly that of Jewish collectors and dealers, without even the semblance of a legitimate transaction. Even to the extent that the illusion of a proper sale was created, such transactions were often illegal. The 1943 London Declaration allowed the Allies and governments-in-exile to nullify certain sales and transfers of property to the occupying Germans and established a presumption that any transactions in Nazi-occupied Europe were invalid.

At the conclusion of the war, special teams of Allied soldiers, known as the Monuments, Fine Arts and Archives officers, collected the artworks stolen by the Nazis and worked to return these to their original owners. This was easier in the case of well-known artworks stolen from public collections (museums, churches, and other institutions) or from prominent private collections, such as that of the Rothschild family. However, it was difficult to return works where the original owners were unknown, the original owners were deceased and their survivors unknown, or the works themselves were not sufficiently distinctive to identify their owners. After a few years, by the late 1940s and early 1950s, the Allies wished to get out of the business of returning art and so turned over the remaining works to the governments of the countries from which the works had been taken by the Nazis pursuant to a policy known as external restitution. In many cases, such as with France, Austria, and the Netherlands, the postwar governments placed obstacles in the way of efforts by survivors to recover their property, including works of art. In addition, the artworks that the Nazi leaders did not want for themselves or for the *Führermuseum* that Hitler planned to build in Linz, Austria, such as Impressionist works, works of the early twentieth century, and works painted by Jewish artists, had been sold onto the international market to raise hard currency for the Nazi war effort. Many of these works disappeared into private collections in the United States and the United Kingdom. It would take a full generation for many of these to pass into public collections, where the survivors and their heirs would have an opportunity to locate and reclaim the work.

As a result, several legal controversies have surfaced in the United States over the past twenty years and continue today. Many of the leading museums in the United States, including the Boston Museum of Fine Arts, the Metropolitan Museum of Art in New York, the Museum of Modern Art in New York, the Art Institute in Chicago, and the Seattle Art Museum, have had claims brought against them. These claims have been resolved through a variety of means, including litigation, initial litigation followed by a settlement, and negotiated settlements. The different resolutions to these disputes illustrate that there are times when objects of intrinsic cultural, religious, or historical value or with particular emotional value cannot be monetized, and sometimes what matters is the narrative that the parties wish to memorialize through the objects.

One particularly poignant example is the litigation concerning a work by Egon Schiele, known as *Portrait of Wally*, painted in 1912. Lea Bondi Jaray, an Austrian Jew and owner of an art gallery in Vienna, acquired *Wally* some time before 1925. Thereafter, although she occasionally showed it in exhibitions, Bondi primarily kept *Wally* hanging in her own apartment. In 1938, soon after the Anschluss, Bondi's art gallery in Vienna was "Aryanized." Although *Wally* was arguably not part of the gallery, the Austrian who took over the gallery insisted on acquiring *Wally* as well, and ultimately Bondi turned it over to ensure that she and her husband would not be stopped from leaving Vienna. At the conclusion of the war, Bondi attempted to recover her property, including *Wally*, which by then had become part of the collection of the Belevedere Museum. Dr. Rudolf Leopold, a Nazi sympathizer, promised to help Bondi in recovering the portrait but instead purchased *Wally* for his own collection, which later became the Leopold Foundation. Between late 1997 and early 1998, the foundation loaned the painting to the Museum of Modern Art as part of an international exhibit. Just before it was scheduled to leave the United States, Bondi's descendants, with the help of both the New York state government and the federal government, attempted to recover *Wally*. The painting went through litigation first in New York state court and then in federal court until the claim was finally settled in 2010. As one commentator has noted, "*Portrait of Wally* may not be Schiele's most important painting, but the legal case has certainly turned it into his most famous one."[1]

Wally returned to Vienna, where it is still on display at the Leopold, and the Bondi heirs were paid monetary compensation in the amount of $19 million. However, two additional conditions are of note. One was that the painting had to be displayed in the Museum of Jewish Heritage in New York before its return to Vienna. Second, when the painting was put on display in the Leopold Museum in Vienna, it had to be permanently accompanied by a full explanation of the history of the painting and of Lea Bondi, including the following statement: "Based on the evidence presented during the case, the United States District Court in New York concluded in 2009 that the Painting was the personal property of Lea Bondi Jaray and that it was stolen from her in Vienna in the late 1930s by Friedrich Welz, who was a member and collaborator of the Nazi party."[2] This case illustrates that while the painting could be monetized through the settlement payment to the Bondi family, some elements could not be monetized. The narrative, the story of the fate of the painting and of its owner and of the efforts to recover the remnants of their life in Vienna before the Holocaust, had to accompany the painting and reestablish the memory in Vienna of the once vibrant Jewish community and its cultural legacy.

This pattern was repeated in other cases involving artworks stolen during the Holocaust. The Art Institute of Chicago and Boston's Museum of Fine Arts, entered into negotiated settlements with the family of Federico Gentili di Guiseppe for a part-purchase, part-donation of artworks (Francesco Mochi's *Bust of Youth* and Corrado Giaquinto's *Adoration of the Magi*, respectively). As a commentator has noted, "Beyond the economics of such a compromise the heirs are also publicly acknowledged as past owners of the artwork which emotionally is priceless. . . . In this type of compromise, the Holocaust survivors or heirs of Holocaust survivors will be acknowledged for the wrongs that have been committed against their families, and will be recognized as owners of the art itself."[3]

Another example in which the intrinsic value of cultural objects cannot be monetized is archaeological artifacts. While archaeological objects may be sold on the market and in that sense they have a monetary value, when they are looted from the ground much more is lost than their economic worth. Controlled, scientific excavation of archaeological sites permits the archaeologist and other scientists to determine the spatial and chronological relationship of the remains and to reconstruct aspects of past life including economics, trade, health, diet, religious ritual and function, burial methods, family structure, political organization, technology, and literature. Artistic and utilitarian objects, faunal and floral remains, architectural features, human remains, and their original contextual relationship to each other are all equally essential. This full body of contextualized information is a destructible, nonrenewable cultural resource. Once it is destroyed, it cannot be regained. The looting of archaeological sites destroys this knowledge and forever impairs our ability to understand our past and ourselves. It is this original archaeological context and the knowledge that it imparts that cannot be monetized or that even restitution of the objects themselves to their country of origin does not provide adequate compensation.

Looted archaeological objects are unknown and undocumented before they appear on the market or in a collection, and this lack of documentation makes such objects particularly suitable for use in criminal activities, such as money laundering. For example, archaeological artifacts were looted from sites in southern Iraq between 2003 and 2008 on an industrial scale, matched now by the looting of sites carried out by all parties (the Islamic State of Iraq and the Levant, the Assad regime, al-Qaeda affiliate al-Nusrah Front, and the rebel forces) to the current conflict in Syria. From a variety of sources, we know that the looting carried out by ISIL provided an income stream to fund its armed conflict and terrorist activities. The undocumented nature of these artifacts also presents particular challenges to the legal system in the effort to reduce incentives for the ongoing looting of sites. This phenomenon therefore requires specialized legal doctrines that supplement the standard legal approaches to the recovery of stolen known artworks and cultural objects. These specialized doctrines serve to decrease market demand and thereby to discourage the looting of archaeological sites. The primary doctrine is recognition of the laws by which many states that are rich in archaeological resources vest ownership in the state. This means that an object that is removed in violation of national ownership is stolen property, and it retains this characterization when it is taken to a market nation, such as the United States or the United Kingdom, for sale.

The prosecution of a prominent New York dealer, Frederick Schultz, in 2002 illustrates both the use of a foreign national ownership law and the losses that the looting of archaeological artifacts imposes. Schultz had been president of the National Association of Dealers in Ancient, Oriental and Primitive Art and maintained a gallery on Manhattan's Fifty-Seventh Street. However, he was also engaged in a conspiracy with a British restorer who would purchase looted artifacts in Egypt, disguise them to look like cheap tourist souvenirs, and smuggle them out of Egypt. When he returned to London, he would restore them in a style of Egyptian artifacts popular in the 1920s and 1930s, and then he and Schultz created an elaborate scheme of a fake "old" collection. Both the British restorer and Schultz were ultimately convicted of conspiring to deal in stolen property, as Egypt had vested ownership of archaeological artifacts in the state. Schultz was subsequently sentenced to thirty-six months in prison, but this case established the U.S. courts' recognition of foreign national owner-ship laws of antiquities as a way of deterring market demand for the acquisition of such artifacts. But neither the return of the artifacts nor the prison sentence and fine imposed on Schultz could compensate for the losses that this conspiracy caused.

The most valuable of the objects involved in the Schultz conspiracy was a sculptural head of the Eighteenth Dynasty pharaoh Amenhotep III. The head of Amenhotep III is an important archaeological and historical object, by virtue of its age (made some 3,350 years ago) and as the image of one of the most renowned of the Egyptian pharaohs who ruled when Egypt was at the height of its international power and artistic achievement. Amenhotep III's accomplishments are extensively documented in ancient texts as well as in stone. During his reign, monumental buildings at Karnak and Luxor were constructed, and the two Colossi of Memnon mark the site of his tomb in western Thebes—sites that have inspired awe among visitors to Egypt for millennia. Considered one of the most artistically productive periods in Egypt's history, the reign of Amenhotep III has been the subject of major museum exhibitions and numerous books.

As a letter from Professor Betsy Bryan of Johns Hopkins University submitted to the district court at the time of Schultz's sentencing indicates, only three other heads of Amenhotep III made from this particular stone are known to exist. This head is a representation of the pharaoh as a god, probably part of a series of life-size god statues used for ritual reenactments. The loss of the find spot and other contextual information means, however, that we do not know where these other statues are nor the location of the temple complex in which these statues were placed. As Professor Bryan wrote, "Sadly, the fact that this head was taken out of context and smuggled out of Egypt means that it will take years, and that is only if we are lucky, to regain the information that was lost by the actions of the looters."

Another well-known example involved the Euphronios krater, an Attic red-figured vase from the sixth century BCE, which was looted from Italy and acquired by the Metropolitan Museum of Art in New York in 1972. Such vases were produced in the region of modern Athens in Greece but exported in antiquity to Italy for consumption by Etruscans. However, it was looted from Italy and eventually made its way through the art market to New York. Some thirty years later, Italy made a claim to recover the krater, and in 2006 the Metropolitan Museum returned it after considerable publicity and pressure was brought to bear on the museum. The director of the museum at the time, Philippe de Montebello, resisted its return, stating that everything we need to know about the pot is on the pot itself. As it happens, we know an unusual amount about this krater. It is highly unusual because both the potter and the painter signed their handiwork, and we know the scene depicted is the death of the warrior Sarpedon, narrated in the *Iliad*, because the characters depicted are labeled. However, we should pause to think about what was lost because the krater was looted. It is hypothesized that most of these vases were buried because of their good condition, but we do not know that for sure. Even if the vase came from a burial, if it had been excavated we would know who was buried in the grave: a man or a woman, young or old, cause of death, nutrition and health, the religious and mortuary practices involved in the burial, perhaps the occupation of the person, and the other goods that can indicate levels of technology, artistic achievement, and trade and economic patterns. All this information was lost—and it cannot be recovered, not through restitution of the looted artifacts and certainly not through monetary compensation.

In his landmark book *Zakhor: Jewish History and Jewish Memory*, Yosef Hayim Yerushalmi posits a distinction between the history of facts and events as contrasted with the way in which history is remembered and honored. The Jewish experience teaches us the value of cultural tradition. One can steal or destroy an object of historical value and its owner could be given compensation for its monetary value, but Jewish experience directs us to appreciate losses for which there cannot be adequate compensation. An object of antiquity, looted from its site of burial, has lost the irretrievable context of its history. A work of art stolen by the Nazis from its Jewish owners might have a market value that the heirs can recover, but the vibrant Jewish culture of pre–World War II Europe is lost forever.

NOTES

1. Tom Freudenheim, "What Is Lost When Works Are Trophies," *Wall Street Journal*, July 27, 2010, D7.

2. Stipulation and order of settlement and discontinuance, *United States of America v. Portrait of Wally, a painting by Egon Schiele, Defendant in Rem*, 6–7, https://www.unodc.org/res/cld/case-law-doc/trafficking-culturalpropertycrimetype/usa/usa-vs--leopold-museum_html/Case_Note_2013_Portrait_of_Wally.pdf.

3. Erica B. Marcus, "Nazi Looted Art: Setting Precedence for Museum Decisions" (master's thesis, Seton Hall University, 2010), 44, 48, http://scholarship.shu.edu/cgi/viewcontent.cgi?article=1251&context=theses.

31

EMBRACING DAVE RAMSEY

A Financial Literacy Model
for the Jewish Community

RABBI ALAN FREEDMAN AND RABBI AMY B. COHEN

In Jewish tradition, money is like any other resource.[1] It is not innately good or evil; wealth can be utilized for philanthropic endeavors or selfish desires; it can be handled with wisdom or greed. While money has been a topic of discussion in our sacred texts since the early chapters of Genesis, budgeting enters the conversation shortly after the Israelites have left Egypt, when they are instructed by God to set aside shekels to support the Levites, the priests (Exod. 30:13). The tax imposed a responsibility on the individual Israelite to direct to the greater community. From this we can learn that financial management is an important part of our personal lives as well as our role within the community.

Throughout the Torah, Prophets, Writings, and centuries of Rabbinic literature, we receive guidance on gaining, using, and giving money. While much of Torah and tradition focuses on communal responsibility, there is also a great deal taught about the Jewish attitude toward personal finance. The avoidance of interest when lending within the Jewish community as discussed in the Torah (Exod. 22:24) reflects a concern about the burden of debt. *Kohelet*, Ecclesiastes, reminds us that, far from being evil, the accumulation of wealth is also a gift from

God to be enjoyed (Eccles. 5:17–19). In Proverbs 13:22 we are told, "A good man has what to bequest to his grandchildren." Maimonides instructs us that once we have money, we are to first take care of our families before fulfilling our communal *tzedakah* obligations.[2]

On one level, it is appropriate for a synagogue to teach about financial literacy, because finance and budgeting are foundational elements of Jewish law and tradition. Even more so, synagogue communities are dedicated to the spiritual, social, and psychological welfare of our members. In our Western society, money management impacts the lives of all people. It affects marriages, self-image, and social relationships. In our capitalist society, the accumulation of wealth and discerning its appropriate use is a constant challenge. Where better than a synagogue to discuss this critical element of American life? A temple community has the unique potential to provide a nonjudgmental place of sanctuary, where one can speak freely about financial struggles and find support. As a religious community, a synagogue is also a place for examination of secular values through a Jewish lens.

Too often, discussions about money in congregational communities fail to go beyond dues structures, operational budgets, and donations. What if, as a community dedicated to the spiritual, social, and psychological lives of our congregants, we provide the tools to help our congregants to better take care of themselves and their families, to build wealth and self-worth, and to promote *sh'lom bayit*, peace and stability within the home? Consequently, our congregants might also be enabled to give more *tzedakah* as a by-product of creating healthy financial lives. Contrary to the stereotype that all Jews are wealthy, there are Jewish families everywhere on the socioeconomic spectrum, with differing levels of financial security. From student loans to credit card debt, from living beyond one's means to worries about not having sufficient funds for retirement, many Jewish people are struggling with their financial lives. According to a 2013 Pew Research Center Study, 20 percent of U.S. Jews report household incomes of less than $30,000 per year; about six in ten Jews in this low-income category are either under age thirty or sixty-five or older.[3] And of course, one can easily have a six-figure income and still be drowning in debt. As a result, these financial concerns impact the health and quality of life of our congregants, as well as creating discord in their familial and other relationships.

In Austin, Texas, we frequently see families who ask for exemptions from shared membership dues, families who request loans from the Hebrew Free Loan Association, and families who are expressing deep financial distress. In fact, in the fall of 2017, a Jewish food pantry was opened through our local Jewish Family Services to address this most basic of needs. As *Pirkei Avot* 3:21 teaches, *Im ein kemach, ein Torah*, "If there is no flour, there is no Torah," meaning without sustenance, we cannot be a people devoted to our spiritual lives, our lives steeped in Torah. In response to individuals' and families' current financial needs, Temple Beth Shalom, our Reform congregation, looked for ways to provide a meaningful program for teaching financial literacy.

Lacking a Jewish-based money management course, an active lay leader in partnership with both of us, the congregation's rabbis, began to explore Dave Ramsey's Financial Peace University (FPU), a nine-session Christianity-based financial literacy course. Its topics include "Seven Baby Steps," starting with $1,000 in the bank for an emergency fund, budgeting and cash-flow planning, then getting out of debt, next increasing the emergency fund to three to six months of expenses, and exploring topics related to insurance, retirement savings, saving for children's college educations, buying a house, wealth building, and giving. While primarily focused on those struggling with debt, the program also addresses those who are currently able to take care of their financial needs and therefore may be ready to begin building wealth and leaving a legacy for their children, as well as giving more to institutions that serve the community.

As rabbis, we believed our responsibility was to approach financial lessons through a Jewish lens informed by discussions from the Hebrew Bible, Jewish teachings and traditions, along with Rabbinic perspectives and contemporary Jewish views. We also wanted to be sure those from different branches of Judaism would be comfortable with the content of the course. With this in mind, we asked Ramsey Solutions, the company that developed Financial Peace University, to send us the teaching materials for our review.

Together, we studied the videos and text materials and developed a chart to compare Christian and Jewish statements and references to money. The first column included Dave Ramsey's personal statements about Christianity; the second included Dave's references to Christian translations of the Five Books of Moses and to verses from the Prophets and Proverbs, as well a few references from the Christian Bible. The third column matched each reference from the second column with comparable Jewish translations when there was a match. At the same time, we looked for Jewish references related to each topic offered in the lessons. As the congregation's rabbinic team, we provided a brief text study at the outset of each meeting to set a Jewish context for that evening's session. It is interesting to note that following our examination of the materials, we surmised that the Christian-specific content would not be a problem for members of our own congregation or others who would choose to take the course.

What surprised members of the class was that while we, the congregation's rabbis, shared Jewish teachings and Dave Ramsey (on the videos) shared a Christian perspective, we were all sending the same messages about how to handle money. For example, we sometimes used different language to convey the same lessons. When Dave Ramsey referred to "giving" to one's church, we discussed the laws of *tzedakah*. His theological viewpoint defines the concept of tithing to be the obligation to give 10 percent of one's income to the church, while Jews believe that tithing is the obligation to give 10 to 20 percent of one's income to the needy, as *tzedakah*. A Ramsey budget includes giving to one's church rather than giving to other types of philanthropic causes. While the concepts of charity and *tzedakah* are not identical, the Ramsey course and our congregation's additions explored how much of one's income is expected to be tithed and how one goes about making those decisions within a religious framework.[4]

The remainder of the class session followed the FPU Ramsey format. We would show the videos featuring Dave Ramsey and his team. Afterward, guided class discussions and activities would be assigned, and members of the class would have access to Dave Ramsey's wonderful financial team via telephone and online presentations. Seeing it as essential that members of the class have a Jewish perspective available to them during each week with "experts" for the topics discussed, our lay leader teaching the class arranged for members of our congregation with expertise in such topics as insurance, mortgages, retirement accounts, and *tzedakah* to be "go-to" experts for questions following a session. A psychologist was also available to those with questions about relating to money with spouses and others. These additional experts not only provided a seamless transition between the class topics and real-life experiences, they also acted as a bridge to our larger congregation, strengthening the bonds of the class participants with active congregational lay leaders.

Although the FPU materials would not use this Jewish language, *b'rit*, covenantal relationship, is a hallmark of Financial Peace University. Couples are encouraged to attend together, and those who are single are asked to bring a "financial accountability partner." These partnerships recognize the mutual responsibility to which each individual committed when signing up for the class. Ultimately the partnerships are elevated to a realm of holiness, as individuals hold each other accountable for becoming financial healthy. Financial health allows one to have more space for spiritual and psychological well-being.

We advertised extensively and attracted a mix of Jewish and Christian members, as well as people of other faith traditions. Class participants included both singles and couples, who ranged from their late twenties through early sixties. Class members came with differing levels of financial security and financial well-being; some were in serious debt and living paycheck to paycheck, while others were beginning to build wealth. The cohesiveness of the group was evident by the second session as members of the class reached out to support one another. At first some struggled with whether they could be successful. Others admitted feeling it was a solid program, but they made the decision not to complete all nine lessons. FPU staff members confirmed it is not uncommon that individuals and couples begin the class thinking they are ready to make changes in their financial lives but later decide they are not ready. In community, the class created a safe space where most felt comfortable sharing more than the group leader or even the curriculum requested.

As the class progressed, the students became champions of each other's progress, and they cheered when an individual or couple completed a step. The lay group leader ascertained that if the class would be talking about difficult personal and family issues regarding money management, there needed to be a comfortable environment. In Judaism, food creates community and provides comfort, so that is what our group leader provided. At the end of the ninth session, there was a graduation, complete with a cake decorated with chocolate gelt!

As an interfaith group, students gained a deeper appreciation for the Christian and Jewish perspectives on financial management. Those who were Jewish enjoyed learning about how money management goes back to biblical times and our own tradition's teachings on the topic. When Dave Ramsey, on video, spoke from his Evangelical perspective, Jewish class members shared that they felt comfortable with Dave's speaking to his own community. Those who were Christian said they very much appreciated learning about the Jewish perspectives about money management. Both the Christian and Jewish members of the class felt strongly that the Christian teachings and the Jewish teachings directed them to the same solid money management strategies. The class, with its mix of religious backgrounds, ages, and experiences with money, added new, varied insights to each lesson.

Our goal for our next class is to recruit more members from the Jewish community and to create an atmosphere in which people feel comfortable learning about financial stability within the walls of their own synagogue. We are grateful that, through a partnership with the Hebrew Free Loan Society of Austin, their board has generously offered five scholarships to members of the Austin Jewish Community to sign up for our next class. Our professional staff and lay leaders support the philosophy behind FPU, but we recognize that these types of discussions are not the norm in the Jewish community and that reality has proved to be a barrier to recruiting Jewish individuals and couples.

Class members differed in the extent to which they found success with the course. Accomplishment included progress or achievement of the step(s) for which each single or couple was aspiring. Success for us was evident when couples spoke about how much more communication they had at their "budget meetings" and singles spoke about establishing relationships or becoming closer to relatives or friends whom they chose to be their financial accountability partners, discussing their financial decisions and plans with them.

For those seeking to replicate or to offer their own money management course, every congregation needs to consider its own members and its own community characteristics. In our experience, the success of this class has been gratifying, and another class is already being planned. Recently, Dave Ramsey's outreach team has asked our congregation to create a Jewish supplement to the curriculum. Our students' experiences reflect our values and goals for every congregant who walks through our doors. As one member wrote following the class, "Having the seven steps memorized and being accountable for making my budget has given me the tools to make lifelong changes." And, in a thank-you note received, one woman wrote, "I had avoided this class, because I had heard it was Christian. Finding it at Temple Beth Shalom allowed me to step through the door."

Let us continue to open our doors to the "strangers" among us. Those who seem fine on Friday night may not be able pay their bills after a spouse loses their job the following week. Those who do not want to ask for financial assistance for congregational membership, camp tuition, or religious school fees remain outside our walls. Financial stability throughout the Jewish community is important for us all. Whether a financial course such as Financial Peace University is offered through such entities as synagogues, Jewish Family Services, a

Jewish Community Center, or a Hillel, there is much to be gained for all generations. Let us allow Dave Ramsey, an Evangelical Christian syndicated radio talk show host and motivational speaker, to remind us of our responsibility to turn to the Torah and Jewish teachings to help our community find financial *shalom* as individuals, achieve *sh'lom bayit* within our relationships, and create holy communities ready to fulfill our communal *tzedakah* responsibilities.

NOTES

1. Much gratitude to Anne Corn, our dedicated lay leader and facilitator who initiated this partnership with Ramsey Solutions and encouraged our congregation to offer Financial Peace University. Anne offered numerous insights and lessons that are included in this article.
2. Maimonides, *Mishneh Torah, Hilchot Mat'not Aniyim* 7:13.
3. *A Portrait of Jewish Americans: Findings from a Pew Research Center Survey of U.S. Jews* (Washington, DC: Pew Research Center Religion and Public Life Project, 2013), http://www.pewforum.org/2013/10/01/jewish-american-beliefs-attitudes-culture-survey/.
4. For more about the difference between the Christian and Jewish views of giving money, see Adar, p. 87, and Holo, p. 373.

32

USING JEWISH VALUES TO TEACH YOUR CHILDREN ABOUT MONEY

DEBORAH NIEDERMAN, RJE

When our children were born, my husband and I were very intentional about how to craft a scaffolding so that they could one day build meaningful Jewish lives of their own. We thought long and hard about how we would celebrate the holidays and what ancient and new traditions we would meld for our family. We considered how we would talk about God in our lives to help them find a way to talk about God in theirs. We were intentional about using texts from our tradition to talk about how we made decisions about our life. But we never spoke about money.

Like many parents, we didn't share with our children what, how, and why we were saving; we didn't share with them what, why, and how we were giving to others. Although we were intentional about Jewish values in every other area of child-rearing, we didn't connect Jewish wisdom to this crucial part of our lives.

Children are curious about the subject. As Ron Leiber writes in the *New York Times*, "Money is a source of mystery to children. They sense its power, so they ask questions, *lots of them*, over many years. Why isn't our house as big as my cousin's? Why can't I have . . . Are we poor? Why didn't you give money to the man who asked you for some?"[1]

My husband and I were clearly not alone in our habits. According to a 2017 T. Rowe Price survey, **69 percent of parents have some reluctance when it comes to talking about money with their children.** And only 23 percent of kids say they talk with their parents frequently about money.[2]

Parents don't always know how to respond to questions about money, something with which they may struggle and about which they have their own ambivalence. This is where Jewish text and tradition can help us.

Proverbs tells us, "Train up a child in the way he should go, and even when he is old he will not depart from it" (Prov. 22:6). At its most basic, parenting is about preparing a child to live a meaningful and fulfilled life. Using the teachings from our tradition can provide parents with tools to make sense of this messy and chaotic world, especially concerning money.

One way parents can respond is by listening carefully to the questions our children ask in order to try to answer the question *beneath* what is asked. When they ask, "Are we rich?" children are seeking to understand something about their place in this world. When they ask, "Why can't I have . . . ?" children are inquiring about how they compare to their friends and testing the limits of wants and needs. But, when they ask, they really do want to know, so we, as parents, need to try to have answers to these difficult questions. We need to engage in these conversations, even when they are difficult, in order to help our children discover much about themselves and the world. Sometimes the best we can do is explore the answers with our children.

When teaching our children, we should begin with the basics:

> You shall love the Eternal your God with all your heart, with all your soul, and with all your might. Take to heart these instructions with which I charge you this day. Impress them upon your children. Recite them when you stay at home and when you are away, when you lie down and when you get up. Bind them as a sign on your hand and let them serve as a symbol on your forehead; inscribe them on the doorposts of your house and on your gates.

(Deuteronomy 6:5–9, cited in the daily recitation of the *Sh'ma* and found within the mezuzah and *t'fillin*)

Here the Torah itself reminds us that it has something to teach us about our daily interactions in the world. Wherever we go and however we travel, we are to take Torah, our love of God (which we partly show through our might, or as some translate, possessions[3]), and the diligent teachings of our parents with us. Given the daily encounters we all have with money and its impact on our lives, Jewish text and tradition have much to teach us. The underlying messages of the many texts related to money and business dealings encourage us simply to be ethical people. Later in this same chapter of the Torah we are taught, "Do what is right and good in the sight of the Eternal" (Deut. 6:18). Helping our children understand how these teachings meaningfully apply to their daily lives is crucial to helping our children grow into successful adults with an appreciation of the variety of ways one can flourish in personal and business life.

I have found that one of the greatest difficulties of parenting is being truly transparent and open in modeling the actions I want my children to follow. I have found myself thinking and even saying, "Do as I say and not as I do." I regret not openly and honestly talking about the challenges we have faced when dealing with money and the choices we have made. Joseph Karo teaches, "The good and right course for one to follow is the happy mean, and not the extreme."[4] We have tried to follow a happy mean, but my family is no different from any other; we often wish we had more or better. We sometimes choose not to spend the money we have for values-based reasons, and we can't always give away as much money as we want to help others.

Jewish tradition and Torah have much to teach us about wants versus needs. There are a variety of teachings to help us understand that happiness is found not in seeking more, but in being satisfied with what we have.

Pirkei Avot teaches, "Who is rich? The one who is happy with their portion" (4:1). Rabbi Steven Leder, Pritzker Chair of Senior Rabbinics of Wilshire Boulevard Temple in Los Angeles, teaches what it means to be happy with our lot, to understand wealth beyond dollars:

> No matter what our net worth, all of us can become rich with family, caring and laughter. We can all invest in and achieve the wealth of friendship. We can all spend less time counting our money and more time counting our blessings. We can all lead richer lives, ever more grateful simply to love and be loved.[5]

As parents, we have a responsibility to teach our children to value experiences, feelings, friendship, and love—to create value beyond the tangible. One way to do this is to cultivate a sense of gratitude. You can create time each night before bed or when waking up to encourage your children to think of one thing they are thankful for. There are traditional prayers that encourage this kind of conversation, including the bedtime *Sh'ma* at night and *Modeh Ani* in the morning. At our Shabbat table, after we have lit the candles and welcomed Shabbat, we go around the table each week and have everyone share at least one thing for which they are thankful. One of the most difficult and frequently asked question by children is "Can I have . . . ?" Helping children understand the distinction between wants and needs can provide a means for answering these questions. As parents, we can get just as caught up in "keeping up with the Joneses" as our children, but we also need to remember there is a difference between what is necessary and what is a choice.

Targeted by advertisers and pressured by peers, children will ask for the latest games and fashions. Helping them understand early on the difference between needs and wants will help them make better spending decisions for life. It's important for parents to remember that sometimes we can, and should, say no. It is not helpful to cave in to every whined request or to purchase every item asked for, even if we can afford it. Throughout our lives we will hear no when we make a request, and it's important for our children to acclimate to that experience as well.

British clinical psychologist Dr. Elizabeth Kilbey tells us, "Experts warn against saying you can't afford it. It's easy to use this default response when your child begs you for the latest toy. But doing so sends the message that you're not in control of your money, which can be scary—and create future anxieties." Kilbey suggests that a more appropriate way is to respond, "We choose not to spend our money like that."[6]

One of the challenges children experience is understanding the value something is assigned relative to its costs. For them, every new thing has the same value: It is new! Helping a child understand how much something costs by thinking about how long it might take to make the money to purchase that item teaches delayed gratification and can help a child appreciate its value. For those who provide allowance to their children, help them consider how many weeks of allowance it might cost. For those who do not give their children allowance, assign payment to different household chores and enable the children to earn the money. There is value in earning the money to purchase something for yourself and beginning to understand how to spend your own money. Suddenly, when children are required to spend their own money, they may realize they don't need the item in the way they may have felt if someone else was making the purchase!

What Does Torah and Tradition Tell Us about Giving and *Tzedakah*?

As discussed in depth elsewhere in this book, the word *tzedakah* comes from the Hebrew word for justice and refers to the mitzvah of sharing our money to make the world a more just place. While there are many mitzvot that encourage us to give of ourselves, we are also commanded to give of our money. This significant part of Jewish ethics is perhaps most familiar to families and children through weekly *tzedakah* collection at many religious schools. Planning where the money a child donates should come from (whether from parents or from the child's own funds) can help a child understand we are all obligated to give. According to Jewish tradition everyone is required to give *tzedakah*, even those who receive it.[7]

There are many ideas the Torah shares with us about sharing our money. Perhaps the most important teaching is to be generous: "You must open your hand and lend [to your needy kin] whatever is sufficient to meet the need" (Deut. 15:8). This is the essence of *tzedakah*, and there are many ways to build the habit and fulfill the mitzvah of *tzedakah*. Hopefully your congregational religious school encourages students to bring in money each week and gives students a chance to think about where they will give, to understand the impact that money will have. Just as with understanding the value of a purchase, students can understand the value of a contribution by understanding the difference it can make. You can set up a time to collect *tzedakah* weekly in your home and highlight times throughout the year to consider how you will distribute your funds. In our family we empty the boxes at the start of Rosh HaShanah, the Jewish New Year, and before Passover. We use the funds to purchase food for the local food bank at that time. Many families have a *tzedakah* box on their table each Shabbat and empty their pockets of coins as a way of separating from the workweek before they light Shabbat candles.

Just as with a budget for an organization, the family budget reflects what the family values and priorities. Share your family budget with your children. Be as open and honest as you can when discussing what you spend your money on. When teaching your children about money, it is important to talk about how and why you choose to spend your money as you do and to be clear about where and why you choose to share your money with others. Parents should write *tzedakah* checks in front of their children and share why that organization and what difference their funds will make.

What Does Torah and Tradition Tell Us about How We Will Ultimately Be Judged?

The Talmud tells us that the first question we will be asked upon our death when we arrive at the heavenly gate will be "Were you honest in your business dealings?" (Babylonian Talmud, *Shabbat* 31a). Why business? Business refers to all matters regarding possessions and money. How we interact daily in this realm is considered a test of our ethical bearing. In some way we all deal in business every day, whether it is through direct contact with money or not. Having a Jewish frame for how to face the complicated decisions we make about money can be a powerful tool in this complex world filled with a variety of pressures. As parents, we must consider what the business of childhood is and what we need to do to help our children navigate money and their daily interactions.

Maimonides teaches, "A person ought constantly to associate with the righteous . . . and shun the wicked . . . so as not to be corrupted by their example."[8] This seems to be the lesson of every Disney show I watched with my children as they grew up; if you have good friends—that is, friends who are good people—you can survive and thrive in the competitive halls of middle school and beyond! In truth, I have seen this borne out as my children and the children of my friends grow up. The quality of friends our children choose does help them to succeed and to make choices about "being honest in their business dealings." Part of the business of childhood is about building and maintaining relationships and navigating the end of relationships. This important work will help children succeed in a variety of ways. It is important for children to understand that many things have value beyond dollars and friendships are about intrinsic worth, not financial gain. Of course, we must also model this in the friends we choose. Do we disparage our friends or other adults in front of them? How do we support our friends and their families through difficult times? When we fall out of friendships, how do we explain that to our children? We need to speak openly and honestly about our relationships as well, to help our children understand how and why relationships change and that change is a reality of growth and daily life.

In addition to constant social pressure, children today face pressure to succeed in school in a way that feels different from when we grew up. The tremendous level of competition for grades and success seems to begin earlier and earlier. Given the models students see of athletes, actors, and others who succeed through less than honest ways, children are tempted to cheat. We need to constantly reinforce the values behind the important question, discussed above, we will be asked, "Were you honest in your business dealings?" (Babylonian Talmud, *Shabbat* 31a), as well as the teaching, "Being honest in business fulfills the whole Torah."[9] We must encourage our children to stay far from temptation by not only being happy with their lot, but also being satisfied with whom they are. Ultimately, the ethics of business are completely intertwined with how we engage with others in every other facet of our lives and how we think about ourselves. Creating a mindfulness, based on the teachings of our tradition, of how we spend and share our money is an important part of the knowledge we must pass on to our children. And we must always remember, in all our parental striving, the most important thing we can teach our children is that they are loved just as they are and that they are worthy of being loved.

NOTES

1. Ron Lieber, "Why You Should Tell Your Children How Much You Make," *New York Times*, January 29, 2015, https://www.nytimes.com/2015/02/01/your-money/why-you-should-tell-your-kids-how-much-you-make.html?_r=1.
2. T. Rowe Price, "Parents, Kids & Money Survey," March 16, 2017, https://www.slideshare.net/TRowePrice/t-rowe-price-parents-kids-money-survey.
3. For example, Rashi interprets *m'odecha* as "all your wealth."
4. *Kitzur Shulchan Aruch*, "Moral Laws," 29:2.
5. Rabbi Steven Z. Leder, *More Money Than God: Living a Rich Life without Losing Your Soul* (Chicago: Bonus Books, 2003), 181.
6. Kara Gammell, "Six Tips to Teach Your Child about Money Matters," *Guardian*, November 10, 2014, https://www.theguardian.com/money/2014/nov/10/tips-teach-child-money-matters.
7. *Shulchan Aruch, Yoreh Dei-ah* 249:2.
8. Maimonides, *Mishneh Torah, Hilchot Dei-ot* 6:1.
9. *M'chilta, Vayisa*, chap. 1.

33

MARRIAGE, MONEY, AND MUSAR[1]

Rabbi Barry H. Block

Engaged couples, meeting with a rabbi before their weddings, do not typically believe that they "need" premarital counseling. They come to the appointment looking forward to planning wedding details. Premarital counseling is viewed as a hurdle to jump in order for their chosen rabbi to officiate. In love and careening toward a wedding date, most are less than eager to acknowledge issues in their relationships. The rabbi's role is to facilitate conversation that will identify potential concerns and to help the couple confront them honestly and productively. Occasionally, the rabbi will refer the couple to a licensed marriage and family therapist, which is never a bad idea but is crucial for only a minority of couples.

The challenges revealed in premarital counseling vary. Money, though, is invariably among them. Whatever their ages, backgrounds, genders, or circumstances, few couples have figured out how to manage their shared financial future. Many have not even consciously realized that they will have one.

For more than a quarter century, I have advised couples to share their individual financial situations with one another, to discuss their attitudes toward each other's spending habits, and to explore their expectations about future income and expenses. When one or both of the parties comes from a wealthy family or a family business is involved, I have urged conversations with parents. Under those circumstances, or when one or both partners comes into the marriage with significant assets or debt, I have pointed to the precedent of the *ketubah*, Jewish marriage contract, to encourage consideration of a premarital agreement.

Since I became a student of Musar, in 2011, I have gained a set of tools that are most helpful in understanding the dynamics that cause couples to be in denial about the need to chart a shared financial future. Just as important, Musar offers resources that can help the couple to resolve those issues.

Musar, Jewish ethical discipline, aims at *tikkun hanefesh*, repairing one's own soul, as a path to achieving the holiness for which God has created us in the divine image. Musar students probe their own *midot*, soul traits—studying, repeating daily affirmations, journaling, and then engaging in repeated practice of all these—to refine aspects of the inner life that impact upon behavior and relationships. For couples, exploring *midot* together offers an opportunity to grow as a couple and to get to know one another more deeply. Just as Musar can help couples work through their financial challenges, discussions about money may reveal soul traits that demand a couple's attention.

Almost always, engaged couples have been living together for some time. Almost never do they have a joint checking account. I ask, "How do you handle shared expenses?" One way or another, costs are divided. I follow up by asking if they've considered establishing a joint account. Typically, the couple will confess that they haven't discussed the matter, though they assume that they'll have a joint account one day. In the past, that's where I would have inserted my instruction that they do so sooner than later—after all, they will have a shared financial future.

Now, instead, with the tools of Musar, I invite the couple to explore the reality: They have merged their homes, and so much of their lives, into one present and future. Why not their money? But I don't ask that question directly. Instead, I begin, "If one of you were to be in charge of your joint account, who would that be?" The question is implicitly about the *midah*, soul trait, of *seder*, order. Does one partner's punctiliousness annoy the other? Does one future spouse's disorganization drive the other to distraction? Often, *seder* is addressed quickly and easily: one partner is simply more organized than the other or just "better with money," and everybody's comfortable with that. Deciding who would manage the (as yet theoretical) bank account is easy. Still, the conversation about *seder*, introduced in the area of finances, impacts other areas of shared living: who leaves dirty clothes all over the apartment, and who can't stand seeing even one dish in the kitchen sink, even after it has been rinsed?

Perhaps, though, the issue isn't *seder* but *bitachon*, trust.[2] In Musar literature, the term *bitachon* typically refers to trusting God, not another person. In building a marriage, though, trust between partners is paramount. Frank conversation about the confidence required to let one's partner manage shared money, and conversely about the challenge of being the repository of that faith, may lead to acknowledgment that the marriage must be built on trust. Discussion may then turn to the *bitachon* that will be required in every aspect of married life, critically including emotional safety and sexual fidelity.

The question of the joint bank account may also be about control. Consciously or otherwise, engaged couples are constantly negotiating divisions of labor and power as their relationship matures. Both partners may perceive that the one managing the money is asserting power over the other. Deciding who will manage the money or how to share the task may impact every area of married life. For example, the partner who will oversee the joint account may fear that financial management will be only one example of outsized responsibility or parent-like control. On the other hand, the party letting go of fiscal affairs may be concerned about giving up too much authority, becoming more like a dependent child than an equal partner in marriage.

In the language of Musar, the issue is *anavah*, humility. *Anavah* does not merely require that we rein in our arrogance. Instead, Musar urges us to strive for balance when we confront our humility, like all other traits. The suggested daily affirmation for a Musar practitioner seeking to cultivate the *midah* of *anavah* is "No more than my place, no less than my space."[3] In negotiating the perceived power disequilibrium brought on by one partner's assuming financial management duties, each is trying to answer, "What is my place, and what is my partner's role, in making my decisions, my partner's choices, and our shared direction?"

I have used words like "fear" and "concerned" in several contexts. We tend to think of fear negatively. Upon reflection, though, fear is a soul trait like others, best when brought into balance. For example, we teach children to be sufficiently afraid of the water that they don't dive in unsafely, even as we help them overcome outsized fears in order to swim their first strokes away from the wall. Similarly, engaged couples are healthiest when they are neither cavalier nor petrified as they consider the challenges that marriage may present.

In that light, I present *yirah*, fear, as another soul trait that merits exploration as we discuss money in premarital counseling. As with *bitachon*, I depart from Musar's usual application of the term *yirah* to our relationship with God. The traditional Musar student seeks to hold God in sufficient awe that we abide by divine ordinances. Applying the concept of *yirah* to marriage, we ask whether the partners are not taking marriage as seriously as they might—or, at the opposite extreme, if they're terrified. Individuals in denial about the enormity of the relationship into which they're entering may not recognize necessary steps, such as combining their finances. Those who are afraid may paradoxically evidence the same response: paralyzed by fear, they avoid actions that make their marriage all too real.

Fear may be the reason that many couples haven't even admitted the reality of their shared financial future to their consciousness. Eager to avoid conflict and the need to confront all the soul traits explored here, they behave as if the issues did not exist.

Fear may also motivate a couple to avoid a needed premarital agreement. Years before I possessed the Musar language to describe that fear, I counseled a couple who presented complex issues that inspired me to refer them to a licensed marital therapist. The couple made excuses rather than seeking the help they needed. I sensed that fear of their relationship's failure was the real reason they avoided in-depth counseling, and I told them so, but to no avail. They did accept ordinary rabbinical premarital counseling, which included conversation about money. Learning that one partner was involved in a family business, I suggested a premarital agreement, and both acknowledged the wisdom of that counsel. I wasn't surprised, though, that they again did not follow my advice. Frightened, they avoided a step that would have acknowledged their fear, that is, the very possibility that the marriage could fail—which, sadly, it did in a matter of months.

Couples are not eager to discuss the financial liabilities that each may be bringing into the marriage. One partner may be burdened by significant credit card debt, while the other has substantial student loans. Some have obligations to offspring from a prior relationship, and others may owe spousal support after a divorce. Individuals may think of these liabilities as being theirs alone, not part of the couple's shared financial future, but they are deluding themselves. Prior obligations may limit the amount of money that the couple has available for their own future and may enhance income requirements in ways that interfere with plans for time together.

Conversations about student loans often lead to congenial agreement that this debt should be shared. After all, those loans have purchased an education or two that may pave the way for the couple's financial future. Moreover, when only one partner's education was paid by parents, student loans may be a useful vehicle for productive acknowledgment of the partners' different financial backgrounds and/ or their parents' divergent values, informing their own.

Other financial liabilities, though, offer the rabbi an opportunity to discuss *kaas*, the soul trait of anger. Sometimes, the anger is coming from outside the couple—children who resent the marriage, for example, or a former spouse. More importantly, one partner may be angered by the real or perceived poor choices in their loved one's past. Engaged couples may be eager to deny or avoid anger, when they would be wiser to acknowledge and work through it. Anger that festers is as dangerous as anger that burns out of control, so effort to keep it in balance is worthy. The ability to discuss one's anger over a partner's outsized credit card debt or unfavorable divorce decree may offer a useful entrée for exploring how the couple manages anger more generally.

My favorite "money question" for a couple in premarital counseling has always been: "How does each of you feel about the other's spending? Does one of you consider the other to be a spendthrift or a miser?" No, engaged couples don't happily admit that they apply such pejoratives to one another. However, they frequently describe behaviors that suggest awareness that one or both of them may harbor traits in the direction of one extreme or the other. One partner may be content when contentment is not warranted, needlessly suffering on a bed of springs even though the couple can easily afford to replace that worn-out mattress. Somebody else, though, will have an insatiable appetite for fine wine, not a problem with alcohol but with a budget-busting habit that threatens both financial and marital equilibrium. Musar urges *histapkut*, satisfaction with what we have. As with all traits, both extremes are possible. Musar counsels us to pursue a "golden mean," a moderate path in all traits. Between miserliness and profligacy, couples must strive to find the middle course that works for both partners.

Spending, of course, is only half of any budgetary equation. Therefore, I invite couples to discuss their expectations about future income. Will one partner be more responsible for bringing home the proverbial "bacon" than the other? If the couple has or is contemplating children, how does each partner value stay-at-home parenting, part-time or full-time, compared to earning income at work? With or without children, how will each partner balance time devoted to earning an income with time for other pursuits and for one another? In short, questions about income touch the most important issues of a couple's life.

We return to a focus on *anavah*, humility. Each person's role in the marital household is the real topic when we're ostensibly talking about sources of future income. Entering a marriage, particularly but not only when children may be included, each person must ask, "What will be my role? What place will be mine, and what space will be occupied by my spouse? How can I make space for my spouse in an arena that will be primarily mine? What role will I find for myself in an area that will mostly be my spouse's responsibility?" None should be so naïve as to imagine that the answers contemplated in premarital counseling will necessarily be "the" answers for decades to come. Aware of the questions and understanding the importance of talking through roles, each may resolve to take "no more than my place, no less than my space," whatever those places and spaces turn out to be.

I always query couples about the role that Judaism will play in their marriage. If the couple doesn't mention *tzedakah*, justice achieved through charitable giving, I will ask them to consider generosity, the *midah* that Musar calls *n'divut*. I may kick-start their contemplation by suggesting that they find an act of *tzedakah*—their own, not their parents'—in connection with their wedding. Some, though, require no prompt from me, having already established charitable routines. As with any other spending, some may be miserly, and others, profligate. Whether helping a couple to begin to establish *tzedakah* practices or to work through individual patterns that must now be merged, I ask them to consider the golden mean. As much as I encourage *tzedakah*, I also urge couples not to overdo it, emphasizing that the Talmud places an upper limit on the extent to which one should be charitable (Babylonian Talmud, *K'tubot* 50a).

Money is but one of the significant topics addressed in comprehensive premarital counseling. If approached thoroughly, the exploration of a range of *midot*, soul traits, that arise from discussing financial affairs will open windows to fruitful conversation about matters as seemingly mundane as wedding planning and as intimate as child-rearing.

NOTES

1. Many ideas attributed to Musar throughout this chapter are based on insights I have learned from the writing and teaching of Alan Morinis. For more information about Musar, visit mussarinstitute.org.

2. I am grateful to Alan Morinis, who suggested adding this *midah* after reading an early draft.

3. The precise language is taken from The Mussar Institute's proprietary course "A Season of Mussar," which is not publicly available. The idea is expressed in slightly different language in Alan Morinis, *Everyday Holiness* (Boston: Trumpeter Books, 2007), 45.

34

SAYING GOODBYE

Honoring Your Congregation's Legacy

RABBI DAVID BURSTEIN FINE
WITH BETH BURSTEIN FINE, MSW

> To everything there is a season and a time for every experi-
> ence under heaven: a time to be born and a time to die, a time
> to plant and a time to uproot.
>
> *Ecclesiastes 3:1–2*

As Ecclesiastes reminds us, all experiences and human endeavors follow a rhythm of beginning and ending, bringing with them a rhythm
of human emotion as well. This is certainly true for our houses of
worship. Congregations begin with hopes and uncertainty, experience
periods of growth and challenge, adapting—even transforming—as
the world around them and the needs of their community change.
Congregations may expand and shrink, merge with other groups, adjust
their mission and vision. And yet there are times when the reality is
such that a congregation needs to end, to dissolve or be absorbed by
another. This is certainly a difficult decision for the members of a
community to make. Yet an approach can be taken that honors the
deep sense of connection people feel toward their shared history and
attends to the practicalities of closing that synagogue. This chapter will
address this challenging time in the season of a congregation.

Congregational leadership will notice certain trends and difficulties that lead them to consider making significant changes in the

organization. Membership may be shrinking in numbers or aging without the potential for growth. Revenue, whether from dues or other sources, may no longer be sufficient to meet the needs of the building and staffing. Demographics may be changing, both in the general and Jewish population. Sometimes there are circumstances when the institution is on solid financial footing, but the people just aren't there. Leaders can access the Union for Reform Judaism or respective movement resources, Jewish Federation, or private consultation to determine a plan to address these challenges. Some situations may require changes in staffing, programming, or building, adapting to the new environment in order to meet their members' needs. Other scenarios reveal that the community can no longer support a congregation. Perhaps the Jewish population has moved out of an area or has changed in nature so that the current congregation does not match the community. In this and similar cases, the hard and loving decision needs to be made to carefully dissolve the congregation, while thoughtfully creating a legacy that honors its history.

It is important to approach this loss pastorally, with awareness of the pain it entails. Shifting demographics are not the fault of those who have lived their lives in a community. In fact, the stalwarts have supported that community throughout the years of growth and celebration. It is important to recognize the sense of loss and possibly failure for congregants. Some may feel guilty for not having done more, for not turning the tide, yet the reality is that they need to be recognized for their strength and dedication. Communities will approach this important work in various ways to allow people to grieve, to accept the difficult reality, and to support the necessary work of dissolving the congregation with care.

The process of dissolving a congregation, while emotional, can be shepherded with respect and sensitivity. It is important to recognize and attend to both the human needs and reactions, as well as the practical details that add up to honoring the history of the sacred community. All aspects of this process have both a practical and emotional nature. As the congregation discusses what to do with the Torah scrolls and who will maintain the cemetery, they are also recognizing the years of community life and the present necessity to let go. The symbols of the congregation take on extra meaning, transcending the link between the holy and the mundane, now embodying a link with the past, the significant people and moments in their lives and life of the congregation.

An organization that can be extremely helpful as a congregation goes through this process is the Jewish Community Legacy Project (JCLP). This is a resource for small congregations outside of metropolitan areas that need support in planning their dissolution in such a way as to cover perpetual care of a cemetery, disposition of ritual objects, preservation of historical documents, and development of legacy endowments that reflect the interests and values of the community. Larger congregations in metropolitan areas generally will pursue a merger or absorption with a neighboring congregation rather than dissolution.

Let's turn to the objects that possess meaning and memory for a congregation to consider how to respectfully deal with them. Each congregation will want to consider what those important objects are for them. These may include siddurim, *Chumashim*, the *ner tamid*, Torah scrolls, the ark curtain and other art, photographs, and historical records, even the actual building. The *yahrzeit* board will take on extra significance, as members with a history at the congregation want to ensure that those who have died will still be remembered. Some ritual items can be shared with individual congregants or offered to the wider Jewish community. Colleges, the American Jewish Archives, and other institutions may be interested in various items. As mentioned, the JCLP can be helpful in this process.

Of course, selling the building is a larger decision. While the sale of the building is a legal real estate transaction, it also involves desacralizing, or removing the sacred meaning imbued in the building. How will members gather to share stories and memories, to laugh and cry together? Many congregations have developed beautiful rituals for honoring the years of joyful Jewish life in their building as part of saying goodbye to the sacred nature of the building, which allow members to consider the building as an asset, separate from their sacred connections to it. This brings us to a second question raised by selling the building—what to do with any assets.

The congregation may have proceeds, once any debts are eliminated, from the general fund or the sale of the building and other items. This opens the important and healing possibility of creating a legacy for the congregation. Even though the actual entity is being dissolved, it must be asked: What matters most to its members? What should they create or maintain with the remaining assets? Along with the leadership of the community, the JCLP can be extremely helpful in this area. The important conversation of what is most important to this community as a legacy can lead to closure and the recognition that the values and priorities of the community can continue to live on.

What will the congregation's legacy be? Many congregations have a cemetery and will want to guarantee its respectful maintenance for generations to come, as a sacred trust with those who came before. Other congregations may feel strongly about supporting a Jewish institution in the area, a social cause, a congregation in Israel, Jewish camping, and other efforts to further the causes the membership holds to be most important.

Let's return to the human side of this endeavor. How does a community say goodbye and honor the past? Consider who should be part of this effort; invite former and current members to participate in the planning and execution. Share stories and photos, and discuss ways to preserve these. You may want to create a Facebook community, record stories (à la StoryCorps), or create an electronic scrapbook. Many congregations create a ritual for removing mezuzot or Torah scrolls from the building. The very act of removal is a physical reminder that the building is no longer an active Jewish synagogue. Imbued with emotion and meaning, the extinguishing of the *ner tamid* is a visual reminder, which shouts in one last glimmer that the soul of a congregation no longer resides in the building. Others create a final celebration or service, recognizing the love and joy that grew in that space and that will continue in other ways and in other places.

To return to Ecclesiastes: "Don't say, 'How has it happened that former times were better than these?'" (7:10). Certainly, saying good-bye to a congregation is a sad event, yet this verse reminds us that circumstances change, communal structures come and go, yet the relationships and the history remain in the lives of those enriched by that congregation.

ETHICS IN FOCUS

Ethical Estate Planning

RABBI RICHARD F. ADDRESS, DMIN

The dynamics of contemporary family life often come into challenging focus as one begins to examine how to honor wishes regarding the distribution of assets. For the family that seeks a Jewish approach to planning an estate, a basis of approach can be gleaned from our sacred texts. A halachic understanding of inheritance can be glimpsed in Numbers 27:6–11, the narrative of the daughters of Zelophehad. In addition, these texts make important contributions to our understanding of the topic: Deuteronomy 21:17, which underscores the double portion allotted to the firstborn son; and Job 42:15, which, reflecting the above Numbers passage, notes that Job's estate was to be shared with his daughters as well as his sons. The discussion of the accepted order of inheritance is found within postbiblical Judaism. That order for the distribution of assets is as follows:

Sons and their offspring (and double portion is assigned to eldest son)
Daughters and their offspring
The father of the deceased
Brothers and their offspring
Sisters and their offspring
The paternal grandfather

Paternal uncles and their offspring
Paternal sisters and their offspring
The paternal great-grandfather[1]

The halachic approach to estate planning follows this formula. For the liberal Jewish world, the parameters of tradition might not be our prime guide, especially when they conflict with other important values like egalitarianism or financially providing for a disabled dependent. Our changing family structures, including blended families, same-sex couples, and people living together without marriage, all present a new and wide range of possibilities. There is no "one size" approach, as each family is unique, with its own universe of desires and concerns. With halachah as a guide, we can begin with the foundational idea of *tzedek* (justice). The idea of justice or equity in dealing with families would seem to be obvious. The desire to see the distribution of assets in a just and equitable manner reflects a hope to respect the wishes of the person who is leaving these assets. The issue of being a steward of those wishes is drawn from the tradition's understanding of the fifth commandment of honoring our parents and therefore respecting their wishes. We are asked to do that even if we disagree with those wishes. Yet, there is often a disconnect between what tradition advises and what a family member feels. The value and ideal of justice may be very personal.

A challenge that often emerges in these discussions is the use of money as a factor of control. How do we apportion financial assets in a just manner when money is often a source of stress? Rabbi Michael Chernick offers an interesting look at this challenge in an analysis of the fifth commandment:

> Money is one of the most highly charged commodities known to humankind. It symbolizes the value at more than the economic level. The Talmudic world understood that when it punned about money, which is sometimes called *damin* in Hebrew. "*Damin* is a double entendre," the Sages said, because it means both money and blood. And "the blood is the life." This is not a statement that means that money is worth everything or that life is money. But

it is a statement that means money makes independence possible. Independence fosters a sense of self-worth, and self-worth makes life meaningful.[2]

Thus, we are sometimes presented with the tension between what a person wishes to be done with his or her money and what the family desires. What is just? The tradition tells us that the prime responsibility is the honoring and respecting of the wishes of the person whose estate is being created.

In addition to the value of *tzedek*, I suggest an additional value that may be of greater significance—*l'dor vador*, literally meaning "from generation to generation." This value directs us to consider the essence of one's estate. What is the ethical foundation of creating a legal document that expresses one's wishes? It is a sense of legacy. The distribution of material assets is a way of leaving a lasting legacy, especially if that estate is supplemented by the creation of an ethical will, a written statement of one's values. Then, our own legacies transcend the material, and it is the spiritual aspect of a person that should emerge as the true essence of a human being.

The values of *tzedek* and *l'dor vador* can inform how individuals and families discuss what their wishes may be in this major life transition. Synagogues can stimulate these conversations about the ethical approach to estate planning by offering comprehensive educational programs. Thought-provoking educational programs should cover (1) how to prepare for the discussion with your loved ones, (2) the ethical values found within the context of Jewish tradition, (3) practical instruction regarding secular documents such as one's will, advance medical directive, and family care plan, and (4) how to write an ethical will to accompany your secular documents. Given the opportunities and challenges presented by medical technology and longevity, the Jewish community has a wonderful opportunity to engage our people with a comprehensive ethical approach to decisions associated with the end of life.

NOTES

1. See W. Gunther Plaut, "The Laws of Inheritance," in *The Torah: A Modern Commentary*, rev. ed., ed. W. Gunther Plaut (New York: URJ Press, 2005), 1089; and K. Eli Akhavan, "Basic Principles of Estate Planning within the Context of Jewish Law," *Probate and Property*, July/August 2011, 61.
2. Michael Chernick, "Who Pays? The Talmudic Approach to Filial Responsibility," in *That You May Live Long: Caring for Our Aging Parents, Caring for Ourselves*, ed. Richard F. Address and Hara E. Person (New York: UAHC Press, 2003), 98.

TALKING ABOUT MONEY

A Time to Give, a Time to Refrain from Giving

MARCIE ZELIKOW

To Marcie Zelikow, philanthropy is an expression of love and respect for others, as well as a deeply held Jewish value. As is written in Kohelet, Ecclesiastes, *life has its moments and also its seasons. When circumstances change, acknowledging and honoring those changes and the impact it has on our relationship partners is a necessary act of courage.*

Below is an adaptation of a letter written by Marcie and her husband to a number of philanthropic organizations during a time of change.

Dear Partner,

This is probably an unusual letter for you to receive, but I like to think that Howard and I are fairly unusual philanthropists. First, please note the list of people and organizations receiving this correspondence. I'm writing to all of you because I have the same message for all of you. We care deeply about you and the values you represent. That's why I refer to you as partners. We like to think of ourselves that way. We have been supporters for many years. We know and understand your organizations. We appreciate what you do and what you stand for. We also appreciate how hard you work for the organizations you represent. I too am engaged in fundraising and know how hard you all work for every dollar.

Because we believe in what you do and understand the difficulties of fundraising, Howard and I have always been full-capacity givers. We actually believe in giving enough away so that we notice, so that we have to make lifestyle choices because of our philanthropy. Now, however, we find ourselves in a situation where we have to make some extremely difficult choices. You have all been reading about how the stock market is at an all-time high. Unfortunately, those results don't hold true for everyone. As it happens, we are heavily concentrated in just a few areas, and those are way down right now. We live on our investment income, and at this moment, it's drastically reduced. To speak plainly, we're in a cash-flow crunch. There's no shame in that, we don't get our sense of self-worth from our bank statement, it just is what it is. With luck, this situation will change, but for now, we need to make some changes.

I know you are all aware that we have made a major commitment to Hebrew Union College–Jewish Institute of Religion and have endowed the School of Nonprofit Management. All philanthropists make choices about where to put their money. We thought long and hard about this commitment and thought it was a good one. We still do. Many of you are the reason why. Howard and I believe in nonprofit professionals and the work they do. I don't begin to know the future of the Jewish community going forward. What I do know is it will take professional leadership to get us to a bright future. Our first priority is to honor our commitment to HUC-JIR and finish paying off that pledge. So, for at least this year, we will not be making any more charitable contributions.

I know this is difficult because we are major donors to your organizations. I want you to understand that the cash flow has been tight for a few years now. I truly understand all of your needs and so have been trying to juggle all of you this past year. Increase some, decrease others, but keep everyone happy to some extent. Unfortunately, all it's done is place terrible stress on me. In order to get our life back on track, we have to take a break.

My mentor and friend Jerry Bubis, of blessed memory, used to always teach the nonprofit students about the three "W's." You all know them—work, wealth, and wisdom. You won't have our wealth next year, but you know you can always count on me for advice and any other help we can give. When we feel we can come back as donors, you know we will. Until then, keep up the wonderful work you do. Howard and I value all of you very much.

Best,
Marcie Zelikow

Editor and Contributors

Editor

Rabbi Mary L. Zamore is the executive director of the Women's Rabbinic Network. As part of her work supporting and advocating for Reform women rabbis, she is co-leading the Reform Pay Equity Initiative to narrow the wage gap for all female employees of the Reform Movement. She is also the editor of *The Sacred Table: Creating a Jewish Food Ethic* (CCAR Press, 2011), designated a finalist by the National Jewish Book Awards. She was ordained by Hebrew Union College–Jewish Institute of Religion in New York in 1997.

Contributors

Rabbi B. Elka Abrahamson is the President of The Wexner Foundation. Together with Foundation chairmen Abigail and Les Wexner, she oversees all aspects of the Foundation's work which is focused on developing professional and volunteer Jewish leaders in North America and Public Service Leaders in Israel. She has served congregations in both California and Minnesota and is a highly regarded teacher and public speaker engaging learners in a wide variety of Jewish settings.

Rabbi Ruth Adar was ordained by Hebrew Union College–Jewish Institute of Religion in Los Angeles in 2008, where her rabbinic thesis was "Money and *Menschlikeit*: A Jewish Ethics of Personal Finance." She holds a BA in economics from the University of Tennessee and an MA in religious studies from the University of Chicago. Currently she teaches "Introduction to the Jewish Experience" both locally and online for Lehrhaus Judaica in Northern California.

Rabbi Richard F. Address, DMin, is founder and director of Jewish Sacred Aging® (jewishsacredaging.com) and host of the weekly podcast "Seekers of Meaning." Ordained by Hebrew Union College–Jewish Institute of Religion in 1972, he served congregations in California and New Jersey as well as over three decades on the staff of the Union for Reform Judaism as regional director and as founding director of the Department of Jewish Family Concerns.

Rabbi Daniel R. Allen, *z"l* was the executive vice president emeritus of the United Israel Appeal and served as the senior vice president of the Jewish Federations of North America. He was noted as an expert and practitioner in Israel philanthropy. He was the son, brother, father, and grandfather of Israelis, all by *aliyah*. He was married to Mary Lou Frishberg, and they are the parents of three and the *saba* and *savta* of four. *Editor's Note: We are grateful that Rabbi Allen was able to contribute his chapter before his death on December 16, 2018. May his memory always be for a blessing.*

Elana Altzman, MD, is a board-certified pediatrician. She is the vice president of Youth Programming at Congregation Anshe Chesed of Linden, New Jersey. An active member of Eshel's parent support network, Dr. Altzman has published in *Kveller* about Jewish parenting. A proud mom of four amazing sons, she enjoys knitting and baking.

Amy Asin, vice president of Strengthening Congregations for the Union for Reform Judaism, leads the URJ's initiatives in strengthening congregations, one of the four priorities of the URJ's 2020 Vision. She guides initiatives in leadership development, congregational innovation, congregational networking, and transition and crisis management. She is a thought leader and frequent speaker in the area of congregational life, and has published articles in media outlets such as the URJ's *Inside Leadership* blog and *eJewishPhilanthropy*. She has an MBA with distinction from Harvard Business School and a BA in economics with high honors from Princeton University.

Rabbi Nicole Auerbach is the director of congregational engagement at Central Synagogue in New York City. She is the author, with Dr. Ron Wolfson and Rabbi Lydia Medwin, of *The Relational Judaism Handbook: How to Create a Relational Engagement Campaign to Build and Deepen Relationships in Your Community*. She was ordained by Hebrew Union College–Jewish Institute of Religion, where she engaged in an immersive study of the halachah of *tzedakah* in the *Mishneh Torah* and *Shulchan Aruch*.

Dov Ben-Shimon is the executive vice president/CEO of the Jewish Federation of Greater MetroWest, New Jersey. Born in England, he served as an Air Force rescue combat medic in the Israel Defense Forces, as a diplomat for the State of Israel, and as a Jewish communal professional in Jewish Federations and the American Jewish Joint Distribution Committee.

Rabbi Leah Rachel Berkowitz is the spiritual leader of Congregation Kol Ami in Elkins Park, Pennsylvania. She is a graduate of Brandeis University and an ordinee of Hebrew Union College–Jewish Institute of Religion. She has contributed to several books on Judaism, spirituality, and women's experiences, and is the author of the picture book *The World Needs Beautiful Things*.

Rabbi Barry H. Block serves Congregation B'nai Israel in Little Rock, Arkansas. His work appears in CCAR publications including *The Sacred Encounter*, *Navigating the Journey*, and *A Life of Meaning*. Ordained by Hebrew Union College–Jewish Institute of Religion in New York in 1991, Rabbi Block's passions include the welfare of the CCAR and its rabbis; URJ camps, above all Henry S. Jacobs Camp and Greene Family Camp; Musar study and practice; and being a dad to his sons, Robert and Daniel.

Rabbi Max Chaiken serves Congregation Kol Ami in West Hollywood, California as assistant rabbi. He was ordained in 2018 by Hebrew Union College–Jewish Institute of Religion in Los Angeles, and he earned his BA in economics at Brown University. His rabbinic thesis, "Telling a New Story: A Model for Economic Ethics in Jewish Law," combined his passions for economic thought and Jewish text. He lives with his husband, Rabbi Danny Shapiro, and their dog, Oogie. Read more at www.maxchaiken.com.

Rabbi Amy B. Cohen, MSW, MARE, serves Temple Beth Shalom in Austin, Texas. Raised in Sudbury, Massachusetts, she received a bachelor of arts degree and a master of arts degree in social work from New York University. Rabbi Cohen also earned a master of religious education degree from Hebrew Union College–Jewish Institute of Religion. She was ordained by HUC-JIR in New York in 2012 and has dedicated her rabbinate to bringing vibrant learning experiences to the Austin Jewish community.

Rabbi Jonathan Cohen, PhD, is the senior rabbi of Temple Tifereth Israel in Beachwood, Ohio. Previously, he served as dean of Hebrew Union College–Jewish Institute of Religion and had been director of HUC-JIR's University of Cincinnati Ethics Center. Rabbi Cohen was born in Israel and served in an armored corps unit of the Israel Defense Forces. He has a law degree from the University of Liverpool and was ordained as a rabbi in 2012 by HUC-JIR. Rabbi Cohen was chair of the Central Conference of American Rabbis Responsa Committee in 2017. He is married and has three young children.

Rabbi Edward Elkin has served as the spiritual leader of the First Narayever Congregation in Toronto since 2000. Hailing from Long Island, New York, Rabbi Elkin received his undergraduate degree from Princeton University and was ordained by Hebrew Union College–Jewish Institute of Religion in New York in 1990. His special interests in the rabbinate include Bible commentaries and the relationship between religion and state in the contemporary world.

Beth Burstein Fine is a Jewish educator and writer. She received an MSW from the University of Washington, working as a social worker for years before embracing a career as a Jewish educator. Beth taught Judaics at a Jewish Day School before becoming an administrator with a focus on coaching teachers, the social emotional curriculum and professional writing. She enjoys collaborating with her spouse, Rabbi David Fine, on this project in particular and life in general.

Rabbi David Burstein Fine is a director of consulting and transition management for the Union for Reform Judaism's Strengthening Congregations team. Since joining the URJ more than twenty years ago, he has developed an extensive portfolio advising clergy, lay leaders, and boards on strategic decision-making. Rabbi Fine has particular expertise in consulting with congregational leaders on asset and space management, mergers, and collaboration.

Rabbi Alan Freedman has served Temple Beth Shalom of Austin, Texas, for sixteen years. He contributes Jewish textual content to the Financial Peace University offering at the temple and has often taught in regard to the ethics of finance in adult education programs. In addition to having been ordained by Hebrew Union College–Jewish Institute of Religion, Rabbi Freedman holds a JD from the University of Pennsylvania Law School. His rabbinate is shared with his wife, Lori, three daughters and son-in-law, and a granddaughter.

Stephanie Garry has been affiliated with Plaza Jewish Community Chapel (the only community-owned and commuity-operated not-for-profit Jewish funeral chapel in New York City) since 2002, assuming the role of chief administrative officer in 2014. An actor for twenty-two years, she has appeared in over one thousand commercials, while always being engaged in the Jewish community, having served as president of her congregation in Westchester County. She sits on various boards crossing all denominations and shares her home in Connecticut with her husband, Art Tatge.

Patty Gerstenblith is distinguished research professor at DePaul University College of Law and director of its Center for Art, Museum and Cultural Heritage Law. She served on the President's Cultural Property Advisory Committee in the U.S. Department of State in both the Clinton and Obama administrations. In addition to her BA from Bryn Mawr College, PhD from Harvard University, and JD from Northwestern University, in 2017 she was awarded the Doctor of Humane Letters *h.c.* by Hebrew Union College–Jewish Institute of Religion.

Rabbi Neal Gold is a prolific teacher, writer, and activist based in Massachusetts. He is the Jewish Chaplain and Hillel Director at Babson College, and teaches for Me'ah, a program of adult Jewish learning through Hebrew College. He has worked as Director of Content and Programming for ARZA, the Association of Reform Zionists of America, and was a delegate at the Thirty-Seventh World Zionist Congress in Jerusalem. He recently received his MA in Near Eastern and Jewish Studies from Brandeis University. Neal has led congregations in New Jersey and Massachusetts, and teaches as a visiting scholar in synagogues around the country.

Rabbi Samuel N. Gordon is the founding rabbi of Congregation Sukkat Shalom of Wilmette, Illinois. He is a graduate of the University of Pittsburgh and was ordained by Hebrew Union College–Jewish Institute of Religion in 1980. In 1985 he received an MBA degree from Northwestern University's Kellogg Graduate School of Management. In 2013, President Barack Obama appointed him to the U.S. Holocaust

Memorial Museum Council and reappointed him in 2017. He is a past vice president of the Central Conference of American Rabbis and served for fifteen years as a trustee of the Reform Pension Board.

Dr. Alyssa M. Gray, JD, PhD, is the Emily S. and Rabbi Bernard H. Mehlman Chair in Rabbinics and professor of codes and responsa literature at Hebrew Union College–Jewish Institute of Religion in New York. She is the author of *A Talmud in Exile: The Influence of Yerushalmi Avodah Zarah on the Formation of Bavli Avodah Zarah* and numerous shorter studies on the two Talmuds and various topics in Jewish law and tradition. Her nearly completed new book is tentatively entitled *Charity and Theology in Rabbinic Literature: Righteous Before God* (Routledge). Dr. Gray is also a widely sought-after lecturer to both academic and non-academic audiences.

Rabbi Eric J. Greenberg is a leading interfaith expert and an international award-winning investigative and religion reporter. He has served as the national director of Outreach and Interfaith Affairs for the Anti-Defamation League and National Director of Communication, Programs and Multifaith Engagement for the Multifaith Alliance for Syrian Refugees. He is on the board of the New York Board of Rabbis, and is director of public affairs for Synagogue Connect and the Center for Interreligious Understanding.

Rabbi Arthur Gross-Schaefer, JD, CPA, is a full professor of business law and ethics at Loyola Marymount University, where he has taught for the past thirty-nine years. He publishes and speaks on a diverse number of topics on law, ethics, academic freedom, and conflict resolution. He is the founding rabbi for the Community Shul of Montecito and Santa Barbara, California. In addition, he is the co-founder and president of the Avi Schaefer Fund. He also publishes murder mysteries.

Rabbi Jennifer Gubitz serves Temple Israel of Boston as the director of the Riverway Project, whose mission is to connect twenties and thirties to Judaism and each other through Temple Israel. Ordained by

Hebrew Union College–Jewish Institute of Religion in New York in 2012, she was an HUC-JIR Tisch Rabbinical Fellow and is a graduate of Indiana University's Borns Jewish Studies Program. Rabbi Gubitz grew up as a song leader and educator at URJ Goldman Union Camp Institute in Zionsville, Indiana.

Rabbi Jill Jacobs is the executive director of T'ruah: The Rabbinic Call for Human Rights, which brings the moral voice of two thousand rabbis and cantors and their communities to protecting human rights in North America, Israel, and the occupied Palestinian territories. She is the author of *Where Justice Dwells: A Hands-On Guide to Doing Social Justice in Your Jewish Community* and *There Shall Be No Needy: Pursuing Social Justice through Jewish Law and Tradition*. Rabbi Jacobs holds rabbinic ordination, an MA in Talmud from the Jewish Theological Seminary and an MS in Urban Affairs from Hunter College. She lives in Manhattan with her husband, Rabbi Guy Austrian, and their two daughters.

Rabbi Andy Kahn serves as the assistant rabbi of Temple Emanu-El of New York. Ordained by Hebrew Union College–Jewish Institute of Religion in 2018, he grew up in Tacoma, Washington, received a BA in religion from Kenyon College in Ohio, an MA in religion in modernity from Queen's University, and an MA in Hebrew Bible from the Jewish Theological Seminary.

Michael A. Kimmel has served as the executive director of the Reform Pension Board since January 2015 but has called the Reform Movement his professional home since 2005, previously holding executive positions with the Union for Reform Judaism and Congregation Rodeph Sholom in New York City. Prior to his work in the Reform Movement, he worked in the for-profit sector in finance and management consulting. He holds an MBA from New York University's Stern School of Business and a BS in finance and management from the University at Albany.

Rabbi Zoë Klein Miles serves Temple Isaiah in Los Angeles. She is the author of *Drawing in the Dust* and *The Goblins of Knottingham: A*

History of Challah, along with writings in many collections including *The Women's Torah Commentary, Teen Texts, Lights in the Forest: Rabbis Respond to Twelve Essential Jewish Questions, Making Prayer Real, The Sacred Table: Creating a Jewish Food Ethic*, and *Holy Ground: A Gathering of Voices on Caring for Creation*. Her poems and prayers are used in houses of prayer around the country.

Rabbi Esther L. Lederman is the director of congregational innovation at the Union for Reform Judaism. Prior to that role, she was the associate rabbi at Temple Micah in Washington, DC. Rabbi Lederman also serves on the CCAR Task Force on the Experience of Women in the Rabbinate. She was ordained in May 2008 by Hebrew Union College–Jewish Institute of Religion in New York City.

Rabbi Leah Lewis is the rabbi at Temple Menorah in Redondo Beach, California. Prior to her arrival there in 2017, she served as rabbi and director of lifelong learning at Congregation Shir HaMa'alot in Irvine, California, and as associate rabbi at Leo Baeck Temple in Los Angeles. She was ordained by Hebrew Union College–Jewish Institute of Religion in 2002. She is married to David Lewis, and they have three children.

Rabbi Seth M. Limmer, DHL, serves as senior rabbi of Chicago Sinai Congregation. During his rabbinate he has served as chair of the Justice, Peace & Civil Liberties of the Central Conference of American Rabbis, as vice-chair of the URJ's Commission on Social Action, as dean of faculty for Eisner and Crane Lake Camps, and at the time of publication serves on the Board of Trustees of the CCAR. On behalf of Chicago Sinai Congregation's lead role in organizing the Reform Movement's participation in the NAACP's 2015 America's Journey for Justice, Rabbi Limmer accepted the Rabbi Maurice Eisendrath Bearer of Light Award, the highest honor of the URJ. Author of many articles, 2016 saw the publication of his first full-length book, *Medieval Midrash: The House for Inspired Innovation*.

Rabbi Limmer also served as co-editor of *Moral Resistance and Spiritual Authority*, published by CCAR Press.

Rabbi Joel M. Mosbacher is the senior rabbi of Temple Shaaray Tefila in New York City, having also served congregations in New Jersey and Georgia. He is a 1998 ordinee of Hebrew Union College–Jewish Institute of Religion in Cincinnati, Ohio. He earned a doctorate of ministry from HUC-JIR in 2006. He is on the national strategy team of the Metro Industrial Areas Foundation and is one of the national co-chairs of the Do Not Stand Idly By campaign.

Kevin Moss is the global director of sustainable business at the World Resource Institute. Prior to his involvement in sustainability, his career path included product management, marketing, and corporate strategy. Originally from London, he holds an honors degree in engineering and management from Liverpool University. He and his wife and two wonderful daughters live in Northern Virginia. When not working, he enjoys time spent outdoors and has a passion for music, movies, antiquarian books, and old mechanical devices.

Deborah Niederman, RJE, serves as the associate director of the Leadership Institute for the Union for Reform Judaism. She previously served as a regional educator and consultant at the URJ and is one of the authors of the *CHAI: Learning for Jewish Life* curriculum. She led three different congregations as director of education and also served as coordinator of alumni engagement and career services for the Hebrew Union College–Jewish Institute of Religion Schools of Education. For over twenty years she has served on the board of the Association of Reform Jewish Educators and is a past president. She received her bachelor of arts in Judaic studies and psychology from Washington University in St. Louis, Missouri, and earned a master's in Jewish education from HUC-JIR in Los Angeles.

Rabbi Hara E. Person is the incoming Chief Executive of Central Conference of American Rabbis, having served as its chief strategy officer and Publisher of CCAR Press. She was formerly the editor-in-chief of URJ Books and Music and the managing editor of the award-winning *The Torah: A Women's Commentary.*

Rabbi Sonja K. Pilz, PhD, earned her doctorate from the department of Rabbinic Literature at Potsdam University, Germany; she holds Rabbinic Ordination from Abraham Geiger College, Germany. Prior to joining the Central Conference of American Rabbis as the editor of the CCAR Press, she taught Worship, Liturgy, and Ritual at HUC-JIR, NY; at the School of Jewish Theology at Potsdam University; and in many congregational settings. She has served as a rabbinic intern, adjunct rabbi, and cantorial soloist in congregations in Germany, Switzerland, Israel, and the U.S.

Rabbi Deborah R. Prinz lectures about Jews and chocolate around the world. Her book *On the Chocolate Trail: A Delicious Adventure Connecting Jews, Religions, History, Travel, Rituals and Recipes to the Magic of Cacao* explores how faith traditions shape chocolate consumption, ritual, and business. This best-selling book provided the foundation for the exhibit "Semi[te] Sweet: On Jews and Chocolate," for the Herbert and Eileen Bernard Museum of Temple Emanu-El, New York City, which Prinz co-curated and is now available to travel. Prinz has held a number of leadership positions in the national and regional Reform Movement, having served the Central Conference of American Rabbis (CCAR) as Director of Program and Member Services and the Director of the Joint Commission on Rabbinic Mentoring. Prior to that she was a congregational rabbi for almost thirty years.

Judith Rosenbaum, PhD, is executive director of the Jewish Women's Archive, a national organization that documents Jewish women's stories, elevates their voices, and inspires them to be agents of change. A writer, educator, and historian, Judith earned her doctorate in American studies from Brown University. She teaches and lectures widely on Jewish studies and women's studies and serves on the faculty of the Bronfman Youth Fellowships.

Rabbi Douglas B. Sagal, DD, has been senior rabbi of Temple Emanu-El in Westfield, New Jersey, since 2002. He is a graduate of Wesleyan University, Hebrew Union College–Jewish Institute of Religion, and Yale Divinity School. In 2019 he will be named a rabbinic fellow of the Shalom Hartman Institute in Jerusalem.

Rabbi Ayala Ronen Samuels, PhD, was born and raised in Kibbutz Shamir, Israel, and is the founding rabbi of the Reform congregation T'filat Ha'adam in Caesarea, Israel. She has a BA in Jewish thought and psychology from Haifa University and a PhD in Jewish education from the Jewish Theological Seminary in New York. She was ordained by Hebrew Union College–Jewish Institute of Religion in Jerusalem and loves the challenges and opportunities of being a Reform rabbi in Israel.

Rabbi Noa Sattath is the director of the Israel Religious Action Center, the social justice arm of the Reform Movement in Israel. She is charged with leading the staff of the organization, developing and implementing social change strategies in the fields of separation of religion and state, women's rights, and the struggle against racism. Prior to her work at IRAC, she was the executive director of the Jerusalem Open House, the LGBT community center in Jerusalem. She was also the executive director of MEET, a nonprofit organization that uses technology to create a common language between Israeli and Palestinian young leaders. Prior to her work in civil society, she worked as a leader in the Israeli software industry. Rabbi Sattath is a graduate of the Hebrew University and Gratz College and was ordained by Hebrew Union College–Jewish Institute of Religion in 2014. She is a member of Congregation Kol Haneshama in Jerusalem.

Rabbi Robert Scheinberg, the rabbi of the United Synagogue of Hoboken, New Jersey, teaches liturgy at the Jewish Theological Seminary and the Academy for Jewish Religion. He served on the editorial committees for *Mahzor Lev Shalem* and *Siddur Lev Shalem*, prayer books for Conservative Judaism published by the Rabbinical Assembly.

Rabbi Amy Scheinerman is a hospice chaplain and scholar-in-residence. She is author of *The Talmud of Relationships* (in two volumes). She serves on the CCAR Responsa Committee, as editor of the *CCAR Newsletter* Torah commentary column, and on the editorial board of the *CCAR Journal*. She and her husband, Dr. Edward Scheinerman, have four children and three grandchildren.

Rabbi Amy Schwartzman is the senior rabbi of Temple Rodef Shalom in Falls Church, Virginia, where she has worked since being ordained by Hebrew Union College–Jewish Institute of Religion in 1990. In addition to serving a dynamic congregation, she is involved in leadership roles for her community as well as the Reform Movement. She is especially active in housing issues, mental health initiatives, and supporting those on the fringes of our society. Within the Reform Movement she serves in a number of leadership roles for the Central Conference of American Rabbis, as well as HUC-JIR. Rabbi Schwartzman and her husband, Kevin Moss, live in McLean, Virginia, with their two daughters.

Rabbi Howard Shapiro was ordained by Hebrew Union College–Jewish Institute of Religion in 1968 and began his rabbinate as a chaplain in the U.S. Army at Fort Belvoir and in I Corps Vietnam. Serving Temple Israel in West Palm Beach and Temple Sha'arey Shalom in Springfield, New Jersey, he has been a board member and vice chair of the Reform Pension Board since 1991. Presently a consultant for the Jewish Federation of Palm Beach County, he blogs at Rabbiunplugged.wordpress.com

Rabbi Idit Solomon is the founder and CEO of Hasidah, a nonprofit dedicated to raising awareness about infertility in the Jewish community, connecting people to support, and reducing financial barriers to treatment. She earned her master's degree in Jewish education and ordination from Hebrew Union College–Jewish Institute of Religion in Los Angeles. She has also worked as the Columbus Federation's vice president of Jewish education and director of Jewish community relations and at The Ohio State University Hillel.

Andrés Spokoiny is president and CEO of Jewish Funders Network and a Jewish communal leader with a history of leading successful organizational transformations. He was CEO of Federation CJA in Montreal and previously worked at the American Jewish Joint Distribution Community. Originally from Argentina, he has a multidisciplinary background, including business, education, and rabbinical studies, and is fluent in a number of languages.

Rabbi A. Brian Stoller is the senior rabbi of Temple Israel in Omaha, Nebraska. A dedicated student of Torah and Jewish thought, Rabbi Stoller has published articles on Reform Judaism and Jewish law and is currently pursuing a doctorate in halachah. Before entering the rabbinate, he had a career in politics and served as press secretary to then U.S. senator Peter Fitzgerald of Illinois.

Rabbi Joshua Weinberg serves as the Vice President of the URJ for Israel and Reform Zionism and is the Executive Director of ARZA, the Association of Reform Zionists of America. He was ordained from the HUC-JIR Israeli Rabbinic Program in Jerusalem, and is currently living in New York. Josh previously served as the Director of the Israel program for the Reconstructionist Rabbinical College and as a faculty member of NFTY Heller High School in Israel. Josh is a reserve officer in the IDF Spokesperson's unit and came on *Aliyah* to Israel in 2003. He is married to Mara Sheftel Getz, and together have Noa, Ella, Mia, and Alma.

Rabbi Dvora Weisberg, PhD, is Rabbi Aaron D. Panken Professor of Rabbinics and director of the School of Rabbinic Studies at Hebrew Union College–Jewish Institute of Religion in Los Angeles. She received her BA from Brandeis University and her MA and PhD in Talmud and Rabbinic literature from the Jewish Theological Seminary, and she was ordained by HUC-JIR. Her research focuses on levirate marriage and gender issues in Rabbinic literature.

Marcie Zelikow, a graduate of Temple University and former executive recruiter who started her own business, retired in 2001 to focus on not-for-profit work. She is a former board member at Jewish Family Service, where she served as vice president for fund development and chair of the social enterprise and public policy committees. At the Jewish Federation of Greater Los Angeles, she was part of the Jews in Need committee and former chair of the health and human services committee, LA/Tel Aviv Partnership, and Hillcrest United Jewish Communities (UJC) campaign. She is the national fund development chair for Friends of Yemin Orde and the former vice president of fund development at Temple Emanuel of Beverly Hills. At Hebrew Union College–Jewish Institute of Religion, she and her husband, Howard, endowed the Zelikow School of Jewish Nonprofit Management.